D1582501

The European Union and member states

European Policy Research Unit Series

Series Editors: *Simon Bulmer and Michael Moran*

The European Policy Research Unit Series aims to provide advanced textbooks and thematic studies of key public policy issues in contemporary Europe. They concentrate, in particular, on comparing patterns of national policy processes and policy content, but pay due attention to the European Union dimension. The thematic studies are guided by the character of the policy issue under examination.

The European Policy Research Unit (EPRU) was set up in 1989 within the University of Manchester's Department of Government to promote research on European politics and public policy. The Series is part of EPRU's effort to facilitate intellectual exchange and substantive debate on the key policy issues confronting the European states and the European Union.

The European Union and member states

Towards institutional fusion?

edited by Dietrich Rometsch and Wolfgang Wessels

Manchester University Press
Manchester and New York
distributed exclusively in the USA and Canada by St. Martin's Press

Copyright © Manchester University Press 1996

Published by Manchester University Press
Oxford Road, Manchester M13 9NR, UK
and Room 400, 175 Fifth Avenue,
New York, NY 10010, USA

Distributed exclusively in the USA and Canada
by St. Martin's Press, Inc.,
175 Fifth Avenue, New York, NY 10010, USA

British Library Cataloguing-in-Publication Data
A catalogue record for this book is available from the British
Library

Library of Congress Cataloging-in-Publication Data
The European Union and member states : towards institutional fusion?/
  edited by Dietrich Rometsch and Wolfgang Wessels.
    p.   cm. — (European policy research unit series)
    Includes index.
    ISBN 0-7190-4809-5
    1. European Union countries—Constitutional law. 2. International law and
  municipal law—European Union countries. I. Rometsch, Dietrich. II. Wessels,
  Wolfgang. III. Series
  KJE5076.E95   1996   95-36275
  341.24'2—dc20   CIP

ISBN 0 7190 4809 5 *hardback*

First published in 1996
00 99 98 97 96   10 9 8 7 6 5 4 3 2 1

Typeset in Great Britain
by Northern Phototypesetting Co Ltd, Bolton
Printed in Great Britain
by Bookcraft (Bath) Ltd

Contents

Notes on contributors

Kenneth Armstrong is Lecturer in Law at Keele University.

Simon Bulmer is Professor of Government at the University of Manchester and Visiting Professor at the College of Europe in Bruges.

Christian Franck is Professor of Political Science at the Institut d'Etudes Européennes at the Université Catholique de Louvain.

Marco Giuliani is Lecturer in Political Science at the University of Milan.

Gerhard Göhler is Professor of Political Theory in the Department of Political Science at the Free University of Berlin.

B. J. S. Hoetjes is a political scientist and Associate Professor of Public Administration at the University of Leiden.

Brigid Laffan is Jean Monnet Professor of European Politics at the University College Dublin and Visiting Professor at the College of Europe in Bruges.

Christian Lequesne is Senior Research Fellow at the Centre d'Etudes et de Recherches Internationales in Paris, Lecturer at the Institut d'Etudes Politiques in Paris and Visiting Professor at the College of Europe in Warsaw.

Francesc Morata is Assistant Professor in the Department of Political Science and Public Law at the University of Barcelona.

Luís Miguel Pais Antunes is Director General for Competition and Prices in the Portuguese Ministry for Commerce and Tourism and Professor of International Economic Law at the Universidade Lusíada in Lisbon.

Thomas Pedersen is Jean Monnet Professor at the University of Aarhus.

Dietrich Rometsch is Research Fellow at the Institut für Europäische Politik in Bonn.

Michael Tsinisizelis is Associate Professor of Political Science in the Department of Political Science and Public Administration at the University of Athens.

Alvaro de Vasconcelos is Director of the Institute for Strategic and International Studies in Lisbon.

Wolfgang Wessels is Professor of Political Science at the University of Cologne, Jean Monnet Professor and Chairman of the Trans European Policy Studies Association (TEPSA). He is a member of the managing board of the Institut für Europäische Politik in Bonn.

Tanguy de Wilde d'Estmael is Research Fellow in the Department of Political and Social Sciences at the Université Catholique de Louvain.

Abbreviations

COPA	Committee of Professional Agricultural Organizations
COREPER	Committee of Permanent Representatives
ECJ	European Court of Justice
EEC	Treaty of the European Community of 25 March 1957/European Economic Community
EFTA	European Free Trade Association
EIB	European Investment Bank
EMS	European Monetary System
EMU	Economic and Monetary Union
EP	European Parliament
EPC	European Political Cooperation
ERM	Exchange Rate Mechanism
ESC	Economic and Social Committee
ETUC	European Trades Union Confederation
EU	European Union
Euratom	European Atomic Energy Community
GATT	General Agreement on Tariffs and Trade
GDP	Gross Domestic Product
NATO	North Atlantic Treaty Organization
SEA	Single European Act
TEU	Treaty on European Union of 7 February 1992
UNICE	Union of Industries of the European Community
WRA	Waste Regulation Authority

List of figures and tables

Figures

Tables

Preface

'Do institutions matter?' was the starting point of studies in political science during the 1980s, leading to what is called 'new-institutionalism'.[1] This approach has affected German political science in general and especially research work in the field of European integration. However, regarding the latter, researchers went a step further and shifted the focus of new-institutionalism to the question of 'How do institutions matter?' We made use of these reflections and applied them to the decision-making process in the European Community/European Union, i.e. the preparation, making, implementation and control of binding decisions. The central question was in which ways and to what extent European *and* national institutions are involved and effectively participate in the EC/EU decision-making process.

The main result of the findings in this book is that the EU is moving towards 'institutional fusion' which is, among others, a corollary of the increasing 'Europeanization' of the institutional set-up in the member states. This means that the interaction and exchanges between national *and* European institutions have become increasingly intensive and it no longer seems to be justified – except for purely analytical reasons – to differentiate between a 'European level' and a 'national level' in an institutional context. Both 'levels' are characterized by a close 'interwovenness' and are mutually dependent. National institutions have 'Europeanized', i.e. they have adapted their structures and procedures and are, to a growing extent,

---

[1] See James G. March and Johan P. Olsen, 'The New Institutionalism. Organizational Factors in Political Life', *American Political Science Review*, 78 (1984), pp. 734–49.

oriented towards the activities in Brussels and Strasbourg. There is the expectation that – in quantitative as well as qualitative terms – the increasing extension of the participation of national institutions in the EC decision-making process will continue within this process of institutional fusion. The institutional 'struggle' for influence and the efforts to adapt to the European decision-making process will go on and might even intensify, irrespective of the member states' differences as regards their specific historical, constitutional and political backgrounds. One would expect that the new member states will also be affected by this trend: thus, a new edition of this book is already scheduled, which will then include all of the fifteen (or more?) member states.

The volume presented is primarily the result of a research project of the Institut für Europäische Politik (IEP) sponsored by the Deutsche Forschungsgemeinschaft between 1990 and 1993 (award no. WE 954/3–1) with the title 'Towards a System of Cooperative States – The Dynamics of the EC Institutional System'. The project was part of the special programme on 'The theory of political institutions' which was coordinated by Gerhard Göhler.

One part of the IEP's research project consisted in the analysis of the effect of the European integration process on national institutions in the (at that time) twelve member states. To this end national rapporteurs were encouraged to deliver reports based on a questionnaire by spring 1993 (unfortunately, no rapporteur could be found for Luxembourg). The results of their findings looked sufficiently interesting that the idea was born to make a separate publication out of the national reports. In autumn 1993, the group of national rapporteurs met in Bonn, which was made possible by a generous grant from the Deutsche Forschungsgemeinschaft (award no. 4850/179/93). This allowed for an intensive discussion of the project, and the idea of a common publication took a more concrete shape. It lasted another year until all of the manuscripts could be finalized.

An indicator of the changes which have happened during the creation of the book is the usage of 'EC' or 'EU' (sometimes even 'EEC') in it. The reason is that there has been a dynamic political development which had an impact on science and research. The findings in this book are based on the 'old EC' although we are already in the European Union comprising fifteen member states. It is somewhat frustrating for academics to be (always?) late. However, academics are ahead of time when they contribute to the synthesis of past developments and try to present them at a moment when they might be useful for future development. This is what has been attempted with this book: to examine the institutional reaction and adaptation process in the (old) member states and to draw conclusions from this with regard to a theoretical explanation of the interaction between national and EC institutions and to the further development of the EU's institutional system.

Whenever the authors were referring in their contributions to the most recent developments and the future prospects, the term 'EU' has been used. However, this is not true for the parts on the EC decision-making cycle in each contribution where the authors stuck to 'EC', since the findings, data, interpretations etc. were based on the period *before* 1 November 1993. When both the old EC *and* the new EU after Maastricht have been referred to, the acronym 'EC/EU' has been used as a compromise. If this appears confusing, it should not be so. The basic rule is that the Community has developed over time, starting with the EEC, becoming the EC in the 1970s and 1980s and finally being transformed into the EU in 1993. Depending on which stage of the development or which pillar of the Union one refers to, the appropriate term has to be applied. Decision-making in the first pillar is quite different from that in the second and third pillars. Since most of the observations and data were based on the experiences with the (old) first pillar, the term 'EC decision-making' has been used most of the time.

A further problem in this book – which is also a general problem in comparative political science – is the question of to what extent empirical findings are comparable to each other.[2] Institutions – in this case the national governments, national parliaments, the courts, the regions/local authorities and the national administration – are the 'products' and the 'producers' of specific national contexts and their behaviour is determined by the history of the member state, the functioning of the national political system, the particular constitutional provisions and the configuration in terms of personnel and 'corporate identity'. Seen from this angle each institution has its own national background and can hardly be compared – in the sense of a 'good' or 'bad' institution – to a similar institution in another

---

[2] See on this aspect Giovanni Sartori, 'Comparing and Miscomparing', *Journal of Theoretical Politics*, 3 (1991), pp. 243–57; Simon Hix, 'The Study of the European Community: The Challenge to Comparative Politics', *West European Politics*, 17 (1) (1994), pp. 1–30.

country, since this would presume that both started from the same basis and were acting under the same conditions. This is almost never the case. An extreme example for illustration is the British parliament, sometimes called the 'mother of all parliaments', which already indicates that it had a quite different historical development from that of other parliaments, such as the French 'Assemblée Nationale' or the German 'Bundestag' and 'Bundesrat'. The latter are part of a federal system and differ in terms of function, competences, political weight, political party configuration etc. from the parliament in the United Kingdom. One solution to this problem of national differences would have been to form typologies of political systems – such as the centralized systems, the decentralized systems and the federal systems – and to make a comparison of the interaction process of the countries according to one typology. But even this would have only partly helped to clarify the differences in the political and constitutional conditions. Another solution would have been to start with a comprehensive analysis of the national political systems and to describe the role, function and weight of the national institutions. However, such an approach would be too extensive. Therefore, we have tried to use a more modest approach, i.e. to deal with the countries according to their specific constitutional provisions and political situation without going into the details of each political system. This explains the sequence of the country reports, ranging from the federal member states (Belgium, Germany), to the member states with a regional level or the decentralized member states[3] (Italy, Spain, France, Netherlands) and finally to the centralized member states (Denmark, Greece, Portugal, United Kingdom). The evaluation of the national institutions and their role in EC/EU affairs is primarily based on the expertise of the national rapporteurs.

The realization of this book would not have been possible without the financial help of the Deutsche Forschungsgemeinschaft and the support of many people. We are most grateful to them and we would like to thank them sincerely for their cooperation, their encouragement and untiring assistance. Special thanks are addressed to the series editors Simon Bulmer and Michael Moran who read the

---

[3] i.e. those member states which have a (more or less successful) record of devolution of competences to the regional and local level; see for more details on this Christian Engel and Joseph van Ginderachter, *Le pouvoir régional et local dans la Communauté européenne* (Paris: Edition Pedone, 1992).

entire manuscript and made useful comments. In this respect we are particularly indebted to Simon Bulmer who, in 1994, spent half a year in Bonn and who followed the creation of the book. He helped us with his expert knowledge and gave us much advice. To him we extend our most warm gratitude. Needless to say the contributors to the book deserve the greatest thanks. They had the expertise and 'first hand' information for writing the chapters and had enough patience with the editors in finalizing the book. The latter would not have been possible, of course, without the technical assistance of Mrs Sinda Kapp-Matsukawa who worked numerous hours on the manuscripts. Many thanks to her, too.

Bonn, April 1995   Wolfgang Wessels
                                                             Dietrich Rometsch

Institutions in political theory: lessons for European integration

The theoretical debate about institutions in political science

Political science is primarily concerned with institutions; questions of institutionalizing political order, of the legitimation of institutions, of their rise and decline have been the main subject of political thinking since its beginning. Yet in the Federal Republic of Germany for a long time political theory has failed to undertake a comprehensive explanation and foundation of institutions. Until the 1980s the need of theoretical foundations for the analysis of political institutions had been recognized only occasionally. One had contented oneself with referring more by way of suggestion to some approaches worked out by neighbouring disciplines. The general sociological theory of institutions,[1] even where it had been noticed, had hardly been applied to the systematic analysis of political institutions. Especially in the 1970s German political science generally showed little interest in institutions, but even in the 1950s and 1960s, in contrast to a widely held opinion, the focus on political institutions was not at all dominant.

---

[1] See Emile Durkheim, *Die elementaren Formen des religiösen Lebens* (Frankfurt/M., 1981); Arnold Gehlen, *Der Mensch*, 13th edn (Wiesbaden, 1986); Arnold Gehlen, *Urmensch und Spätkultur*, 5th edn (Wiesbaden, 1986); Maurice Hauriou, *Die Theorie der Institution und zwei andere Aufsätze* (in French 1925; Berlin, 1965); George H. Mead, *Mind, Sell and Society* (Chicago, 1934); Talcott Parsons, *The Social System* (Glencoe, Ill., 1951); Talcott Parsons, *On Institutions and Social Evolution* (Chicago, 1982); Helmut Schelsky, *Zur Theorie der Institution* (Düsseldorf, 1982); Helmut Schelsky, *Zur Theorie der Institution* (Düsseldorf, 1970); Helmut Schelsky, 'Zur soziologischen Theorie der Institution', in Helmut Schelsky, *Zur Theorie der Institution* (Düsseldorf, 1970), pp. 9–26.

According to the common understanding of political science which subdivides it into 'politics' (political processes), 'polity' (political structures), and 'policy' (contents of politics), institutions fall at first under the category of 'polity' as framework for political processes. They are the organized areas and systems of norms within which political actions are carried out. In this way institutions on the one hand do influence the political processes and their results, i.e. the contents of politics – on the other hand their stability and development are dependent on the outcome of political actions. Since the 1980s political science has begun to notice that the institutional factor plays a really significant role in politics and that the underestimation of this fact has led to serious deficits and misjudgements in political analysis. The new assessment of political institutions has found its clearest expression in the new-institutionalist approach.[2] It became clear that the deficit in analysing institutions was at the same time a deficit of theory. The study of political institutions requires a more comprehensive perspective which extends beyond the isolated analysis of single institutions if it is adequately to grasp their institutional character, whether by empirical explanation or even by normative foundation. For this purpose in 1989 a research program entitled *Theory of Political Institutions* was established by the German Research Foundation (Deutsche Forschungsgemeinschaft) in which the Institut für Europäische Politik participated with a project entitled 'Towards a "System of Cooperative States" – the Dynamics of the EC Institutional System').[3] It had been intensively prepared by the 'Section of Political Philosophy and the History of Political Ideas' within the German Political Science Association, and continued until 1995. The aim of the research program may be shortly described as follows: in order to understand the institutional factor systematically and to clarify its role in politics, the research program investigates political institutions at a level which is basic for the study of each of them. In an analytic sense it is concerned with patterns of development, the structure, and func-

[2] See James G. March and Johan P. Olsen, 'The New Institutionalism. Organizational Factors in Political Life', *American Political Science Review*, 78 (1984), pp. 734–49; James G. March and Johan P. Olsen, *Rediscovering Institutions. The Organizational Basis of Politics* (London, New York, 1989); P. Evans, D. Rueschemeyer and T. Skocpol (eds.), *Bringing the State Back In* (Cambridge, 1985).

[3] See Wolfgang Wessels and Dietrich Rometsch, *Auf dem Weg zu einem 'System kooperativer Staaten' – Zur Dynamik des EG-Institutionen Systems*, unpublished report to the Deutsche Forschungsgemeinschaft (Bonn, 1995).

tional conditions of political institutions; in a normative sense it deals with justification, discussion, and critique of the institutional arrangements of political order. The precondition is a comprehensive understanding of political institutions from the point of view of the social sciences. In this way a theoretical framework for the research on political institutions will be developed.

A new concept of political institutions

Usually, political science starts with a very concrete understanding of institutions which corresponds largely to common sense. The inquiry is concerned with entities such as parliament, government, the President, the Supreme Court, etc. There are no 'ifs and buts' about it, but the common-sense understanding of political institutions is not sufficient for political science because it does not signify a theoretical concept. By common sense each political institution can at best be viewed isolated, i.e., from its own origin, behaviour patterns and regulation mechanism. But what is common to political institutions is not understood by this point of view. Exactly for this reason a theory of political institutions is needed. It deals with the question of what is characteristic of all political institutions: that is, to identify what is *institutional* and what is *political* in political institutions. Even if it sounds banal, these are the two basic components of the concept of political institutions, and considerable theoretical efforts are required to determine them sufficiently. In this respect the outcome of the research program can be qualified as follows: first of all, a definition of political institutions has been developed out of the context of social sciences; secondly, a symbolic dimension was added in order to supplement a deficit in the definition; finally, in order to proceed in this direction a more precise understanding of symbols is required.

The concept of political institutions in the context of social sciences

The definition of what political institutions are has been accomplished during the progress of the research program in two steps. Firstly, in order to grasp institutions in a full sense a comprehensive concept is needed. It has to be taken from the general theory of social institutions. Especially in the field of sociology several concepts have been developed which may be fundamental also for political science.

Even if they are very different from each other a basic core which will be of use for our purposes can be singled out.

Social institutions are relatively persistent patterns of behaviour and carriers of meaning stabilized by internalization; they serve a regulating and orienting function in human interaction. Institutions are relatively stable and therefore exhibit a certain duration. The stability is based on a temporary reinforcement of patterns of behaviour. They are internalized to the extent that people who are addressed by them orient their expectations to the inherent meaning which is expressed by them. Institutions are principally transpersonal; they structure human behaviour, and in this way they produce social order.

The second step in the definition is related to the concept of politics. Politics is understood as the scope of human interaction in which binding decisions for the society as a whole are generated, regulated and carried out. This understanding stresses the focus of decisions, their binding nature, and the involvement of the whole society in order to distinguish political from social institutions. It carries on the German tradition of the concept of 'state' founded by Max Weber, Carl Schmitt, and Hermann Heller.[4] The distinguishing characteristic of obligation is derived from Max Weber's concept of 'authority'. It describes the political association which continuously guarantees its existence and the validity of its order within a given territorial area by the application and threat of physical force and – in the case of the state – through the monopoly of the legitimate use of it. The distinguishing characteristic of the involvement of the whole society refers to an aspect of Carl Schmitt's concept of politics, namely the intensity of conflicts. Not every conflict can be categorized as political, but only those conflicts which reach an extreme intensity. This point can be accepted by understanding it in a merely sociological sense so that Carl Schmitt's existential distinction between friend and foe can be avoided. The most important characteristic in defining politics is that politics are concerned not only with deliberation and

---

[4] See Hermann Heller, 'Politische Demokratie und soziale Homogenität', in *Gesammelte Schriften*, vol. 2 (Leiden, 1971), pp. 421–33; Hermann Heller, *Staatslehre* (Leiden, 1934); Carl Schmitt, *Römischer Katholizismus und politische Form,* 2nd edn (München, 1925); Carl Schmitt, *Die geistesgeschichtliche Lage des heutigen Parlamentarismus* (originally 1926; Berlin, 1979); Carl Schmitt, *Der Begriff des Politischen,* 3rd edn (Hamburg, 1933); Max Weber, *Wirtschaft und Gesellschaft,* 5th edn, ed. J. Winckelmann (Tübingen, 1972).

coordination, but in the last analysis with definitive decisions relating to the community. This contribution to the concept of politics derives from Hermann Heller's theory of state as the 'organized unity of decisions and their execution' (*organisierte Entscheidungs- und Wirkungseinheit*).

Combining this concept of politics with the definition of social institutions outlined above leads to the following definition of political institutions. Political institutions are systems regulating the generation and carrying out of binding decisions which concern society as a whole. Politically the regulating function of social institutions operates as the transformation of interests into decisions for the whole society with binding authority. The persistence and internalization of social institutions imply on the part of political institutions a certain level of actual power, legal order, and acceptance by those concerned. All this requires at the same time a certain level of consensus concerning political order and, at least in modern times, real opportunities for the citizens to participate. Although political institutions work transpersonally, political decisions are made by specific persons within political institutions. That means: political institutions are the framework within which these persons act.

The symbolic dimension of the concept of political institutions

As became evident during the work of our research program, political institutions were not yet adequately described by the concept used until now. Thus I would like to draw attention to the work of Arnold Gehlen.[5] It is in particular his concept of institutions which gives evidence of another dimension to be taken into account. Gehlen grounds his concept of institutions on two different anthropological contexts. The second of them introduces a dimension which has usually been overlooked: the symbolic dimension of institutions.

The first context in Gehlen's concept of institutions is *instrumental*. While acting rationally men arrive at a division of labour which can only be carried out within a framework of institutions which relieve and stabilize human behaviour. This aspect of Gehlen's concept is well known. The second anthropological context is *ideal* and is called by Gehlen 'ideative' (*ideativ*). It is especially relevant for our

[5] See note 1 above.

purposes. In archaic cultures men express their reactions to the impact of their surroundings by rituals. Gehlen calls this 'ritual representation' (*rituell-darstellendes Verhalten*) and he describes it as symbolic, without specific purposes (*zweckfrei*), but effecting mutual obligation between the members of a group. In the common action of rituals they express their situation in a stylized and overemphasized manner, and it is precisely through rituals that they recognize what they have in common and, as a consequence, what they are themselves (see Hegel: 'to recognize oneself in another'). Similar to the results of the instrumental function of institutions, but in a quite different way, the ritual representation stabilizes human behaviour and holds interactions together. It is of major importance that in rituals symbols are expressed. Rituals are symbolic activities; the symbols in use extend beyond singular and changing contents and therefore make visible what is common and persistent for all members of the community. This representation of the unity, which due to the symbols is as concrete as it is generally binding, ensures all members feel at home and secure. It is here that they find the orientation they need and long for. Institutionalization by ritual representation is without specific purpose on the part of those concerned even if not completely without motivation. It does not depend on and is not even influenced by instrumental considerations; it is an end in itself. Yet secondarily, indirectly, and not in a subjective but in an objective sense, this kind of institutionalization is extremely useful: it is the institutional precondition for organizing society.

We do not need to discuss here to what extent Gehlen's anthropological theory of the foundation of institutions, which was developed for archaic cultures, is appropriate also for modern societies. In the view of Gehlen the modern shift to the dominance of 'subjectivity' is very dangerous for the effectiveness and even the existence of institutions because subjectivity tends to make use of the world in a discretionary manner and therefore loses its stable external support. What can also be left out of consideration is Gehlen's extremely conservative bias. He restricts himself to a merely static understanding of institutions. Either he contents himself with recognizing the existent institutions as leading systems without questioning them, or he simply laments the lack of them. This attitude may be considered primarily an ideological burden while the basic terms of his concept of institutions need not necessarily be ideological.

Gehlen's significance for the understanding of political institutions can be summarized as follows: the twofold concept of institutions goes beyond a merely technically defined understanding. Gehlen's argument stresses the requirement of a more complex understanding of institutions in which the importance of the symbolic dimension of institutions is given significance. It is necessary that institutions not only function technically; also and even more they must work symbolically, in a non-instrumental sense. The reason for this is to be found in the condition of human existence, and it is the merit of Gehlen's concept of institutions to bring attention to this aspect.

The consequences of this approach are far-reaching although they are more ambiguous than in Gehlen's opinion. The existence and the effectiveness of institutions do not simply depend on the consciousness and the intentions of the individuals. The symbolic level of institutions is to a certain degree removed from direct and personal influence. On the other hand there is no doubt that institutions are permanently subject to social pressure. The symbol systems of institutions do not hover in space lifted up like clouds in the sky. Concrete societies create their specific symbols which express and maintain the principles of order, and in this way they form specific institutions. This is especially true for modern societies. Through social change due to the struggles of social interests, symbols are continuously revalidated; institutions can change their character without losing their basic function as institutions. Nevertheless we can learn from Gehlen that institutions, specifically due to their symbolic dimension, are less open to change than they would appear to be when viewed only from an instrumental point of view. To this extent, even in modern societies institutions cannot be formed at one's convenience – overblown attempts in this direction may lead to self-deception.

Why is Gehlen's concept important especially for political institutions? Because we can find in one outstanding principle of political order, which is closely connected to political institutions, the analogous twofold structure. This is the principle of political representation; it also has to be conceived in terms of an additional symbolical dimension in order to comprehend its nature. This aspect has especially been recognized by the German tradition of constitutional law, but in the concept of political representation these insights were hardly brought together and much less applied to political analysis.

Taken in its broadest sense the concept of representation means to bring something which is absent to presence, which also means to

make something visible which is invisible. The concept of representation is normally used in a narrower sense; representatives do articulate the wishes, suggestions, and concrete interests of the citizens
because in a larger state due to purely technical reasons these cannot
be brought into effect directly by themselves. But this is only one side
of the general concept. Representation also requires that the principles which are constitutive for the community must be made visible.
This is the symbolic performance of representation which is the precondition for political integration. It is the merit of a German tradition of political thinking to have stressed this point.

Eric Voegelin argues that by decisive political symbols the meaning of the existence of a society is expressed.[6] Symbols represent the
experience that only by participating in the whole and surpassing his
own particular existence does man become human in the fullest sense.
In this way the self-perception of societies by symbols is an integrative component of social reality. A political society comes into existence when it articulates itself and when representatives are brought
forth. Representation understood as symbolic representation defines
for each society the 'truth' of its order (which for Voegelin can have
only a transcendental origin). It is fundamental for all types of legitimate political power to be secured and stabilized by recognized symbols. In this way symbolic representation is an existential form of
representation which is the basis of all technical forms of representation.

Carl Schmitt conceptualizes representation as existential: 'Representation means to make an invisible being visible by a publicly present being and so to bring it for its part to presence'.[7] Only a being of
higher rank and of special value can be represented. This is, in the
understanding of Schmitt, 'the people' (*das Volk*) which in its existence as a 'political unity' lives much more intensely than is the case
when merely living together as an unrelated group of men and women.
Carl Schmitt's theory of existential representation may be problematic
due to his connections with National Socialism. However, even
Siegfried Landshut, who as an emigrant is not under suspicion of har-
bouring National Socialist tendencies, refers to Carl Schmitt and Maurice Hauriou and characterizes representation as a relation in which

---

[6] See Eric Voegelin, *Die neue Wissenschaft der Politik/The New Science of Politics*
(München, 1952).
[7] See Carl Schmitt, *Verfassungslehre* (Leipzig, 1928), p. 209.

the representative brings to actuality what is not visible and in this respect not 'there' without it: something ideal and mental, which is the obligating idea of life in a community. Only when the idea is represented by a symbol does it become existent and effective.[8]

The historical background of the concept of existential representation was the crisis of parliamentarism in continental Europe during the 1920s. The failure of parliamentarism, its decline in credibility, and its lack of integrating ability raised the question of whether the parliament could still be regarded as an actual representative institution. The main problem was whether any other institution could be found which would be able to fulfil the function of representation. The question had to be asked: what is the function of representation in creating and maintaining political unity? Exactly this is the issue addressed by symbolical and existential representation. It cannot be denied that some authors were definitely anti-liberal and anti-democratic. In fact, the citizens who are represented have to endure passively the representation of the existential type.[9] It is not an active achievement of the citizens and not a democratic process. For this reason it seems to be especially appropriate for legitimizing authoritarian or totalitarian regimes. If representation is reduced exclusively to the existential, symbolically mediated type, so that symbolic representation finally would replace and eliminate the idea of acting in the interest of the citizens as formulated by Western constitutionalism instead of founding it – then symbolic representation is in fact a principle of order which is politically very dangerous.[10] But that's only half the truth of it. As a political fact which cannot simply be eliminated by incantation of its dangerous potential, symbolically mediated existential representation is a principle of order which is indispensable for understanding political events, especially issues of political identity of societies. Everything depends on the successful combating of ideological exaggerations and on the democratic explication of the principle of symbolically mediated representation in a normative sense. Should a political order intend to create by the symbolic representation of its leading ideas the existence of a *democratic* society, citizens must be able to recognize themselves and their own

---

[8] See Siegfried Landshut, 'Der politische Begriff der Repräsentation', in H. Rausch (ed.), *Zur Theorie und Geschichte der Repräsentation und der Repräsentativverfassung* (Darmstadt, 1968).

[9] See Hans-Julius Wolff, *Organschaft und Vertretung* (originally 1934; Aalen, 1968).

[10] See Hannah F. Pitkin, *The Concept of Representation* (Berkeley, 1972), p. 109.

intentions in the symbols of such a society. They must be empowered to exercise self-determination. In this way this very German tradition has to be incorporated in a strictly democratic understanding of representation.

On the other hand it is equally inadequate to emphasize only the negative aspect of symbols in politics as is done in the influential 'theory of symbolic politics', i.e. the symbolic use of politics.[11] Admittedly, symbolic representation relates mainly to aspects of politics which are based on feelings and identifications. This does not exclude rational forms of agreements and decision-making. On the contrary, it is constitutive for them. Edelman emphasizes only the negative aspects of symbolic representation when he characterizes symbolic politics in the last analysis as obscuring the actual events because it awakens mainly emotions, fears, and uncritical acceptance. This view describes only the degenerated form of the misuse of symbols in politics. Edelman neglects the positive integrative function. In all forms of political communication symbols serve to represent meaning, to provide orientation, and to enable control and regulation by condensing beliefs and values into a visible form.[12]

Altogether we have to broaden the concept of political institutions by taking two aspects into consideration. In the first place, the theory of political institutions is a theory of the fundamentals of establishing political order in a society. Institutions determine and persistently fix the way in which a society will be organized politically, i.e. the way in which by representation the wishes and interests of the citizens will be articulated publicly and the results of the formation of opinion are effected for the community in the form of political decisions. In the second place, the theory of political institutions is a theory of the fundamentals of providing orientation for the members of a society. Political institutions express the society's formative principles, they make them visibly present and ascertainable for all citizens, whether in the fashion of a flag or – to mention the most important example for modern democracies – of the written constitution. This second dimension has not been part of the concept of political institutions used until

[11] See Murray Edelman, *Politik als Ritual. Die symbolische Funktion staatlicher Institutionen und politischen Handelns* (Frankfurt/M./New York, 1990); Ulrich Sarcinelli, *Symbolische Politik* (Opladen, 1987); Ulrich Sarcinelli, 'Symbolische Politik und politische Kultur', *Politische Vierteljahresschrift*, 30 (1989), pp. 292–309.
[12] See Pierre Bourdieu, 'Symbolic Power', *Critique of Anthropology*, 4 (1979), pp. 77–85; Pierre Bourdieu, 'Social Space and Symbolic Power', *Sociological Theory*, 7 (1989), pp. 14–25.

now, and it is this lack which has led to serious deficits. The understanding of political institutions as 'systems regulating the making and implementing of binding decisions which concern the society as a whole' stresses only the aspect of control and remains therefore one-dimensional. For this reason the definition of political institutions must be extended to include the aspect of social integration. Political institutions, comprehended in the context of social institutions, are *systems regulating the generation and carrying out of binding decisions which concern the society as a whole, as well as authoritative forms which represent symbolically the basic orientations of a society*. The first part of the definition formulates the aspect of control, the second part the aspect of integration.

Towards a more precise understanding of symbols

The connection between political institutions and symbolic representation is based, however, on a specific concept of symbols. In his *The Philosophy of Symbolic Forms* the German philosopher Ernst Cassirer argues that symbols are constitutive for reality because social reality is in its basic structure symbolically mediated and interpreted.[13] Reality itself is a product of the human mind without which it would not exist. Symbols create a connection between man and world. Symbols enable the perception of our surroundings not only fragmentally but as interrelated. Only in this way can we orient ourselves and form the world. This is a very philosophical theory which belongs to the tradition of Kantian transcendentalism.

This has been expressed in more concrete terms by the French sociologist Pierre Bourdieu in his concept of habit.[14] 'Habit' is the sum of dispositions of an individual or a group which serve as schemes of perception and instruments of drawing distinctions in everyday life. The reason why society does not disintegrate into different habits is that in all distinctions the basic structure of society is represented by the same perception patterns. For Bourdieu they are not of transcendental origin (as they are for Cassirer), but the concrete result of

[13] See Ernst Cassirer, *Philosophie der symbolischen Formen*, 3rd vol., 2nd edn (Darmstadt, 1953–4).
[14] See Pierre Bourdieu, *Zur Soziologie der symbolischen Formen* (Frankfurt/M., 1983); Pierre Bourdieu, *Sozialer Raum und 'Klassen'* (Frankfurt/M/., 1985); here: pp. 7–46.

struggles for symbolic power in society. Those symbols which have gained supremacy are now dominating the perception of social reality both for the winners and for the losers. Groups which dominate a society are the exclusive deliverers of the symbols offering interpretation of the world. In this way, symbolic representation does not emerge from a universe of ideas beyond time and space, but rather is related to social interests and struggles; the political order is the outcome which offers its symbolic form of interpretation. The symbols are part of the effectiveness of the order, and probably the most important one.

The crucial point is to clarify more closely what symbols are and the way they work. In my argument the concept of symbolic representation only makes sense if the understanding of symbols goes beyond the semiotic theory of signs. Symbols are signs, but not all signs are symbols. Like all signs symbols are part of social reality and in the last analysis it is through them that social reality is constituted. At the same time, symbols contain a certain surplus beyond mere signs. Symbols are not definite and final in their meaning, they always have to be interpreted. They are signs which are conceivable only by hermeneutics. That is the reason why they are not 'denotative', but rather 'connotative' (as has often been observed). With symbols it is not so much the case of signification (which is the subject of semiotics), but rather of interpretation (which is the subject of hermeneutics).[15]

This aspect is particularly important in understanding the political effects of symbols. In contrast to rules, as in the legal system, symbolization does not regulate unambiguously; it leaves a widened scope of interpretation and allows a variety of emotional involvement. Symbols constitute a common social reality, but not a uniform one. If used properly they guarantee the persistence of plurality within integration. In symbols the emotional and the expressive component are included, so that the citizens are involved not only in an abstract role, but in their whole context of life. These symbols offer orientation which can be accepted or rejected. The most important fact is that symbols can vary in their meaning for individuals, that symbols can be interpreted differently without destroying the unity needed by the community. They actually provide the conditions which ensure and even promote integration under the condition of pluralism because they allow variations. The political institutions are

---

[15] See Gerhard Kurz, *Metapher, Allegorie, Symbol*, 2nd edn (Göttingen, 1988).

the carriers of these symbols; how they present them is at least as important as their concrete efficiency.

Consequences for the understanding of integration

The preceding considerations lead to a broader concept of political integration. The symbolic dimension of political institutions is closely connected with its function of integration. By using symbols political institutions have to provide the required fundamental orientations for the citizens for living together in a community. This inclusion of the aspect of social integration in the concept of political integration may appear unusual. In discussing problems of European integration the focus normally lies on coordination, standardization, and concentration of the rules and activities of the member states, that is, on the function of control. Only scarcely has the focus been directed to symbolically mediated orientations of the citizens. Taking the symbolic dimension into account also makes the social aspect of political integration apparent. In this way we come to consequences for the theory of political integration which generally remain overlooked.

The twofold concept of integration is very closely illustrated by Norbert Elias. The author of 'The Process of Civilization' reflected shortly before his death about questions of integration which may be helpful for our subject.[16] He studies the process of social integration in a sweeping investigation from archaic tribal units through the nation state of modern Europe up to supra-national units like the European Community and the United Nations Organization. He demonstrates that the development of forms of integration into units of a higher level corresponds to a process of differentiation. The organization form becomes more and more complex while the individual obtains a drastically increasing value of its own. The self-identity (*Ich-Identität*) surpasses both in value and in emphasis the collective identity (*Wir-Identität*) by far. Nevertheless a balance of these two kinds of identity is needed so as to maintain the integration of the individuals into the society. Given the definition – that by which the individuals distinguish themselves one from another is their self-identity; what they share in common is their collective identity – how then is a balance between the two to be established? Obvi-

---

[16] See Norbert Elias, 'Wandlungen der Wir-Ich-Balance', *Die Gesellschaft der Individuen* (Frankfurt/M., 1987), pp. 207–315.

ously the individuals form a collective identity complementary to their self-identity even under the conditions of modern societies. Taking this for granted, integration at a higher level implies not only the establishment of new and more effective forms of organization. It depends in fact upon a corresponding development of a collective identity.

In this way Elias uses a twofold concept of integration. At first, integration means the organization of the survival of a group. In modern times this kind of organization is connected with the nation state which is at the same time the point of reference for the collective identity of the individuals. This is the second dimension, and here arises the main problem of integration for the present. To the extent that in our times supranational organizations are replacing the organizational form of the nation state, the question arises whether the collective identity has accordingly changed its character. Whether or not the collective identity corresponds to the organizational form of the community depends on the social habit of the citizens which often lags behind the degree of organizational integration. Collective identity is based on a common personality structure of the individuals. In their social habit people show special dispositions which they share with each other. The social habit depends not only on rational dispositions, but also on the emotional and the expressive part of human behaviour which all derives from whole context of life. The social habit changes at such a slow pace that people, if they already are incorporated into an organization with a higher level of integration, are delayed in developing the corresponding level of collective identity. This analysis of Elias aims to make the actual problems of integration plausible. He notices a nearly irresistible tendency for social development to replace the nation state by supranational forms of organization, but he is also forced to acknowledge that this new form of integration beyond the nation state is limited first to processes of regulation. The collective identity of the citizens which depends mainly on their social habit remains generally on the previous lower level which is the integration of the citizens in their national state. Elias's analysis is based on experiences prior to the late 1980s. His diagnosis that the difficulties of the European integration in surpassing the nation state are to some extent the result of the lagging behind of the development of a collective European identity has not lost its relevance after 1993, even after the Maastricht treaties.

Integration through formation of a collective identity is closely connected with the symbolic function of political institutions. The essentials of this concept of integration were formulated by Rudolf Smend, one of the famous German professors of constitutional law during the Weimar Republic period. Central for him was the question of how the constitution can be conceived in relation to the fundamental problem of national unity which is the problem of integrating the citizens.[17] He pointed out that interpreting the constitution should not be restricted to rational intention. It has to be taken into account that functional and often unconsciously working values, which are to some extent irrational, play a decisive role in integrating the members of the community. In reference to Litt[18] he assumes that the bonds tying the citizens to the state are not so much of a rational nature, but are even more the result of collective experiences. Litt and Smend assert that the connections of society result so much from rational discourses, but rather from intersubjective acts of imagination, empathy, and feeling. Therefore integration, whether we are aware of it or not, works in a much wider than purely rationalistic way. It follows that in the state, political institutions not only integrate the citizens by providing rational forms of decision-making processes. An even more important function of political institutions is to provide participation by means of creating a feeling of common identity. In this way the structure of integration is more fundamental than is expressed simply in terms of organization. Integration is effected in general by conveying symbolically a feeling of collective identity. Symbols are the essentials of integration. They are particularly necessary when the number of citizens to be integrated is so large that a direct experience of participation processes is not assured. In small communities identification is assured by direct participation. In larger societies this feeling of identification must be produced by symbols which can bridge time and space. Providing social unity becomes a problem in all cases where the identity cannot be experienced immediately by the citizens themselves. The consequence is the need to effect integration by using symbolic means. A national symbol such as a flag or a written constitution serves such a function of providing this experience of identity which is not immediately felt by means of political organization. Obviously this way of using symbols to orient people in their political actions has an indis-

[17] See Rudolf Smend, 'Verfassung und Verfassungsrecht', *Staatsrechtliche Abhandlungen*, 2nd edn (Berlin, 1968), pp. 119–276.
[18] Theodor Litt, *Individuum und Gemeinschaft* (Berlin/Leipzig, 1919; 3rd edn, 1926).

pensable integrative function in modern mass societies which are so anonymous and heterogeneous.

To sum up: taken in its broadest sense the concept of integration means that a collective unity as a frame of reference for individual behaviour must be established and kept effective continuously. Integration is based both on organization and on orientation of the citizens. In a technical sense unity is established through the coordination and organization of collective action. Those involved act according to the same rules and submit to commonly binding decisions. One may call it the result of a 'successive integration'. In a symbolic sense integration is related to orientation; one may call it 'continuous integration',[19] i.e. the result of a reiterative process. It arises when the citizens direct their actions – as far as others or the community are concerned – according to a commonly shared value system of the society. They need not be consciously aware of it. The action patterns can be found in a corresponding social habit, namely in specific forms of expression, styles of thinking, and types of behaviour. The orientation to commonly shared values and principles of political order requires a symbolic expression so that to a certain extent there exist visible and ascertainable guideposts which continuously offer an orientation for collective action. In this sense political institutions are means of symbolic orientation. They are to be measured not only by their organizational functionality and effectiveness. In addition they have to bring to expression the basic values and principles of political order. That is the second and sometimes even more important criterion of their real effectiveness.

This is true for social as well as for political integration. In general, political unity is associated mainly with control and therefore with technical integration, and social unity mainly with symbolic integration. When considering the problems of European integration we should be aware that this distinction is obsolete from the point of view of politics. The subject of politics is to come to decisions which are relevant and binding for the society as a whole. So it cannot do without providing orientation too. Symbolic integration is required at the national as well as at the supranational level, and this kind of integration is often neglected when analysing the present situation and future trends of European integration.

I would like to summarize the structure and the functional condi-

---

[19] See the contribution of Dietrich Rometsch in this book.

tions of political institutions which I have presented by discussing symbols, symbolic representation, and symbolic integration. It is obvious that *symbolic integration* is closely connected with *symbolic representation*. Symbolic representation makes visible the principles of living together in an expressive manner which goes beyond the pure description of political order. Symbolic integration provides and maintains in this way an orientation which holds the community together. This integrating orientation is offered by those principles of order which are expressed and kept present by symbolic representation. Thus symbolic integration and symbolic representation are interrelated. Briefly, in the context we are discussing here, symbolic integration is the functional complement of symbolic representation which is required in the formation of societies. Accordingly symbolic representation, symbolic integration, and political institutions are interrelated. To the extent that the principles of order are persistently established and confirmed by internalization, they are institutionalized. In this way every society develops its own systems of institutions in which symbols are incorporated. Based on symbolic representation and by means of symbolic integration the institutions offer symbolically mediated orientation. The orientation is political and has to be provided by political institutions when related to the community in the sense of definitive and generally binding decisions. It is one of the results of the work of the research program on 'Theory of Political Institutions' to have drawn attention to these interrelations. In this way, new perspectives are opened for the analysis of national and supranational institutions, and even for the problems of European integration.

Select bibliography

Bellah, Robert N. et al., *Habits of the Heart* (Berkeley, 1985).

Bermbach, Udo, *Demokratietheorie und politische Institutionen* (Opladen, 1991).

Böckenförde, Ernst-Wolfgang, *Demokratie und Repräsentation* (Hannover, 1983).

Buchheim, Hans, *Theorie der Politik* (München/Wien, 1981).

Castoriadis, Cornelius, *Gesellschaft als imaginäre Institution* (Frankfurt/M., 1990).

Dörner, Andreas, 'Die Inszenierung politischer Mythen', *Politische Vierteljahresschrift*, 34 (1993), pp. 199-218.

Douglas, Mary, *How Institutions Think* (Syracuse, NY, 1986).

Eco, Umberto, *Zeichen* (Frankfurt/M., 1977).

18   *The European Union and member states*

—— *Semiotik und Philosophie der Sprache* (München, 1985).

Elias, Norbert, *Über den Prozeß der Zivilisation. Soziogenetische und psychogenetische Untersuchungen*, 2 vols. (Frankfurt/M., 17th edn, 1992).

Fraenkel, Ernst, *Zur Soziologie der Klassenjustiz und Aufsätze zur Verfassungskrise 1931–32* (Darmstadt, 1968).

—— *Reformismus und Pluralismus* (Hamburg, 1973).

—— *Deutschland und die westlichen Demokratien* (7th edn, Stuttgart, 1979; extended version Frankfurt/M., 1991).

Göhler, Gerhard, 'Soziale Institutionen – politische Institutionen. Das Problem der Institutionentheorie in der neueren deutschen Politikwissenschaft', in Wolfgang Luthardt and Arno Waschkuhn (eds.), *Politik und Repräsentation* (Marburg, 1988), pp. 12–28.

—— 'Politische Repräsentation in der Demokratie', in T. Leif, H.-J. Legrand and A. Klein (eds.), *Die politische Klasse in Deutschland* (Bonn, Berlin, 1992), pp. 108–25.

—— 'Politische Institutionen und ihr Kontext. Begriffliche und konzeptionelle Überlegungen zur Theorie politischer Institutionen', in Gerhard Göhler (ed.), *Die Eigenart der Institutionen. Zum Profil politischer Institutionentheorie* (Baden-Baden, 1994), pp. 19–46.

Göhler, Gerhard (ed.), *Grundfragen der Theorie politischer Institutionen* (Opladen, 1987).

—— *Die Eigenart der Institutionen. Zum Profil politischer Institutionentheorie* (Baden-Baden, 1994).

Göhler, Gerhard and Schmalz-Bruns, Rainer, 'Perspektiven der Theorie politischer Institutionen (Literaturbericht)', *Politische Vierteljahresschrift*, 29 (1988), pp. 309–49.

Göhler, Gerhard, Lenk, Kurt, Münkler, Herfried and Walther, Manfred (eds.), *Politische Institutionen im gesellschaftlichen Umbruch. Ideengeschichtliche Beiträge zur Theorie politischer Institutionen* (Opladen, 1990).

Göhler, Gerhard, Lenk, Kurt and Schmalz-Bruns, Rainer (eds.), *Die Rationalität politischer Institutionen. Interdisziplinäre Perspektiven* (Baden-Baden, 1990).

Hartmann, Volker, *Repräsentation in der politischen Theorie und Staatslehre in Deutschland* (Berlin, 1979).

Hofmann, Hasso, *Repräsentation. Studien zur Wort- und Begriffsgeschichte* (Berlin, 1974; 2nd edn, 1990).

Langer, Susanne, *Philosophy in a New Key. A Study in the Symbolism of Reason, Rite, and Art* (Cambridge, Mass., 1942).

Lau, Ephraim Else, *Interaktion und Institution. Zur Theorie der Institution und Institutionalisierung aus der Perspektive einer verstehend-interaktionistischen Soziologie* (Berlin, 1978).

Leibholz, Gerhard, *Das Wesen der Repräsentation* (Berlin, New York, 1973).

Mantl, Wolfgang, *Repräsentation und Identität* (Wien, New York, 1975).

Münch, Richard, *Die Struktur der Moderne. Grundmuster und differentielle Gestaltung des institutionellen Aufbaus der modernen Gesellschaften* (Frankfurt/M., 1984).

Peters, Bernhard, *Die Integration moderner Gesellschaften* (Frankfurt/M., 1993).

Podlech, A., 'Repräsentation', in Brunner/Conze/Koselleck (eds)., *Geschichtliche Grundbegriffe*, vol. 5 (Stuttgart, 1984).

Rehberg, Karl-Siegbert, 'Institutionen als symbolische Ordnung. Leitfragen und Grundkategorien zur Theorie und Analyse institutioneller Mechanismen', in Gerhard Göhler (ed.), *Die Eigenart der Institutionen. Zum Profil politischer Institutionentheorie* (Baden-Baden, 1994), pp. 47–84.

Rödel, Ulrich, Frankenberg, Günter and Dubiel, Helmut, *Die demokratische Frage* (Frankfurt/M., 1989).

Rüther, Günther u.a., Die *'vergessenen' Institutionen* (Melle, 1979).

Schmalz-Bruns, Rainer, *Ansätze und Perspektiven der Institutionentheorie. Eine bibliographische und konzeptionelle Einführung* (Wiesbaden, 1989).

Schmölz, Hans-Martin (ed.), *Der Mensch in der politischen Institution* (Wien, 1964).

Schneider, Heinrich, 'Europäische Integration: die Leitbilder und die Politik', in Michael Kreile (ed.), *Die Integration Europas* (Opladen, 1992), pp. 3–35.

—— 'Europäische Identität. Historische, kulturelle und politische Dimensionen', *Integration*, 14 (1992), pp. 160–76.

Schülein, Johann August, *Theorie der Institution. Eine dogmengeschichtliche und konzeptionelle Analyse* (Opladen, 1987).

Sellin, Volker, 'Politik', in Brunner/Conze/Koselleck (eds.), *Geschichtliche Grundbegriffe*, vol. 4 (Stuttgart, 1978).

Waschkuhn, Arno, *Zur Theorie politischer Institutionen*, Ph.D thesis (München, 1974).

Willms, Bernard, *Funktion – Rolle – Institution* (Düsseldorf, 1971).

—— *Selbstbehauptung und Anerkennung. Grundriß einer politischen Dialektik* (Wiesbaden, 1977).

—— *Einführung in die Staatslehre* (Paderborn, 1979).

Wolff, Hans-Julius, *Organschaft und Vertretung* (Aaler, 1968).

Institutions of the EU system: models of explanation

The dynamic framework: the EC/EU as a growing politico-administrative system

The West European states and their political institutions are undergoing fundamental changes. Major features determining these evolutions are the dynamics of the integration process within the EC/EU framework. For looking at political institutions in Europe we therefore need to be aware of the relevance and the basic characteristics of the EU. My major thesis is as follows:

The development of the EC system from the early ECSC (European Coal and Steel Community) times towards the EU can be seen as a process in which political institutions have fused their competences and powers for, on a broadening scale and with growing intensity, preparing, making, implementing and controlling binding decisions[1] for public policies by using state-like instruments.[2] The EC/EU has thus evolved into a state-like politico-administrative system.

We thus apply traditional notions of political analysis, such as the term 'political system' for the EC/EU as defined by Max Weber's 'monopoly of legitimate coercion'[3] and by Easton's 'authoritative allocation of values'[4] or – in line with this argument – by the output of legally binding acts. We also look at major phases within such a policy cycle.

---

[1] See 'Einleitung: Politische Ideengeschichte – institutionentheoretisch gelesen', in Gerhard Göhler, Kurt Lenk, Herfried Münkler and Manfred Walther (eds.), *Politische Institutionen im gesellschaftlichen Umbruch* (Opladen: Westdeutscher Verlag, 1990), pp. 7–19.

[2] See Ernst-Hasso Ritter, 'Das Recht als Steuerungsmedium im kooperativen Staat', *Staatswissenschaft und Staatspraxis*, 1 (1990), pp. 50–88.

[3] See Max Weber, *Wirtschaft und Gesellschaft, Grundriss der verstehenden Soziologie*, ed. J. Winkelmann, 4th edn (Tübingen: Mohr, 1956).

[4] See David Easton, *A Systems Analysis of Political Life* (New York: John Wiley, 1965).

The constitutional set-up

The major bodies

One essential feature for any institutional analysis is what might be called the 'constitutional set-up' or the overall institutional configuration. Figure 2.1 shows the institutions, organizations and bodies of major importance within the EU. With regard to the overall composition of this set-up and to the procedural division of labour among them in the policy cycle, we are faced with a unique set-up.

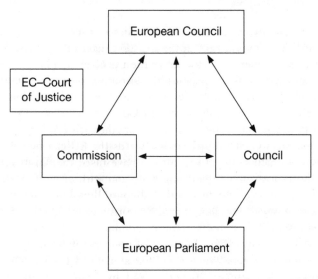

Fig. 2.1 Institutions of major importance within the EU

As opposed to traditional 'international organizations' and 'confederal systems', one of the unique features of the EC set-up is that three institutions – the Commission, the European Parliament (EP) and the European Court of Justice (ECJ) – which take part in the policy cycle are *de jure* and to a large degree *de facto* independent of national governments or other national bodies; this implies that 'sovereign' states have to deal with political actors which are outside their immediate control. Individual national governments are no longer fully in charge of the preparation, taking, implementation and control of decisions which are binding upon them. The role of these independent bodies has been extended, both in terms of legal powers and political and administrative functions in the policy cycle, and in terms of policy areas in which they are getting active.

This feature, however, does not imply that national actors are being pushed out of the policy cycle. Quite the contrary: national governments are striving for a central role in several bodies.

The 'highest authority' of national representation, the European Council, is outside the 'constitutional checks and balances' of the EC/EU since it is – legally speaking – not a body of the European Community and it is not subject to the control of the European Court of Justice. This body nevertheless takes *de facto* basic decisions for the Community;[5] it is the arena in which the highest political leaders and representatives of the member states have over the years increased their involvement in the EC/EU considerably. Ministers of national governments participate in the EC Council which after the Maastricht Treaty is the responsible decision-maker in all three pillars of the EU. The number of sessions of this body has increased considerably over the history of the EC/EU from twenty-one (1960) to ninety-five (1993).

In contrast to traditional confederal systems, the Council takes decisions in important policy areas increasingly by majority votes (1994: forty-eight decisions by qualified majority) or, at least, can threaten to do so. This means that the traditional doctrine of unanimity in international bodies – a symbol for sovereign states – has been eroded.

In such an institutional set-up it is very difficult to identify *the* decision-maker of the system. There is no president, no prime-minister or chancellor who – at the end of the day – would be able to take the final decision and would have to defend it. Given the complexity, decisions are always taken by several bodies of different composition, making it difficult to identify *the* persons responsible for the EU policies. There is a benevolent 'diffusion of responsibility and accountability'.[6]

---

[5] See Simon Bulmer and Wolfgang Wessels, *The European Council. Decision–Making in European Politics* (London: Macmillan, 1987).

[6] See Fritz Scharpf, 'The Joint-Decision Trap: Lessons from German Federalism and European Integration', *Public Administration*, 66 (Autumn 1988), pp. 239–78; here: p. 270.

Constitutional models

This set-up is neither static nor interpreted in one way only, but several models are presented in the political and academic debate which serve as a way of analysing and assessing the present set-up as well as options for future constitutional strategies.

The *intergovernmental model* of what one might call a 'confederal Europe' (see Figure 2.2) is based on the notion of the national sovereignty of member states. According to this concept, there would and should be no fundamental transfer of areas of competences from nation states to the Union which could then be exercised by independent European institutions. A confederal Europe is simply based on a 'pooling of sovereignties', the member states, as the 'masters of the game', are always keeping the final say. There is only one legitimacy involved, that of national governments, which is derived from national elections and transferred by national parliaments. In terms of its institutional evolution in the EU, this pooling of national authorities finds its ultimate representation in the European Council. This body should become – *de facto* or even *de jure* – the central decision-making locus which would take decisions by unanimity only.

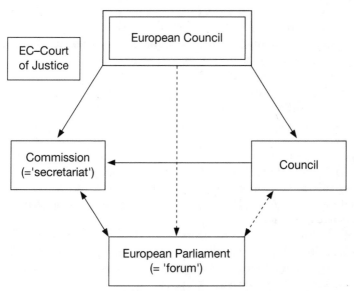

Fig. 2.2 Intergovernmental model of a confederal Europe

The Council would also be of major importance taking the legally binding decisions. It is supported by the Council Secretariat, the Committee of Permanent Representatives (COREPER) and its working groups; some kind of formal authority representing the Union to the public and to the external world is located in the Presidency. The Commission would become something like an expert bureaucracy which would be able to work within the Council machinery and which might be asked to implement certain jointly agreed-upon decisions. The European Parliament would become a forum for public debate but without co-decision-making powers. The European Court of Justice would or should not play any major role as it would imply a higher authority than that of national governments which is not acceptable according to the basic notions of this constitutional model. The demand for unanimity would create quite considerable hurdles for decision-making efficiency, which would go on to influence the overall effectiveness of the future EU. With consensus as the only decision-making modality, distributional bargaining would lead to solutions sub-optimal in terms of rational decision-making. Quite often the proponents of this system stress that the effectiveness of implementing common acts will be higher as this is done by competent national administrations without being bothered by an independent bureaucracy such as that of the Commission.

Such a model might be perceived as a valid description, though with slight variations, in the area of the Common Foreign and Security Policy (second pillar), taking into account the fact that the Commission is 'fully associated'. The same model is generally compatible with the legal set-up of the cooperation in areas of Justice and Home Affairs (third pillar). Also in the original EC Treaty as amended by Maastricht (first pillar), some approximations to this model can be found, such as in the area of economic cooperation in the context of the Economic and Monetary Union. Some would argue that this model would be very useful, or at least relevant, in view of the further enlargements to include less 'federalist' countries and for all crucial areas of national sovereignty, especially those of 'high politics' like defence, foreign policy and monetary policy. This constitutional strategy would propose to reinforce all those bodies and procedures which strengthen the role of the member states. The subsidarity principle should work downwards and the IGC '96 should reverse some steps taken by the Maastricht Treaty.

Such a model as part of a downward revision is of major importance in the current debate. It may well find a stronger 'renaissance' should the Maastricht Treaty fail to be fully implemented. In contrast to the view of intergovernmentalists the traditional federal strategy is proposing a different constitutional option.

The *federal model* of the 'United States of Europe' (see Figure 2.3) would imply a total rearrangement of the present institutional set-up along the traditional lines of classical federations. The Commission would turn out to be a government; the head of this government would be directly elected by the European Parliament with no say or only a limited say by the Council; this person would then appoint other 'ministers'. In terms of the relative weight of the respective bodies, the European Parliament would become the first chamber, the Council merely a second chamber which would have an equal status only in certain rather limited areas of remaining concurrent competence. The seats of the European Parliament would be distributed among member states by strict proportionality which would lead to a strong representation of the populations of larger member states. To compensate this shift, the Council, as a second chamber, could be based on a more equal representation such as that of the German Länder in the Bundesrat (i.e. different number of votes depending on the size of the population), or even going in the direction of the US Senate by which each member state would have the same number of votes in the Council. The application of a strict proportionality in the EP, as the dominating body, could lead to worries in small member countries which would not be counter-balanced sufficiently by more equal rights in the Council, especially if the importance of this body were reduced.

In this model the basic source of legitimation would be the direct elections to the European Parliament and, via the parliament, the link between the citizens and the European government. Legitimation by traditional national sources would be of secondary importance. The historical West European nation state would, to a considerable degree, be substituted by the 'European Federation'.

This model is based on a clearly formulated transfer of competences to the level of the 'United States of Europe', leaving competence only for a limited number of areas to the national level. The basic notion is that the pre-existing national states would become similar to those which are known in the United States as 'states' or as 'Länder' in the Federal Republic of Germany. A constitutional court would be of major importance for 'intergovernmental' relations between the different levels of government and for disputes among the institutions of the Union. Efficiency and effectiveness are supposed to be high since decisions could be taken swiftly and adequate instruments would be available to the then government of the United States of Europe. The basic problem, however, would be the implementation process by national or regional administrations and the legitimacy involved in it. Without proper participation in the policy cycle, the acceptance of binding decisions taken 'far away' in Brussels or Strasbourg might be low by the administrations and populations concerned; the overall capacity to deal with problems might then be rapidly eroded. The relative clarity of the constitutional arrangements would then contrast with the lack of social acceptance and proper implementation. To establish a Community bureaucracy, specifically to supervise in detail the implementation of Community acts in all member countries, would, indeed, create a 'super-bureaucracy' which looks neither acceptable nor effective.

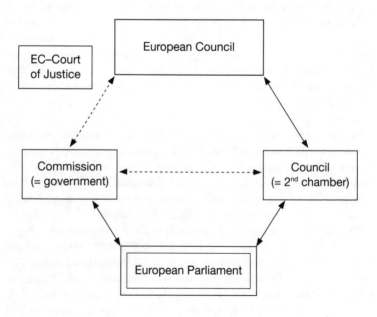

Fig. 2.3   Federal model of a United States of Europe

The trends of the EC/EU in the last years, including the post-Maastricht development, give some indications of a 'real world' evolution in the direction of this federal model. The European Council and the Council have remained central decision-making bodies. There are, however, some steps towards a (pre-) parliamentary government system by giving the European Parliament a say in the Commission's elections, though this is neither the only nor the final say. Of high relevance also are the co-decision and the assent procedures which considerably increase the weight of the EP. The clearest step forward in the direction of this model is the decision concerning the Monetary Union with an independent central bank system at the European level; at least in terms of the transfer of competences, Monetary Union follows the strategy of the federal model.

The *cooperative federal model* of a 'merged Europe' (see Figure 2.4) is based on the concept of dual legitimacy, i.e. that of the member states and that of the Community, which both have a decisive say in preparing, making, implementing and controlling binding decisions for the combined use of instruments located originally either at the EC or at the national level. Following this dual principle, all major decisions, subdivided into five groups of legal acts – be they of a legislative, budgetary, elective, external treaty-making or constitutional nature – would be taken by the European Parliament and the Council in a *joint* way. Nearly all constitutional treaty changes in the last decades have supported the trend towards a co-decision-making power of the EP. In the future the principle of equal status of both bodies could be applied in several ways. Taken together, the 'weaker' body would be able to block a decision by certain quota which would be fixed according to the hierarchy of acts.

Besides this duality the Commission would move into the direction of a government; however, the head of the government would be elected by both the European Parliament and the European Council. The other members of this 'government' would be nominated by the head of the Commission and would at least require an approval by both other bodies in the way the US Senate approves 'Secretaries' in the Washington administration. The European Council would become – as already indicated in the provisions for EMU – a 'higher level chamber' of the Council, but would be integrated into some kind of constitutional 'checks and balances'. The European Parliament would be elected on what is called the 'regressive proportionality', i.e. that the distribution of voters among member states is taken into account more than in the present EP, but not fully to the degree of a strict proportionality such as in the federal model of the United States of Europe. Thus, there would be a minority protection of the smaller countries in the Parliament, but also – compared at least with the status quo – more fairness for larger countries. The

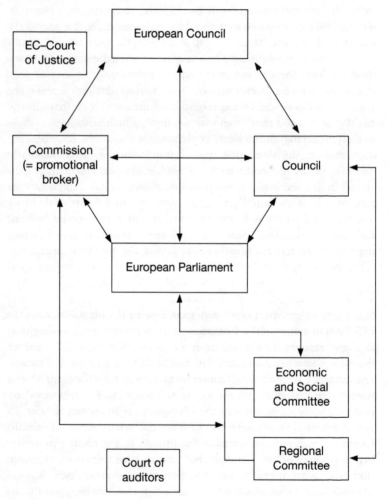

Fig. 2.4 Cooperative federal model of a merged Europe

same applies to the weighted voting in the Council. The present distribution of votes among member countries might be kept, though the
respective majorities needed might have to be adapted. The Court
would play an important role, especially in conflicts between the different institutions which would inevitably arise. The transfer of areas
of competence would be less clear in this model: national and Community areas of competence are mixed. Any attempt to make, more
or less once and for all, a clear-cut division of areas of competence
between the national and the community level (or even the sub-
national levels) is viewed by advocates of this model as a rather futile
exercise.

In terms of performance, we expect a mixed balance for this
model. Given majority voting in all institutions, the efficiency of decision-making within each of these bodies would be considerable. The
major problem would be the relationship between the institutions of
equal status and, thus, the way to find agreements among those
bodies, especially on the election of the Commission (= government).
The new co-decision procedure (established by the Maastricht
Treaty) already demonstrates the problems of conciliation and of the
conciliation committee. It would be necessary to have some kind of
mechanism which would – in crucial situations – be able to de-block
any kind of institutional 'impasse'. In particular, this would be done
by giving one of these bodies a certain prerogative, but also by offering specific procedural functions to the President of the Commission.

Institutions in the policy cycle

Starting from an 'ideal type' policy cycle, we can also identify for the
EC the four major phases of decision-preparation, decision-making,
decision-implementation and decision-control (see Table 2.1), though
the role of institutions is different from traditional national patterns.

The policy cycle of the Community concerning the 'first pillar' only
starts after a proposal by the Commission. In the EC areas of competence the Commission has the monopoly of initiative, which is a
very influential instrument for shaping the final output. Inside the
Commission there are complex horizontal and vertical procedures
between Directorates General and Cabinets for preparing the decisions which are taken by the college. The commission services look
normally for close contacts with civil servants, lobbies, diplomats
from third countries, etc., whilst preparing proposals. The Commis-

sion has established a loose system of so-called 'expert groups' (around 600) in which national civil servants and representatives of interest groups are invited to comment on first drafts. The Commission itself seeks to build up a system of 'engrenage' (meshing) with these persons who might act as some kind of 'coalition partners' for the next phases of the policy cycle.

The procedures in the decision-making phase vary according to the rules applied. Important actors are the Council and – to a varying, though increasing degree – the European Parliament. The Maastricht Treaty on European Union has strengthened the powers of the EP and enlarged the areas of their application. In 1994 the Commission launched ninety-one proposals in the complex co-decision procedure (189b TEU). The co-decision procedure has been applied sixty times in 1994, the co-operation procedure fifty-three times and the consultation procedure, which gives the least powers to the EP, was used 168 times.

The decision-making process within the Parliament is dominated by committees and party groups. Unlike the dominant pattern in the parliaments of the member states, there is no clear cleavage between those parties which support the government and those which are in opposition. Several lines of cleavages exist in the EP. The left/right cleavage dominates in only a few cases. Given the heterogeneity of the parties involved, a clear ideological demarcation which would cut across all areas is difficult to identify and maintain; cleavages can also be found along certain policy sectors, such as the agricultural and regional policies which have different lobbies.

Since the Single European Act of 1987 we can identify one basic pattern of great importance to the internal working of the EP: a *'grande coalition'* between the European Socialists and the Christian Democrats (called the European People's Party). This is largely induced by the constitutional provisions of the EC Treaty: the opinions of the European Parliament need an 'absolute majority' now of 314 if they are to be of further legal relevance, when the 'cooperation' (see Article 189c TEU) the 'co-decision' (see Article 189b TEU) and the 'assent' procedures at least for accessions (see Article O TEU) are applied.

For the Council it is useful to make a distinction between two phases in the internal decision-making. In the *first phase*, the proposal by the Commission and the opinion of the European Parliament are sent via COREPER (the Committee of Permanent Representatives of EC Member States) to working groups (1994: 238 working groups) in

Table 2.1 Stages of the politico-administrative decision-making process of the EU

Level	I. Decision-preparation	II. Decision-making				III. Decision-implementation		IV. Control	
		(a) Pre-parliamentary deliberations	(b) Parliamentary deliberations	(c) Preparation	(d) Decision-making	(a) Transposition	(b) Implementation	(c) Execution	(d) Control
Interstate level (Community level)	*Com* 20 members Cabinet DG (23) Expert groups (around 600)	*Committee of the Regions* (222 members) *ECOSOC* (222 members)	*EP* (626 members) Party Groups (10) Committees (20)	*Council* Secretariat General	*Council* Presidency A + B Points	*Com* Supervision	*Com* Implementation Implementation Committees	*Com* Supervision	*ECJ* Jurisdiction
Intra-state level (National level)	Civil servants and interest groups Municipalities Regions European Associations/Federations		National parliaments Political parties federations	COREPER and working groups (around 250)	National ministries and administrations	National governments, parliaments and administrations	7 basic types (around 300)	Execution through national (incl. regional) administrations	National Courts of Justice

Phase

which civil servants of the national governments, together with the respective experts of the Commission, discuss and negotiate the draft texts word by word. It is in this phase that the majority of articles of a legislative act are agreed upon.

The *second phase* of the Council's decision-making consists of the final decisions taken by the ministers themselves. On the Council's agenda we find so-called 'A' and 'B' points. The 'A' points are those drafts which need no further deliberations because a consensus has been reached on a lower administrative level. In those cases ministers simply 'ratify' the agreements of their civil servants. As for 'B' points, different voting modalities must be respected. Of particular importance is the qualified majority with weighted votes. Its application was extended by the Single European Act and the Maastricht Treaty on European Union to more and more fields of EC activity. The 'real life' patterns so far show that direct voting in the Council 'by raising hands' takes place only on very rare occasions; normally the President of the Council concludes a debate in the Council by indicating that the conditions for achieving an agreement have apparently been met, which means that an act has been passed if there is no outright and open opposition to this statement. Such a procedure in the Council, which is animated by the possibility of using majority voting, places each member government and national administration under strong pressure to act and react quickly in order to avoid being suddenly outvoted or being caught in an uncomfortable minority position. The President of the Council and the chairs of the groups are of crucial importance for moving the dossier through the machinery and – as neutral brokers – for coming to an agreement.

The *third phase* of the EC policy cycle is the decision-implementation which is often neglected in most analyses of Community procedures. We should distinguish at least three different phases:

1 EC legal acts, especially directives, must be transposed into national law, or at least into national administrative acts. The Commission carefully and comprehensively supervises this transformation which is done by national governments, administrations and parliaments. National institutions are thus under direct surveillance.

2 Once an act has become legally valid, the Commission is responsible for the implementation of these acts. For this phase the Council has established a system of committees (the so-called 'comitology')

which is highly complex (currently more than twelve types exist, which are supposed to be reduced to seven basic types). The differences within this set of procedures are due to the powers of a committee to delay or to block the implementation acts of the Commission. There are around 310 committees (1994) in which national civil servants and experts of the Commission try to put the legal provisions into operative practice.

3 The day-to-day implementation of legislative acts is done by national, regional and local administrations, e.g. national customs officers are applying the Community regulations on customs duties. The Commission as the 'guardian of the Treaty' has the function of controlling the proper implementation of Community acts.

The legal control, the *fourth phase*, is performed by the European Court of Justice as well as by national courts. It is in this phase that the supranational binding character becomes especially evident. One basic feature becomes clear: in each place political institutions from both the EU and the national level, are closely involved in some kind of multi-level cooperative effort.

The politico-administrative system in growth

The system as described is not static, but we observe an extensive growth of the decisions by the Council and the Commission – also in comparison with the national legislation. The Council's decision-making capacity increased from ten decisions, regulations and directives in 1960 to 546 in 1993. In a very rough comparison to this, the German Bundestag's legislative activity remained rather stable, ranging from 424 laws which were adopted between 1957 and 1961 to 314 laws between 1990 and 1993, i.e. an average of approximately 100 laws a year.

The EC/EU's decisions add up to the '*acquis communautaire*' which has considerable relevance for the member states, for the economic and social actors, as well as for the individual citizens. The EU system also produces other decisions of what some might call 'soft law'; declarations by the European Council or decisions taken in the area of the Common Foreign and Security Policy (CFSP), i.e. the second pillar, and in the area of Justice and Home Affairs, i.e. the third pillar, are examples of this output. Those are not subject to control by the European Court of Justice, but have nevertheless some kind of binding character and impact. Also in the first pillar of the EC there are less binding agreements such as 'action programmes'.

Also the scope of traditional and new public policies being pursued by the institutions of the EU has increased considerably from the early 1950s to the early 1990s. The number of state sectors dealt with at the European level is approaching that covered normally by Western European states, at least since the Maastricht Treaty on European Union has come into force.

Not only the classical issues of the European Economic Community (like the internal market) but also traditional core areas of national sovereignty – internal order (see third pillar), external defence (see second pillar) and monetary autonomy (see first pillar) – are in some way or the other dealt with by the EU; newer areas of public interest, such as environmental issues and consumer protection, are also subjects which concern the European Union. There are very few political issues on the national agenda which are not also addressed – albeit with varying intensity and procedures – by the EU institutions.

The scope of policies dealt with is not identical with the legal power to take binding decisions. The major types of 'state-like instruments' are laws and budgetary appropriations.[7] Competences for operating public policies have increasingly been transferred upwards to the level of the European Union by new treaties, treaty reforms such as the Single European Act and the Maastricht Treaty on European Union, incremental adaptations using Art. 235 EEC and legal 'mutations' by the ECJ.[8] This upward trend is, however, not leading to the traditional division of competences known from classical federal constitutions. We are confronted with a 'messy' and ambiguous vertical fusion of national and EU competences and even more with a highly differentiated 'mixture' of public instruments located on several levels. The transfer process is not based on a federally inspired blueprint for framing a constitution but on 'package deals',[9] which combine several national interests – not necessarily in a coherent and consistent way.

    [7] See Ritter, *op. cit.*
    [8] See Joseph Weiler, 'The Transformation of Europe', *The Yale Law Journal*, 8 (1991), pp. 2403–83.
    [9] See Helen Wallace, 'Making Multilateral Negotiations Work', in William Wallace (ed.), *The Dynamics of European Integration* (London, New York: Pinter, 1990), pp. 213–28; Wolfgang Wessels, 'Staat und (westeuropäische) Integration. Die Fusionsthese', in Michael Kreile (ed.), *Die Integration Europas*, special issue of *Politische Vierteljahresschrift*, 23 (1992), pp. 36–61.

We also witness a growth of institutions and procedures which has reached over the years a high degree of 'byzantine' variety. After Maastricht the EC Treaty alone contains twenty-five combinations of voting modalities in the Council and forms of participation of the EP. Many procedures – such as the budgetary procedure (Art. 203 TEU) and the co-decision procedure (Art. 189b TEU) – are quite complex, documenting a carefully weighted relationship between member-state-dominated institutions and independent EC/EU institutions. More and more actors from national institutions participate in the policy cycle. The relative intensity of participation of the German administration has on average more than doubled since 1960 at least when taken from rough quantitative indicators.[10]

National institutions and the EC system: Europeanization, fusion and convergency?

So far we have looked at the institutions from a 'Brussels perspective': we have tried to identify the actors in the EU arena from the European level. In the following chapters we will observe the roles and behaviour of institutions on the national level, i.e. from the perspective of the national capitals. The focus will be on the extent and intensity of participation by national institutions in the EC/EU decision-making process. Given the features and the dynamics of the EC/EU evolution, we expect to find generally observable trends in the ways national institutions react and adapt to the challenges of the EC/EU. For the chapters on national institutions we formulate three hypotheses:

The Europeanization hypothesis

We expect that the overall number and the number of respective groups of national actors involved in the policy cycle on the national and the EC/EU level have and will increase considerably as will the intensity of their European engagement. National actors will not react by resistance to the integration process of the EC/EU but by raising demands for an adequate participation on the national and

[10] See Wolfgang Wessels, *Die Öffnung des Staates. Modell zwischenstaatlicher Verwaltungsstränge* (working title, forthcoming).
[11] See for these categories Albert Hirschmann, *Exit, Voice and Loyalty. Responses to Decline in Firms, Organizations and States* (Cambridge, Mass.: Harvard University Press, 1970).

European level. The attention given to the EC/EU arena will grow: actors will raise 'voice' and not look for 'exit'.[11] A 'pull' by the EC/EU will turn into a 'push' to participation. Such a 'Europeanization' will affect all national actors in a rather similar way, which means we do not expect an asymmetry among national institutional actors. 'Europeanization' in our definition is at first only a shift of attention and participation, not a change in the positive or negative attitudes towards the integration process of the EU.[12]

The fusion hypothesis

In a second step we expect the patterns of participation to lead to a 'fusion' of national and EU institutions in the policy cycle. This means for national institutions that they increasingly share responsibilities with other institutional actors outside their own control, be they national actors from other member states or from independent bodies, and that their way of interacting vertically and horizontally is increasingly influenced by the EC/EU arena. A change of policy styles is a logical corollary to this development.

The convergence hypothesis

In a third step we expect that the constitutional and institutional set-up of member states will converge towards one common model, which is not yet achieved but which is – as a result of the Europeanization and the fusion – 'in the making': in response to similar challenges given by the policy cycle in the EC/EU arena, political institutions in the EU member states will undertake constitutional, institutional, procedural, organizational and behavioural innovations and adaptations which lead in a similar direction. The pre-existing differences among member states will slowly, and partly unnoticed, disappear.

In the following chapters we will look on the basis of this three-fold working hypothesis, at how national institutions have developed as part of the EC/EU evolution.

---

[12] See for a slightly divergent definition Robert Ladrech, 'Europeanization of Domestic Politics and Institutions: The case of France', *Journal of Common Market Studies*, 32 (1) (1994), pp. 69–88; here: pp. 69f.

Belgium

Fundamentals of Belgium in EU affairs

To understand the Belgian decision-making process in EU matters, one must have in mind two main features of the politico-institutional system of the kingdom: firstly, since the end of the last world war, Belgium has always been acting as the 'good pupil' of European integration to promote its federalist vision of European construction. The idea that 'what is good for Europe is good for Belgium' is shared by all political parties of the country and is also spread among public opinion. Secondly, the transformation of Belgium into a federal state, in progress since 1970 and formally achieved in 1993, has not changed this way of thinking. However, it complicates the decision-making in European issues and the implementation of Community law.

Next to the language cleavage that has led to the federalization process, the working of political institutions in Belgium is still characterized by the so-called theory of 'pillarization', which means that policies are more the result of compromises between the three dominant 'sociological pillars' (Christian, socialist and liberal) composing the Belgian socio-political structure,[1] than the result of debates in the

---

[1] The 'pillars' express the adherence to 'spiritual groups' which are a kind of *Weltanschauungsgruppen* or 'sociological worlds' that cross the whole politico-social field and have an influence on most of the organized structures (trade unions, trade associations, social security mutual insurances, schools, universities, political parties). The effective power belongs to the 'pillars' despite the formal autonomy of the executive and the legislative. On the theory of 'pillarization', called *'verzuiling'* in Dutch (*zuil* means pillar) and *'mondocratie'*, *'théorie des mondes sociologiques'*, *'pilarisation'* or *'pluralisme segmenté'* in French, see, among others, J. Meynaud, J. Ladrière and F. Perin (eds.), *La décision politique en Belgique. Le pouvoir et les groupes* (Paris: Cahiers de la Fondation nationale des sciences politiques, 1965); V. R. Lorwin, 'Conflits et compromis dans la politique belge', *Courrier hebdomaire du CRISP*, 323 (1966); L. Huyse, *Passiviteit, pacificatie en verzuiling in de Belgische politiek* (Antwerpen: Standaard, 1970); J. Fitzmaurice, *The Politics of Belgium. Crisis and Compromise in*

parliament or in the regional chambers. Nonetheless, decisions in EU matters generally meet a wide consensus that does not require difficult compromises, in the search for which Belgian politicians have always shown a particular skill. To summarize, the definition of European policies in Belgium is largely facilitated by a national consensus on European integration that transcends the political and linguistic cleavages, even though the EC/EU decision-making process takes place now in a new federal reality in Belgium. Therefore, the main challenge to the implementation of the Maastricht Treaty lies in the effective participation of all the components of the Belgian state in any decision relevant to their competence.

Promoting European integration
Since the birth of the European Coal and Steel Community, Belgium has adopted European integration as an aim in itself.[2] It has always been supporting progress in the development of the Communities, defending proposals that emphasize the supranational elements in the European institutional structure. This political line, defined by Paul-Henri Spaak in the early 1950s, has been pursued by all subsequent governments, irrespective of the political parties in power. Several significant initiatives of Belgian leaders who have played key roles in the history of European integration can be mentioned.[3] The last one was the Belgian memorandum on the European construction sent in March 1990[4] to the Irish presidency by Mark Eyskens, Foreign Minister in the last government of Wilfried Martens (1988–1991). The memorandum was the first paper to propose the opening of an intergovernmental conference on political union in order to complete the planned intergovernmental conference on economic and monetary union. Relayed by the Kohl-Mitterrand letter on political union of

a Plural Society (London: C. Hurst and Company, 1983); A. P. Frognier and M. Collinge, 'La problématique des mondes sociologiques en Belgique', *Cahiers du CACEF*, 114 (1984), pp. 3–12; L. Huyse, *De verzuiling voorbij* (Leuven: Kritak, 1987) and S. Govaerts, 'Le débat sur le verzuiling en Flandre', *Courrier hebdomadaire du CRISP*, 1329 (1991).

[2] See P. de Schoutheete, 'Sovereignty and Supranationality', in M. A. G. van Meerhaeghe (ed.), *Belgium and EC Membership Evaluated* (London: Pinter Publishers; New York: St Martin's Press, 1992), p. 113.

[3] For instance: the initiatives of Spaak at the Messina conference in 1956; the Davignon report on European Political Cooperation in 1970; the Tindemans report on European Union in 1975.

[4] 'Aide-mémoire sur la construction européenne du 20 mars 1990', *Agence Europe. Europe-Documents*, no. 1608 (29 March 1990).

April 1990,[5] the Belgian memorandum was, without doubt, the first determinant step in the process leading to the Maastricht Treaty. The strong European commitment of the different Belgian governments has received wide approval within the country. In parliament, European integration is the only non-controversial field of foreign policy, in contrast to the African policy or the security policy. The programme of every political party contains the aim of a federal Europe. Even the Flemish nationalists and the Walloon regionalists are advocating the European federal idea because they are in favour of a (utopian) Europe of the regions. Public opinion also agrees with this consensus on European integration. An explanation of this fact can be found both in the small-power status of Belgium and in its open economy.

After the compulsory neutrality commanded by the European powers from 1830 till 1914, and the unsuccessful neutrality policy decided in 1936, Belgium saw in Atlantic and European multi-lateralism a better way to guarantee peace[6] and to intensify its participation in international affairs. Hence the participation of Belgium in European integration, where an attractive common sovereignty is exercised by the member states. Indeed, attachment to national sovereignty does not characterize the political culture of the Belgian citizens.[7] Being part of a small state, Belgian people realize that their country exerts more influence on world politics within a 'European integrated whole' than by a policy focusing on itself. They also know that Belgian statesmen have acquired an international dimension by their action within the framework of the European Community and that Brussels' world reputation is partly due to the presence of the European institutions in the Belgian capital. Besides, the economic life of a country whose exports represent half of the gross domestic product, and whose intra-Community trade reaches 70% of external exchanges, profits on a large scale from the trade effects of the Common Market. Already in 1973, Etienne Davignon, future member of the European Commission, recognized that Belgium was lucky

[5] See *Agence Europe*, no. 5238 (20 April 1990).

[6] Neither the neutrality status dating from the nineteenth century, nor the 'free hands' (strict neutrality) foreign policy conducted between the two wars, has avoided the invasion and the occupation of the country in 1914 and 1940.

[7] P. de Schoutheete (*op. cit.*, p. 114) summarizes very well this attitude: 'Belgium, a bilingual State at the crossroads of Europe, long used by its neighbours as a preferred battlefield, has always had a lesser degree of national self-conciousness and identity than other more monolithic and less-exposed nations'.

because its economic interests were often headed in the direction of European integration. So, the absence of noticeable national interests which must be defended most of the time facilitates Belgian action in European institutions.[8] Criticism of European integration is an exception that proves the rule of consensus. Some people express the wish to enhance the existing EU system by more efficiency and democracy. Sometimes national debates are about particular European issues. For instance, the chance given by the Treaty on European Union (TEU) to every citizen of the Community to vote in local elections in the member states is only contested in Belgium where it would possibly change linguistic majorities in the municipalities. This perspective makes the Dutch-speaking parties anxious. They fear the non-national residents' votes around Brussels will favour the French-speaking parties.[9]

Another worry has recently appeared in Belgium about the functioning of the EU institutions. The increasing role of the European Council, confirmed by the Maastricht Treaty, and the tendency of some large countries' European leaders to meet outside the EC/EU agenda about Community matters, gave rise to the spectre of a European '*directoire*' composed of four or five states, insidiously dominating the smaller countries. To prevent any extension of this tendency, Belgium voices strong opposition to every project aimed at changing the majority voting rules to the benefit of the large states or at limiting the use of every European language inside the European institutions. Belgium does not accept any institutional reform that does not respect the principle of equality between member states. To avoid any diminution of the political influence of the small countries inside the European Union after the next widening, the Belgian government, together with The Netherlands and Luxembourg, presented a memorandum insisting on this matter at the European Council of Lisbon in June 1992.[10]

[8] 'Nous avons une chance, c'est que nos intérêts économiques vont souvent dans le sens de l'intégration européenne. Si nous devions défendre de difficiles intérêts nationaux, cela nous compliquerait la tâche. Cela dit, nous ne cherchons pas le compromis pour le compromis. Quand un compromis possible ne va pas dans le sens de nos objectifs, nous ne l'appuyons pas.' *Agence Europe. Europe Documents*, no. 713 (January 1973), p. 7.

[9] See, on this question, T. de Wilde d'Estmael and C. Franck, 'Du mémorandum belge au traité de Maastricht', in C. Franck, C. Roosens and T. de Wilde d'Estmael (eds.), *Aux tournants de l'Histoire. La politique extérieure de la Belgique au début de la décennie 90* (Brussels: De Boeck-University, 1993), p. 59.

[10] See 'Mémorandum des pays Benelux concernant les décisions à prendre sur l'élargissement de l'Union européenne', *Agence Europe. Europe Documents*, no. 1789 (27 June 1992).

This critical debate does not mean an erosion of the favourable consensus which has prevailed so far in EC/EU affairs in Belgium. Quite the opposite, in fact: it only aims at preserving the federal vision of the founding fathers of European integration.

The federal structure

From 1970 to 1993, Belgium evolved from a unitary state towards a federal state. Several stages were necessary to achieve the federal metamorphosis of the country. The main constitutional revisions took place in 1970, 1980, 1988–89 and 1993. Since 5 May 1993, the federal identity of Belgium has been formally inscribed in the Constitution.[11] The radical specificity of Belgian federalism lies in the coexistence of two different kinds of federate entities: regions and communities. Their material competences are distinct while their respective areas of jurisdiction cover overlapping but non-identical territories. To render this *sui generis* federalism understandable, it is essential to show the difference between regions and communities before presenting their patterns of participation in the EC process.

Regions are territorial entities that divide Belgium into three parts: the Flemish region in the north (13,512 square kilometres), the Walloon region in the south (16,844 square kilometres) and the region of Brussels-Capital (162 square kilometres) that is located in the centre of the country, enclaved in the Flemish region. Two kinds of prerogatives lie within the competences of the regions: territorial matters (e.g. environment, water policy, town-planning) and economic matters (e.g. public works and transport, energy policy). The area of jurisdiction of each region is strictly determined by its geographical borderlines.

[11] The first article of the Belgian constitution now states: 'La Belgique est un Etat fédéral qui se compose des communautés et des régions'. On the Belgian state reforms, see, among others, for a political explanation of this peculiar phenomenon of dissociation federalism, X. Mabille, *Histoire politique de la Belgique. Facteurs et acteurs de changements* (Bruxelles: Éditions du CRISP, 1992); for a comprehensive view of the institutional reforms, C.E. Lagasse, *Les nouvelles institutions politiques de la Belgique et de l'Europe* (Louvain-la-Neuve: Artel, 1993); for a first comment on the reforms of 1993, F. Delpérée (ed.), *La Constitution fédérale du 5 mai 1993* (Brussels: Bruylant, 1993) and F. Delpérée, 'La Belgique est un Etat fédéral', *Journal des Tribunaux* (1993), pp. 637–47. Because of the numerous reforms adopted since 1970, the Belgian constitution had become nearly unreadable by 1993. The length of some articles and their complex numeration (article 59 *septies* and 107 *ter-bis*, for instance) have made the text very clumsy. Therefore, the constitutional text was completely reviewed and rearranged on 17 February 1994; the different articles appear now with a new numeration. See 'Constitution cordonnée', *Moniteur belge*, 17 February 1994.

Communities are groups of persons united by the use of the same language. Two major linguistic groups live in Belgium: the Dutch-speaking people (about 5·7 million) who form the Flemish community and the French-speaking people (more than 4 million) who constitute the French community.[12] Besides, about 60,000 Belgian citizens use the German language to form a small German-speaking community. As federate bodies, the Belgian communities hold competences relevant to the individual: education, cultural matters, use of language, broadcast media, parts of the youth protection policy and the health policy, for instance. The communities' areas of jurisdiction are essentially determined by the localization of the linguistic groups. So, the borderline of the communities does not correspond with those of the regions. The Flemish region falls under the sole jurisdiction of the Flemish community, even though a numerous French-speaking minority lives around Brussels. The population of the Brussels-Capital region includes about 85% French-speaking people and about 15% Dutch-speaking people. Both major communities may exercise their competences inside the Brussels area. Finally, the French community acts within the French-speaking Walloon region, except for a small part in the east of the region where the German-speaking Belgian people are living. This part of Wallonia, clearly limited (854 square kilometres), forms the area of jurisdiction of the German-speaking community. In short, people in the same area are dependent on both a region and a community.

This complex distribution of competences also multiplies the institutions in charge of their exercise. The overlapping structure of the regional and community institutions is difficult to understand for a foreign observer generally minded to limit the Belgian issue to the basic linguistic cleavage (Dutch-speaking versus French-speaking). In fact, each region and each community has its own government, called 'executive' till 1993, and a legislative assembly, the council.[13] In pursuance of their autonomy (in the literal sense of the word: the ability to make law on several matters), the institutions of the components of

[12] The term 'French community' is ambiguous. It might lead one to think of an association of Frenchmen living in Belgium. In fact, the name 'French community' comes from the wording that was at first used in 1970: 'cultural community of French language'. It has been shortened to 'French community' since the constitutional reform in 1980.
[13] Except the Flemish region, whose competences for reasons of simplification are exercised by the government and the council of the Flemish community.

the Belgian state have been more and more concerned and involved in the EC decision-making process, at the beginning with regard to the preparation of the decision and the implementation of Community law, and since the Maastricht Treaty, with regard even to decision-taking.[14]

In state reform after state reform, most of the governmental leaders have elaborated an ideological linkage between the Belgian federalization process and the construction of Europe. Under the catch-phrase 'la Belgique fédérale dans une Europe fédérale', political speeches have tried to show that the Belgian experience presages the federal Europe in the near future. So it is said that Belgian federalism is preparing European solidarity or that the Belgian bi-national coexistence constitutes a precursory mark for European integration. This ideological parallelism aims at justifying the merits of the constitutional reforms but, in reality, European integration and Belgian federalization are relying on opposite dynamics. The EC/EU process brings together nations having identical values and interests, establishes progressively a common sovereignty between member states and sets up a European citizenship beyond national identities. Now precisely the increasing powers devolved to the Belgian regions and communities reinforce the national identities: new autonomies are put forward by a centrifugal movement. Consequently, before foreshadowing a hypothetical federal Europe, Belgian federalism must give a clear indication of willingness to strengthen solidarity and the coexistence between its component parts.

The EC decision-making cycle and the participation of national institutions

The respective participation of the federal, regional and community institutions in the EC decision-making process is basically determined by the nature of the matters discussed at the European level. The degree of participation of each power level during the preparation of the decision, the decision-taking and the implementation of the EC legislative acts varies according to the internal distribution of competences. Thus, some EC matters concern only the federal level (e.g. provisions regarding economic and monetary union), others lie essentially within the competence of the communities (e.g. culture) or the

---

[14] See the section on 'The regional and community governments', below.

regions (e.g. industrial policy) and others belong to both federal and federate bodies (e.g. agriculture).

Since the TEU has come into force, the participation of the regions and communities in the EC decision-making process has increased for two main reasons:

- new EC competences lie more and more within their internal prerogatives (e.g. education, culture, industry);[15]
- both the Maastricht Treaty (new article 146 TEU) and the Belgian Constitutional Act concerning the international relations of the communities and the regions allow them to occupy the Belgian seat in the Council of Ministers.[16]

In horizontal terms, the role of the different authorities varies at every stage of the decision-making process. During the preparation of the EC decisions and during the implementation of EC legislative acts, the (federal, regional and community) civil service plays a key role, especially the federal Foreign Department, in coordinating the actions at each level. The parliament and the regional and community councils (legislative assemblies) intervene little during the preparation of EC decisions, but their role is essential for what concerns the implementation of EC legislative acts. Besides, the parliament and, since 1993, the regional and community councils have to approve the EC treaties and any other EC agreements in the field of external relations for which national ratifications are necessary. As for the rest, they do not directly act in EC decision-making. The federal government and, in the limits of their jurisdiction, the regional and community governments hold in their hands the effective decision-taking power in EC affairs. They benefit from the preparatory work of the civil service to define the Belgian position in the EC framework and also give an impulse to the legislative work of their assemblies in order to implement Community law quickly. The federal government pays particular attention to this issue. Indeed, only the Belgian state is responsible for any default or delay concerning the implementation of the Community law, even if the default or the delay is due to the regions or communities. To prevent the sentences of the Court of Justice in pursuance of the infringement proceedings, the federal gov-

---

[15] See J. Van Ginderachter, 'Les accords de Maastricht. Une évaluation du point de vue régional', *La Revue politique*, 6 (1991), pp. 43–9.

[16] See the section on 'The regional and community governments', below.

ernment has an exceptional power at its disposal: it may implement the Community law instead of the delaying region or community. This 'substitution power' does not take into consideration the internal distribution of competences and constitutes thus a limitation of the autonomy of the regions and the communities.

Despite the important prerogatives devolved to the regions and communities, the federal institutions remain the most influential in the EC decision-making process. The federal civil service has more experience in EC matters than its regional and community counterparts which focus on managing their new internal competences without being aware of the European reality. Only the federal parliament has elaborated original forms of political control of EC affairs. And, finally, the federal government keeps on playing the key role within the EC framework, especially during the Belgian EC presidency.

After this overview of the roles and the patterns of participation of the Belgian institutions in the EC decision-making process, the following paragraphs will describe in more detail the working of these institutions in the EC process.

The federal government

Most of the final decisions concerning EC affairs are made by the federal government. The federal government also takes the main initiatives aimed at implementing EC legislative acts. Inside the government, the key role is played by the Minister of Foreign Affairs who has been helped in his task, since 1965, by a minister or secretary of state competent for European Affairs. The latter does not head a ministry, and has neither a special budget nor a civil service at his or her own disposal. The European Affairs Minister's or European State Secretary's mission consists in preparing, conceiving and implementing the Belgian policy in EC matters, in collaboration with the Foreign Affairs Department.[17]

[17] The government composed by Wilfried Martens in May 1988 presented a peculiarity. Next to the traditional '*Secretary of State for European Affairs*' one could notice the presence of a Secretary of State '*à l'Europe 1992*', associated with the Minister of Foreign Trade. According to the holder of this new position, Anne-Marie Lizin (in *Socialisme*, no. 212–13, March–June 1989), her action aimed at 'coordonner les instances administratives impliquées dans la réalisation du marché intérieur, ainsi qu'à informer les milieux concernés pour leur permettre de se préparer et de répondre aux perspectives du marché intérieur. Les interlocuteurs du secrétariat d'Etat sont donc, par priorité, les adminstrations publiques, le monde économique et social, la jeunesse qui est à l'aube de sa vie active, et le grand public'.

Inside the Belgian council of ministers, internal decision-making is governed by the rule of consensus. This rule is absolutely necessary to governments composed of a coalition of political parties and counting the same number of Dutch-speaking and French-speaking ministers.[18] Consensus means neither unanimity nor majority. It implies a deliberation aimed at founding an understanding between opposite points of view. The decision is thoroughly negotiated and needs concessions from everyone to lead to a compromise. Once adopted, the decision demands solidarity between the members of the government: every minister has to defend the decision taken. For what concerns EC matters, consensus is generally reached without difficulty. The proposals coming from the civil service are often adopted without debate. The preparatory work of the civil service is thus essential both upstream (decision-making) and downstream (implementation).[19]

Since the federalization of the Belgian state, federal ministers often have to coordinate their actions with their regional and community colleagues, in particular when the complex distribution of competences requires close cooperation in order to manage EC matters coherently. To this aim, inter-ministerial conferences, inspired by the German system, were created in 1989.[20] These conferences gather federal, regional and/or community ministers, mostly under the chairmanship of a federal minister. As far as EC affairs are concerned, the conferences allow for a better cooperation between the different power levels interested in EC matters (exchange of information, coordinated actions, cooperation mechanisms).[21]

The 'substitution power' of the federal government, mentioned above, concerns the implementation of EC legislative acts in the scope

[18] The Prime Minister is not counted in the compulsory linguistic balance of the Belgian government according to article 99 (former article 86 *bis*) of the Belgian constitution.

[19] See the section on 'The administration', below.

[20] On the working of these inter-ministerial conferences, see A. Alen and M. Barbeaux, 'Le comité de concertation: bilan à la lumière de l'expérience', in *Les conflits d'intérêts: quelle solution pour la Belgique de demain?* (Bruges-Bruxelles: La Charte, 1990), pp. 167–70, 261–5.

[21] Fifteen inter-ministerial conferences were created in 1989 ('Circulaire ministérielle du 3 juillet 1989 relative aux conférences interministérielles', *Moniteur belge*, 3 May 1990). Under the government of Jean-Luc Dehaene, they are now sixteen in number ('Circulaire ministérielle du 31 mars 1992 relative aux conférences interministérielles', *Moniteur belge*, 23 June 1992). The main conferences involved in the coordination of EC matters in Belgium are the following: conferences concerning foreign policy, environment, agriculture, scientific policy, public health, media.

of regional or community competences.[22] The autonomy of each level, prior to the reforms of 1993, forbade the federal government to act *ultra vires*, namely in the place of the region or the community in default. But this new exceptional power depends on several conditions:

- the Belgian state must have been sentenced by the European Court of Justice;
- the region or community in default must have been fully associated both in the preparation of the decision in Belgium concerning the EC legislative act and in the procedure pending before the Court of Justice;
- the region or community concerned by the infringement must have received, three months before, a formal notice from the federal government threatening the use of its substitution power.[23]

Considering these strict conditions, the substitution power seems to be, in reality, a way to force the regions and communities to implement quickly the EC legislative acts which concern them. The federal government might never use it because the perspective of a loss of power, even provisional,[24] could be sufficient to ensure haste from the regions and communities as regards the implementation of Community law.

The administration
We have already pointed out the important preparatory work achieved by the civil service in the decision-making process and the implementation of Community law.[25] Most of the ministries involved in the EC decsion-making process have set up a special division in

[22] The implementation of Community law in Belgium requires legislative acts (federal act or regional and community decrees). So, the substitution power belongs both to the federal government and the federal chambers but the initiative will come from the government which plays the main role in this procedure.

[23] See article 169 (former article 68.7) of the Belgian constitution and the Constitutional Act concerning the international relations of the communities and the regions ('Loi spéciale sur les relations internationales des communautés et des régions du 5 mai 1993', *Moniteur belge*, 8 May 1993).

[24] The decisions taken in pursuance to the substitution power become ineffective when the region or community in default has complied with its European obligations.

[25] On this subject, see the elaborate study of Y. Lejeune, 'Le cas de la Belgique', in S.A. Pappas (ed.), *Procédures administratives nationales de préparation et de mise en oeuvre des décisions communautaires* (Maastricht: Institut Européen d'Administration Publique, 1994), pp. 59–112.

order to prepare the EC dossiers. The administrative coordination of all administrative departments dealing with European affairs takes place inside the *P.11 service* (called '*coordination Europe*') of the Foreign Department (administrative direction of European affairs). This service ensures the weekly inter-ministerial preparation of the meeting of the EC Councils of Ministers. All civil servants of the Belgian permanent representation to the European Communities, as well as the deputies of different (federal, regional and community) concerned ministries and ministers' departmental staffs take part in these preparatory coordination meetings. With regard to the increasing significance of EC matters and their implications on several aspects of the internal administrative work, the P. 11 service often meets five times a week with twenty or thirty participants. Besides this, the EEC group of the inter-ministerial economic commission (Commission économique interministérielle or CEI), composed of specialists from the ministries dealing with economic matters, *sensu lato*, under the direction of a civil servant coming from the Economic Affairs Department, prepares the Belgian positions in the more technical matters.

After the Single European Act (SEA) and the new challenge consisting of the application of numerous EC directives, the administrative coordination assumed by the P. 11 service and the CEI has improved. Since 1990, each ministry has nominated a civil servant in order to manage and to supervise the implementation of the EC binding legislation concerning his department. The *European coordinator* (Coordinateur européen) permanently stimulates the services of his or her department to get a fast application of EC directives. Furthermore, the P.11 service and the CEI meet together every two or three months with a double purpose:

- to assess immediately, during the preparation of an EC legislative act, the technical problems apt to occur in Belgium at the time of the implementation, and to inform the Belgian delegation about it in order to amend the projected act;
- to ensure real administrative follow-up of all (former, new, projected) EC legislative acts necessitating an implementation in Belgian law.

During the common meetings of P. 11–CEI, a *pilot department* (Département pilote), namely a leader department, is designated. It has to prepare the texts aiming at implementing EC acts and to organize the coordination between all (federal, regional or community) competent authorities in order to implement the Community law. In the same way, the pilot department, in collaboration with the lawyers of the Foreign Department, is responsible for taking appropriate action in accordance with the judgments of the Court of Justice against the Belgian state. Each meeting of P. 11–CEI is an opportunity to make an assessment of the implementation of Community law in Belgium on the basis of information coming from the pilot departments.

These increasing efforts undertaken at the administrative level aim at enhancing the situation of Belgium regarding the implementation of Community law. The paradox is well known: Belgium, an EC member state characterized by a pro-European attitude, is also one of the least reliable countries in applying binding EC legislation. The 'good pupil' of the European school has internal weaknesses that render the implementation process very slow, namely the absence of a department exclusively devoted to EC affairs, an under-staffed civil service in general and a federal system without normative hierarchy necessitating a permanent coordination between the federal, regional and community level. In consequence, a great number of judgments have been pronounced against Belgium by the European Court of Justice according to the infringement procedure.[26] The breaches of Community law decided by the Court consist mostly of delays in the application of EC directives.[27]

At the beginning of 1992, the Belgian situation with regard to the White Paper of the European Commission on the Internal Market was still worrying. Therefore, the government formed by Jean-Luc Dehaene in March 1992 adopted an emergency programme in order to improve still further the administrative coordination and to accelerate the parliamentary work. All these measures began to give results in 1993. For the first time for years, Belgium has reached fourth place in the table concerning the application of EC directives

[26] After Italy, Belgium is the most sentenced state by the Court of Justice concerning non-implementation of Community law. More than sixty judgments have been pronounced against Belgium since 1962.

[27] The most serious difficulties have appeared in the implementation of EC directives concerning environmental matters. For a comprehensive view on this issue, see H. Bocken and D. Ryckbost, *L'élaboration et l'application des directives européennes en matière d'environnement* (Bruxelles: Story-Scientia, 1990).

by the member states.[28] So, the Union's 'good pupil' seems to have matched the words with action.

The federal parliament

The Belgian parliament (Chamber of deputies and Senate) participates directly in EC decision-making by giving its approval to the EC treaties and to the EC external agreements binding both the Community and the member states. This is an indicator of how wide the Belgian consensus about European integration is. Indeed, treaties or external agreements concerning the European Community are often approved by a large majority (including members of the non-governing parties). Moreover, the Chamber and the Senate play determinant roles in the implementation of EC law when they adopt the necessary national legislation. In this respect, the parliament's intervention is situated at the end of a process which began inside the civil service (preparatory work) and was relayed by the legislative initiatives of the federal government.

In order to keep a closer eye on the government's actions at the European level, as well as to prepare well in advance the implementation of Community law, the latest state reform provided for a system involving the parliament earlier in EC decision-making. The government has to communicate the proposals for EC legislative acts to both chambers immediately after their transmission to the EC Council of Ministers. To the same end, the parliament is informed about the opening of negotiations with the intention to revise the EC treaties. Thus, the Chamber and the Senate become acquainted with the draft treaty before it is signed. This new provision is the consequence of criticisms which appeared in Belgium during the negotiations of the Maastricht Treaty. The preparatory phase of the EC treaties revision took place at the governmental level with the help of two intergovernmental con-

---

[28] Until 1992, Belgium has always occupied one of the last four positions concerning the application of EC law (see, for 1992, *European Report*, 5 December 1992). In February 1993, Rober Urbain, Belgian Minister of European Affairs, was obviously satisfied to be able to announce the expected change. This evolution reinforced indeed the credibility of his country among the EC member states, just before the starting of the Belgian presidency in July. By a press release produced on this occasion (19 February 1993), Rober Urbain declared precisely: 'ce progrès a pu être réalisé grâce à l'efficacité du plan d'urgence mis en place par le gouvernement depuis mars 1992. Ce sont surtout les départements de l'Agriculture, de la Santé publique et des Finances qui, sous l'impulsion des Affaires européennes, ont fourni un remarquable effort (...). Nous devons maintenant défendre notre bonne position. En effet, dès le 1er juillet, la Belgique assumera la présidence européenne et nos réalisations dans le cadre du marché intérieur devront alors accentuer la crédibilité de nos convictions européennes.'

ferences, keeping the parliament essentially outside the European talks until the signature of the Maastricht agreements. In the future, this undemocratic method will be impossible in Belgium.[29]

Furthermore, the Belgian parliament has set up special parliamentary commissions concerning EC affairs, called advisory committees on European issues (*comités d'avis chargés des questions européennes*).

The Chamber of deputies created the first advisory committee in April 1985. It is composed of ten national deputies and ten Belgian members of the European Parliament. The Belgian electoral law has established an incompatibility between national and European mandates. It is interesting to gather national deputies and Belgian members of the European Parliament who have, year after year, acquired experiences in EC affairs. The advisory committee holds hearings of the members of the federal government with regard to their European policy. Next to this classical political control, the advisory committee produces elaborate reports aimed at getting public opinion's or government's attention on particular issues. For example, a critical report concerning the problems of delay in the implementation of Community law, written by the advisory committee in 1986,[30] had an important repercussion in Belgium. It led to a reaction by the concerned authorities.[31]

In March 1990, the Senate also created an advisory committee on European issues. Its role is identical to the role of the advisory committee of the Chamber but its composition differs (twenty-two

---

[29] See article 168 (former article 68.6) of the Belgian constitution and the special act on the international relations of the communities and the regions. All the considerations developed above with regard to the action of the parliament in the EC decision-making process can be applied, *mutatis mutandis*, to the regional and community councils (therefore the following section concerning the federate bodies will only approach the question of the participation of the regional and community governments in the EC decision-making process). Since the latest state reform, the regional and community assemblies play, in the scope of their competences, the same role as the federal parliament concerning the treaties approval and the implementation of Community law. They also have to be informed by their government about EC draft acts or revision projects of the treaties. In consequence, any future revision of EC treaties will need the approval of seven different legislative assemblies before coming into force in Belgium. This could delay the Belgian ratification process if the assemblies do not proceed to concomitant approvals.

[30] 'L'application par la Belgique du droit des Communautés européennes', rapport fait au nom du comité d'avis chargé des questions européennes, *Documents Parlementaires, Chambre*, 1986–1987, no. 739/1. Other interesting reports, with regard to the Treaty on European Union and the preparation of the Belgian presidency, have also been produced by the advisory committee (see, *Documents Parlementaires, Chambre*, 1991–1992, no. 460/1; 1992–1993, no. 1097/1).

[31] See the section on 'The administration', above.

national senators without participation of Belgian members of the European Parliament). Both advisory committees organize common meetings more and more often, especially in order to control the European policy of the ministers and to benefit from the experience of Belgian Euro-deputies in more technical matters.[32]

The regional and community governments

The participation of the regional and community governments in the EC decision-making process has radically changed since the latest state reform and the implementation of the Treaty on European Union. Until 1993, the federate governments were only involved with the preparation of the EC decision-making process in Belgium, without taking part in the meetings of the EC's Councils of Ministers.[33] Both the national constitution and the European Treaties excluded this possibility. The EC Council, under a strict obligation, had to be formed by members of the national government.[34] The Maastricht Treaty now states that the Council will be composed of a representative of each member state at 'ministerial level', entitled to take binding decisions for the government of that member state.[35] The members of regional and community governments are, without any doubt, Belgian representatives 'at ministerial level' and the Belgian special act on the international relations of the communities and the regions entitles them to take binding decisions for the Belgian government.

Beyond this principle, the question is: who will do what and how in the EC's Councils of Ministers? Which minister: federal, regional or community? Which kind of Council? Which rotation system between the different regional and community ministers and which internal cooperation to prepare the Belgian votes?

In this respect, the Belgian special act has provided a compulsory

---

[32] Such advisory committees do not exist inside the regional and community councils.

[33] Since 1989, the cooperation between the federal government and its regional and community homologues has taken place inside interministerial conferences (see the section on 'The federal government', above). Progressively, the participation of the federate governments has evolved. In the limits of their competences, regional or community representatives have been included in the Belgian delegation according to the matters approached by EC Councils or EC working groups. Thus, the regional and community governments had sometimes 'a word to say' within the EC framework, but they never had voting rights or the ability to bind the Belgian state.

[34] Article 2 of the Merger Treaty (former article 146 EEC).

[35] New article 146 TEU.

cooperation agreement between the federal state, the regions and the communities that could answer these three questions. This cooperation agreement[36] was signed on 8 March 1994. The cooperation agreement distinguishes first the EC Councils of Ministers according to the internal distribution of competences. Four cases may occur:

- Councils concerning exclusively federal competences (type I), namely general affairs, economy and finance, budget, justice, telecommunications, consumers, development, civilian protection and the fishing industry;
- Councils concerning exclusively federate (community or regional) competences (type IV), namely tourism, housing and country planning, culture, education, and youth;
- Councils concerning both federal and federate competences with a predominance of the federal competences (type II), namely agriculture, the internal market, health, energy, environment, transport and social affairs;
- Councils concerning both federal and federate competences with a predominance of the federate competence (type III), namely industry and research.

According to the types of Councils, the Belgian representative holding Belgium's right to vote will be (type I) a federal minister, (type II) a federal minister, called 'sitting-minister' (*ministre siégeant*), accompanied in the Belgian staff by a federate minister, called 'assessor-minister' (*ministre-assesseur*), (type III) a federate minister (sitting-minister) accompanied by a federal minister (assessor-minister) and (type IV) a federate minister. The assessor-minister will assist the sitting-minister during the EC Council, without the right to vote. As the case may be, the sitting-minister will authorize him or her to take the floor in order to make the Belgian position clear. Moreover, the assessor-minister will keep in touch with his or her power level during the EC talks. Thus he/she will be able to inform the sitting-minister correctly as the negotiations go along. Table 3.1 describes in detail the pattern of participation of the federal, regional and community governments according to the types of EC Councils of Ministers.

[36] On the legal status of such cooperation agreements, see T. de Wilde d'Estmael, 'Les accords de coopération comme moyen de prévention et de solution des conflits', in Les *conflits d'intérêts, op. cit.*, pp. 91–122.

Table 3.1 Pattern of participation of the federal, regional and community governments in the Councils of Ministers of the EU

EU Council	Belgian representative
Type I	
General Affairs	FM
Ecofin	FM
Budget	FM
Justice	FM
Telecommunication	FM
Consumers	FM
Development	FM
Civilian Protection	FM
Fishing	FM
Type II	
Agriculture	FSM/RAM
Internal Market	FSM/RAM
Transport	FSM/RAM
Energy	FSM/RAM
Environment	FSM/RAM
Social Affairs	FSM/CAM
Health	FSM/CAM
Type III	
Industry	RSM/FAM
Research	CSM/FAM
Type IV	
Tourism	RM
Housing and Country Planning	RM
Culture	CM
Education	CM
Youth	CM

Key: FM = Federal minister; RM = Regional minister; CM = Community minister; FSM/RAM = Federal sitting-minister and regional assessor-minister; FSM/CAM = Federal sitting-minister and Community assessor-minister; RSM/FAM = Regional sitting-minister and federal assessor-minister; CSM/FAM = Community sitting-minister and Federal assessor-minister.

A rotation system will be organized between the regional and community ministers (sitting or assessor-ministers) participating in the EC Councils (types II, III, IV). The rotation will take place every six months. It will correspond to the rotating presidency of the Council of Ministers (January–June and July–December). This lapse of time would normally be sufficient to avoid fits and starts in the work of the Belgian representatives. Six months seem enough to manage EC affairs smoothly and thoroughly. A close cooperation will be necessary between the federal state and its component entities before each Council of types II and III.[37] Indeed, the minister-sitting at the European level, whoever he or she may be, is entitled to take binding decisions for the Belgian state. Therefore his or her action and vote inside the Council cannot consist in a plea *pro domo*. As Belgian representative, the minister will have to defend the point of view and the interests of every authority (as the case may be, federal and/or regional or community) affected by the Council. This will imply, in fact, permanent connection between all the component parts of the Belgian state. The objective of this coordination is to lead to a coherent European policy that does not weaken the position of the Belgian state within the EC/EU framework. In this respect, rapid internal consensus is necessary to ensure the credibility of the new federal Belgium *vis-à-vis* the European partners. Furthermore, the creation of the new Committee of the Regions[38] is an additional element for the strengthening of the regional and community presence within the EC framework. The Belgian government in September 1993 set up the list of the twelve Belgian members of the Committee of the Regions. Logically, the Belgian delegation will be composed of regional and community ministers.[39]

The courts

The most important contribution of the Belgian courts in EC affairs has been to determine the status of Community law, namely its primacy and direct applicability in Belgium. Indeed, the Belgian constitution does not contain any provision guaranteeing explicitly the primacy of Community law over conflicting national legislation. The *Cour de Cassation* has established the primacy of Community law in Belgium by its famous decision of 27 May 1971.[40] The principle con-

---

[37] This system will render administrative coordination still more essential during the preparation of the EC Council to define the Belgian position. In this respect, the vertical and horizontal coordination task of the administrative direction of European affairs (P. 11 service, see the section on 'The administration', above) and the cooperation taking place within the interministerial conferences (see the section on 'The federal government', above) will increase.

[38] New article 198, TEU.

[39] The list is composed of seven Dutch-speaking ministers (six members of the Flemish government and one member of the government of Brussels-Capital) and five French-speaking ministers (two members of the Walloon government, two members of the government of the French community and one member of the government of Brussels-Capital). Every two years, one member of the government of the German-speaking community will take first a Dutch-speaking minister's place and then a French-speaking minister's one.

[40] 'Cassation belge', 27 May 1971, *Pasicrisie* (1971), p. 886.

sists of the precedence of Community law over inconsistent national legislation.[41] Furthermore, the preliminary ruling procedure (article 177, TEU) has often been used by the Belgian courts (281 questions from 1958 till June 1992). There have not been significant cases of explicit defiance of courts of last instance which declined to refer a question to the European Court of Justice.

Public opinion, political parties and interest groups

With respect to the so-called 'pillarization' of the Belgian politico-institutional system,[42] political parties and interest groups which are important elements within the 'pillars' have an underlying influence on the definition of the Belgian EC policy. The voting system, which uses proportional representation, means that governments assemble a coalition of several parties. Therefore federal, regional and community governments will follow the main lines of the programmes of their component parties. Compromises are necessary between the political parties to determine governmental action. However, compromises concerning EC policy are easy to reach because of the similar European concepts of the main political parties.

The interest groups (trade unions, trade associations, industrial lobbies, farming lobbies, employers' organizations etc.) intervene in EC decision-making by means of lobbying actions to the political institutions. They appeal to the ministers or try to make the public aware of some problems in diffusing memorandums on certain issues. Pressure groups also take advantage of the presence of European institutions in Brussels to approach directly the European Commission. One cannot easily perceive the impact of these interest groups on the EC decision-making process in Belgium. It is certain that the minister sitting in the EC Council takes every lobbying action into account, but the negotiation between the national representatives often leads to political compromises that lie far from the economic interests defended by pressure groups. Sometimes too, the interests of

---

[41] This wide-ranging question cannot be fully described in the scope of this analysis. See further, among others, K. Lenaerts, 'The Application of Community law in Belgium', *Common Market Law Review* (1986), pp. 254–62. For a recent overview on the application of Community law in Belgium, see P. Wytinck, 'The Application of Community law in Belgium (1986–1992)', *Common Market Law Review* (1993), pp. 981–1020.

[42] On this subject, see the section on 'Fundamentals of Belgium in EU affairs', above.

Table 3.2 Comparison of attitudes in Belgium and the EC to membership of the EC/EU[44]

(a) Membership of the EC/EU

	% June 1992		% November 1992		% June 1993		% July 1994	
	B	EC	B	EC	B	EC	B	EC
Good thing	69	65	63	60	64	60	55	53
Bad thing	7	10	7	12	7	12	11	12
Neither good nor bad	22	19	25	23	23	23	30	27
Don't know	3	6	5	5	5	5	5	8

(b) For or against the Maastricht Treaty[45]

	% June 1992 B	% September 1992 B	% November 1992		% June 1993	
			B	EC	B	EC
For	47.5	42.8	53	43	47	41
Against	15.5	13.4	11	27	16	24
Undecided	37	43.8	35	30	36	35

(c) Interest in European politics, June 1993[46]

	% B	% EC
A great deal	6	8
To some extent	31	33
Not much	43	39
Not at all	18	18
Don't know	1	2

the different groups are contradictory, so that the results of the lobbying actions look like a zero sum game.

The degree of acceptance of the European Community/European
Union as a whole is very high among the Belgian population. The reasons for this wide consensus characterizing Belgian public opinion
have been already exposed above.[43] According to opinion polls, most
of the Belgian people think that Belgium's membership of the EC/EU
is a good thing. As can be seen from Table 3.2, recent figures show
that attitudes to national membership in the EC are more positive in
Belgium than in the European Community/European Union as a
whole.

European integration seems to be a generally accepted idea in Belgium, but this idea is so perfectly accepted that it is only rarely the
subject of a discussion. Interest in European politics is in fact lower
in Belgium than in the other member states. Table 3.2 shows that a
high percentage of the Belgian population is undecided with regard
to the Maastricht Treaty, even if the percentage of favourable opinion is higher than the EC average. One may also notice in 1993 the
weak interest of Belgian people in European politics in comparison
with the EC average. Therefore, on the occasion of the French referendum on the Maastricht Treaty, the Belgian government launched a
large information campaign with regard to the EU. Several means
have been used to explain the EU's institutional system and the Maastricht Treaty (brochures, strip cartoon, television and radio broad-
casts, 'didactic bags' for teachers, and so on). This 'awareness
campaign' has been pursued during the Belgian presidency in the
second half of 1993.

Conclusion

'To be and to become oneself within the EU framework' – this purpose seems to be the main challenge for Belgium in the post-Maastricht period: to be a kind of paragon of European integration; to be
a member state where the positive consensus in EC/EU affairs has

    [43] See the section on 'Promoting European integration', above.
    [44] *Eurobarometer*, 37, 38/1992, 39/1993 and 41/1994. Concerning the Eurobarome-
ter of July 1994 the figures have been taken from the question on membership in the
'European Union (European Community)' as in table 15c, p. A 28.
    [45] *Le Soir*, 17 September 1992 (Marketing-Unit polls), *Eurobarometer*, 38/1992 and
39/1993.
    [46] *Eurobarometer*, 39/1993.

always been wide, both within the political institutions and public opinion; and to remain, despite the federalization of Belgium, this small state of the European Community/European Union endowed with a special skill in crafting difficult compromises between the other member states in order to put forward the integration process of Europe.

The purpose is to become within the EU institutions what Belgium has become inside its borderlines: a federal state. This mutation involves organizing the participation of all the component entities of the Belgian state in the EC/EU decision-making process. The state reform of 1993 ensures this power-sharing. The Belgian constitution and the special act on the international relations of the communities and the regions take the European dimension of the foreign policy into account. Several new mechanisms aim at coordinating at best the actions of every power level involved in the EC/EU decision-making process. In this respect, significant progress has already been noticed in the field of the application of EC directives in Belgium. It remains to be seen whether the actions of different kinds of ministers (federal, community and regional) inside the Council can maintain the coherence of the Belgian EC policy. The credibility of Belgium will depend on the efficiency of the internal coordination between the federal state, the regions and the communities. In the future, Belgium has to prove to its European partners that its peculiar centrifugal federalism does not constitute a weakening inside the EU framework.

Select bibliography

Bocken, H. and Ryckbost, D., *L'élaboration et l'application des directives européennes en matière d'environnement* (Brussels: Story-Scientia, 1990).

Delpérée, F. and Lejeune, Y. (eds.), *La collaboration de l'Etat, des communautés et des régions dans le domaine de la politique extérieure* (Louvain-la-Neuve: Academia, 1988).

Franck, C., 'La prise de décision belge en politique extérieure: cohésion, tensions, contrôles et influences', *Res Publica*, 29 (1987), pp. 61–84.

François, A., Vandercammen, D., Alvarez, L. and de Visscher C., 'Belgique', in H. Siedentopf and J. Ziller (eds.), *L'Europe des administrations? La mise en oeuvre de la législation communautaire dans les Etats membres,* vol. ii (Maastricht: Institut Européen d'Administration Publique, 1988), pp. 11–88.

Lejeune, Y., 'Belgium', in H. J. Michelmann and P. Soldatos (eds.), *Federalism and International Relations. The Role of Subnational Units* (Oxford:

Clarendon Press, 1990), pp. 141–75.

—— 'Belgique' in Y. Charpentier and C. Engel (eds.), *Les régions dans l'espace communautaire* (Nancy: Presses universitaires de Nancy, 1992).

—— 'Le cas de la Belgique', in S. A. Pappas (ed.), *Procédures administratives nationales de préparation et de mise en oeuvre des décisions communautaires* (Maastricht: Institut Européen d'Administration Publique, 1994), pp. 59–112.

Nagant de Deuxchaisnes, D., 'Fédéralisme belge et intégration européenne', in Centre européen universitaire de Nancy (ed.), *Impact de la construction européenne sur l'organisation administrative française*, Actes des journées d'études des 1er et 2 décembre 1992 (Nancy: Centre européen universitaire de Nancy, 1993), pp. 31–51.

Standaert, F., *Les relations extérieures dans la Belgique fédérale* (Brussels: Groupe Coudenberg, 1990).

Van Meerhaeghe, M. A. G. (ed.), *Belgium and EC Membership Evaluated* (London: Pinter Publishers; New York: St Martin's Press, 1992).

de Wilde d'Estmael, T. and Franck, C., 'Du mémorandum belge au traité de Maastricht', in C. Franck, C. Roosens and T. de Wilde d'Estmael (eds.), *Aux tournants de l'Histoire. La politique extérieure de la Belgique au début de la décennie 90* (Brussels: De Boeck-Université, 1993), pp. 41-65.

The Federal Republic of Germany

Fundamentals of Germany in EU Affairs

In the 1950s when the Community's development began with the foundation of the European Coal and Steel Community (ECSC), integration from a German perspective had both an economic and a political meaning which were strongly interrelated. The recovery of the German industry within the ECSC and the reconstruction of West Germany as a whole would strengthen the newly founded Federal Republic and in the long run would lead to the reunification of Germany. To this so-called 'magnet-theory' which was mainly conceived under Konrad Adenauer add four other specific German motivations to participate in European integration: political stability, acceptance in international affairs, gain in sovereignty and reconciliation with its neighbours.[1] This early understanding of European integration was explicitly mentioned in the preamble of the German constitution (the 'Basic Law' or '*Grundgesetz*'), with the formula

> to serve the peace of the world as an equal partner in a united Europe ...

Though this provision lost somewhat in importance, it never vanished, and became an underlying common assumption in German politics. From the 1960s onwards European integration became increasingly an aim in itself and was much less considered as an instrument for reunification. It became a political concept with the idea of a federal union based on democracy, law and respect for human rights. It was this understanding of integration which under-

---

[1] See Rudolf Hrbek and Wolfgang Wessels (eds.), *EG-Mitgliedschaft – ein vitales Interesse der Bundesrepublik Deutschland?* (Bonn: Europa Union Verlag, 1984), pp. 45–51.

pinned the German 'permissive consensus'[2] in the 1970s and 1980s. When German unification came in 1990 it was an unexpected surprise which did not constitute the final aim of the German integration policy – though there have been many doubts – but the *'finalité politique'* which had been formulated in the 1970s and 1980s prevailed and was again reiterated in the process leading to the Maastricht Treaty.

After German unification the economic weight and the political role of Germany in Europe changed considerably. A discussion started as to what extent this had changed the conditions in Europe as a whole and which were the major conclusions to draw.[3] In Germany itself a discussion started about its new role and the definition of a new foreign policy after gaining full sovereignty. The outcome of this debate on the implications of German unification for the Federal Republic, Europe and the international system are not yet clear. One observation so far is that Germany would like to 'normalize' its role within the European Union, and the German government stresses more than in the past the close political and economic interdependence of Germany and the European Union, or as Chancellor Kohl put it repeatedly: 'German unification and European integration are two sides of the same medal'. Thus Germany is very keen on showing to the inside and outside world the continuity of its European commitment. It has adapted its internal decision-making procedures in EC/EU affairs to the post-Maastricht situation with the introduction of the new Art. 23 into the Basic Law. And the Federal Constitutional Court (*Bundesverfassungsgericht*) – though with some curious wording – gave a positive judgment on the Maastricht Treaty on European Union and thus opened the way for its final ratification. However, it cannot be overlooked – as the reactions to the war in former Yugoslavia and the UN peacekeeping actions in Somalia have shown – that Germany is in the process of searching for a new identity in foreign policy.

---

[2] See Leon N. Lindberg and Stuart A. Scheingold, *Europe's Would-Be Polity. Patterns of Change in the European Community* (Englewood Cliffs, NJ: Prentice-Hall, 1970), pp. 249ff.

[3] See Anne-Marie Le Gloannec, 'The Implications of German Unification for Western Europe', in Paul B. Stares (ed.), *Germany and the New Europe* (Washington: The Brookings Institution, 1992), pp. 251–78; Christian Deubner, 'Die Wiedervereinigung der Deutschen und die Europäische Gemeinschaft', in Cord Jakobeit and Alparslan Yenal (eds.), *Gesamteuropa. Analysen, Probleme und Entwicklungsperspektiven* (Bonn: Bundeszentrale für politische Bildung, 1993), pp. 393–413.

Taken together the relationship between the Federal Republic of Germany and the European Community has been described as being one of 'complex interdependence', in both economic and political terms.[4] This is essentially due to the history of Germany but also to its specific social and economic structure. Even after unification the basic motivations for European integration are still valid – though they have changed some of their original meaning[5] – and it seems difficult to agree with those who argue that Germany will go its 'own way' (*Sonderweg*) while it is still involved in a complex interdependence with the European Community and its European neighbours.

Another result of developments since 1989 is the different perception in East and West Germany concerning European affairs: it seems that, as for the West Germans in the 1950s and 1960s, integration has a strong economic function for the East Germans. This is certainly linked to the economic misery there and the fact that East Germans have first to 'digest' the adhesion to the Federal Republic and the acquisition of a new national identity before being able to deal adequately with Europe. It might only be a question of time until the East Germans have a similar understanding of integration as being the process towards a European political union.

Concerning terminology, a clear and ever valid definition of the term 'integration' does not exist in the German language. One reason for this is certainly that the term 'integration' itself is a 'foreign' (= Latin) expression in the German language which has been used quite differently depending on the context. In its origin the term 'integration' in German did not have a European background.[6] The first to introduce the term was the sociologist Albert Schäffle who defined integration as a 'social unity of individuals or groups'.[7] Other scientists followed Schäffle and developed different concepts of integra-

---

[4] See Simon Bulmer and William Paterson, *The Federal Republic of Germany and the European Community* (London: Allen and Unwin, 1987), p. 13.

[5] E.g. 'international rehabilitation' has become 'international acceptance of German unification'; the acquisition of full sovereignty is still going on in the sense of becoming a 'normal' country of the international community according to its size and economic strength. The debate on a permanent seat on the UN Security Council and the use of German troops in Somalia is an indicator of this.

[6] See the contribution of Gerhard Göhler in this book.

[7] See Albert Schäffle, *Bau und Leben des socialen Körpers*, 4 vols. (Tübingen: Laup 1875–1878, 2nd edn in 2 vols., 1896), quoted after Heinrich Schneider, *Leitbilder der Europapolitik, vol. 1: Der Weg zur Integration* (Bonn: Europa Union Verlag, 1977), p. 232.

tion.[8] More important was the development of the so-called 'integration theory' (*Integrationslehre*) of the lawyer Rudolf Smend who based his thoughts on the social and cultural philosophy of Theodor Litt.[9] According to Smend integration is a process of unification which is the basic process for the existence of a state. The reality of a state consists in being permanently integrated and built up by and through its members. Thus 'integration' is the *'creatio continua'* of the state, the process of existence of a state which works against the naturally existing disintegrating forces.[10] In contrast to this the term 'integration' in the English language has a quite clear meaning: it is the process towards the establishment of a social and political unity, especially of states. It is thus the *'creatio successiva'* i.e. a step by step process towards unity whereas the original German understanding assumes an already existing unity which is kept together by an ongoing process of integration of its members, especially of people (i.e. by *'creatio continua'*). The *'creatio successiva'* was originally the American understanding of the term 'integration' which in connection with the European Community has become today also the common understanding of integration in the German language.

However, the terminological difference between the Anglo-Saxon and the German understanding has won some new relevance today: the accession of the five East German Länder to the Federal Republic is called a 'process of unification' (*Einigungsprozess*) or the restoration of the 'German unity' (*Wiederherstellung der deutschen Einheit*). None would call the German unification the 'German–German integration', except maybe in a purely economic context. In contrary to this one can use in German the term 'European unification process' (*europäischer Einigungsprozeß*) as well but the term 'German integration process' (*deutscher Integrationsprozeß*) has not been applied to describe the German unification after 1989. It seems that the more technically sounding term 'integration' is especially

[8] See Leopold von Wiese, *System der Allgemeinen Soziologie als Lehre von den sozialen Prozessen und den sozialen Gebilden der Menschen (Beziehungslehre)*, 2nd edn (Munich/Leipzig: Duncker and Humblot, 1933); Max Huber, 'Beiträge zur Kenntnis der soziologischen Grundlagen des Völkerrechts und der Staatengesellschaft', *Jahrbuch des öffentlichen Rechts*, vol. iv (1910, book edn 1928), p. 56; Franz Oppenheimer, *Der Staat*, 4th edn (Stuttgart: G. Fischer, 1954).

[9] See Theodor Litt, *Individuum und Gemeinschaft. Grundlegung der Kulturphilosophie*, 3rd edn (Berlin/Leipzig: Teubner, 1926).

[10] See Rudolf Smend, *Verfassung und Verfassungsrecht* (Berlin: Duncker and Humblot, 1928), quoted after Schneider, *op. cit.*, pp. 232f.

applied to an economic step by step process and is specifically used in connection with the European Community – at least concerning the post-war period[11] – whereas the creation of one German state since 1989 is exclusively called 'unification' or 'unity' (such as *deutsche Einheit*).

The EC decision-making cycle and the participation of national institutions

When analysing the participation of German institutions in EC decision-making it seems necessary to mention some central factors of policy-making in the political system of the Federal Republic. There are at least four factors which seem to be decisive for the German policy-making in EC affairs:

1 the vertical division of competences due to the federal structure of the country;
2 the horizontal division of competences due to the autonomy of national actors (such as the Bundesbank, the Constitutional Court and individual ministries);
3 a relatively consensual attitude towards European politics on the part of the political elite (in spite of coalition governments) and to a minor degree also of public opinion;
4 in the past the issues raised by German–German relations and, since 1989, by the ongoing German unification process.

1 As a corollary of its federal structure there are different levels which intervene in the policy-making process in Germany. Policy-making power is distributed between the federal level, the Länder level and the local level which all have specific competences and functions which are mentioned in the Basic Law of the Federal Republic. The vertical division of power in the Federal Republic has led to a complex system of 'political interwovenness' (*Politikverflechtung*)[12] in which there is no single decision-making centre but in which different levels interact and participate in the decision-making process.

---

[11] See on the older use of the term 'integration' again the contribution of Gerhard Göhler in this book.
[12] See Jens Joachim Hesse (ed.), *Politikverflechtung im föderativen Staat. Studien zum Planungs- und Finanzierungsverbund zwischen Bund, Ländern und Gemeinden* (Baden-Baden: Nomos 1978); Fritz W. Scharpf, Bernd Reissert and Fritz Schnabel, *Politikverflechtung. Theorie und Empirie des kooperativen Föderalismus in der Bundesrepublik* (Kronberg/Ts.: Scriptor, 1976).

2 To this is added the horizontal division of power between the different ministries and institutions on each level. According to the principle of ministerial autonomy (*Ressortprinzip*) the ministries on the federal level are relatively independent actors which makes it difficult to have a coherent approach to EC policy-making. To this is added the autonomy of the German Federal Bank (*Deutsche Bundesbank*) in conducting an independent monetary policy. Although the Bundesbank does not act in a 'political vacuum' but is aware of the needs of the federal government (and thus knows the position of the Ministry of Finance and the Economics Ministry), of the economic and social partners and especially of Germany's European partners, it primarily follows the rules of preserving the stability of the German currency. Moreover there is the specific function of the Federal Constitutional Court (*Bundesverfassungsgericht*) to watch over the 'constitutionality' of federal laws and thus to interpret the 'Basic Law'. To appeal to the Bundesverfassungsgericht in case of party political disputes has become a common feature in German politics, though the Court has repeatedly stated that political disputes have to be decided by majorities in parliament and not by the court. However, like the Bundesbank, the Federal Constitutional Court plays a political role and its decisions are of major political importance, as could be seen during the ratification process of the Maastricht Treaty on European Union. Thus EC policy-making in Germany is characterized by an 'institutional pluralism'[13] which is apparent on different levels and which explains the lack of a central agency being responsible for formulating a coherent European policy.

3 Surprisingly enough – and in spite of the apparent contradiction with German reunification – the EC and European policy-making have almost never become a conflictual issue in German politics. On the contrary Germany always tried to be a kind of 'paragon' (*Musterknabe*) in European integration, based on a large permissive consensus in public opinion concerning EC affairs. There was and still is a strong general support for the European integration process by the major political parties in Germany (CDU/CSU, FDP, Grüne, SPD). Although since 1949 there has been a prevalence of coalition governments in the Federal Republic, the only significant party conflict over European matters dates back to the 1950s when the SPD rejected the Schuman plan and the adherence of the Federal Repub-

---

[13] See Bulmer/Paterson, *op. cit.*, p. 17.

lic to the European Defence Community. Since then the social democrats have gradually accepted the German '*Westintegration*' and during the social–liberal coalition from 1969–1982 – especially under the chancellorship of Helmut Schmidt who was one of the architects of the European Monetary System – became full supporters of the European integration process. Even the arrival of the Greens and the spread of some post-materialistic beliefs did not decisively alter the rather pro-European attitude in Germany. It is only recently that the favourable attitude towards European integration has decreased and that one can observe an erosion of the permissive consensus which prevailed so far on Europe among the German public.[14] The more critical debate within the political parties – particularly on the part of the Bavarian CSU – concerns the question of immigration and the stability of the Deutschmark which became more and more politicized especially in the context of the 'electoral marathon' in 1994. Critical statements were also emerging from economic circles who called into question the use of EMU for Germany's economic interests.

4 In spite of the pro-European attitude in the Federal Republic, German–German relations had never been completely neglected in the last 35 years. Quite the opposite: in the Paris treaties of 1954 the allies recognized the aim to have a 'unified Germany' which would be an integrated part of Western Europe. And in the Treaty of Rome, Bonn managed to make its European partners recognize that there are special relations with the GDR and that EC membership does not affect the intra-German trade. The start of European Political Cooperation (EPC) in the 1970s was paralleled by the German government's launching of the Ostpolitik, aiming at the normalization of its relations with the GDR. Thus the German–German division did play a role in the FRG's attitude towards European integration and contributed to some more or less strong suspicion among its European partners with regard to Germany's 'European credibility'. Since unification the political situation has changed completely, though it seems that the process of unification has put some similar – if not

---

[14] The four standard indicators of support for the European Community used by Eurobarometer – i.e. support for the unification of Western Europe, EC membership a 'good thing', benefit of one's country from EC membership and attitude if the EC is scrapped – all show a downward trend. In fact, between 1990 and 1993 all four indicators have lost between 10% and 20%; see *Eurobarometer*, no. 40, December 1993, p. 16.

larger – constraints on German policy-making in EC matters compared to the past. The economic and financial burden of unification is the reason that Germany has to concentrate on its internal problems. However, it is quite clear, from a German point of view, that in the long run German unification and European integration are 'two sides of the same coin' and that both processes have to be pursued in parallel. The problem at the beginning of the 1990s is that in times of economic recession and after a period of quite successful European integration, the German unification process – especially in the light of important national elections which took place in 1994 – has some kind of priority compared to the European integration process. This might explain why the stability of the German Deutschmark is currently prevailing over the future creation of the EMU which – and this seems to be the current belief in Germany – may have to come into existence a few years later than scheduled.[15]

After these preliminary remarks on the context of German EC policy-making, the focus will now be on the different patterns of participation of German political institutions in the different phases of the EC decision-making process. A first observation is that the above mentioned 'institutional pluralism' has resulted in a rather divergent participation of the different institutions in EC affairs according to the level and the phase in decision-making. National institutions participate to a varying degree and intensity in the preparation, taking and implementation of EC decisions.

Table 4.1 Participation in EC decision-making in the Federal Republic of Germany

Actors	Phases		
	Preparation	*Decision-taking*	*Implementation*
Central government	++	++	+–
Bundestag	–	–	+–
Länder/Bundesrat	+–	–	+
Administration/Civil servants	++	+	++
Interest groups	+	—	+
Political parties	–	+–	–

Key: ++ very high + high +– medium – low — very low

[15] Statement of Chancellor Kohl at the beginning of August 1993 in connection with the change in the fluctuating margins of the EMS.

In fact Table 4.1 suggests, very roughly, that there are apparently 'winners' and 'losers' when it comes to participation in EC decision-making. It seems that the government and the administration are involved in nearly all phases of the decision-making process, whereas the parliament, the Länder and the political parties are virtually outside the decison-making process. Interest group involvement is only in the preparatory phase and in the implementation phase but does not play any role in the phase of decision-taking. This is a very rough characterization which might vary, depending on the policy field and the particular issue at stake. In the following discussion we will examine more closely the different national institutions and their role in EC decision-making.

The government and the ministerial bureaucracy

Complexity and sectorization   The German government – defined as the Chancellor, the ministers, ministers of state, supported by the ministerial bureaucracy – is one of the central actors in German EC decision-making. This is certainly due to the fact that important decisions are still taken in the Council of Ministers where the government is exclusively represented (with the exception of the 'Länder-Observer' who might be present, and the four councils, i.e. culture, education, research, internal affairs, in which Länder ministers can take decisions for the Federal Republic as a whole: see below).

According to Article 65 of the Basic Law the Chancellor disposes of the so-called '*Richtlinienkompetenz*' i.e. the competence to set the guidelines of government policy. However, in the past, few Chancellors made use of their right to set the guidelines of EC affairs[16] and very often delegated this matter to the Foreign Minister (who was at the same time Vice-Chancellor). To this must be added the fact that the ministerial bureaucracy is very much involved in the preparatory drafting of EC legislation within the numerous working groups of the Commission (more than 500) and the Council (about 300). Those ministries which have to deal with policy matters in which the Community has extended competences dispose of specific European

---

[16] With the exception of Adenauer and Schmidt; the latter made use of the '*Richtlinienkompetenz*' in imposing, against harsh internal criticism, the European Monetary System.

departments or sections: in the Economics Ministry, since 1958, department E; in the Ministry for Agriculture, since 1981/82, department 7 concerning EC agricultural policy, international agricultural policy and fishery policy; in the Ministry for Employment and Social Affairs, department VII, called European and international social policy since 1992; in the Finance Ministry since 1993 department IX concerning currency and finance relations, and financial relations with the EU; in the Foreign Office, since May 1993, the European department; other ministries such as environment, traffic, development and education and research have at least one or two sections (*Referate*) dealing with European affairs. The chancellery which is a kind of 'administrative sub-structure' of the Chancellor has itself within its foreign relations department (*Abteilung 2*) a unit dealing with European integration including CFSP and bilateral relations with the EC member states. The main function of the European unit in the chancellery is to coordinate and to consult with the different ministries and to brief the Chancellor before meetings of the European Council.

Table 4.2 Participation in EC decision-making according to the different levels of government

Government levels	Phases		
	Preparation	Decision-taking	Implementation
Cabinet/Ministers	–	++	—
State Secretaries	+	–+	—
Head of Department	++	–	+–
Section Heads	++	—	++

Key: ++ very high + high +– medium – low — very low

According to the phase in decision-making each level within the government plays a different role in EC affairs (see Table 4.2). The ministerial level is mostly involved in the phase of decision-making and much less in the phase of preparation and implementation; and even then they deal above all with important political matters and try to find a compromise with their European counterparts. The secretaries of state might quite often replace the ministers in their function in the Council and frequently consult their European counterparts in order to solve political problems and important questions of substance. The heads of department and the heads of section are mostly involved in the preparation and the implementation of decisions and much less in their making. They deal above all with day-to-day questions and to this end they are in permanent contact with their European colleagues, with other national ministries and with civil servants in the permanent representation in Brussels. Owing to the so-called '*Ressortprinzip*', whereby the different ministries dispose of a rather large autonomy, and due to a wide range of informal contacts with civil servants in Brussels and in the other European capitals, the ministerial bureaucracy at this level might play a rather independent role.

The '*Ressortprinzip*' is also mainly responsible for the fact that the Foreign Office does not play a preponderant role in EC affairs. For historical and also political reasons – i.e. defence of the social market economy! – the Economics Ministry is mainly responsible for the distribution of information and documents to the other ministries and the Bundestag, the Bundesrat and the Länder-Observer. Moreover the Economics Ministry chairs the inter-ministerial committees on EC affairs and it is responsible for transferring the instructions of this committee to the diplomats and other civil servants in the Permanent Representation in Brussels. Although it is the Foreign Office which has the primary function of ensuring the overall coordination among the ministries and which, to this end, chairs the *Committee of State Secretaries for European Affairs* and may report to the Cabinet on EC developments, it competes in EC affairs with the Ministry of Economics. Very roughly it can be said that the Foreign Office is responsible for the more political questions, whereas the Economics Ministry deals with questions of a more technical nature.[17] However, since EC affairs have become increasingly technical in nature, there is a trend for the Foreign Office in the long run to continue to lose some of its influence in EC/EU affairs. To this must be added the fact that under Chancellor Kohl who is a dedicated 'European' and the rather weak Foreign Minister Kinkel, German EC policy has become increasingly influenced by the chancellery and the chancellor himself.

The specialized and rather independently acting ministerial bureaucracy, the comparatively weak Foreign Office and the '*Ressortprinzip*'

---

[17] This goes back to an agreement in 1958 between the then ministers von Brentano and Erhard; see Christoph Sasse, Edouard Poullet, David Coombes and Gérard Deprez, *Decision Making in the European Community* (New York: Praeger, 1977), p. 11.

explain why there is a 'sectorized policy making' in Germany in European affairs.[18] A further indicator to this is that the Länder bureaucracies are more and more looking for their chance to participate in EC/EU affairs since the Community has extended its activities to policy fields which belong to their exclusive competences. One consequence of the Maastricht Treaty is that a new Article 23 has been introduced in the Basic Law of the Federal Republic which extends – via the Bundesrat – the power of the Länder in EC affairs. Thus we witness on the executive level – which includes the ministerial bureaucracy of the Bund and the Länder – a complex system characterized by

- an institutional complexity, i.e. various ministries, the chancellery, the Länder ministries as well as the Bundesbank are involved;
- a sectorization, i.e. policy-making is done by individual ministries and policy networks in a specialist manner;
- a specialist policy-making and less a political policy-making, i.e. there are strong technical ministries and a (compared to other member states) rather weak political role played by the Foreign Ministry and the chancellery (though both show a tendency since Maastricht to become more influential in European affairs).

This complex system might even be exacerbated by party political rivalries due to the coalition government in Bonn and the various Länder governments where the opposition parties have the majority and form coalitions which combine different 'political colours'.

Problem of coordination   From the German policy-making machinery described so far, one can easily deduce that the coordination of the activities of the different actors on the different levels in the various decision-making phases is of utmost importance. However, it seems that this is one of the weaknesses of the German policy-making system. Although there is a regular process of coordination on the horizontal level between the ministries, it seems that this does not result in a 'positive coordination' in the sense of a common policy but rather in a 'negative coordination' in the sense of a 'zero sum game' in which each actor tries to protect its own sphere of influence.[19] If one takes

---

[18] See Bulmer/Paterson, *op. cit.*, pp. 25–42.
[19] See Elfriede Regelsberger and Wolfgang Wessels, 'Entscheidungsprozesse Bonner Europapolitik – verwalten statt gestalten?', in Rudolf Hrbek and Wolfgang Wessels (eds.), *EG-Mitgliedschaft: ein vitales Interesse der Bundesrepublik Deutschland?* (Bonn: Europa Union Verlag, 1984), pp. 480–1.

into account that Maastricht has extended the scope of the policy fields dealt with at the Community level and that, as a corollary, new ministries (Ministry of Justice, Ministry of Internal Affairs) and new 'territorial actors' (regions, local communities) will be involved in the decision-making process, then it is obvious that the whole coordination process at the national and at the Community level will also considerably increase in time and substance and will become more complicated.[20]

So far the coordination function has been fulfilled on the different governmental levels by different bodies which have different functions and which vary in importance (see Table 4.3). The *Cabinet Committee on European Policy* has only convened a few times and does not play an important role in the coordination of Germany's EC policy. This is explained by the fact that EC/EU matters have become increasingly important and are almost permanently on the agenda of the cabinet. The convening of a specific cabinet meeting has therefore not proved to be necessary. Only issues which are disputed between the ministries or which are delicate in terms of public opinion are discussed in the cabinet.[21] The bulk of the coordination work – at least as far as important political issues are concerned – is done by the inter-ministerial *Committee of State Secretaries* (*Europa-Staatssekretäre*). This committee is almost always composed of the state secretaries of the Foreign Affairs Ministry, the Economics Ministry, the Agricultural Ministry and the Finance Ministry (the 'four musketeers' in EC affairs) as well as by the Permanent Representative in Brussels and the state secretary responsible for community affairs in the Federal Chancellor's Office; depending on the agenda, state secretaries and senior civil servants from other ministries might join the meetings. The committee's task is to settle conflicts between ministries, to prepare documents on political aspects involved in Council meetings and to draft outlines of Germany's negotiation strategy in the Council. The committee's decisions, which are taken by common accord, are binding for the ministries.[22] From this it follows that the com-

[20] One civil servant in the Foreign Office estimated that 40–50% of his working time is spent on the internal coordination process i.e. intra-ministerial and inter-ministerial coordination.

[21] Such as the so-called 'holiday directive' which in summer 1993 suddenly reached the cabinet and was immediately transposed into national law. The reason was that German tourists were stranded at airports without any help, after their holiday operator had gone bankrupt.

[22] See Sasse et al., *op. cit.*, p. 12.

mittee's main function is an 'internal' one in the sense of solving inter-ministerial conflicts and establishing a coherent European policy; however, it is less successful as an instrument to put forward an active European policy, the lack of which is one of the weaknesses of the German EC policy, which has therefore been described as being mostly a 'reactive policy'.[23]

Table 4.3   Inter-ministerial coordination committees in EC policy-making

	Date of creation	Function	Frequency of meetings and presidency
Cabinet Committee for European Policy	1973	important political matters; global strategy	one session in October 1973 and in the 1980s [CH]
State Secretaries' Committee (Europa-Staats-sekretäre)	1963	controversial political questions; preparation of political documents	approximately every four weeks; during presidency more often [AA]
Europe-Delegates (Europa-Beauftragte)	1971	exchange of information	approximately every four to six weeks [BMWi]
Tuesday Committee (heads of section)		detailed technical matters	weekly meetings

Key: CH = chancellor; AA = Foreign Office; BMWi = Economics Ministry

There is a sophisticated sharing of work between the Foreign Office and the Economics Ministry: while the Committee of the State Secretaries is chaired by the Minister of State in the Foreign Office, its secretariat is part of department E in the Economics Ministry. The function of chairman of the committee is very often to deputize for the Foreign Minister in the General Foreign Ministers' Council in Brussels; moreover the Minister of State might report in this function to the full cabinet meetings of the government. Thus the chairman plays an important role as a bridge between the administrative level and the political level.

As far as the irregular meetings of the *Europe-Delegates* (*Europa-Beauftragte*, i.e. the heads of department or deputy heads of sub-departments) and the weekly meetings of the *Tuesday Committee*

[23] See Bulmer/Paterson, *op. cit.*, pp. 19–20.

(heads of section, i.e. *Ressortleiter*) is concerned, neither of them has the political authority to solve inter-ministerial conflicts. The meetings of the Europe-Delegates are chaired by the head of department E in the Economics Ministry; they deal with non-political matters which are more general in nature and are of cross-sectoral importance. The Tuesday Committee is the forum to discuss more technical matters and especially the agenda of the COREPER in Brussels. Its main function is to coordinate the instructions for the Permanent Representative in Brussels. Depending on the points on the agenda, the instructions are drafted by the competent ministries and are then rubber-stamped by the head of department E in the Economics Ministry which is the central agency for giving instructions to the Permanent Representative in Brussels.

The principle of the main responsibility of a department or sub-department in an issue (i.e. the *Federführung*) might help to produce a relatively clear decision-making procedure although this principle does not prevent conflicts arising between different ministries. Before an issue reaches COREPER the decision-making process in the Council working groups is rather decentralized. At the lower level civil servants are rather specialized which does not facilitate finding a solution if problems arise between ministries. Interministerial meetings at this level are chaired by the department which is responsible for the specific issue (i.e. the *federführendes Ressort*). Meetings are nearly permanently composed of civil servants from the 'four musketeers' but also irregularly from other ministries which have to deal with European affairs (Social Ministry, Environmental Ministry, Ministry for Science and Research etc.). The Deputy Permanent Representative in Brussels also takes part in meetings as well as representatives from the Länder.[24] It is quite clear that in such large and relatively heterogeneous groups it is difficult to coordinate the divergent views and to come to a common position in policy-making or to develop a common strategy with regard to Brussels. Too many actors and issues are involved on an irregular basis which makes it difficult to formulate a coherent standpoint. Thus very often the coordination gets stuck in the 'morass of technical details' and ministerial self-interest prevails. This might explain why the German

[24] The 'Länder Observer' sits in the meetings of the Europe-Delegates and in the Tuesday Committee there are two Länder civil servants: one from a Land of the A-group (i.e. SPD-led Länder) and one from a Land of the B-group (i.e. CDU-led Länder).

position in Brussels is often based on individual ministries and why even in the permanent representation civil servants often show a higher loyalty to 'their' ministry (the Foreign Office and Economics Ministry each provide only ¼ of the senior staff in the permanent representation in Brussels) than to a coherent European policy of the Federal Republic. The lack of an effective coordination of *the* European policy might lead to the paradox of the Agricultural Ministry asking for more money from Brussels for its farmers whereas the Ministry of Finance at the same time reminds its European partners that the EC has to reduce its expenditure. And this situation might even become more complicated when the Länder are representing Germany in the Council and bring up their specific concerns on issues. In one sentence: Germany's day-to-day European policy-making is characterized by a weak horizontal coordination leading to a 'bureaucratized policy-making' which lacks – with some exception during the Council presidency – strong political impetus.

The Bundestag

Preparatory phase   In Germany there is a clear preponderance of the executive compared to the legislative in EC affairs. However, it cannot be overlooked that the Bundestag has made increasing efforts in the context of Maastricht – especially with the introduction of the new Arts. 23 and 45 in the Basic Law – to strengthen its influence on EC legislation.

In the past various traditional instruments were available to the German Bundestag to influence the government's EC policy:[25]

- 'minor' or 'major' interpolations of the government (*große und kleine Anfragen*) or orally presented questions;
- discussion of EC affairs during the 'question hour' (*aktuelle Stunde*);
- influence over EC affairs through the voting of the national budget;
- influence on (some) treaties of the EC and on amendments to the Treaty of Rome through the voting of the act of ratification.

The different types of interpolations and the question hours are control instruments for the Parliament of the government's actions.[26]

---

[25] See Regelsberger/Wessels, *op. cit.*, pp. 469–99.
[26] Any member of the Bundestag has the right to address an orally presented question to the government (1949–87: 62,000 in total). Small and big inquiries can only be

They have only been used marginally in order to influence the government's EC policy.[27] As for the voting of acts of ratification such as on the Rome Treaties, the SEA and the Maastricht Treaty on European Union, they have a post-action character.

Concerning more specifically the preparation of EC decisions, the most important instrument has been Art. 2 of the Act of Ratification of the Treaty of Rome. According to this article the government had a duty to inform the Bundestag (and the Bundesrat, see below) before any decision which will become binding law in Germany.[28] 'Information' in this context means that all kind of initiatives of the Commission which are transferred to the Council (proposals for EC legislation, written statements, reports, programmes and memoranda etc.) and become Council documents are channelled to the Bundestag and then to the specialist committees. However, this clause could never be applied very efficiently. One reason was that the Bundestag was only informed about a Commission proposal at a relatively late stage i.e. after its publication and transfer to the Council. The timing of further steps depended on updated information from the government which was difficult to obtain. Another reason was, and still is, the sluggishness of the Bundestag itself in dealing with EC legislation. In fact the procedures of handling documents inside and outside the German Bundestag do not seem to be adapted to the fast and growing legislative output of the Community. The time lag between the publication of a Council document and action by the reponsible committee in the Bundestag is several weeks.[29] Moreover, few parliamentarians are really interested in

---

done by the political factions in the Bundestag (*Fraktionen*). Between 1949 and 1987 there were 695 big and 4,725 small inquiries in the Bundestag. The question hour was only used 117 times. Unfortunately no figures are available yet on how many times these instruments have been used in European affairs. See Joachim Jens Hesse and Thomas Ellwein, *Das Regierungssystem der Bundesrepublik Deutschland*, 7th edn, vol. i (Opladen: Westdeutscher Verlag, 1992), pp. 234–5.

[27] Interview with a senior civil servant of the German Bundestag.

[28] See Bulmer/Paterson, *op. cit.*, p. 167.

[29] The route of documents being sent from the Council of Ministers to the German Bundestag is as follows: (1) Outside the Bundestag they go from the Council Secretariat to the Permanent Representation, then to the Economics Ministry, the Chancellery and to the administration of the Bundestag and Bundesrat. (2) Inside the Bundestag documents are formally transferred to the office of the President of the Bundestag and then to the Secretariat of the Bundestag which has a special unit dealing with EC affairs ('Fachbereich XII'). This unit sends the documents to the committees asking whether they would like to deal with those documents. Then the committees

dealing with the sometimes rather technical EC legislation which
needs expert knowledge and which, in electoral terms, is not very
profitable to deal with. Thus, in many cases, parliament found out
at a late stage that a legislative act of the Community had been
adopted.[30] Discussion of an EC bill in the Bundestag scarcely dis-
guised its growing powerlessness in EC legislation.[31]

However, this does not mean that the German Bundestag was
not interested in EC affairs. Because of the great quantity of information (Commission proposals, reports and resolutions of the European Parliament, regulations, directives and decisions of the Council
of Ministers) and the amount of work with its own national legislation, the Bundestag had a selective approach to EC legislation. In
fact, in approximately 80% of the cases the Bundestag just took note
of a document without further action. In general the Bundestag concentrated especially on laws which were of internal political importance and on the debates in plenary on the progress reports of the
government on integration and its European policy.

According to the new Art. 23 in the German Basic Law, which contains the provisions for the participation of the Bundestag in EC
affairs and which was defined in more detail by a special implemen-

---

inform the EC unit about their intentions and the EC unit XII prepares a document
about the committees' working intentions and reports to the Council of Elders
('Ältestenrat') of the Bundestag. This latter makes a proposal to the plenary of the
Bundestag as to which committee should be responsible ('federführend') in an affair.
Only after a decision by the Bundestag and thus the official assignment will a committee really start its deliberations on a document and prepare a proposal for the plenary. Since the committees only have weekly sessions and the Council of Elders
convenes even less frequently, and including the various holidays etc., the whole procedure within the Bundestag takes several weeks. The paradox is that according to §93
of the rules of procedure of the Bundestag there is an 'accelerated procedure' concerning EC documents, i.e. the Council of Elders can directly transfer documents to
the committees but the latter will start deliberations only after the official assignment
though they have the documents already 'in their hands'.

[30] Between July 1980 and July 1986 2,506 bills were transferred to the Bundestag out
of which 256 (i.e. 10%) were dealt with in plenary on the proposal of the committee
which was responsible. Of those 256 bills 167 had already been published in the *Official Journal* when the Bundestag was passing a resolution on them. See Klaus Hänsch,
'Europäische Integration und parlamentarische Demokratie', *Europa-Archiv*, 7 (1986),
pp. 191–200; here: p. 197.

[31] See Alwin Brück, 'Europäische Integration und Entmachtung des Deutschen Bundestages: Ein Unterausschuß ist nicht genug', *Zeitschrift für Parlamentsfragen*, 2 (1988),
pp. 220–4.

tation law,[32] the Bundestag will have access already in the prepara-tory phase of an EC decision to 'comprehensive' and 'earliest possi-ble' information which the government – now by force of the constitution – is obliged to provide. Moreover, according to Art. 23 § 3, the government must enable the Bundestag to vote on a resolu-tion *before* a decision is taken in the Council. The government is obliged to 'take into account' the resolutions of the Bundestag in the negotiations in Brussels. An evaluation of the concrete application of these provisions has not yet been made; however, it is believed that the participation rights of the Bundestag in the preparatory phase of the EC decision-making process have been improved.

The establishment of the *Commission on Europe* (i.e. the Europa-Kommission since 1983)[33] in the German Bundestag took twenty-six years and even then was only non-binding in character.[34] It was only in September 1991 that the German Bundestag established a regular *Committee on European Affairs* (the EG-Ausschuß) – thirty-four years after the signing of the Treaty of Rome[35] – in which amend-ments to the Treaty of Rome or issues of high political importance could be scrutinized and discussed. One reason for this late reaction was that the Foreign Affairs Committee feared a loss of competence in EC affairs. Therefore in May 1987 only a sub-committee on Euro-pean affairs had been established which was not able to fulfil the nec-essary coordination function in EC affairs. It contained twenty-six members out of the Bundestag (fourteen were at the same time in the Foreign Affairs Committee and the others in various other commit-tees) and thirteen German members out of the European Parliament who had no voting rights. The first task of the EG-Ausschuß after its foundation in 1991 was to monitor closely the work of the two inter-

[32] Law on the Cooperation of the Federal Government and the German Bundestag in Affairs of the European Union, 12.3.1993. See Thomas Läufer (ed.), *Europäische Gemeinschaft, Europäische Union. Die Vertragstexte von Maastricht* (Bonn: Europa Union Verlag, 1993), pp. 278–97.

[33] Before that all bills concerning EC legislation had been dealt with in the different specialized committees of the Bundestag.

[34] From 1987 to 1990 a sub-committee to the Foreign Affairs committee was estab-lished to deal with questions of the European Community. The sub-committee had extended rights compared to its predecessor the 'Commission on Europe'.

[35] And even this only happened after hard fights by some 'Europeanists' in the Bun-destag and was apparently the result of the specific situation in summer 1991 (inter-governmental conference, new Bundestag after elections in 1990 and thus weak foreign affairs committee) and of a kind of accidental majority in the Bundestag. A senior civil servant therefore called the EC committee the 'unloved late-born child'.

governmental conferences on European Monetary Union and Political Union. To this end the Foreign Minister and various other ministers had been invited to the committee sessions in order to report on the negotiations and the government's European policy.[36]

The new Art. 45 of the Basic Law was introduced in connection with the ratification of Maastricht foresees the creation of a new *Committee for Affairs of the European Union* (Ausschuß für Angelegenheiten der Europäischen Union, so-called '*Unionsausschuß*') which, together with the Committee on Foreign Affairs, the Committee of Defence and the Petition Committee, is one of the four committees of the Bundestag which are explicitly mentioned in the Basic Law. The new committee convened for the first time in December 1994 and is composed of thirty-nine regular members and eleven associated members of the European Parliament. What is new about the 'Unionsausschuß' is that the plenary of the Bundestag can authorize it to take over the rights of the Bundestag as a whole with regard to the government in European affairs. The idea is that the Bundestag should be enabled to react quickly to legislative drafts coming from Brussels. By December 1994 it was not yet clear what would be the specific competences of the 'Unionsausschuß' especially in relation to the existing specialized committees of the Bundestag (Fachausschüsse) and under which conditions it would get what kind of authorization – general or partial – of the rights of the Bundestag.[37] This last point is important since a *general* delegation of the rights of the Bundestag to the 'Unionsausschuß' as mentioned in Art. 23 would make it a quite powerful body. In December 1994 an amendment to § 93 of the rules of procedure of the Bundestag was decided on, including the introduction of a new § 93 on the 'Ausschuß für Angelegenheiten der Europäischen Union'. According to these new provisions the 'Unionsausschuß' has in principle the main responsibility (*Federführung*) for the treatment of EC documents and it can invite to its deliberations, in addition to the eleven associated German MEPs, further German members of the EP.

The relatively limited involvement of the Bundestag in EC matters was probably also due to the fact that, before the 1979 direct Euro-

[36] See Eberhard Schoof, *Stichwort eg-ausschuß. Der Deutsche Bundestag und die Europäische Gemeinschaft*, ed. public relations department of the Deutsche Bundestag (Bonn: SZ, 1993), pp. 19–20.

[37] See Sven Höhlscheidt and Thomas Schotten, 'Der Unionsausschuß des Deutschen Bundestages – Gestaltungsprobleme', *Integration*, 4 (1994), pp. 230–3.

pean elections, members of the Bundestag were sent to the European Parliament and disposed of double mandates. Thus there had been established a general feeling of enough interest representation on the EC level through party colleagues in the EP. After the introduction of the direct elections, the European Parliament was considered strong enough to follow EC legislation closely. It was only after the 1985 White Book and the Single European Act that it became increasingly evident that the European Parliament was not able to participate effectively in EC decision-making and to control the executive. A debate started on the so-called 'democratic deficit' of the Community. Maastricht again did not fulfil the expectations of a stronger European Parliament which, as a consequence, led to the conviction that a stronger involvement of national parliaments would be necessary. Thus the Bundestag strengthened its participation in EC legislation with the introduction in December 1992 of the new Art. 23 in the Basic Law.

Experts estimated in the 1970s that 10–15% of the committee work in the Bundestag (and the Bundesrat) was taken up by EC matters. Due to the increasing importance of EC legislation and the extension of the policy fields this figure, it is estimated, must be considerably higher today. In fact the number of documents (so-called 'EG-Vorlagen') sent over from Brussels and dealt with in the Bundestag grew between the 1970s and the 1980s from about 1,100–1,700 per legislature to about 1,800–2,400 during the 10th and 11th Bundestag (1983–1990).

Implementation phase During the phase of decision-taking the German Bundestag is absent since it is not represented in the Council. However, as far as the implementation phase of the EC decision-making process is concerned, the Bundestag – but also the Bundesrat and the parliaments of the Länder – plays an important role. In all cases in which a Council directive must be incorporated into national law, the Bundestag, in cooperation with the administration on the federal and on the Länder level, might use its room for manoeuvre to adapt EC law to the national peculiarities and traditions and thus have an influence – though a rather marginal one[38] – on the shaping

---

[38] See on the problem of the direct applicability of EC directives Heinrich Siedentopf and Jacques Ziller, *Making European Policies Work*, vol. i: *The implementation of Community Legislation in the Member States* (London: Sage, 1988), pp. 8ff.

of EC policies. In many cases the room for manoeuvre consists only in technical details and quite often the Bundestag has to transpose EC legislation directly into national law without any national discretion. Furthermore, the incorporation of EC law into national law is often done by the executive through secondary legislation (*Rechtsverordnungen*) in which, under specific circumstances, only the Bundesrat participates. Studies on the implementation of EC legislation have shown that the German Bundestag is quite quick in incorporating EC law into national law compared to the other member countries,[39] though the real problem is the application and control of EC law by the various national authorities which very often fall into the realm of competences of the Länder and the local authorities.

The Länder and the Bundesrat

Bund and Länder In general terms it seems that the German Grundgesetz (GG) contains a basic dilemma with regard to the integration process: on the one hand there is the federal structure of Germany which according to the Basic Law is not alterable (Art. 79 §3 GG), and on the other hand the Bund has the power to represent Germany in foreign affairs (Art. 32 GG) and to transfer competences by simple law to a supranational level (Art. 24 GG). The latter competences of the Bund necessarily include actions which affect the content and the sense of the former just as the competences of the Länder affect the right of the Bund to exert its power fully in the integration process. EC policy-making in the Federal Republic, therefore, is a policy to find the right balance between the internal structure, i.e. the distribution of competences between Bund and Länder, and the external functioning, i.e. the pursuance of an effective EC policy.[40]

Concerning more specifically the distribution of competences, the German political system is characterized by a vertical division of power between the federal level, the Länder level and the local level (Bund–Länder–Gemeinden). Each level has specific competences

---

[39] See Siedentopf/Ziller, *op. cit.*, vol. ii: *National Reports*; see also the graph on the implementation of the Commission's White Book in the *Seventh Report of the Commission on the Implementation of the White Book on the Realization of the Internal Market*, Com (92) 383 of 2 September 1992, Annex VII.

[40] See Rudolf Hrbek and Uwe Thaysen (eds.), *Die Deutschen Länder und die Europäischen Gemeinschaften*, Symposium of the German Association for Parliamentary Questions (Baden-Baden: Nomos, 1986), pp. 17–20.

which are more or less clearly defined in the Basic Law or which have been officially confirmed by decisions of the Federal Constitutional Court as in the case of the competence of the Länder in cultural affairs ('*Kulturhoheit der Länder*' which includes schools, education, universities, art, science, media etc.). The most important division of competences in this connection concerns legislative power where the Basic Law differentiates between the 'exclusive legislative power' of the Bund (*ausschließliche Gesetzgebung*, see Art. 71 and 73 GG, i.e. in the fields of foreign affairs, nationality, currency, customs, federal police etc.) and the 'concurrent legislative power' of the Bund and the Länder (*konkurrierende Gesetzgebung*, see Art. 72 and 74 GG, i.e. in the fields of civil and criminal law, right of establishment for foreigners, use of atomic energy, real estate, roads, hospitals – to mention only a few). In these fields the Länder can take legislative action as long as the Bund does not do so.

The catalogue of competences in the Basic Law (Art. 73 and 74 GG) which suggests a clear-cut division of power between Bund and Länder is essentially of theoretical value today and does not correspond to reality. In fact in many 'dominions' of the Länder the Bund intervenes today more or less directly, either through 'framework legislation' (*Rahmengesetzgebung*, see Art. 75 GG) as in the field of the universities or through its financial contribution to environmental projects, the construction of roads, and other infrastructural projects. Moreover, according to Art. 91a of the Basic Law there are 'common tasks' (*Gemeinschaftsaufgaben*) in which the Bund participates, though they fall partly into the competences of the Länder (such as regional funding, agriculture, construction of universities and hospitals). Thus there is a complex system of overlapping competences and functions which only in theory allows differentiation between the Länder level and the federal level; in practice however German policy-making is characterized by a sharing of competences in a system described as 'cooperative federalism'.[41]

The Länder on the other hand are very often responsible for the administrative implementation of laws decided by the Bund: a system which is described by the term 'administrative federalism' (*Verwaltungsföderalismus*).[42] In fact the Basic Law contains specific provi-

---

[41] See Scharpf, Reissert and Schnabel, *op. cit.*
[42] See Hesse and Ellwein, *op. cit.*, pp. 86–90.

sions in which the Länder either execute federal laws as 'own affairs' (*eigene Angelegenheiten*, see Art. 84 GG) or 'by order of the Bund' (so-called '*Bundesauftragsverwaltung*', see Art. 85 GG). These provisions are important for the implementation of EC legislation and they show to what extent the Bund depends on the administrative cooperation of the Länder without which any policy decision of the Council would have no effect.

Although in Germany a legalistic approach prevails on the part of the administration towards binding law and the application of specific regulations is very strict, it might happen that because of an unsatisfactory involvement of the Länder in EC policy-making – especially in the *preparatory phase* – there is a certain unwillingness of the Länder to comply with EC measures on whose substance they have not had any influence.[43] In fact, so far the participation of the Länder – especially of the Länder parliaments[44] – in EC policy-making has been fairly marginal and has been mostly limited to the *phase of implementation and control* by the Länder administrations. However, in any conflictual case, when executing federal laws the Länder are bound to the Bund by the principle of 'federal loyalty' (*Bundestreue*). As a kind of last resort the Basic Law foresees in Art. 37 the possibility of the Bund forcing a Land – after the consent of the Bundesrat – to fulfil its duties (*Bundeszwang*).

On the basis of these constitutional provisions the Länder have developed different instruments in order to participate more effectively in the EC decision-making process. They primarily made use of the second chamber, the Bundesrat, which is composed of representatives of the Länder governments.[45] Compared to the Bundestag the Bundesrat, it seems, has been better equipped when dealing with EC affairs; since 1957 the Bundesrat has had a *Committee on Questions of the European Community* (i.e. the Ausschuß für Fragen der

[43] See Sabine Pag and Wolfgang Wessels, 'Federal Republic of Germany', in Siedentopf and Ziller, *op. cit.*, vol. ii, pp. 163–229; Siedentopf and Ziller, *op. cit.*, vol. i, pp. 5ff and 26ff.

[44] See the President of the Landtag of Nordrhein-Westfalen (ed.), *Die Landtage im europäischen Integrationsprozeß nach Maastricht. Vorschläge für eine Stärkung der europapolitischen Rolle*, Schriften des Landtags Nordrhein-Westfalen, vol. v (Düsseldorf, 1992).

[45] This might be ministers, but in most cases there are civil servants sitting in the Bundesrat. According to Art. 51 GG each Land has at least three votes; those Länder with more than 2 million inhabitants have four votes, those with more than 6 million inhabitants have five votes and those with more than 7 million inhabitants six votes.

Europäischen Gemeinschaften) and thus was the first second chamber of an EC member state to undertake such a step.[46] The Länder
were stimulated to deal effectively with EC affairs by their basic concern to preserve their federal rights and freedom of action.[47] In order
to understand the Länder's new powers since Maastricht, a look back
at the development of the different instruments and their adaptation
to the European integration process is necessary.

Article 2 procedure   The most important instrument prior to Maastricht has been Article 2 of the Act of Ratification of the Rome
Treaties (so-called '*Zuleitungsverfahren*' or '*Bundesratsverfahren*')[48]
which included the Bundesrat in the government's duty of information. Although the Bundesrat – like the Bundestag – was also concerned with the question of timing of EC draft legislation because of
the rather long-distance information flow,[49] it seems that the Bundesrat – especially its *Committee for EC affairs* (Ausschuß für Fragen
der Europäischen Gemeinschaften) – made use of this procedure
rather successfully. The Article 2 procedure led to an intensive
exchange of information between the federal government and the
Länder governments and has been evaluated quite positively.[50]

One reason for this seems to be that the Bundesrat is less politicized in its committee work compared to the Bundestag, i.e. issues
are handled less by politicians who would like to profit from it in
political terms than by senior civil servants from the Länder governments. Moreover, reports on specific issues – according to the functional specialization within the Bundesrat – are handled by two
Länder.[51] They control each other, thus preventing one Bundesland
exploiting any matter for its own benefit. Though the expert-domi-

---

[46] See Klaus Pöhle, 'Parlamente in der EG – Formen der praktischen Beteiligung',
Integration, 2 (1992), pp. 72–82; here: p. 73.

[47] It has happened for example in the field of regional policy that, contrary to the
German government and the Bundestag who were rather against the introduction of
the regional policy, the Bundesrat was in favour if the Länder could participate in the
allocation of funds and if the development areas within the Federal Republic were at
the same time extended. See Sasse et al., *op. cit.*, p. 46.

[48] See the wording of Art. 2 of the ratification law of the Treaty of Rome in Hrbek
and Thaysen, *op. cit.*, doc. 1, p. 222.

[49] See above note 29.

[50] See Rudolf Hrbek, 'Doppelte Politikverflechtung: Deutscher Föderalismus und
Europäische Integration. Die deutschen Länder im EG-Entscheidungsproezß', in Hrbek
and Thaysen, *op. cit.*, pp. 17–36; here: p. 25.

[51] The so-called 'A-Länder' have an SPD government, whereas the 'B-Länder' have
a CDU government.

nated handling of EC affairs in the Bundesrat functioned quite smoothly, it seems that the influence of resolutions of the Bundesrat on Germany's position in the Council and thus on EC policy-making was limited. An important 'balancing effect' in this respect came from the federal government's attitude to avoid quarrels with the Länder. The government depended on the Länder's agreement in the legislative process in other fields; this was particularly true for bills requiring the consent of the Bundesrat (*zustimmungspflichtige Gesetze*). Since the opposition parties have mostly had the majority in the Bundesrat, the federal government had an interest in taking into account the Länder's concerns. So there was a more informal political influence of the Länder on the government's positions which was also symbolized by the attendance of representatives of the federal ministries at committee meetings of the Bundesrat.

The Länder-Observer   The already mentioned Länder-Observer (*Länderbeobachter*) who is appointed by the Conference of the Economics Ministers of the Länder – this happened for the first time in 1956 – provides useful information to the Bundesrat and the Länder through his or her participation in Council meetings and contacts with the various institutions and permanent representations in Brussels. However, as the title indicates, he or she is essentially an 'observer' who has no decision-making power or voting right. Due to the observer's function and rather modest administrative equipment he or she is not a key figure in the EC decision-making process. The establishment of representations in Brussels by all Länder since the mid-1980s must be considered as a competitive element to the 'Länder-Observer' which weakens the latter's information task.

Länder participation procedure   In 1979 a new procedure was introduced – the participation procedure of the Länder (*Länderbeteiligungsverfahren*) – after complicated juridical negotiations with the Länder who were pushing the federal government for a guaranteed participation in EC affairs. However, the only outcome was a letter of the Federal Chancellor – at that time Helmut Schmidt – in which he agreed to a kind of voluntary obligation of the Bund to respect the principle of 'federal loyalty' (*Bundestreue*) in dealing with EC affairs. More specifically he stated in this letter[52] that in all matters which concern the exclusive competences of the Länder or which are of spe-

---

[52] See doc. 5 in Hrbek and Thaysen, *op. cit.*, p. 237.

cific interest for the Länder (especially in issues which have financial implications) there will be a 'close and confidential cooperation' of the Bund and the Länder. The most important element of this new procedure was – and this was certainly an improvement for the Länder compared to the already existing Article 2 procedure – that the obligation to inform the Länder on EC legislation should be met at a much earlier stage, i.e. in the *preparatory phase*. Although this contributed on the one hand to solve the 'timing problem', on the other hand it meant that the Länder had to respond to a legislative draft coming from Brussels in a 'reasonable time period', i.e. much quicker than before. The Bund was obliged to respect the standpoint of the Länder governments in all cases which concerned the exclusive competences of the Länder and only for 'compulsory reasons concerning external affairs or European integration' could it deviate from the Länder's opinion. There was also the possibility of including representatives of the Länder in official German delegations, although this depended entirely on the willingness of the Bund. Moreover the new procedure introduced a new article in the common standing orders of the federal ministries stating that the Länder-Observer would receive all information transferred to the federal ministries by the services of the Commission.

The new 'Länderbeteiligungsverfahren' did not have the expected impact. In part this was due to the difficulty for the Länder of co-ordinating their own views and seeking common solutions in specific working groups. Another reason was that the Bundesrat was not involved in this procedure which led to a duplication of information and participation of the Länder which was not very efficient. The Bundesrat seemed to be the more effective 'channel of participation' due to its established contacts with the Bundestag, the European Parliament and the other EC institutions.[53]

Cooperation since the SEA The ratification of the SEA constituted for the Länder an opportunity to extend their rights of participation in the EC decision-making process. This step was not really convincing since the SEA did not contain the transfer of substantially new competences to the Community which touched upon the exclusive competences of the Länder. Nevertheless, after complicated juridical negotiations with the Bund in which it became clear that the exten-

---

[53] See Hrbek and Thaysen, *op. cit.*, pp. 29–31.

sion of the Länder's participation rights in EC affairs was above all a political matter, the Länder managed to improve their situation with regard to the EC legislative process. In contrast to the past, the Länder applied a strategy of concentrating their efforts on the role of the Bundesrat and of finding an arrangement with the Bund based on law. The result was Art. 2 of the Act of Ratification of the SEA and the agreement between Bund and Länder of December 1987.[54] Compared with the preceding Länder participation procedure, the Länder could improve their situation with the help of the Bundesrat with regard to the following points: (1) the amount and the substance of EC documents transferred to the Bundesrat was specified as well as the procedure for distribution; (2) the participation of representatives of the Länder in the working groups of the Council and the Commission was extended, i.e. their participation was made possible not only in cases where the exclusive competences of the Länder were involved but also in cases in which 'substantial interests of the Länder' were concerned; (3) on the basis of the agreement of December 1987 the Bundesrat established a special committee – the *'Europe-Chamber'* (EG-Kammer) which could be empowered to take decisions for the Bundesrat as a whole; thus the Bundesrat could deal more effectively with EC affairs and within the required time limits. Taken together, the Länder could, above all, through the 'formalization' and the further 'legalization' of the existing provisions and practices, extend their participation in the EC decision-making process after the SEA.

Art. 23 GG and the Bundesrat   A qualitative step to extend further the Länder's rights in EC/EU decision-making consisted in the introduction of a new Art. 23 in the German Basic Law (see also above on the Bundestag). With the amendment of the Basic Law after Maastricht the Länder continued their strategy of enhancing the Bundesrat's role in EC/EU decision-making and – together with other new provisions and instruments at their disposal in European affairs – one could have the impression that the 'Länder were striking back'.[55] In fact with the completion of the Internal Market and the intergovernmental conferences on EMU and Political Union, which

[54] See doc. 7 and 8 in Rudolf Morawitz and Wilhelm Kaiser, *Die Zusammenarbeit von Bund und Ländern bei Vorhaben der Europäischen Union* (Bonn: Europa Union Verlag, 1994), pp. 157–65.
[55] See Charley Jeffrey, *The Länder strike back: Structures and Procedures of European Integration Policy-Making in the German Federal System*, unpublished paper presented at the Sixteenth IPSA World Congress (Berlin, August 1994).

both had their effects on the competences of the Länder (such as in the fields of education and culture, health and consumer policy) and touched upon their interests (such as in the fields of the trans-European networks and regional policy), the Länder were no longer willing to be kept outside the EC decision-making process which to an increasing extent produced binding law for them. During the process leading to Maastricht, the Länder were applying a lobbying strategy, combining four core elements, which were fed into the discussion inside and outside Germany: (1) the principle of subsidiarity; (2) the opening of the Council for ministers for the sub-national level; (3) the establishment of a 'regional chamber' at European level; (4) the right of the regional level to appeal to the ECJ.[56] The outcome of this strategy was successful and had its impact on the amendment of the German Basic Law. In short the following provisions are of importance to the Länder for their participation in EC/EU decision-making:[57]

1 According to Art. 23 § 2 GG the government is obliged to inform the Bundesrat in a 'comprehensive' and 'earliest possible' way on affairs of the EU;
2 According to Art. 23 § 5 GG the government has the duty 'extensively to take into account' (*maßgeblich zu berücksichtigen*) the position of the Länder in its negotiations in Brussels in case exclusive legislative competences of the Länder are affected;
3 According to Art. 23 § 6 GG the Länder may – via the Bundesrat which appoints a member in the rank of a minister of the Länder – represent the Federal Republic in the Council and directly participate in decisions on EC legislation in cases in which exclusive competences of the Länder are involved (e.g. in the fields of culture and education, health, regional projects etc.).

These provisions of the Basic Law were settled in more detail in the law of March 1993 concerning the cooperation of Bund and Länder in affairs of the European Union, and the special agreement between Bund and Länder of October 1993.[58] Thus it is now possible for a

[56] *Ibid.*, p. 7.
[57] See for a more detailed presentation of the new constitutional provisions Wolfgang Fischer, 'Die Europäische Union im Grundgesetz: der neue Artikel 23', *Zeitschrift für Parlamentsfragen*, 1 (1993), pp. 32–49; Ulrich Everling, 'Überlegungen zur Struktur der Europäischen Union und zum neuen Europa-Artikel des Grundgesetzes', *Deutsches Verwaltungsblatt* (1 September 1993), pp. 936–47.
[58] See for the text of both: Bundesrat (ed.), *Handbuch des Bundesrates 1993/94*

minister of one of the Länder to speak and decide in the Council of Ministers in the name of the Federal Republic *as a whole*. This corresponds to the contents of the new Art. 146 TEU on the composition of the EU Council. The general rule since Maastricht is that the Länder, via the Bundesrat, participate in EC legislation to the same extent as they participate in or are competent for purely national legislation. However, the new rights, according to Art. 23 § 6, must be applied 'with the participation of' and 'in accordance with' the federal government.

The Länder fully apply these provisions and are also represented in other EC/EU forums. In January 1995 there were 125 representatives of the Länder in working groups of the Council and 229 in those of the Commission.[59] There were further amendments to the Basic Law which directly concerned the Länder[60] and of which Art. 52 § 3a on the *Europe-Chamber* was among the most important, though it only 'constitutionalized' an already existing practice (see above). Taken together the Länder reached their aim of not only being present in Brussels but also being directly and actively involved in the national process of the preparation and the making of EC/EU decisions.

Conference of Europe-Ministers   A new 'post-Maastricht body' of the Länder is the *Conference of the Ministers of the Länder dealing with European Affairs (Europaministerkonferenz)* which was established in October 1992.[61] Although there had already been in the past conferences of ministers of the Länder, including the respective federal minister, dealing also with specific affairs related to the Community *(Fachministerkonferenzen)*, the new conference of the *'Europaminister'* of the Länder has a permanent character and must be seen in the light of the specific political context of its creation. Whereas the other thirteen *'Fachministerkonferenzen'* are essentially instruments to coordinate the views of the Länder and to discuss important issues together with the Bund, the *'Europaministerkonferenz'* (EMK) has in addition to that a preparatory function of artic-

[59] See Bundesrat, Ausschuß für Fragen der Europäischen Union, *Gremien des Rates und der Kommission, zu denen der Bundesrat Ländervertreter benannt hat*, internal document (January 1995).

[60] Such as Art. 50 on the Bundesrat and the EU, Art. 28 § 1 on the right of EU citizens to vote and Art. 24 § 1 on the transfer of competences to international institutions.

[61] See Florian Gerster, 'Die Europaministerkonferenz der deutschen Länder: Aufgaben – Themen – Selbstverständnis', *Integration*, 16 (2) (1993), pp. 61–7.

ulating the Länder's views towards Brussels. This latter point is not explicitly mentioned, but it cannot be denied that the Länder have established the EMK at a moment when they were strengthening their presence in Brussels within the new Committee of the Regions. However, the main function of the EMK is to coordinate the Länder's European activities, to have a common interest representation with regard to Bonn and Brussels and to watch strictly over the application of the subsidiarity principle on the European level.

The development since the SEA and Maastricht indicates that the Länder have considerably increased their power in EC/EU affairs and in the future the scope of activities on the EC level in which the Länder 'have a word to say' will certainly further extend. This means that the responsibility of the Länder in EC/EU affairs will also increase considerably which raises the central question of their 'European preparedness' ('*Europafähigkeit*') to participate more extensively in EC/EU decision-making and to play a constructive role in the European integration process. This will, among other things, depend on the Länder's ability to coordinate their views internally and to find common positions with regions and local authorities in the other member states.

The record of implementation of EC law

Against the background of the highly complex German decision-making system in European affairs which has been analysed so far, it is interesting to examine briefly its effectiveness in terms of the incorporation and the application of Community law. One way of measurement consists in the analysis of the infringement proceedings which have been put forward against Germany according to Art. 169/170 EEC (see Table 4.4).

The infringement procedure according to Art. 169/170 EEC becomes relevant not only in cases of violation of primary legislation, i.e. the Treaty of Rome as amended by the SEA and Maastricht, but also in cases of non-conformity with secondary legislation, i.e. the so-called '*acquis communautaire*'. In this latter respect the infringement procedure is particularly relevant concerning the incorporation of binding EC directives into national law. Concerning the total EC this amounts to approximately 75% of all infringement procedures brought to the ECJ.

There has been a considerable growth in the application of Art. 169/170 EEC since the foundation of the Community. The increasing use of the infringement procedure, especially since the beginning of the 1980s, is due to the growth of EC legislation in general – and of directives in particular because of the '1992 Internal Market' project – but also because of a stricter control by the Commission on the full application of existing Community law.

Table 4.4   Comparison of infringement proceedings against Germany and EC member states in total according to Art. 169/170 EEC 1988–1992

Year	Letter with deadline			Decisions of the ECJ		
	Germany	EC	%	Germany	EC	%
1988	55	567	9.7	3	56	5.3
1989	56	691	8.1	0	27	0
1990	61	964	6.3	3	38	7.8
1992	97	1210	8.0	6	50	12.0

Source: Tenth Annual Report of the Commission to the European Parliament on Monitoring the Application of Community Law 1992, COM (93) 320 final, 28.4.1993, p. 154.

Concerning more specifically the Federal Republic, it seems that though there has been an increase in the number of infringement proceedings in the Community, the number of infringement proceedings against the FRG has been slightly reduced. However, this observation is only true concerning the *first phase* of the infringement proceedings, i.e. the phase of setting a final deadline for incorporation. In fact the number of the German infringement proceedings with regard to the total number of infringement proceedings in the Community has decreased; expressed in terms of percentage it fell from approximately 10% in 1988 to nearly 6% in 1990 and increased slightly to 8% in 1992 (Table 4.4). However, concerning the *decisions* of the European Court of Justice the record of the Federal Republic is much less convincing. In relation to the total number of infringement proceedings in the Community in this phase, the German share has increased from 5.3% in 1988 to 12% in 1992. In more general terms it seems that the relative number of infringement proceedings which are initiated against member states does not always correspond with the relative number of decisions of the ECJ, i.e. a low number of 'Letters with a deadline' does not necessarily mean that there is also a low number of ECJ 'decisions'.

There have been six decisions of the ECJ against Germany in 1992. Compared with the record of the other member states Germany ranks

Number of decisions

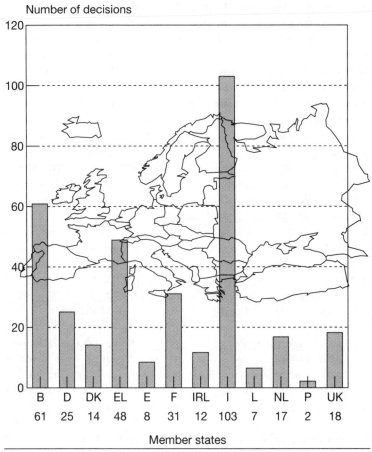

Fig. 4.1 'List of sinners': Article 169 decisions of the ECJ against EC member states 1980–1993

Source: Fifth and Eleventh Annual Report of the Commission to the European Parliament on Monitoring the Application of Community Law.

fourth worst after Greece, Italy and Belgium.[62] However, the figures of the 'List of Sinners' for the period 1980–1992 indicate that Germany is among those countries with the lowest number of infringe-

---

[62] See Tenth Annual Report of the Commission to the European Parliament on Monitoring the Application of Community Law, COM (93) 320 final, 28.4.1993, p. 154.

ment decisions from the ECJ.[63] In more general terms it seems that some countries which are known for their pro-European attitude – such as Italy and Belgium – are especially those countries which are the least reliable in applying binding EC legislation; whereas those countries such as Great Britain and Denmark which are known for their sceptical attitude towards Europe are those countries which have the best record concerning the implementation and application of Community law.

If one looks more closely at the German case there are three policy fields in which most of the infringement proceedings were initiated against Germany:[64] internal market, agriculture and environment/nuclear safety. Calculated on the basis of the figures from the *phase of setting a deadline*, those three policy fields together make up about 70–80% of all infringement proceedings against Germany. This corresponds to the general trend in the EC. Compared to the number of *decisions* of the ECJ against Germany, nearly all of them have also been made in the above mentioned fields. In total there have been twenty-one decisions by the ECJ between 1988 and 1992, out of which eight were in the field of environment, five were in the field of the internal market and three in agriculture; five decisions have been in other fields. Out of those twenty-one decisions ten have been because of an infringement of a treaty, a decision or a regulation and eleven because of the non-satisfactory incorporation of a directive. The latter concerned especially the field of the environment, whereas the infringements of binding regulations and treaties have mostly been committed in the field of the internal market and agriculture.

The reason for the relatively high number of infringement proceedings in the field of the environment[65] might be that in this field very often competences of the Länder are involved which could explain the difficulties – or even unwillingness – in incorporating a directive. This is quite understandable in the case of the directives on ground water[66] and on surface water[67] in which the Länder are asked to fulfil certain technical standards – especially the content of nitrate

[63] Concerning the figures in this graph it must be kept in mind that Spain and Portugal joined the Community only in 1986.

[64] See Tenth Annual Report, *op. cit.* , pp. 148–52.

[65] There were eight new environmental directives, not taken into account in this calculation, for which the incorporation deadline had already elapsed and which were not (yet) incorporated into national law; see *ibid.*, p. 111.

[66] See directive 80/68/EEC on ground water.

[67] See directive 75/440/EEC on surface water.

in the water – which is linked to considerable investments in order to reach the required water quality of the EC, if the Länder want to avoid the closure of certain waterworks. Concerning both directives Germany has been condemned by the European Court of Justice and the procedure according to Art. 171 EEC has been initiated after which Germany might have to pay a fine.[68] Until 31 December 1993 the German authorities had not undertaken further steps in order to comply with the Court's decisions, though since January 1991 Germany has a new national regulation on drinking water but which apparently does not fulfil the requirements of Community legislation. A similar issue is the Court's decisions on the protection of wild birds in which the required national law has been passed by Germany but has not yet been implemented by some of the Länder's administration. Other decisions of the Court are about to be followed by the German authorities, such as the decision on the import of French 'paté',[69] the decisions on air pollution[70] and on the import of pharmaceuticals by private individuals.[71] Compared with the number of judgments (by 31 December 1993) which are not complied with in other member states, Germany has a rather bad record, ranking on place nine among the twelve; only France, Italy and Belgium are worse.[72] This is in contrast to the above shown 'List of sinners' where Germany was better placed. Thus it seems that, although there are an average number of decisions by the ECJ against Germany – though we have seen that their number has increased during the 1990s – once a judgment has been made, Germany has problems complying with it. The above mentioned cases do not constitute very problematic cases; however most of them have in common the fact that the Länder and/or the Bundesrat are involved. A preliminary conclusion therefore could be that the complex internal decision-making process in Germany and the distribution of competences between the Bund and the Länder contribute to a lack of conformity with EC legislation. To qualify this, one has to add that in the past there have

---

[68] See decision of 28 February 1991, case C-131/88 and decision of 17 October 1991, case C-58/89.

[69] See decision of 2 February 1989, case C-274/87.

[70] See decision on sulphur dioxide of 30 May 91, case C-361/88, and decision on lead of 30 May 91, case C-59/89.

[71] See decision of 8 April 1992, case C-62/90.

[72] See Eleventh Annual Report of the Commission to the European Parliament on Monitoring the Application of Community Law 1993, OJ C 154, 6 June 1994, Annex V, pp. 169ff.

been other cases – such as the 'purity of the German beer', the tax problem of so-called 'butter trips' and the question of substitutes for milk – which were less a problem of Länder involvement than of national traditions and of consumer protection. Thus, it seems – and in this respect further empirical studies are needed – that a mixture of structural, i.e. linked to the complex politico-administrative German system, *and* policy reasons, i.e. linked to the specific substance of an issue, are responsible for some of the problems Germany has in its efforts to implement EC legislation and to comply with decisions by the ECJ.

The courts

A further indicator for the relationship between the Community's institutional system and the member states is the reactions of national courts towards Community law. Decisions of the Community are only fully applied if the national jurisdictions take existing Community law into account and if they are willing to respect its application according to their national legal system. One method of measurement is the use of the preliminary ruling procedure according to Art. 177 EEC.

Table 4.5   Legal acts brought to the ECJ according to Art. 177 EEC 1988–1993

Year	Germany	EC/EU	%
1988	34	183	18.5
1989	47	125	37.6
1990	34	140	24.2
1991	52	182	28.5
1992	62	157	39.4
1993	57	204	27.9

Source: Annual Reports of the Commission to the European Parliament on Monitoring the Application of Community Law.

The development of legal acts brought to the European Court of Justice on the basis of Art. 177 EEC shows an upward trend between 1988 and 1993 (see Table 4.5). This is an indicator of the growing acceptance of Community law by the member states. In fact it seems that national courts are increasingly addressing questions to the ECJ on the interpretation and application of Community legislation in a specific case. Thus national courts not only make use of binding Community law but they also respect the role of the ECJ as the 'protector' of the legal system of the Community.

As far as German courts are concerned Table 4.5 indicates that they increasingly made use of the preliminary ruling procedure. In fact between 1991 and 1993 approximately ⅓ of all cases brought to the ECJ on the basis of Art. 177 were undertaken by German courts. Out of the fifty-seven German preliminary rulings in 1993 approximately ⅕ came from courts of last instance (four from the Federal Court of Justice, one from the Federal Administrative Court, six from the Federal Finance Court and two from the Federal Social Court).[73] This is an additional indicator of the relatively 'high' respect of German courts for the legal system of the EC.

However, there have been some controversial judgments of high German courts. There is above all the so-called 'Solange-I-Decision' of the German Constitutional Court in 1974 in which it expressed some doubts about the preservation of fundamental rights in the EC's legal system and the role and function of the ECJ. The same is true for the Constitutional Court's decision on the Maastricht Treaty in October 1993 which again contained some concerns as to the preservation of the standard of fundamental rights in the Union. This was surprising since the Court had already stated in its 'Solange-II-Decision' in 1986 that it accepted the ECJ's role in this respect. In addition to that, the Court's intention to exert its jurisdiction concerning fundamental rights in future in 'cooperation' with the ECJ created certain ambiguities. 'Cooperation' in this sense has been interpreted as the Bundesverfassungsgericht's 'general' control over the standard of fundamental rights, whereas the ECJ would only precede in this respect.[74] Others have evaluated the Maastricht decision as a step towards the 'renationalization of the protection of fundamental rights' by the German Constitutional Court.[75]

Another case concerned the behaviour of the Federal Finance Court which in 1985 did not fully respect the decision of the ECJ as regards the direct applicability of a directive on value added tax. In 1987 this

[73] *Ibid.*, p. 174.

[74] See Ulrich Everling, 'Das Maastricht-Urteil des Bundesverfassungsgerichts und seine Bedeutung für die Entwicklung der Europäischen Union', *Integration*, 17 (3) (1994), pp. 165–75; here: p. 170.

[75] See Manfred Dauses, 'Die Rolle des Europäischen Gerichtshofes als Verfassungsgericht der Europäischen Union', *Integration*, 17 (4) (1994), pp. 215–29; here: p. 218.

decision was abolished by a decision of the German Constitutional Court because of the 'objective arbitrariness' of the Finance Court. However, those incidents were exceptions – though the Maastricht decision of the Constitutional Court left some 'bitter aftertaste' – and do not alter the overall picture that in general German courts respect the primacy of the EC's legal system and fully respect the role of the ECJ as regards the interpretation of Community law. It remains to be seen to what extent the application of Art. 177 TEU develops towards a more decentralized control mechanism of EC/EU legislative acts, thus shifting the focus of compliance control away from Art. 169/171 TEU and giving national courts a more important role.

Interest groups and political parties

Interest groups

The role of interest groups in German politics has been a rather ambivalent one. On the one hand they were accepted in the late nineteenth and at the beginning of the twentieth centuries as necessary actors who mostly articulate the interests of the different economic and social forces and who have an influence on parliament and government. On the other hand interest groups in Germany have always been accompanied by a certain suspicion since they constitute also elements of differentiation of the society and do not seek the welfare of the state as a whole.[76] The Federal Republic has been accused of a 'sense of shame regarding interest groups' (*Interessenverbandsprüderie*)[77] and interest groups call themselves mostly 'unions' (*Verbände*), thus stressing their broader perspective and denying in some respects their lobbying character. This dichotomy concerning the role and function of interest groups has been reflected in social science in the debate on the theories of pluralism and public welfare. It was the merit of neo-corporatist contributions that they went beyond a mere analysis of the influence of interest groups in the legislative decision-making process.[78] They developed the understanding of a 'system of

[76] See Hesse and Ellwein, *op. cit.*, pp. 145–6.

[77] Ernst Fraenkel, *Die Stellung der Verbände im demokratischen Rechtsstaat* (Düsseldorf, 1968), p. 204.

[78] See Philip Schmitter and Gerhard Lehmbruch, *Trends Towards Corporatist Intermediation* (London/Beverly Hills 1979); Ulrich von Alemann and R.G. Heinze (eds.), *Verbände und Staat. Vom Pluralismus zum Korporatismus. Analysen, Positionen, Dokumente* (Opladen: Westdeutscher Verlag, 1981); Gerhard Lehmbruch and Philip Schmitter (eds.), *Patterns of Corporatist Policy-Making* (London/Beverly Hills, 1982).

association' (*Verbundsystem*) and 'informal concertation' (*formlose Konzertierung*) among societal groups which interact in the political decision-making process. This approach enabled them to explain the close cooperation of political bodies and associations of labour and capital particularly in Germany.

Because of the sectorized nature of European policy-making in Germany and the decentralized and pluralistic character of the German constitution there is in general an intensive form of cooperation between the administration and the relevant interest groups in the policy-making process. The reason for this is that the early involvement of interest groups in the decision-making process is not considered as negative – in the sense of possible corruption – but as a positive contribution in the sense of conflict avoidance and the exchange of information and useful expert knowledge. The Common Rules of Procedure of the Federal Ministries (*Gemeinsame Geschäfts-ordnung der Bundesministerien*) explicitly mention the consultation of umbrella organizations of the private interest. This explains the 'rationalist consensus'[79] which exists between administration and interest groups with regard to the major economic policy principles (especially concerning the German macro-economic policy, the so-called '*Ordnungspolitik*') and the substance of most European policies which facilitate cooperation. In most policy fields with financial implications there are well-established networks between civil servants and interest groups that are particularly active in the preparatory phase of the EC legislation and to some extent also in the implementation phase. However, the consequence of this is that some interest groups are better informed and more involved in policy-making than others. This is for example the case for the close relationship between the Agriculture Ministry and the German Farmers' Union (*Deutscher Bauernverband*). The latter has a disproportionally large influence – measured against the weight of agriculture for German PNB and the number of people working in this sector – on the German agricultural policy in Brussels compared to the views of the German consumer interests and the interests of German wholesalers and exporters.[80] The reason for the over-representation of the farmers' interest is on the one hand the result of the high awareness of public opinion with regard to the situation of Germany's agricul-

[79] See Bulmer and Paterson, *op. cit.*, p. 104.
[80] *Ibid.*, pp. 104–5.

ture, and on the other hand the comparative weakness of the other interest groups in articulating their views and influencing the Agriculture Ministry and the agriculture committee in the Bundestag.

Most of the German interest groups are members of transnational interest groups which are located in Brussels. However, their role and utility in influencing policy-making on the European level seem to be limited. There are structural reasons for this which explain that European interest groups play more the role of 'forums' than of real 'actors' in EC policy-making.[81] They are mainly considered as 'listening posts'[82] who collect information about the legislative intentions of the Commission and whose activities are thus mostly effective in the preparatory phase of the EC decision-making process. Depending on the policy field the predominant focus of German interest groups remains the national level and here especially the government and the ministerial bureaucracy. Though there has been an increase in the participation of German lobbying in the EC policy networks at Brussels – also on the part of large German firms – it seems that as soon as sensitive issues of vital interests for the German economy are involved, interest groups shift their attention to the national administration in order to have their concerns pursued in intergovernmental bargaining.[83] There are long established and cooperative relations between civil servants and representatives of interest groups which are consensus-orientated and which are particularly helpful for the bigger German interest groups such as the German Farmers' Union or the Federation of German Industry (BDI). Others, like the trade unions, have been less successful in this respect and also failed so far to organize their views with the help of an effective lobby group on the European level.[84] German trade unions play a more indirect role in the EC policy-making process through the process of conflict solving with the employer's organization on the national level (through the autonomy to negotiate wages and working conditions, i.e. the so-called '*Tarifautonomie*') and the influence of their views – in the final instance expressed through strikes – on the political parties.

[81] See Beate Kohler-Koch, 'Interessen und Integration. Die Rolle organisierter Interessen im westeuropäischen Integrationsprozess', in Michael Kreile (ed.), 'Die Integration Europas', *Politische Vierteljahresschrift*, 23 (1992), pp. 81–119; here: p. 97.

[82] See Bulmer and Paterson, *op. cit.*, p. 102.

[83] See Beate Kohler-Koch, 'Germany: Fragmented but Strong Lobbying', in M. C. P. M. Van Schendelen (ed.), *National Public and Private EC Lobbying* (Aldershot: Dartmouth Press, 1993), pp. 23–48.

[84] See Kohler-Koch, 'Interessen und Integration', *op. cit.*, p. 85.

Political parties

As is indicated above there are scarcely any major differences in opinion over the objective of European integration among the political elite in Germany. Though the legislature is less involved in EC decision-making than the executive, this is in a sense tolerated by the 'general consensus' in German politics over European integration which also transcends the dichotomy of majority and opposition. It was only the foundation of the European Coal and Steel Community in 1951/52 which caused some disagreement. At that time the governing CDU under Adenauer considered the ECSC as a chance to integrate Germany as an equal member into the democratic Western part of Europe whereas the SPD in opposition under Schumacher saw membership of the ECSC as a decision against the possibility of a peaceful reunification of Germany. However, in 1957 the CDU and the SPD were both in favour of membership in the EEC and only the Liberals at that time voted against. The establishment of the EC Committee of the Bundestag in 1991 was realized by a common motion of the parliamentary groups of the CDU/CSU, the SPD and the FDP.[85] The ratification of the SEA and the Maastricht Treaty on European Union was reached by a large majority in the Bundestag of the 'traditional' parties (CDU/CSU, SPD, FDP); parts of the Greens abstained and Maastricht was rejected by the whole PDS (i.e. the follow-up party of the SED, the former Communist Party in the GDR) which formed a group of seventeen representatives in the Bundestag after the 1990 elections.[86] The nomination of the former trade union leader and member of the SPD, Monika Wulf-Mathies, as member of the new Commission under President Santer is a further indicator of the consensus-oriented attitude of the political parties towards European Union. Chancellor Kohl nominated a candidate who is close to the party in opposition and who has the necessary profile. The CDU, although it plays a leading role in the governing coalition in Bonn, does not have 'its' commissioner in Brussels.

In terms of day-to-day decision-making in Brussels political parties do not play an important role. There are of course party political links especially between the members of the European Parliament and the Bundestag but those informal contacts do not result in decisive impacts on the EC/EU decision-making process. However, polit-

---

[85] See Schoof, *op. cit.*, Annex 1.

[86] See Thomas Läufer, 'Bundesrepublik Deutschland', in Werner Weidenfeld and Wolfgang Wessls (eds.), *Jahrbuch der Europäischen Integration 1992/1993* (Bonn: Europa Union Verlag, 1993), p. 301.

ical parties do play a role as far as the general 'European atmosphere' is concerned. This was particularly true when the so-called 'Schäuble-Lamers-Paper'[87] on the future development of the European integration process was presented to the public. Though it was meant to be some 'reflections on European politics' and officially had only been worked out by a small group of CDU parliamentarians, in the other EU member states it was perceived as the opinion in Germany on Europe and contributed to a large debate and the shaping of a more pronounced attitude, especially among the German public, as regards the further way the European integration process should take.

Conclusion

Germany's policy-making in EC/EU affairs is highly complex. There is not one central actor but a plurality of actors representing various institutions on different levels who are involved in formulating, deciding, implementing and controlling the European policy of the Federal Republic. The complexity of the policy-making process is certainly due to the federal structure of Germany but also to some peculiarities of the German political system. The relatively high autonomy of the German ministries, the rivalry between the Foreign Office and the Economics Ministry, and the relatively technically thinking staff have led to a 'sectorization' of German policy-making in EC/EU matters. The strength of such a system certainly is that many actors are involved which might lead to a broad consensus and might help to find a solution even for highly problematic cases. The weakness of such a system is that it is slow and, in cases where there is no consensus, it lacks the necessary legitimacy and there might be incoherence of Germany's position in Brussels. Thus the efficiency and effectiveness of the process of coordination and internal deliberation is of utmost importance for Germany.

The Länder are part of this internal decision-making process, although in the past they only rarely succeeded in effectively influencing the federal government's positions in Brussels. In connection with Maastricht the Länder have shown a great willingness to participate more effectively in EC affairs and have successfully adapted their instruments of participation. The rear of the German institutional system in terms of participation in EC/EU affairs is brought up

---

[87] See CDU/CSU-Fraktion of the German Bundestag, *Überlegungen zur Europapolitik* (Bonn, 1 September 1994).

by the Bundestag. Though the Basic Law has been amended with the new Arts. 23 and 45 GG and although a new 'Committee on Affairs of the European Union' has been established, there are still many hurdles to take in order to participate effectively in the preparation, making and implementation of EC decisions and really to make use of the new possibilities. However, in all parts of the German institutional system an increasing 'Europeanization' could be observed, in the sense of a more active participation in EC/EU decision-making and a more intensified exchange with EC/EU institutions.

Germany certainly does not belong to the 'bad Europeans' in spite of its complex structure and some curious features of its political system. The record of implementation of EC legislation and the behaviour of the German courts show that there is a highly developed pattern of participation and a wide range of activity on behalf of the national institutions within the Communities' institutional system. Nor does Germany belong to the 'good Europeans' as can be seen when examining more closely the Constitutional Court's decision on Maastricht and the record of compliance with decisions against it by the ECJ. With regard to the future, Germany has to deal with these points. Its successful participation in EC/EU affairs will to a large degree depend on its ability to solve some of the internal coordination problems and to find the right balance between federal interests and regional demands.

Select bibliography

Bulmer, Simon and Paterson, William, *The Federal Republic of Germany and the European Community* (London: Allen and Unwin, 1987).

Deubner, Christian, 'Die Wiedervereinigung der Deutschen und die Europäische Gemeinschaft', in Cord Jakobeit and Alparslan Yenal, *Gesamteuropa. Analysen, Probleme und Entwicklungsperspektiven* (Bonn: Bundeszentale für politische Bildung, 1993), pp. 393–413.

Gaddum, Eckart, *Die deutsche Europapolitik in den 80er Jahren. Interessen, Konflikte, Entscheidungen der Regierung Kohl* (Paderborn: Schöningh, 1994).

Heisenberg, Wolfgang (ed.), *German Unification in European Perspective* (London: Brassey's, 1991).

Hellwig, Renate (ed.), *Der Deutsche Bundestag und Europa* (München: Aktuell, 1993).

Hesse, Joachim Jens and Ellwein, Thomas, *Das Regierungssystem der Bundesrepublik Deutschland*, 7th edn, vol. i (Opladen: Westdeutscher Verlag, 1992).

Hrbek, Rudolf and Thaysen, Uwe (eds.), *Die Deutschen Länder und die Europäischen Gemeinschaften*, Symposium of the German Association for Parliamentary Questions (Baden-Baden: Nomos, 1986).

Hrbek, Rudolf and Wessels, Wolfgang (eds.), *EG-Mitgliedschaft: ein vitales Interesse der Bundesrepublik Deutschland?* (Bonn: Europa Union Verlag, 1984).

Hubel, Helmut (ed.), *Das vereinte Deutschland aus internationaler Sicht: eine Zwischenbilanz*, working paper no. 73, Forschungsinstitut der Deutschen Gesellschaft für Auswärtige Politik (Bonn: Europa Union Verlag, 1993).

Janning, Joseph, 'Bundesrepublik Deutschland', in Werner Weidenfeld and Wolfgang Wessels (eds.), *Jahrbuch der Europäischen Integration 1993/1994* (Bonn: Europa Union Verlag, 1994), pp. 305–12.

Jeffrey, Charlie and Sturm, Roland (ed.), *Federalism, Unification and European Integration* (London: Frank Cass, 1993).

Kaiser, Karl and Maull, Hans W. (eds.), *Die Zukunft der deutschen Außenpolitik* (Bonn: Forschungsinstitut der Deutschen Gesellschaft für Auswärtige Politik, 1993).

Lankowski, Carl F. (ed.), *Germany and the European Community. Beyond Hegemony and Containment?* (New York: St Martin's Press, 1993).

Lippert, Barbara, Günther, Dirk, Stevens-Ströhmann, Rosalind, Viertel, Grit and Woolcock, Stephen, *Die EG und die neuen Bundesländer. Eine Erfolgsgeschichte von kurzer Dauer?* (Bonn: Europa Union Verlag, 1993).

Morawitz, Rudolf and Kaiser, Wilhelm, *Die Zusammenarbeit von Bund und Ländern bei Vorhaben der Europäischen Union* (Bonn: Europa Union Verlag, 1994).

Pag, Sabine and Wessels, Wolfgang, 'Federal Republic of Germany', in Heinrich Siedentopf and Jacques Ziller (eds.), *Making European Policies Work*, vol. ii: National Reports (London: Sage, 1988), pp. 163–229.

Schweitzer, Carl-Christoph and Karsten, Detlev (eds.), *The Federal Republic of Germany and EC Membership Evaluated* (London: Pinter, 1990).

Stares, Paul B. (ed.), *Germany and the New Europe* (Washington: The Brookings Institution, 1992).

Italy[1]

Fundamentals of Italy in EU affairs

As one of the six founding members of the European Community, Italy has always been an ardent participant in every integration effort. However, except for the sustaining role normally assigned to De Gasperi in the 1950s, history does not recognize this country as a leading force in that process. Always present, somehow curiously, when the Community jumped to higher degrees of cohesion – just think of 'dramatic' summits like the ones held in Rome or Milan – Italy has rarely been considered a real protagonist of 'Europeanization'.[2]

The Italian position inside the European Community has been marked by many ambiguities and paradoxes. With a foreign policy deeply involved in supporting the European integration process, Italy has long searched for a 'third way', able to link this natural inclination with its predisposition towards the countries of the other side of the Mediterranean and with its political dependence on the United States.[3] Being the fifth nation in the world in terms of GNP, it takes part in the G-7 meetings and, even institutionally speaking, is one of the four biggest countries of the Community, but it is much less influential than its partners in these international arenas. Italy is a well-known Euro-enthusiast but, at the same time, its government has always had many problems in fulfilling EC obligations. It pushed for the agreement regarding the European Monetary Union (EMU)

---

[1] This chapter was updated in February 1994, although subsequent events do not seem to contradict my arguments.

[2] See Alberta Sbragia, 'Italy/EEC. An Undervalued Partnership', *Relazioni Internazionali*, 2 (June 1992).

[3] See IAI (Istituto Affari Internazionali), *L'Italia nella politica internazionale* (Milano: Franco Angeli, various years), or, more briefly, Luigi Vittorio Ferraris, 'Italian-European Foreign Policy', in Francesco Francioni (ed.), *Italy and EC Membership Evaluated* (London: Pinter, 1992), pp. 131–6.

notwithstanding its precarious economic situation, one that even threatens the possibility of respecting the conditions arranged for the payment of the second instalment of the EC loan subscribed at the beginning of 1993. It has major problems of unemployment and rein-dustrialization, but it has been unable to make effective use of the already allocated structural funds.

There have been a few explanations of these kinds of paradoxes. The Italian exceptionalism in the EC arena has been depicted as the result of the same problems that have gained this country the appellation of a 'difficult democracy':[4] alienated and fragmented culture, delayed modernization, polarized party system, governmental instability, blocked majorities, inefficient administration, byzantine procedures and so on.

We surely won't question the fact that national and international arenas are strictly interconnected, and that, often, domestic features affect EC/EU decision-making dynamics, but we do contest the hypothesis that those factors – normally considered singularly as unique causes of every political problem – are able to explain much of the Italian participation in EC/EU affairs. The question is not whether 'politics matter' or not, but whether the same variables that are beginning to be disputed even as far as the internal policy-making is concerned,[5] can be recycled at the European level.

In the following pages, together with a brief description of the institutional relationship between the Italian and the EC/EU decision-making systems, we will try to advance an alternative explanation of the paradoxes previously mentioned.

Sketch of the institutional framework
As a clear reaction to the fascist period, the 'founding fathers' of the Italian Republic included in the 1948 constitution a complex system

[4] Frederic Spotts and Theodore Wieser, *Italy: A Difficult Democracy* (Cambridge: Cambridge University Press, 1986). It is possible to perceive the same type of evaluation in quite a few major works on Italy, where it is described as 'backward', 'eccentric' or 'without government'. See Edward Banfield, *The Moral of a Backward Society* (Glencoe: The Free Press, 1958); Percy Allum, *Italy: Republic without Government* (New York: Norton, 1973); Giuseppe Di Palma, *Surviving Without Governing: The Italian Parties in Parliament* (Berkeley: University of California Press, 1977); Gian Enrico Rusconi and Sergio Scamuzzi, *Italy Today: An Eccentric Society* (London: Sage, 1981).

[5] See, for example Bruno Dente and Gloria Regonini, 'Politics and Policies in Italy', in Peter Lange and Marino Regini (eds.), *State, Market, and Social Regulation* (New York: Cambridge University Press, 1989), pp. 51–79; Gloria Regonini and Marco Giuliani, 'L'Italie: au-delà d'une démocratie consensuelle?', in Bruno Jobert (ed.), *Le tournant néo-libéral en Europe* (Paris: Harmattan, 1994).

of checks and balances that put in the hands of the parliament, as the most representative institution, the power to control every possible abuse of autonomy from the executive. This control is exercised not only through the necessary vote of confidence to the government but, day by day, maintaining an almost absolute monopoly on the whole legislative process, on every issue up to its technicalities. The executive has no reserved powers, and 'very little room for manoeuvre is left to delegated legislation or statutory instruments'.[6]

Notwithstanding the potential difficulties encountered by each legislative proposal (due to the necessity of facing an open political debate), and in spite of the fact that the two chambers, both elected and with equal powers, have to approve the bill in the same version before passing it,[7] the Italian parliament can be considered as one of the most prolific representative institutions in the world. It has been estimated that in Italy 'the number of laws currently enacted is around 100,000', with a gap in comparison with the amount of other countries' legislation that is constantly increasing.[8]

This generous productivity has not been hindered either by the high number of parties – whose presence inside the parliament was assured, till the recent (1993) institutional reforms, by a highly proportional electoral mechanism – or by the impressive governmental turnover that has characterized these forty-five years of the Republic.[9] In fact, party fragmentation and levels of political litigation have produced a confrontational legislative style only in a minor number of cases. Helped by the traditionally consensual work of permanent commissions, that in Italy may (and often do) have legislative powers, most of the bills have always been passed with the contribution of both majority and opposition parties.[10]

[6] Sabino Cassese, 'Hypotheses on the Italian Administrative System', *West European Politics*, 16 (July 1993). We shall return later to this point, since an extended use of delegated legislation has been recently introduced to comply with EC directives.

[7] And, in case of disagreement, there is no procedure to stop the potential endless 'shuttling' (*navette*) between the two chambers.

[8] Sabino Cassese, *op. cit.*; Heinz Schaffer and Attila Racz (eds.), *Quantitative Analyses of Law: A Comparative Empirical Study* (Humanities Press International, 1990); Richard Rose, *Understanding Big Government. The Programme Approach* (London: Sage, 1984); Paul Furlong, 'Parliament in Italian Politics', *West European Politics,* 3 (1990).

[9] There have been 47 different governments in 11 legislatures: less than one a year.

[10] See, for example, Massimo Morisi, *Le leggi del consenso. Partiti e interessi nei primi parlamenti della Repubblica* (Messina: Rubbettino editore, 1992); Alessandro Pizzorno, *Le radici della politica assoluta* (Milano: Feltrinelli, 1993), ch. 8.

We have mentioned some of the most important characteristics of the political system, mainly because they have often been proposed as self-evident reasons for the poor Italian performance in EC/EU matters. From our point of view, these features are sometimes secondary factors and, more often, simple alibis for that same performance. But we will return to this point later.

Italy is a country with a regional level of government. Obviously, this has nothing to do with federal states, but each of the twenty regions (five of which have special autonomy for their peculiar geographical location) has legislative powers in particular policy areas. The majority inside the elected assemblies appoints the regional government ('*giunta*') divided into different departments ('*assessorati*'), establishing a polity that reproduces, at a decentralized level, the same political structure and labour division existing in the capital. But the relation between centre and periphery[11] is not at all so simple. Geographically identified in the 1948 constitution, regions – at least the fifteen ordinary ones – were politically activated only in 1970 with the first regional election, but have been authorized to legislate autonomously solely since a decree of the President of the Republic in 1977.[12] These thirty years have not been enough to clarify distinctly the competences of the two levels of government, especially in those grey areas where the limit between central coordination and regional delegation or conveyance of powers remains unclear. The Constitutional Court has been called more and more frequently to settle controversies due to this kind of situation, mostly because regions complain about formal and informal attempts at 're-centralization' by the national government. As we shall see, the monopoly held by the latter in the matter of foreign relations makes EC/EU politics and policies one of the main occasions of litigation between the central and the regional level.

Which institutional style?
We have drawn attention only towards certain macro-characteristics

---

[11] To use the expression adopted by Sidney Tarrow, *Between Center and Periphery. Grassroots Politicians in Italy and France* (New Haven: Yale University Press, 1977).

[12] See, for example, Robert Putnam, Robert Leonardi and Raffaela Nanetti, *La pianta e le radici. Il radicamento dell'istituto regionale nel sistema politico italiano* (Bologna: Il Mulino, 1985); Robert Putnam, *Making Democracy Work. Civic Traditions in Modern Italy* (Princeton: Princeton University Press, 1993).

of the Italian institutional framework. Our scope was limited to the necessity of anticipating some of the background elements of the relationship between the national and the EC/EU decision-making systems. One point should be added to this scheme, namely what we can call, with what is probably a rough neologism, the 'institutional style'. With this term we refer to the logic that has guided the transformations introduced in the last decade to cope with the increasing importance of the European Community for internal affairs. The issue of institutional reform has been in Italy the leading topic of the political debate in these last years, absorbing the energies of politicians and intellectuals, and regaining the political attention of citizens. The fact is that, somehow differently from the renewed interest shown in the international literature for institutions, these have been reductively considered as 'juridical architectures', as 'sets of norms pertaining to the organization and to the formal competences of parliaments and executives'.[13]

This type of bias has prevented institutions from being viewed in their 'relational character', as 'formal (and informal) rules, compliance procedures and standard operating practices that structure the relationship between individuals in various units of the polity and economy', or as 'conventions and codes of behaviour'.[14] A strictly juridical conceptualization of institutions has probably had major spill-overs on the way problems connected to the Italy–EC relationship have been tackled, that is establishing new and specialized offices or departments, and arranging *ad hoc* procedures. Linking structures to presumed functions and splitting competences seems the way, the 'institutional style', adopted in answer to the new challenges coming from Brussels. Coordination, representation, communication and information – unfamiliar terms for a juridical tradition – look like having had a minor impact on the definition of the Italian approach to EC policy-making.

[13] On this point, see Gloria Regonini, 'Alla scoperta delle istituzioni: senza sbagliare continente', *Stato e Mercato* (August 1993).

[14] For these less formal and more flexible meanings, see Peter Hall, *Governing the Economy: The Politics of State Intervention in Britain and France* (New York: Oxford University Press, 1986), p. 19; Douglass C. North, *Institutions, Institutional Change and Economic Performance* (Cambridge University Press, 1990), p. 4; James G. March and Johan P. Olsen, *Rediscovering Institutions. The Organizational Basis of Politics* (New York: The Free Press, 1989).

The EC decision-making cycle and the participation of national institutions

What do statistics really tell us?

The easiest way to look at the relationship between a country and the European Community is to read the statistics regularly produced by the Commission in its reports. The most used indicator in this regard is the rate of transposition of EC directives: it is simple, concise, immediately understandable and it is possible to determine the position occupied by each member state in a hypothetical classification of EC performance. Unfortunately, at least for some member states, these types of data turn out to be completely insufficient, if not misleading. Take, for example, the diagrams presented in Figure 5.1, in which we present the evolution of the Italian record relative to (a) the general transposition of EC directives, and (b) the 1992 project, compared to the performance of the other eleven members of the Community.

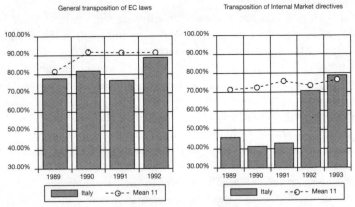

Fig. 5.1   Rates of transposition of EC legislation

Source: Com(90)288, Com(91)321, Com(92)136, Com(93)320 for the first graph, and Com(89)422 (situation at July 1989), Com(90)90 (February 1990), Com(91)237 (May 1991), Com(92)383 (August 1992) and Memo 93/56 (December 1993) for the second.

Following these figures, we could easily argue, as did many journalists and observers, that Italy had in the past a lot of problems in respecting the Internal Market's obligations (much more than for the whole EC legislation), but that, since 1992, the situation has improved a lot, so as to transform that same country into a model for other more reluctant governments. According to this view, it would be possible to advance the hypothesis that the way the Italian

policy-making system relates itself to the Community constitutes –
for the improvement allowed – a sort of repeatable 'ideal type'.

Things are obviously not so easy. First of all, we should shape a
more complete image of that relationship considering other indicators,
such as the number of infringement proceedings or the percentage of
assigned EC funds effectively spent. Secondly, official statistics are
often produced for reasons other than those of scientific research, and
need to be taken cautiously.[15] They lack in 'temporal perspective' (we
don't know anything about the path that has led to improvements or
declines); they are dichotomous (two countries may have, at a certain
time, the same transposition ratios in spite of very different
approaches); and they tend to hide the 'quality' of the process of
national adaptation to European standards. Finally, the whole process
of mutual influence between EC and national legislation results is lev-
elled out by these statistics, as if it were a matter of respecting the EC's
will, whereas anticipating or following (perhaps with delays) EC directives are symptoms of contrasting decision-making styles.

We certainly won't deny that the data presented in Figure 5.1, as
far as Italy is concerned, do suggest a certain progress, but for a
better comprehension of their exact meaning we need a more in-
depth analysis. For our purposes, and as a starting point, a source of
multiple suggestions lies in the possibility of considering thoroughly
the process of adaptation to Internal Market measures as a sympto-
matic field in which to verify the relationship between national and
EC decision-making systems.[16] Comparing the dates at which every
country has adopted the legislative or administrative acts necessary
for the application of each directive, with the time of EC approval

[15] This is particularly true for Italy because, since 1990, EC legislation has been
incorporated through a unique annual law, called 'Legge Comunitaria', which mainly
consists of the delegation of legislative powers to the government. As a result, time and
manner of data collection on behalf of the Commission tend to influence the Italian
record in the statistics presented in the annual reports. On a more theoretical ground
the point is made by Douglas E. Ashford, 'Of Cases and Contexts', in Douglas E. Ashford (ed.), *History and Context in Comparative Public Policy* (Pittsburgh: University of
Pittsburgh Press, 1992).

[16] We have included in this analysis all the directives (expired before 30.4.1993) considered by the same Commission pertaining to the realization of the Internal Market,
that is, the ones contained in the data base INFO92 (and not necessarily included in
the White Paper). The publication to which we have referred is: Commissione delle
Comunità Europee, *Misure nazionali di recepimento per l'applicazione del libro bianco
della Commissione sul completamento del mercato interno – Situazione al 30 aprile 1993*
(Luxembourg, 1993).

and with the scheduled limits for their national implementation, we can identify four pure types of situation (see Figure 5.2).

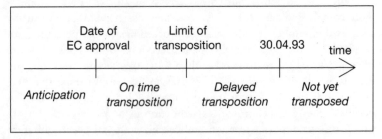

Fig 5.2 The process of national transposition of EC directives

The first one arises in the event that a country's normative framework anticipates the legislative intervention of the European Community, having probably influenced the contents of that same intervention. In this case, it is completely unnecessary to adopt any new norms, being sufficient to inform the Commission of the existence of the measures already in effect. In the second case, a country adapts its legislation according to the introduced EC standards and respecting the time limits for transposition set in the directive considered. In the third one, the EC intervention has already come into force with its incorporation in the national law, but only after its fixed deadline. The condition of delay can be even more serious if, at the time data have been collected – 30 April 1993, that is after the nominal completion of the Internal Market project – it has not adopted any national measure of transposition.

This simple scheme, that reveals the temporal process underlying the mutual adaptation of the two policy-making systems, can help to distinguish policy style differences and decision-making nuances that in the ordinary dichotomic statistics cannot be identified. In Table 5.1, as anticipated, it has been applied to all the directives pertaining to the Internal Market project, adding a fifth category, in case of insufficient information for a correct attribution of national transpositions.[17]

[17] Since our analysis is political, and not strictly juridical, when we found mixed situations for the same directive, that is multiple measures adopted in different periods (e.g. one before and one after the due date), we have chosen to consider them benevolently as signs of political attention, assigning them to the most favourable category. The same methodology has been applied, where possible, to partial transpositions.

Table 5.1 National transposition of Internal Market's directives

	Anticipation		On time transposition		Delayed transposition		Not yet transposed		Don't know		Total
	No.	%	No.	%	No.	%	No.	%	No.	%	
B	19	7·1	71	26·7	120	45·1	52	19·5	4	1·5	266
D	79	29·4	53	19·7	61	22·7	62	23·0	14	5·2	269
DK	61	23·0	84	31·7	77	29·1	35	13·2	8	3·0	265
E	32	12·3	55	21·1	110	42·1	60	23·0	4	1·5	261
EL	8	3·0	51	19·3	119	45·1	82	31·1	4	1·5	264
F	58	21·7	62	23·2	80	30·0	64	24·0	3	1·1	267
I	15	5·6	59	22·1	138	51·7	48	18·0	7	2·6	267
IRL	42	15·7	51	19·0	89	33·2	77	28·7	9	3·4	268
L	13	4·9	57	21·3	128	47·8	65	24·3	5	1·9	268
NL	47	17·5	62	23·1	81	30·2	57	21·3	21	7·8	268
P	32	12·3	49	18·8	111	42·5	66	25·3	3	1·1	261
UK	61	22·8	58	21·7	78	29·2	49	18·4	21	7·9	267

Source: See note 15 (situation at 30.4.1993).

It would be possible to comment on these figures with greater attention, but we prefer to use them as starting points or as suggestions for successive analysis. It is here sufficient to remember four points:

1 The data just presented do not seem to contradict the picture portrayed by the most recent Commission reports.[18] In particular, Italy has really improved its situation, becoming one of the most law-abiding countries of the Community. Only Denmark has done better, failing to transpose around 13% of the directives compared to the 18% of Italy.

2 Countries normally considered as having the greatest abilities in coping with EC obligations – Denmark, Germany, France and Great Britain – appear to be challenged not only by Italy, but by other 'non-model' nations. Belgium is in 'fourth position', immediately after the United Kingdom; Spain and Germany have the same record; France is closely pursued by Luxembourg and Portugal.

3 Having non-dichotomous figures we are able to distinguish more clearly what exactly links that same group of four countries. They do not have the same transposition ratios, but they are the only countries that have been able to anticipate more than 20% of the

[18] Actually, there are a few differences, our percentages of transposition being normally lower than the one produced directly by the Commission, but the discrepancies seem to be limited to physiological levels.

Internal Market's directives. That early intervention probably means that their respective governments succeeded in influencing the same formulation of EC policies, relieving their internal legislative and administrative processes of an important part of the EC burden. This remark helps to explain why Denmark, Germany, France and Great Britain still hold the first four positions if we add the number of anticipated directives to the ones correctly incorporated before their due date.[19]

4 Considering the low number of early transpositions (less than 6%), the recent Italian improvement loses part of its brilliance, while it is possible to shed new light on its European behaviour. Using one of the two dimensions of the concept of 'policy style' proposed by Richardson,[20] we could now advance the hypothesis that Italy has adopted towards the European Community a clear reactive style. In the following pages we will try to bring new evidence to our argument, specifying it more precisely.

Preparing and taking decisions in the EC

The public policy literature has long demonstrated that the decision-making process should be considered as a 'seamless web',[21] and that seems particularly true for EC politics, where the relation between agenda setting, formulation and implementation dynamics is particularly strong. Nonetheless, it remains analytically fruitful to distinguish between an ascending phase of the process, where national positions are prepared, discussed and bargained, and a descending phase, with EC policies being transposed, applied and implemented in the national arenas.

In the case of Italy, this separation reveals itself to be more than an analytical expedient, since the two phases are, even institutionally, considered separately. Incidentally, the actual segmentation of the policy process is one of the main features of the Italian approach towards the Community, accounting for a great part of the ambiguities and paradoxes described in the introduction. In the preceding

---

[19] It would even be possible to argue that delays or non-transpositions can be considered part of national preferences or strategies.

[20] Jeremy Richardson (ed.), *Policy Styles in Western Europe* (London: George Allen and Unwin, 1982).

[21] The image has been proposed by Giandomenico Majone and Aaron Wildavsky, 'Implementation as Evolution', in Jeffrey Pressman and Aaron Wildavsky, *Implementation* (Berkeley: University of California Press, 1979).

paragraph we have considered the limited anticipation capabilities of the Italian government as an indicator of its lack of influence in the day-to-day bargaining that happens at the decision stage.[22] This lack of influence, that cannot be attributed to minor weight at the EC level, mostly stems from insufficient or fragmented preparation of Council meetings. The Permanent Representation complains of the fact that, often, ministers arrive in Brussels without knowing the position they have to defend and, contrary to any correct division of competences and responsibilities, they have to be acquainted with the measures under discussion. Some Italian Commission officials have even suggested that Italy seems to have adopted a new type of the well known 'policy of the empty chair', opposite in its effects to the French boycott of the mid-1960s, since it consists in being present without having a say in the matter.[23]

Sometimes the exact opposite happens, with different ministers or government deputies, having divergent personal views on the same matter, supporting in Brussels different positions, in a sort of internal competition exported at EC level.[24] The same Permanent Representation should receive coherent instructions from the Italian Council of Ministers and from the Inter-ministerial Committee for Economic Planning *(Cipe)*, but instead they receive them directly from the single departments, without any coordinating effort. 'There is a wide heterogeneity in the organisational forms [of the Italy–EC

[22] Alberta Sbragia, *op. cit.*, reminds us that Italy has been an effective agenda setter in particular policy areas, but that observation can't be generalized to the greatest part of EC legislation. For example, a survey realized at the end of the 1980s shows that Italian civil servants used to meet their foreign colleagues 'for operative reasons due to the 1992 project' only in a minor number of cases; see Censis, *Note e commenti*, 9–10 (1989).

[23] The comment has been reported in an authoritative economic newspaper (*Il Sole 24 Ore*, 7.12.1992), suggesting that nothing has changed since the similar consideration made, two decades earlier, by Helen Wallace, *National Governments and the European Communities* (London: Chatham House, 1973). On the same point see Senato della Repubblica – Giunta per gli affari delle Comunità Europee, *Indagine conoscitiva sulla partecipazione dell'Italia alle fasi formativa ed applicativa del diritto comunitario* (Roma, 1991).

[24] See Maurizio Ferrera, 'Italia: Aspirazioni e vincoli del "quarto grande"', in Maurizio Ferrera (ed.), *Le dodici Europe. I paesi della Comunità di fronte ai cambiamenti del 1989–1990* (Bologna: Il Mulino, 1991); Sabino Cassese, 'Poteri divisi: amministrazione europea e amministrazioni nazionali', in Giuliano Amato and Massimo Salvadori (eds.), *Europa conviene?* (Bari: Laterza, 1990); and the inquiry realized by Giulia Mariani, 'Italia, pubblica amministrazione: a che punto siamo per il 93?', *Queste istituzioni*, 85–6 (1991).

relationship], structured on the basis of multiple solutions,[25] that intersect and link themselves in various manners and, as a consequence, that cause a marked fragmentation of the intervention at the Community level. Each administration works autonomously and follows different operating procedures, thus determining duplications and overlaps, competence gaps, resource dispersion, conflicts and coordination problems.'[26] The overall effect is quite predictable: unclear positions, unreliable promises and reduced margins for defensible strategies widen the space for non-satisfactory compromises.

There have been efforts to rationalize the system through the concentration of responsibilities in a unique institution, establishing a department for the coordination of EC policies at the Presidency of the Council, but centrifugal dynamics and the wish of the Ministry for Foreign Affairs (whose directorate for economic affairs is normally responsible for politically sensitive matters regarding the Community) not to lose its prerogatives prevented complete implementation of the reform. Actually, the Ministry for EC policies has almost no competences as far as the ascending phase is concerned. Even the flow of information coming from Brussels and regarding the issues continuously discussed in the COREPER and in the working groups does not arrive directly at the Department for the coordination of EC policies. The documentation should be collected at the Ministry for Foreign Affairs (whose officers make up more than half of the Permanent Representation) and passed to the competent administrations, but many ministries prefer to rely on direct relations with their own officers in Brussels, sometimes duplicating communication channels and sometimes losing important information.

If administrative segmentation and under-coordination seem to be the most striking characteristics of the ascending phase of Italian

[25] Some ministries (e.g. Post and Telecommunications, Transportation, State Investment, Budget and Economic Planning) have specialized offices in EC relations; others (e.g. Environment, Agriculture and Forestry, Foreign Trade, Labour and Social Security, Industry, Public Education, University and Scientific Research) entrust those relations to the offices of each directorate; others have adopted a mixed organization (e.g. Finance and the General Accounting Office inside the Treasury).

[26] Claudio Franchini, *Amministrazione italiana e amministrazione comunitaria* (Padova: Cedam, 1993), pp. 71–4. On the problem of political and administrative fragmentation, see Maurizio Ferrera, 'The Politics of EC Membership. An Explanation of some Italian Paradoxes', paper presented at the conference of the College of Europe, *The Institutions of the European Community after the Single European Act*, Bruges, 28–30.6.90, and Natalino Ronzitti, 'European Policy Formulation in the Italian Administrative System', *The International Spectator*, 4 (1987).

participation in EC policy-making, another important factor should be considered, namely what we can call, adopting a familiar term of the EC literature, the 'Italian democratic deficit'. Notwithstanding its legislative power, crucial in the transposition phase, the Italian parliament is almost totally excluded from the preparation of the national position on EC matters. We have to recognize that, according to a survey conducted at the end of the 1980s, most MPs seemed unaware of the impact of the European Community on Italian society and, as a consequence, were quite uninterested in EC affairs,[27] but the same institutional organization prevents them being better informed. According to the so-called 'Legge La Pergola' (1989),[28] every six months the government should present a report to the parliament in which it explains, for each policy area, its preparatory work, its bargaining position and the main lines of intervention for the following semester. Actually, those reports usually contain only a brief *ex-post facto* account of what has been approved in the last Council meetings and of the positions presented or defended by the other eleven governments.[29] They have often not been presented regularly at the time due; and they are not submitted to the assemblies' scrutiny but to the attention of the two specialized but not powerful committees (the *Giunta per gli affari delle Comunità europee* of the Senate, and the *Commissione speciale per le politiche comunitarie* of the low Chamber). In practice, these reports, of limited interest for any *ex-ante* will of influence, have a very limited circulation and, in spite of being the unique instrument of coordination between parliament and government, remain almost completely unknown.

[27] See Claudio Radaelli, 'Europeismo tricolore', *Relazioni Internazionali*, 4 (1988), and Gian Franco Ciaurro, 'Strumenti di collegamento tra il parlamento nazionale e le istituzioni comunitarie', *Affari sociali e internazionali*, 4 (1986). We should add that, till recently, the national system of incentives has always rewarded domestic and not European careers; Italian MEPs and top civil servants have often considered their engagement in Strasbourg or Brussels as temporary, preferring to compete in national elections or for a governmental seat rather than to work in the European arena.

[28] The law takes its nickname from the Minister for the coordination of EC policies in charge at that time, Antonio La Pergola. For optimistic comments on this point, see Vincenzo Guizzi, 'La legge La Pergola n. 86/89: una impostazione nuova del circuito decisionale e operativo Italia–Comunità', *Rivista di diritto pubblico europeo*, 1 (March 1990), and 'Parlamento italiano e Comunità europea nei meccanismi introdotti dalle nuove norme dei regolamenti parlamentari', *Rivista di diritto pubblico europeo*, 2 (June 1991).

[29] Nor could they be anything different, since their drafting is done by a diplomat at the Department for the coordination of EC policies who can't clearly commit the government to positions that, as we have already noted, are often decided at the last minute. Answering to a parliamentary request, reports have been recently adapted to more prospective needs, but they still remain an 'under-usable' instrument.

If the parliament, that is the institution that will have to adopt the necessary measures to conform to EC legislation, is kept to the margin of the ascending phase of the decision-making process, this is all the more true for the regional level of government which is practically excluded from that process. Regions cannot establish own representation agencies in Brussels because foreign relations are the exclusive competence of the state,[30] and if regional officials have direct contact with EC institutions, their mission requests have to be approved at the centre through complex procedures. The only instrument that permits their participation in EC affairs is a State–Region Conference, established in 1989 by the same 'Legge La Pergola', to be held twice a year. In these conferences, the presidents of the regional bodies, which – we remember – are regularly elected assemblies with their own governmental structures, are consulted only to give non-binding opinions on the general lines of Community acts concerning regional competences. Unfortunately, and quite symptomatically, the minister for the coordination of EC policies has convened the conference only twice since 1989: the first time in December 1989, and the second time in April 1991.

It is true that, since the approval of Law 183 in 1987, regions should be informed on every EC proposal before their discussion and approval, but the transmission of the relevant documents by the government takes place too late to be effective and, anyway, their eventual observations would have no legal recognition.[31] The discontent of the regional bodies in respect to this situation, considered a patent example of the efforts of 're-centralization' discussed in the second paragraph, became all the more evident in 1993, when regions succeeded in abolishing, through popular referendum, two major central ministries – Agriculture and Tourism – mainly considered ineffective instruments for the protection of regional interests at the international level. At the end of 1993 the most 'EC-sensitive' issue was

[30] The meaning of 'international relevant activities', that is the only kind of actions regions are allowed to perform, has been actually broadened but, 'in fact, the power in question reminds one much more of a tradesman advertising his goods, rather than some sort of departmentalized foreign policy'; Giovanni Grottanelli de Santi, 'The Impact of EC Integration on the Italian Form of Government', in Francesco Francioni (ed.), *op cit.*, p. 188.

[31] There have been a lot of juridical studies on the role assigned to Italian regions in the EC policy process. See, for example, Maria Valeria Agostini, 'The Role of the Italian Regions in Formulating Community Policy', *The International Spectator*, 2 (1990); and the articles published in two special issues of *Le Regioni*, 20 (3), 20 (5) (June and October 1992).

solved through the establishment of a new 'Ministry for Agricultural, Alimentary and Forestry Resources', which clarifies the distribution of funds between central and regional level but doesn't touch the problem of the external representation of local needs.[32]

To conclude this section we can advance the hypothesis that, in the last decade, the Italian political and administrative system has not deeply modified its style in the preparation and making of EC decisions. There have been a few formal changes, constantly overvalued by jurists, but the substance has remained the same. We can find a further indirect proof of this statement observing in Figure 5.3 the trend of the 'anticipation ability' of the Italian government, that is, the number of measures approved before the corresponding EC intervention, compared to that of the four leading countries (Germany, Denmark, France and United Kingdom). In spite of the reforms introduced, it is impossible to state any progress in this crucial indicator of the influence exercised in the ascending phases of the decision-making process.

Implementing and controlling EC legislation

To examine the descending phase of the EC policy-making process, we ought to distinguish analytically between three very different moments: (1) the incorporation of EC measures (transposition); (2) the factual application and the substantive impact of those measures (what, in the politicological – but normally not in the EC – literature is called implementation); (3) the juridical evaluation of moments (1) and (2) (control).

The transposition phase, as already noted, has received in Italy the greatest attention, with apparently undeniable results, whereas the other two moments have been mostly neglected. For a better understanding, we can try to break down the progress shown in Figure 5.1 using our Internal Market's data, analysing, year after year, how many directives have been transposed on time and how many have been incorporated only after their expiring dates or have not yet been transposed (see Table 5.2 and Figure 5.4).

The evolution of the transposition style is evident. Looking either at absolute values or at percentages, the year 1991 represents the turning point after which EC obligations seem to have been taken

---

[32] Regions declared themselves only partially satisfied with the chosen solution, and found new material for complaints in the poor results of the GATT agreements.

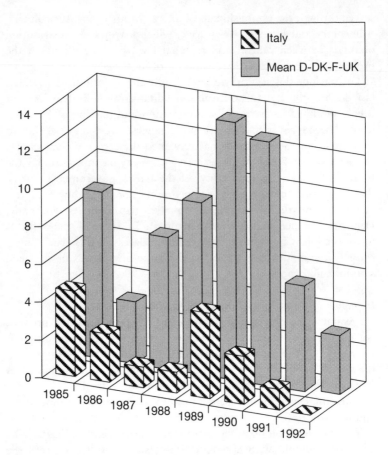

Fig. 5.3 Diachronic comparison of anticipation abilities

Source: see note 15. The x-axis reports the years EC directives have been adopted: the y-axis reports the number of directives 'anticipated'.

seriously. Even if we take into consideration only the directives incorporated after their time limits, observing their actual postponement, we can advance similar reflections. Actually, the mean delay, always above a year till the end of the 1980s (forty-eight months in 1986, thirty in 1988, eighteen in 1990), became much lower starting from 1991 (eight months in 1991 and five in 1992).[33]

Table 5.2   The evolution of the Italian transposition style

Type of transposition	1985	1986	1987	1988	1989	1990	1991	1992	1993
On time or anticipated	1	3	1	7	6	4	8	20	23
Delayed or not yet	5	8	20	11	20	29	39	45	10

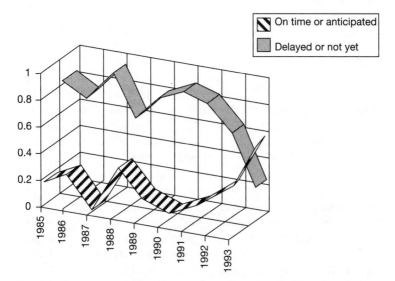

Fig. 5.4   Percentage of directives transposed on time or delayed

Source: see note 15; the x-axis reports the years in which EC directives expire

These figures confirm the positive judgments expressed by many observers and by the same Commission, since they testify to the increasing efficiency of the transposition process. But is that process, besides being efficient, even effective? Before answering this crucial question, we have to explain how the recent compliance progress has been realized and which factors account for that improvement.

First of all, let us sweep away possible misunderstandings. During the 1980s, the Italian inability to cope with EC obligations has been often explained in terms of backward bureaucratic culture, fragmented legislation, juridical problems, lack of crucial positions held

---

[33] From a methodological standpoint, this kind of comparison is not completely correct, since we cannot predict when the directives still not transposed will be incorporated. Actually, in its substance, the argument is completely defensible, since during the 1980s 'less than one-year delays' were extremely rare, whereas in the 1990s they are the praxis.

in the Commission, centrifugal tendencies due to the multiparty political system, etc.[34] Since none of these variables has undergone in the last few years major transformations, we can conclude they are not (and probably were not) influential in the process considered. According to another widespread opinion, the chronic deficiencies of the Italian system would have stemmed from the supremacy of a highly heterogeneous parliament over a weak and non-autonomous coalition government, and from the unavoidable and repeated rigidities of parliamentary procedures. For this reason, in 1987, the government succeeded in passing a norm (Law 183/1987) which tried to cope with the heavy legislative charge inherent in the Commission's White Paper by (1) ensuring administrative incorporation of directives not affecting matters covered by law, (2) delegating normative powers to the same government, and (3) granting 'force of law' to particular directives. Since these measures did not appear to be sufficiently effective, a new comprehensive law had to be passed two years later, containing 'General provisions on the Italian participation in the Community legislative process and on the procedures for the incorporation of Community obligations' (Law 86/1989, the so-called 'Legge La Pergola'). Its main innovation concerned the expanded use of the delegation instrument and of direct administrative implementation and, more important, the introduction of the so-called 'Annual Community law' (*Legge comunitaria*) in which to transpose all the directives expected to expire in the first semester of the following year.

The approval of packages of EC measures is not at all something new, since it had already been used at least twice before 1989, incorporating each time almost 100 directives, but its novelty resides in the routinization of that practice. The mechanism is quite simple and straightfoward. The minister for the coordination of EC policies draws up the bill containing four types of measures: articles that incorporate directives or abrogate non-conforming norms, others that

[34] See, for example, Fausto Pocar et al., 'Italie', in Heinrich Siedentopf and Jacques Ziller (eds.), *Making European Policies Work. The Implementation of Community Legislation in the Member States*, vol. ii (London: Sage, 1988); Emil Noël, 'Italy-EC. Vices and Virtues of a Founding Member', *Relazioni Internazionali, 2* (June 1990); Natalino Ronzitti, 'The Internal Market, Italian Law and the Public Administration', *The International Spectator*, 1 (1990); Maria Valeria Agostini, 'Italy and its Community Policy', *The International Spectator*, 4 (1990); David Hine, 'Italy and Europe: The Italian Presidency and the National Handling of EC Matters', in Fausto Anderlini and Robert Leonardi (eds.), Italian Politics. A Review, vol. vi (New York: St Martin's Press, 1992).

permit the adoption of administrative acts, others that delegate legislative power to the government and articles that directly give force of law to existing directives (as if they were regulations or technical measures). After its examination and approval by the Council of Ministers, the bill should be presented in parliament each year before the beginning of March, and then follows the normal 'shuttle' procedure between the two chambers. There are no time limits for its discussion in the numerous commissions involved[35] or for its final approval, but after its adoption, the government has normally another year to fulfil the legislative delegations received. Is this really the 'most radical way of trying to cope with the obligations of the Internal Market', as suggested a couple of years ago,[36] or can it be better conceived as the result of the tempting, but misleading, attraction of synoptic problem-solving? To answer this question we first have to verify how this new approach towards EC decisions worked in practice. Some crucial figures in this regard are given in Table 5.3.[37]

Table 5.3 Annual Community laws

Annual law	Date of presentation	Date of approval	Directives included	of which	(1)	(2)	(3)	(4)
1990	08.03.1990	20.12.1990	134		93	39	2	–
1991	01.03.1991	28.01.1992	95		52	12	29	2
1992	05.10.1992	17.12.1992	33		23	7	3	–
1993	12.07.1993	09.02.1994	171		49	40	82	–

Key: (1) Delegation of legislative power to the government; (2) governmental regulation; (3) administrative act; (4) direct transposition.

First of all, the almost fixed timetable has not always been respected and, notwithstanding the fact that the process never

[35] The commissions specializing in EC matters in both chambers have only coordinating tasks.

[36] Christian Engel, 'The Changing Patterns of Interaction between EC Institutions and the Member States: The Debate about Subsidiarity and Federalism', paper presented at the conference of the College of Europe, *The Institutions of the European Community after the Single European Act*, Bruges, 28–30.6.90; see Massimo Morisi (ed.), *L'attuazione delle direttive CE in Italia. La 'legge comunitaria' in Parlamento* (Milano: Giuffrè, 1992).

[37] Actually, the 1992 Community law was never approved, but only presented at the Senate. After the political elections of April, the government decided not to bring in that bill, but to push for a quick approval of a reduced version (immediately called *'mini-comunitaria'*), as is evident from the number of directives reported in Table 5.3.

required a double examination from both chambers, parliamentary scrutiny has gone well beyond expectations.[38] External events, such as the closing of the Italian semester of presidency (1990), anticipated political elections (1992, 1994), scandals and ministerial turnovers (1993) have often crossed the law-making process, sometimes speeding it up and sometimes blocking it. In the end, annual Community laws have always been perceived as emergency measures, with the government trying to push the package towards a 'quick' approval and, for that same reason, accepting without discussion many of the amendments advanced in parliament.

In fact, remembering that the Community law does not transpose EC directives directly but, as pointed out in Table 5.3, mainly assigns legislative powers to the government, its discussion becomes almost the only occasion on which MPs, belonging to the opposition as well as to the majority coalition, can have a say in EC politics. Moreover, this kind of package deal has other troublesome effects: non-problematic issues are treated together with highly political matters, suffering the same problems and delays of the latter; logrolling dynamics are favoured;[39] the same 'quality' of the norms risks being endangered, since the contemporary and one-shot analysis of about a hundred directives is inevitably less accurate than the constant review of the flow of EC obligations. Finally, there is no control over the definitive use of delegated powers on behalf of the government, and that accounts for the fact that, till 1992, the number of delayed transpositions has always exceeded that of on-time incorporations.

To return to the problem of the relationship between efficiency and effectiveness in respecting EC obligations, we can now advance the following argument. Establishing specialized statutes, procedures or norms may certainly increase the speed of the transposition process but, as we have tried to underline, has numerous counterproductive spill-overs. This 'non-consensual' style,[40] applied both at the central level towards elected representatives and at the local level towards regional govern-

---

[38] Its length is all the more incredible considering that, in fact, the annual Community law is a sort of empty box, a procedural trick with which the government asks the parliament for the authorization to legislate according to (more or less) the same prescriptions already stated in Brussels.

[39] Eventually, annual Community laws have always been approved in parliament with large majorities: 93% of the MPs voted in favour of the 1990 Community law, 98% in 1991, 70% in 1992 and 91% for the 1993 law.

[40] We introduce here the second dimension of the already quoted policy style's typology proposed by Richardson.

ments,[41] creates rigidities that may hinder the correct implementation of the adopted measures. In fact, introducing new regulative policies, such as those normally derived from EC legislation, has never been the real problem in Italy: over-regulation and not under-regulation is the recognized praxis.[42] Difficulties always begin when these policies have to be put into practice, and trying to isolate the transposition phase from the preceding (preparation) and following (implementation) moments of the decision-making process, risks being a palliative or a simple postponement of harder problems. Only case study analyses are able to illustrate this point with due precision.[43] Here we can just refer to the number of infringement proceedings as a possible indicator of contrasts between the juridical transposition of EC norms and their practical application (see Table 5.4 and Figure 5.5).

The first thing we have to note is that, in spite of the increasing rate of transposition, the number of infringement proceedings initiated against Italy has not decreased as expected, and even its capacity to settle cases at an early stage has not dramatically improved. Moreover, if we look at the first step of that procedure (the issuing of letters of formal notice sketched in Figure 5.5), we can recognize the stability of the number of cases opened not for lack of transposition but for incorrect application of EC legislation (always around a half of the total infringements), and its high level compared to that of the other eleven member states. Actually, street-level implementation problems met by EC measures tend to remain invisible,[44] there

[41] Regions are allowed to implement directives only 'within the limits of the general principles that will be pointed out either by the "general law for the implementation of Community norms" that every year will have to be adopted by Parliament, or by other specific state law implementing directives. [Eventually], in most cases the regional role is reduced to the adoption of norms of implementation of state norms implementing Community rules with a margin of discretionary power that does not need any comment'; Giovanni Grottanelli de Santi, *op. cit.*, pp. 187–8.

[42] On this point, see Marco Giuliani, 'Regolazione senza regole. Il caso italiano e le possibili interpretazioni', *Rivista Trimestrale di Scienza dell'Amministrazione*, 4 (1989).

[43] Just as an example, in the transposition of directives regarding the quality of drinking water or bathing prohibitions, Italy has always chosen the most rigid parameters within the range suggested. But this praiseworthy behaviour is of no use if, as it has really happened, the chemical analyses of the water are rare, unreliable or self-contradicting, or if nobody enforces the prohibitions, or if the causes of pollution remain out of control, or, what is worse, administrative decrees temporarily suspend the validity of the norm.

[44] We should probably look at judgments passed by national – especially administrative – courts. In this regard, as a further indirect proof of the problematic implementation of EC measures, we can remember that Italian courts have always been very active in asking the ECJ for preliminary rulings (Art. 177 TEU): ten in 1989, twenty-five in 1990, thirty-six in 1991 and twenty-two in 1992.

being no reliable quantitative evidence in this regard, but we suggest that the procedural reforms already introduced in Italy do not seem to affect them directly.

Table 5.4 Infringement proceedings per stage of the process

	1987	1988	1989	1990	1991	1992
Formal notice	73	107	115	111	115	137
Reasoned opinion	27	70	58	62	76	40
Reference to the ECJ	21	14	36	25	24	11
Court rulings	14	15	9	10	18	10

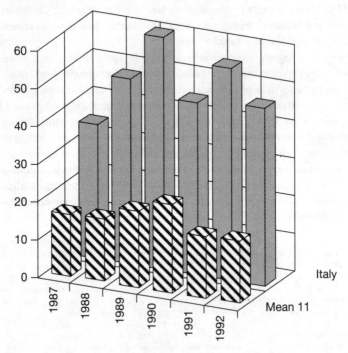

Fig. 5.5 Letters of formal notice for incorrect application of directives, treaties, regulations and decisions

Source: Com(91)321, Com(93)320.

Politics, political parties and public opinion – a different equilibrium?

The outlined framework confirms some of the paradoxes pointed out in the introduction: the most evident deficiencies have been put under control establishing new *ad hoc* procedures and institutions, but the overall situation still depicts a country which participates untidily in EC affairs. How can this arrangement hold? How can it be convenient, both for Italy and for its EC partners, if the internal costs of compliance seem so hard to meet, and if its participation in the construction of Europe sometimes looks like an obstacle to the realization of a common good?

Lacking a precise and clearly established criterion, political costs and benefits are hardly valuable.[45] From the perspective of recognizing the revealed preferences of the public, of the different parties and of other political and economical elites, we should simply accept the fact that, somehow, even the present configuration seems to be satisfactory. Surveys regularly confirm the positive attitude that Italians have towards the Community.[46] European matters have never been an occasion for partisan confrontations and, even if the two most extremist parties have voted against the ratification of the Maastricht Treaty, no party platform is explicitly against the integration project.[47] Together with the Italian government, even trade unions, employers' organizations and public interest groups have all confirmed their support for the European integration project, without any severe criticism. Evidently, political actors have success and performance indicators that are different from the ones normally adopted by jurists or academics. Put differently, most commentators believe that the institutional setting represented by the relation between two (or many) linked decision-making systems[48] (here, EC

[45] See Maurizio Cotta, 'European Integration and the Italian Political System', in Francesco Francioni (ed.), *op. cit.*, pp. 204–15.

[46] We could even conceive it a sort of 'European faith', considering the fact that most people have only a vague idea of what the EC/EU actually is and how it works. See Eurispes, *Rapporto Europa. L'Italia in Europa: scenari e prospettive* (Roma: Koinè edizioni, 1993); Sonia Stefanizzi and Guido Martinotti, 'Governo senza confine. Le opinioni dei cittadini europei sull'integrazione europea', *Quaderni di sociologia*, 2 (1993).

[47] Philip Daniels, 'Italy and the Maastricht Treaty', in Stephen Hellman and Gianfranco Pasquino (eds.), *Italian Politics. A Review*, vol. viii (New York: St Martin's Press, 1993). Each party – from the PDS to the Lega Lombarda, from the Christian Democrats to the right-wing Alleanza nazionale – declares itself as the real interpreter of the European evolution.

[48] For the concept of linkage see James Alt, Robert Putnam and Kenneth Shepsle, 'The Architecture of Linkage', and Fritz Scharpf and Andreas Ryll, 'Core Games, Connected Games and Networks of Interaction', both papers presented at the workshop on *Connected Games: Theory, Methodology and Applications*, Max-Planck-Institut für Gesellschaftsforschung, Köln 17–18.11.1988.

and member states) should realize a 'Pareto efficient' solution. If that unique optimal framework is not established, as in the case of Italy, actors should feel the necessity to move towards its realization.

On the contrary, we think that a complex multi-level decision-making system presents different points of equilibrium, that is, situations which no one (at least not the most relevant actors) wants to modify, even if they do not maximize their preferences. From our point of view, the relationship between Italy and the EC has reached one of these satisfactory points of equilibrium. Its configuration is substantially different from that attained by other countries, but it is similar as far as its internal logic is concerned. Looking for other, more efficient solutions is obviously possible and sometimes needed, but it may be risky. In this sense, the established institutional setting is the result of past strategies and, at the same time, constrains the actors' *modus operandi*. It is simultaneously the effect and the shaper of their preferences. The equilibrium slowly produced by the sedimentation of Italian attitudes towards the Community is not made by active participation in the decision-making process (as for some of the northern countries), nor by a conscious defence of particular policy areas (as for some Mediterranean nations). We can imagine it as the constant search for and accumulation of political resources to be spent reactively in the national arena or in future EC/EU bargaining on single policy issues. The statement that Italy's EC policy is somehow the 'prosecution of internal politics by other means' should be carefully specified. It is not a matter of embracing a realist paradigm of politics, but rather to understand that apparently incoherent behaviours become intelligible once we consider them as the complex results of nested decision-making systems, each with its internal political logic.[49]

Not implementing EC measures that have been defended and sustained in the Council should not be simply regarded as the effect of administrative deficits, liturgical Europeanism or schizophrenic policy style. Not hampering the projects of EC partners immediately stimulates their 'good will', and can be thought as a sort of political invest-

---

[49] See George Tsebelis, *Nested Games. Rational Choice in Comparative Politics* (Berkeley: California University Press, 1990); Shlomo Weber and Hans Wiesmeth, 'Issue Linkage in the European Community', *Journal of Common Market Studies*, 3 (1991).

ment to be spent on more pressing matters of internal concern.[50] At the opposite side, the lack of EC investigating and sanctioning powers makes national obstructionism a worthwhile strategy, especially if, as frequently happens in Italy, the prevailing reactive style discounts future implementation costs at a very high rate. Failing to meet one's obligations can always be justified in the European arena as being the result of factors outside the government's control, such as parliamentary byzantinism, procedural fragmentation or administrative inertia. In spite of a few criticisms, more symbolical than effective, the other eleven partners are normally unwilling to investigate further in one's internal problems, and even the Commission has often shown itself to be somehow 'sympathetic' towards one of its regular allies. After all, no one really wants to risk the loss of a 'taken-for-granted' support in the Council, even if the sustained positions sometimes reveal themselves to be self-contradictory.

In the domestic arena the game can be played the other way round, ascribing costs and responsibilities for unwelcome decisions to the partners, and stressing one's resistance or the benefits obtained. Whereas this type of political dynamics is always present in every two-level system,[51] the Italian framework makes it particularly appealing and effective: uninformed public opinion is unable to distinguish 'cheap talks' from 'real intentions',[52] parties are normally not conflictual on EC matters, and the lack of coordination between national and European decisions favours the reciprocal opacity between the two arenas. Only 'insider policy takers' can realize the actual stringency of the measures adopted and, if necessary, their experience normally suggest to them how to escape the most harmful effects. A similar mechanism is at work when political elites are unable to impose certain types of necessary sacrifices, mainly in the sphere of fiscal or monetary policy, because they do not want to bear

[50] Such as delaying the closure of a steel plant (e.g. Bagnoli or Taranto), ignoring ecological standards (e.g. directives on water quality), negotiating the payment of fines (e.g. for excessive milk production) or the assignment of economic subsidies (e.g. to public-owned industries). To be more precise, according to this reactive style, matters need some sort of national or European adjustment only *ex-post*, when the mobilization of interests jeopardizes the internal 'calculus of consent'.

[51] Robert Putnam, 'Diplomacy and Domestic Politics: The Logic of Two-Level Games', *International Organization*, 41 (1988).

[52] The argument is well explained in Lange's analysis of the EC social policy: Peter Lange, 'The Politics of the Social Dimension', in Alberta Sbragia (ed.), *Euro-politics. Institutions and Policymaking in the 'New' European Community* (Washington: The Brookings Institution, 1992), pp. 225–56.

their political costs. 'Europe' and its proclaimed requirements have revealed themselves as efficient political anaesthetics because of the benefits automatically ascribed to EC membership by Italian people.[53] The confidence always shown towards European institutions, compared to the alienation or negative attitudes shown towards national governments, is obviously a key factor in understanding this second type of 'costs discharge'.

Let's take another kind of paradox, namely the well known fact that Italy has been unable to spend most of the funds assigned by the European Community.[54] It is probably true that administrative and procedural problems have prevented better results, but it is possible to put forward an alternative explanation. Structural funds, Integrated Mediterranean Programs, EIB loans are obviously useful resources and are actively searched to integrate national programmes, but if EC funds are assigned and controlled through strict procedures, the same has not happened for national policies. Using the words of a Commission official, 'many of the Italian regions have from the state considerable financing that are much easier to obtain than from the Community. A "personalised" and less honest handling of EC money is far more difficult than what happens for funds coming from Rome'.[55] Not using already assigned EC resources and dissipating the ones allocated through national uncontrolled distributive policies are the two faces of the same coin. As demonstrated by political scandals,[56] internal subsidies have often been the occasion for irregularities which would not have been allowed by the EC scrutiny. Illegitimate party financing, corruption, costs escalation, unrealized (but paid) projects, etc., used to produce a self-sustained illegal equilibrium which favoured all the involved actors: politicians, civil ser-

[53] See Giuliano Urbani and Maurizio Ferrera, 'L'Europa alle soglie del '90: quali istituzioni politiche?', in Giuliano Amato and Massimo Salvadori (eds.), *op. cit.*, pp. 33–66.
[54] Clear figures in this regard can be found in the last report of the Court of Auditors, OJ 309/93, 16.11.1993. See 'L'Italia e l'utilizzo dei fondi comunitari per lo sviluppo regionale: cronaca di un'ordinaria follia', in Eurispes, *op. cit.*, pp. 401–19. Incidentally, even regional administrations have adopted in these circumstances a reactive style, as demonstrated by the absence of *ex-ante* evaluations of the projects to be realized; see Manuela Crescini, 'Il ruolo della valutazione nella spesa regionale con particolare riferimento al caso dei Programmi integrati mediterranei', in Massimo Florio and Lorenzo Robotti, *Valutazione della spesa regionale e riforma dei fondi strutturali Cee* (Bologna: Il Mulino, 1993), pp. 189–224.
[55] *Il Sole 24 Ore*, 6.12.1990.
[56] We mainly refer to the 'Tangentopoli' inquiry, and to the so-called 'clean hand operation'.

vants, regional administrators and entrepreneurs. Compared to national policies, EC funds have (fortunately) never ensured the same flexibility and, for that same reason, could have been considered less appealing resources. We can add two more considerations on this point. First of all, Italy has always been at the top position as far as the number of EC frauds is concerned. Secondly, in spite of its poor record, the Italian government has defended the amount of EC funds assigned quite effectively: notwithstanding the fact that the deadlines fixed for a quick recovery of EC spending have never been respected, the Commission has not carried out its threats entirely.[57] Generally speaking, the contrast between two different distributive styles, the Italian and the EC ones, has prevented a better use of existing resources. Whereas the number of frauds is an indicator of that kind of incompatibility, the success in preventing a radical redistribution of the funds can be considered a further sign of the consensual attitudes produced by the strategy (and the equilibrium) we have tried to sketch.

Conclusion

In the preceding pages we have examined the institutions and the political dynamics that characterize the relation between the Italian and the EC decision-making systems. Not satisfied by the ordinary explanation that views administrative and procedural factors as independent variables affecting the Italian performance, we have suggested that the same 'specific organizational characteristics' which have created in the Italy–EC relationship a particular institutional and policy style came to prevail in the internal arena. The slow adaptation of the institutional framework to the challenges and the increasing requests of the European environment demonstrates its internal strength.[58] Actors involved in the network, including those belonging exclusively to the European arena, preferred to maintain the realized equilibrium as stable as possible rather than to risk potentially damaging reforms. Synthetically, it worked because the establishment of a 'protected political and policy market' satisfied the

---

[57] Funds have not been cut as expected, and even the question regarding the exclusion of an Italian region (Abruzzi) from Objective 1 financing has been solved in favour of Italy.

[58] As suggested by Douglass North, *op. cit.*, those kinds of frames are self-reinforcing even if they are socially inefficient.

most crucial participants, quite independently from the widespread social costs. Probably, the continuous growth of these same costs is already representing the most powerful challenge to the outlined framework: if not for the coherent recognition of their relevance, at least for the practical contradictions they imply, or for the impossibility of managing the increasing requests singularly and reactively, as happened in the past.

Retaining this 'spill-over overload' in the background, we can identify two more tension factors, the first coming from the national arena and the second from the European one.

Firstly, after an unrestful period of instabilities, Italy is in the midst of major political transformations. The new majoritarian electoral law will probably spread its effects even on EC/EU matters, although it will not have the traumatic consequences that many expect. Actually, even without any formal turnover, there have already been signs of a different attitude towards the European Community, at least starting from the government guided by the former president of the central bank, Azaglio Ciampi. The pressing requests for the diffusion of EC responsibilities, coming both from the parliament and from the regional level, may represent, in this regard, accelerating factors. The same 'political atmosphere' established after the inquiries that, revealing the illegalities committed during the 1980s, have involved almost half of the Italian political elites, can be considered a challenge to the persistence of the strategies that have prevailed in the preceding decade.

Secondly, there are other factors coming from the new European Union dispute, in particular those that permit it to further its 'sanctioning powers' beyond the formal competences of the European Court of Justice. We mainly think of the possibility of linking benefits to compliance, something implicit in the binding provisions characterizing the monetary union or in the constraints put forth by the Commission for the EC loan subscribed by the Italian government at the beginning of 1993. The same extension and institutionalization of majority procedures, decreasing the importance of the assent given by single countries, may force Italy to adopt a more active anticipatory decision-making style. From our point of view, the 'key' for an effective improvement in Italian participation lies not in the invention of new specialized offices or procedures, but in the genuine 'Europeanization' of policy-making experiences. Institutions have obviously to undergo gradual transformations if they want to cope with the deepening of the integration process, but here, as we have argued in the third section, the term 'institution' should be correctly understood in its informal and extended meaning. The task remains complex, but not impossible.

Select bibliography

Amato, Giuliano and Salvadori, Massimo L. (eds.), *Europa conviene?* (Bari: Laterza, 1990).

Dente, Bruno (ed.), *Le politiche pubbliche in Italia* (Bologna: Il Mulino, 1990).

Eurispes, *Rapporto Europa. L'Italia in Europa: scenari e prospettive* (Roma: Koinè edizioni, 1993).

Franchini, Claudio, *Amministrazione italiana e amministrazione comunitaria* (Padova: Cedam, 1993).

Francioni, Francesco (ed.), *Italy and EC Membership Evaluated* (London: Pinter Publishers, 1992).

Lange, Peter and Regini, Marino (eds.), *State, Market and Social Regulation* (New York: Cambridge University Press, 1989).

Morisi, Massimo, 'L'attuazione delle direttive CE in Italia. La "legge comunitaria" in Parlamento' (Milano: Giuffrè, 1992).

Regonini, Gloria and Giuliani, Marco, 'L'Italie: au-delà d'une démocratie consensuelle?', in Bruno Jobert (ed.), *Le tournant néo-libéral en Europe* (Paris: Harmattan, 1994).

Senato della Repubblica, *Partecipazione dell'Italia alle fasi formativa ed applicativa del diritto comunitario* (Roma: 1991).

Spain

Fundamentals of Spain in EU affairs

The constitutional structure

Spain is a decentralized state divided into seventeen Autonomous Communities (regions). National legislative power is vested in two Chambers, the Congress (Congreso de los Diputados) and the Upper Chamber (Senado) which, despite constitutional provisions, cannot be defined as a territorial Chamber. Including sixteen ministries, the central government structure is headed by the president and the vice-president. According to the constitution, the president of the government conducts domestic policy, foreign relations, civil administration and national defence while the vice-president assumes the president's office management and coordinates the several ministries in preparation for the Council of Ministers' weekly meetings. After the transition to democracy which was led by the centrist party UCD, the socialist party (PSOE) enjoyed an absolute majority from October 1982 until June 1993. As a consequence, the parliament's role has declined somewhat while the national executive and central administration powers have become more significant. However, since the general elections of 1993 only gave the socialist party a relative majority, the decision-making power of the central government to a large extent depends on political support from other parties.

The division of powers between central and regional institutions is the most controversial aspect of the Spanish constitution. This establishes a hybrid system which is neither federal nor regional, but based on the to some extent contradictory principles of the 'unity of the Spanish nation' and 'the autonomy of the nationalities and regions which constitute it'. The conflict between both principles expresses the difficulties faced by the parties in reaching a satisfactory agreement as to the territorial organization of the state. In fact, the rather complex and ambiguous division of power has been a source of constant political and judicial controversy, especially during the 1980s, in which the Constitutional Court has been playing a prominent role as policy-ruler. The statutes of autonomy fall into two main categories, special and general. The first one covers the three national minorities (the Basque country, Catalonia and Galicia) and Andalusia, which have 'full' autonomy statutes ratified by referendum. The general form, applying to eleven regions, is intended to be transitional since the regional authorities can request more powers. In addition, the national parliament can transfer at any moment legislative and executive functions to regions, as already happened in the cases of Valencia and the Canaries in 1983, and again with the lesser autonomous regions in 1993. Because of the constitutional recognition of its traditional (medieval) rights, Navarre also enjoys a full autonomy regime.

The constitution establishes that each autonomous community shall have a legislative assembly elected by universal suffrage, a government headed by a president, and a high court of justice. Most of the constitutional functions are shared between the central government and the regions according to two lists (sections 148.2 and 149.1 of the constitution). Under the first one, all the regions can take responsibility for many policy areas such as industry, public works, communications and transport, environment, regional development, banking and credit, agriculture and fisheries, tourism, housing and urban planning, etc. Under section 149.1 those regions with full autonomy can have further responsibilities in the fields of education, health, local administration and police. However, in addition to the federal traditional functions such as foreign policy, defence, monetary policy and general communications, the central state is empowered to set basic legislation or principles in most of these fields. Moreover, the central government and the higher autonomy regions are fully competent in research and development policy and culture. In contrast to German federalism, central administration retains field executive services at the regional and provincial levels to deal with matters which have not been transferred to the regions. However, central control over regional administration is just limited to those functions delegated from the centre. Following the precepts of federalism, there are mechanisms for the representation of regional interests at the central level. Some members (20%) of the Senate are chosen by regional parliaments and the latter have the right to propose bills in the lower chamber of the national parliament. Regions enjoy financial autonomy even though the central government controls the main revenue sources. Following an intergovernmental agreement negotiated in 1993 each region receives 15% of the income tax revenue collected in its territory. In addition, a national equalization fund is designated to reduce regional disparities. The Basque Country and Navarre enjoy a special financing system which allows them to collect general taxes. Periodical arrangements with central authorities fix their financial contribution to the national budget. Presently, the regions are responsible for 25% of total public expenditure and for about one-third of total public investment.

In many regards the Spanish territorial system expresses a difficult attempt to incorporate the national minorities into the general framework of the new democratic state. However, the Spanish constitution does not provide for effective integration of regional concerns into the national decision-making system. The Senate is, in fact, a non-specialized chamber where national party interests dominate. In contrast with the German model, the integration of regional concerns via the Senate is not feasible because of the lack of territorial representation. This situation weakens institutional cohesion, leads to both centrifugal and centralist tendencies and, in short, undermines the system's ability to function. While decision-making is highly fragmented, efficient mechanisms of vertical and horizontal cooperation do not exist and consensus-building, which is normally reached on a bilateral basis, consumes a lot of energy. The need for comprehensive institutional reform has become increasingly evident. This explains why the national parliament agreed in 1993 to transfer both new functions and financial resources to the regions with the lesser degree of autonomy. However, the immediate reaction of those regions already enjoying substantial autonomy was to call for more competences and for the removal of central administration services from their territories. Since the socialist party depends on the Catalan nationalist coalition's (CiU) support to pass national legislation it is likely that regional autonomy will substantially increase in the near future. Thus, the Spanish institutional system is permanently on the move depending on centre–periphery relations. Finally, the constitution guarantees administrative autonomy for municipalities and provinces. According to the Local Government Act of 1985, local authorities are responsible for many activities. However, the effective range of local powers is fixed by central and regional legislation. This double dependence poses serious problems, especially as regards the organization of the local system, local finance and intergovernmental coordination.

Basic impact of the EC/EU

The horizontal division of powers among Community institutions has affected the distribution of functions in Spain. Firstly, as a result of its prominent role at the European level, the central government has concentrated decision-making functions which constitutionally belong to the national parliament. Secondly, Spanish participation in the EC has had important consequences for the vertical distribution of functions. The institutional position of the regions has been weakened by the transfer of internal competences to the Community. The loss of regional powers affects many areas, especially after the enforcement of the SEA and the Maastricht Treaty on European Union: finance, agriculture and fisheries, industry, regional policy, transport, research policy, environment and consumer policy. At the same time, however, the regions are involved in the implementation of Community policies and in the management of structural funds.

Major changes and peculiarities

The Spanish government has been quite active in adapting its behaviour to the requirements of the new Community decision-making process. It has to be remembered that Spain's entry into the EC coincided with the negotiation and the enforcement of the SEA. In January 1989 the Spanish government assumed its first semester of Community presidency – quite successfully, bearing in mind its inexperience – which was followed soon after by the setting-up of the two intergovernmental conferences that opened the way to the EU treaty. In other words, unlike the old member states who were accustomed to the unanimity rule, rapid adaptation to the new institutional procedures has characterized the Spanish government. This has proved its ability to negotiate some relevant issues to which it attached great importance for domestic concerns such as the reform of the structural funds in 1988 or the Maastricht compromise on the cohesion fund, after the initial failure of a Spanish proposal aiming to establish a compensatory fund among member states. Both regional and central authorities have had to adapt their structures and standards to Community requirements. Another important consequence of Spanish participation in the EU is the regional activism at the European level.

Last, but not least, Spanish regional and environmental policies are closely linked to entry into the European Community. Ironically, before 1986, Spain lacked any consistent policy designed to correct territorial imbalances. On the other hand, the Spanish government did not attempt to negotiate special provisions in the accession treaty granting delay or other derogations on the execution of Community environmental policy. Consequently, the relevant directives came immediately into effect. This has created serious problems for the different levels of Spanish government, as can be seen by the increasing number of infringement procedures initiated by the Commission against Spain.

The EC decision-making cycle and the participation of national institutions

The central government

In Spain there is neither a ministry vertically responsible for EC matters nor a specific committee. Since 1986, the Secretary of State for the EC (SSEC), which depends on the Ministry of Foreign Affairs, has been in charge of coordinating state action in the EC institutions while the General Secretary of Foreign Policy retained responsibilities for coordinating European Political Cooperation. This does not, however, prevent other departments from exercising their own powers when these affect EC matters. A Secretariat General depending on the SSEC is divided into two General Directions both responsible for technical coordination and judicial and institutional coordination. The first one looks after sectoral Community policies (agriculture and fisheries, economic, financial and social affairs, trade and customs, industry, energy, transports and communications). The second body is in charge of coordinating judicial affairs and institutional relations inside central administration. The SSEC also chairs the Interministerial Committee for Economic Affairs related to the EC, which was created to improve intragovernmental coordination. To the extent that the SSEC officials have been recruited in the different ministries, coordination is facilitated because of their working experience in the departments. Senior officials representing the Presidency of the government and the Ministries of Economy and Financial Affairs, Agriculture, Trade, Industry and Energy, and Labour and Social Security serve on the Committee as do other representatives of any other department involved in the items on the agenda for a particular meeting. The Committee essentially coordinates economic affairs and provides information. This organizational framework reflects the central government's effort to maintain the criterion of unified action abroad through the Ministry of Foreign Affairs, while recognizing the special competences and political influence of the individual ministries. However, it does not prevent interministerial conflicts which are triggered by major EC decisions. The Interministerial Committee is sometimes unable to define the Spanish position vis-à-vis items on the agenda of the COREPER and the Council of Ministers. Negotiating is mostly a matter of informal contacts between the Spanish permanent representatives, members of the SSEC and the officials of the ministries involved. In addition, there is a Follow-up and Coordinating Committee for affairs related to the EC Court of Justice. This body, made by representatives of the Office of the Presidency, the SSEC, the Ministries of Justice, Economy, and any other interested department, studies all proceedings brought against Spain as well as those that could in any way affect the country. Most of the central ministries are involved in Community policies although Foreign Affairs, Economy and Financial Affairs, Industry and Energy, Public Works, Transport and Environment, Agriculture, and Health and Consumer Affairs are the most active players in the Community arena. The various departments are staffed with experts – usually lawyers and economists – on EC matters, generally ranked as sub-directors and advisors who are part of the ministerial staff. The officials do not act in Brussels beyond the permanent representative and other structures of technical and political support.

The administration
Until recently the implementation of Community policies was seen as a routine issue by public officials. Nevertheless, since 1991 there is a growing awareness about the effects of the internal market on public administration in terms of transnational political administrative competitiveness and internal institutional cooperation in Community matters. A public survey conducted in 1991 among 650 senior public officials[1] showed quite a clear degree of dissatisfaction regarding both the impact of the European integration process on central administration and the setting-up of the new model of state. The conclusions

---

[1] *Reflexiones para la Modernización de la Administración* (Madrid: Ministerio para las Administraciones Públicas, 1991).

stressed the need to improve the implementation structures of Community acts, intragovernmental coordination and cooperation with regional administrations. This preoccupation expresses the growing difficulty of implementing Community decisions in Spain, especially when they disrupt traditional schemes and compel them to meet higher standards. A broader model of management is needed which can encompass subsidiarity and partnership with the regions. Despite the efforts made in recent years at both central and regional level to transpose Community directives, serious doubts remain about their effective application, as can be seen from the numerous complaints made by the Commission, and the warnings given to the Spanish administrative bodies, some of which have reached the European Court of Justice.[2] In recent years, some efforts have been made to improve intra- and intergovernmental coordination. For example, since 1992, a telematic data base and an electronic mail service link the Permanent Representation in Brussels and the Secretary of State for the European Communities (SSEC). It provides direct Community information to central ministries and, with some restrictions depending on the 'confidential' nature of some issues, to regional governments. Moreover, the SSEC systematically evaluates the administrative implications of any Community document, which includes the detection of the involved central services.

Community pressures have had a consistent impact on Spanish administration. As a response to the complaints from the EC about the increasing number of infringements (see Table 6.1) especially in the field of environmental directives, the central government has had to resettle its organizational structure. Firstly, a General Secretary for the Environment was created in 1990 within the Ministry of Public Works and Housing. However, this organizational change was not sufficient. Renewed pressures from the Commission to provide it with

---

[2] During the period 1986–1992, eight judgments have been pronounced against Spain and none in favour of it. The Spanish breaches on Community law include the following cases: (1) Case 31/89, VAT on imported cars; (2) Case 119/89, non-taxable persons: deduction of residual VAT paid in the member state of exportation; (3) Case 258/89, control measures: catches of fish stocks subject to a tag or quota outside the Community fishing zone; (4) Case 313/89, failure to fulfil obligations: directive 80/155/EEC, training of midwives; (5) Case 35/90, VAT-directive 77/388/EEC: national law not complying therewith; (6) Case 192/90, failure to fulfil obligation: containers of liquid for human consumption, implementation of a directive in national law; (7) Case 24/91, directive 71/305/EEC: award of public works contracts, publication of notice of contract; (8) Case 96/91, exemption and remission of turnover tax in international travel.

a competent interlocutor led to a new revision of the organizational framework in 1991. This change involved moving responsibility for the environment to the level of the Secretary of State for Water and Environmental Policies. Finally, in 1993 the government decided to give ministerial status to 'Environment' with the new ministry of 'Public Works, Transport and Environment'.

Table 6.1 Infringement proceedings against Spain (1986–93)

	86	87	88	89	90	91	92	93	86–93	EC–12
Letters of Formal Notice	22	32	31	53	114	79	127	107	565	6,582
Reasoned Opinions	–	8	11	8	15	30	39	28	139	2,150
Cases to the ECJ	–	1	1	5	3	2	5	5	22	553

Source: European Commission, Annual Reports to the European Parliament on Monitoring the Application of Community Law, 1990–1993, COM (91) final, 16.10.1991; COM (92) 136 final, 27.5.1992; COM (93) 320 final, 28.4.1993; COM (94) 500 final, 29.3.1994.

Cases 258/89 (concerning fishing outside the Community fishing zone) and 192/90 (concerning containers of liquid for human consumption) have been perceived as of particular importance by national authorities. It is worth noting that both are cases of non-compliance with the judgements of the ECJ. Fishing is one of the main Spanish industries. This explains the reluctance of Spanish authorities to support any attempt to limit such activity. According to this particular directive, member states are obliged to inform the EC about the number of fish captures in order to preserve the international fishing reserves out of the 200-mile area. However, as Spanish fishing capacity heavily exceeds the national quota corresponding to the international agreements negotiated by the Commission, the Spanish ships have been used to fishing outside the national fishing grounds. In October 1991, the Spanish authorities agreed formally to comply with the Community norms. Concerning the liquid containers for human consumption, the Spanish government is still negotiating with the Commission the effective implementation of Community technical requirements which seem to create serious problems for the national industry. Once a judgement has been pronounced against Spain, internal authorities enforce Community norms through the usual channels (mostly 'decrees'). The operation usually requires about one year. According to national officials, the infringement procedure is considered to be an effective mechanism of control, especially after the new draft of Article 171 TEU.

The national parliament

The national parliament is not directly involved in the EC decision-making process. Its role is mainly symbolic-reactive as the information generally comes after the definition of the official Spanish positions. A Mixed Committee for European Affairs ('*Comisión Mixta para las Comunidades Europeas*') of the upper and lower chambers, created in 1986, is in charge of monitoring EC policies. Its follow-up action includes checking legislative decrees presented by the central government to enforce EC regulations and directives. However, it does not monitor the decrees or any other administrative measure taken by the executive, which constitute the usual way of implementing Community legislation. The Secretary of State appears bimonthly before the Upper House Budget Committee and the Mixed Committee in order to answer questions. After each Community summit, the President of the government reports to the Congress and responds to the questions addressed by the parliamentary leaders. This generally produces agreements on resolutions and recommendations aiming to guide the Spanish positions in Brussels. According to a proposal of resolution which was presented in November 1993 by the opposition Popular Party, the Mixed Committee for European Affairs should be closely involved in the preparation of the intergovernmental conference which will have the duty of reviewing the Maastricht Treaty in 1996. Up to now the Senate has not been involved in the Community process except for questions addressed to the central government on EC issues affecting the autonomous communities such as the new Committee of the Regions. After the ratification of the Maastricht Treaty the upper chamber has taken the decision to set up a special committee entrusted to report on regional participation in Europe. MPs do not generally have permanent channels of communication to EU institutions. They tend to get in touch with Brussels or Strasbourg when they need information and usually make contacts through the SSEC, MEPs or their proper political parties.

The regions

According to the internal distribution of functions, the regions implement Community policies within their own areas of competence. After the accession of Spain to the EC, the adaptation of previous regional legislation in order to cope with Community rules ('*acquis communautaire*') has only affected Catalonia and the Basque Country because of their higher level of competences. Nevertheless, as entry into the EC had been taken for granted since the early 1980s, in both regions there was an anticipatory voluntary adaptation. Until now regional parliaments have been excluded from both EC decision-making and implementation. As at the central level, regional executives remain the main Community actors. Parliamentary activity regarding the EC is usually devoted to debating the general or sectoral impact of the integration process (such as the Single Market or the European Union). This results in the adoption of initiatives, resolutions or recommendations designed to shape the behaviour of the executive internal aspects (i.e. the regional administrations' response to EC policies) as well as the relationship with central authorities vis-à-vis Community matters affecting regional competences. In some cases (Catalonia, the Basque Country, Galicia, Valencia, Andalusia and the Canaries), permanent non-legislative committees have been created in order to follow up European affairs.

As regards regional participation in the EC, faced with pressure from regions, the central government proposed in 1986 an 'Agreement for cooperation in Community matters'. Negotiations came to a standstill in 1988. The proposal, based on the 'Länder procedure'[3] in force in Germany from 1980 to 1986, provided for the transfer of Community information affecting regional matters. Regions would inform central government of their policy preferences, aiming to incorporate them in the Spanish position, and would coordinate their own positions and cooperate through a regional conference. This latter could propose the designation of an 'observer' and 'extra observer' as members of the Spanish permanent representation in Brussels. The technical shortcomings of this proposal were rather obvious. The main problem was that Catalonia and the Basque Country, the two most powerful regions, wanted their own representatives to have more autonomy with respect to the Spanish repre-

---

[3] See the contribution on Germany of Dietrich Rometsch in this book.

sentation. The central government's refusal to accept such a proposition blocked any agreement. All that had been achieved was the
compromise to respect the internal distribution of functions in matters relating to the EC. There was also an intergovernmental agreement aiming to guarantee internal coordination on breaches of
Community law and on public grants.

Regional claims led in 1988 to a new arrangement with central
authorities establishing an informal Conference on Community
Affairs. Regions and central government agreed in October 1992 to
institutionalize regional participation in Community affairs through
the Conference. Following the German model, the Conference is a
cooperation body between both levels of government. According to
the final declaration, the Conference will concentrate on the following tasks:

- 'the common information and discussion about the development
  of the European integration process;
- the institutionalized regional participation in Community matters;
- the impulse and monitoring of regional participation in each Community policy through the sectoral conferences already existing'.

The Conference, which is set up at the ministry level, will be
assisted by a permanent working group, the Committee of Coordi-
nators on Community Affairs. Central authorities are represented by
the Minister for Public Administrations who is not a permanent
member of the main central decision-making structure, the Interministerial Committee for Economic Affairs relating to the EC. The real
partner of the regions is obviously the SSEC as it reveals its growing
relations with regional authorities. Thus, despite the Conference, the
regions continue to develop bilateral contacts with the SSEC. In spite
of multilateral arrangements, Catalonia and the Basque Country have
not given up hope of getting direct representation in Brussels. Since
1994, the nationalist–socialist coalition government of the Basque
Country has been negotiating with central authorities a special status
in the EU. A common demand is the need to establish a bilateral relationship with the EU which should include issues such as taxes, transport, infrastructures and police. Basque participation should also
include the negotiation of structural and cohesion funds as well as the
Schengen and Trevi groups. Both parties stress the need to include
regional representatives in the Commission's advisory committees,
one observer of the autonomous communities in the Spanish perma-

nent representation and the possibility that a regional minister could represent Spain in the Council meetings when regional competences are concerned.

Since they are not directly involved in the Community decision-making process, regional governments try to influence Community decisions both at the domestic and at the EC level using formal as well as informal channels. Most of the regions have adapted their organizational structures in order to carry through the implementation of Community policies and the management of European funds. The office of the Presidency generally assumes the political representation of the region at the European level. Only in Catalonia is one ministry officially in charge of 'external activities'. These include frequent contacts with Community institutions and developing networks of relations with regional authorities inside and outside the Community. In spite of the formal opposition of central authorities, the Spanish regions have established regular, informal contacts with Community institutions. Indeed, the direct involvement in the application and management of European policies makes it inevitable that they should have contacts with Commission officials interested in following up regional policies on the ground. The nine regional offices set up by Catalonia, the Basque Country, Galicia, Andalusia, the Canary Islands, Murcia, Asturias, Castille and Valencia allow constant contacts with European decision-making centres. Furthermore, the integration of interest groups in the implementation of EC policies is seen as a political priority by most of the regional administrations. In preparation for the internal market, some autonomous communities have forged a dense network of transregional relations, including not only participation in European organizations of the regions but bilateral or multilateral cooperation agreements. The Catalan government is the one which has been the most active at the European level, concentrating on the preparation of the Single Market. The President of Catalonia has chaired the Assembly of European Regions (ARE) since June 1992, while the mayor of Barcelona has chaired the Assembly of Municipalities and Regions of Europe since January 1992. Ironically, two Catalan antagonist politicians have been negotiating the composition of the Committee of the Regions and Local Authorities which was decided in Maastricht. According to the final decision taken by the central government the twenty-one seats that correspond to Spain are shared between the seventeen autonomous communities and the mayors of Barcelona, Bilbao, Madrid and Seville. This represents a

difficult compromise valid until 1996 which has been strongly criti-
cized by the local government's lobby, the Spanish Federation of
Municipalities and Provinces.

Moreover, there are the 'Four Motors of Europe', a mutual cooperation agreement established in 1988 between Baden-Württemberg,
Catalonia, Lombardia and Rhône-Alpes. The agreement covers
diverse matters such as foreign economic relations, economic cooperation, technology transfer, promoting research and design, environment and culture policies. By working together and acting as a
public lobby, the four regions aim to play a major role in European
integration. Another initiative was the creation in 1989 of a trans-
Pyrenean Euroregion which includes Catalonia, Languedoc-Roussil-
lon and Midi-Pyrénées. The three regional governments combine
forces to carry out joint ventures in some areas such as communications and telecommunications infrastructure, occupational training,
research and technology transfer, culture, sports and tourism.

At the local level, in the later 1980s the city of Barcelona has been
very active in creating a transnational network made up of the forty
major European cities, named 'Eurocities'. Barcelona is also promoting a network with five other French and Spanish cities (Montpellier,
Toulouse, Palma de Mallorca, Valencia and Zaragoza) known as C-
6, whose objective is to promote a macro-Mediterranean region
within the framework of the EU. This network is currently involved
in several projects mainly designed to promote economic and cultural
exchange, to protect the environment and to develop new technolo-
gies, communication and social welfare.

With regard to some matters, the internal division of functions
sometimes causes special problems at both central and Community
level. The most striking example is the environmental policy, where
the main responsibilities belong to the regional authorities. Decentralization has generated considerable complexity in environmental
management. Within the autonomous communities there is a variety
of organizational and managerial arrangements whilst mechanisms
for horizontal coordination among regions to address common problems are lacking. As a result, neither central government nor the
Commission are in a position to monitor effectively the implementation of Community directives at the regional level.

The courts
Despite the growing impact of European law on Spanish society,

there is little evidence about the adaptation of national courts to Community law. Since preliminary ruling procedures provide an interesting indicator of the degree to which Community law is applied, Spain shows a poor performance during the period 1986–1993 when only twenty-seven questions were brought to the ECJ by national courts, of which eight were by the High Court. This is not due to any kind of reluctance vis-à-vis Community legislation but, to a large extent, simply to the unawareness of the procedure. The fact that 90% of the total preliminary ruling procedures have been brought to the ECJ after 1989 seems to prove this impressionistic view. It is interesting to note that both the administrative section of the Spanish High Court and the Constitutional Court have expressed serious doubts about their effective competence to bring preliminary ruling procedures to the ECJ. Arguing that it has exclusive jurisdiction on administrative acts and regulations, the former has refused to bring a question to the ECJ since the answer could have been to consider the application of a legal norm, given that the Constitutional Court is the only one which can address such a question to the ECJ. Nevertheless, the Constitutional Court did not agree on such an interpretation, arguing its incompetence to decide on the compatibility between the national law and the Community law which is not included in the Spanish constitution. In short, the Constitutional Court has refused to control the application of Community law except for protecting fundamental rights. The Constitutional Court has had, however, to intervene frequently in disputes dealing with the impact of Community acts on the internal division of functions between the central government and the regions. Problems arise when both levels of government claim exclusive competence to enforce Community directives on shared matters according to the constitution and the statutes of autonomy. The Constitutional Court has insistently pointed out that the accession of Spain to the EC did not mean any reassignment of internal powers to the benefit of the central government. The latter is only responsible for the negotiation of supranational agreements which involve the whole institutional structures and for guaranteeing their fulfilment, not for the effective enforcement itself.[4]

---

[4] 'La garantía de la ejecución del Derecho Comunitario y las Comunidades Autónomas', *Noticias/CEE*, 106, 1993.

Public opinion, political parties and interest groups

Public opinion

Acceptance of the EC institutional system is quite high in Spain. Belonging to the EC has become a strong shared feeling among Spaniards and also had a positive effect on the general attitude towards the EC/EU (see Table 6.2). Entry into the EC in 1986 has been perceived as the final step of the democratization process as well as the end of the secular isolation from Europe that has characterized Spain since the last century, and especially during the Franco regime. Most of the political parties and social forces share common pro-European attitudes which pervade public opinion. Moreover, until now Spain's income from the EC budget has been higher than its outlays. While most of the population ignores the institutional framework of the EC/EU and its current workings, the general perception tends to link economic prosperity of the 1980s with participation in the Community system, with the structural and cohesion funds being its most expressive outcomes. However, in Spain there is a relatively low interest in EC politics although several issues such as environmental policy, social policy, the effectiveness of the Single Market and Economic and Monetary Union are generating political debate, forcing social groups to take clearer positions *vis-à-vis* the EU.

Although the European Parliament is quite well known, its functions and utility remain unclear for public opinion. The institution appears too far away from the citizens' interests. This probably explains the rather low participation (59.6%) registered in the European elections of 1994. Furthermore, Spanish MEPs are not very popular among the public probably due to the scarce attention paid to them in the media. The Council of Ministers and the European Council are more popular because of the frequent public appearance of national leaders attending the different meetings. In fact, during the 1989 Spanish Council Presidency 78% of the Spanish people thought that this was an important event; only the Portuguese reached with 85% a higher score throughout the whole Community during their presidency in 1992. This does not mean, however, that there is a clear comprehension of the crucial role the Council or the European Council play. Their acceptance is more a matter of fact than a conscious recognition of any kind of legitimacy. The Commission is frequently perceived as a synonym of a weak and distant 'European executive', meaning a sort of naïve champion of Community interests facing strong national governments. The European Parliament and Commission have in common that from 1992 onwards the so far relatively good impression they made in Spanish public opinion became subject to a sharp decline. There are many reasons for this phenomenon, which can also be observed in other member states, the most important of which seems to be a general dissatisfaction with the 'output' of the institutional system and the growing complexity of its functioning. The European Court of Justice is almost unknown in Spain as a Community institution. Some unaware media even tend to confuse it with the European Court of Human Rights.

Table 6.2 General attitude in Spain towards the EC/EU and its institutions*

	1984 %	1986 %	1988 %	1990 %	1992 %	1994 [6/1993] %
EC/EU membership of Spain is a good thing	54	64	66	67	61	50
Spain has benefited from EC membership	–	15	26	54	44	38
Quite good impression of the EP based on what has been read or heard	–	48	51	58	58	[45]
Quite good impression of the European Commission based on what has been read or heard	–	–	50	57	48	[37]
For a future European Government responsible to the EP	–	–	53	64	59	55

* The figures for the columns 1984–92 represent the average per year taken from the Eurobarometer Trends 1974–92.

Source: Eurobarometer Trends 1974–92, April 1993; Eurobarometer no. 39, June 1993; Eurobarometer no. 41, July 1994.

Political parties

Until now European integration has enjoyed a large consensus among political parties although their attitude regarding Community affairs has been quite reactive and their participation limited. This includes the socialist party which usually supports governmental initiatives. Even though the leader of the Spanish socialist MEPs was the former

Minister of Foreign Relations in the first socialist cabinet (1982–6), its influence on the party, and especially on the government is quite irrelevant. Moreover the EP has become a sort of 'golden retirement' for some conservative MEPs who were involved in the Franco regime. As in other member states, however, recently national parties have 'discovered' Europe as a consequence of the unexpected negative impact of the Maastricht Treaty on public opinion. The socialist party has been one active promoter of the new European Socialists' Party while the conservative Partido Popular (PP) has recently succeeded in joining the European Popular Party despite the initial reluctance of the Catalan Christian democrats and the Basque Nationalist party which already belonged to the European Christian democrat family. In addition, the PP is indirectly involved in Community policy-making since it shares with the socialist party the two seats which correspond to Spain in the European Commission.

Spain is represented in the European Parliament by sixty-four MEPs. After the 1989 European elections and as a result of a pact with the European conservatives, a member of the socialist group, M. Barón Crespo, served as President of the Parliament for the first half of the 1989–94 legislature. The European elections of 1994 gave the relative majority (twenty-eight seats) to the conservatives, although they were in opposition. The rest was shared among the governing socialists (twenty-two) – which was in fact perceived as a clear defeat for González – the Communist Party and its allies (nine) and the Catalan and Basque nationalists (five). Since 1986 Catalan and Basque parties have been unsuccessfully calling for the establishment of regional constituencies – as in Germany, Belgium and Italy – for the European elections.

Interest groups
Spanish tradition regarding relations between private interests and public administration is still far from that of Northern Europe. Participation of the private sector in the decision-making process is seen as an obstacle in the achievement of the so-called 'public interest' which is soundly founded in the administrative culture. However, the negotiation of EC policies is shifting this perspective. Ministries involved in the negotiation of Community acts increasingly tend to establish contacts through informal procedures with interest and pressure group representatives with the aim of formulating the Spanish 'technical' positions and facilitating the implementation of direc-

tives, especially those linked with the Single Market. Banks, Chambers of Commerce and Industry, the employers' peak associations, small and medium companies, farmers' organizations and the big sectoral associations are among the most active private lobbies. The involvement of territorial interest groups is seen too as a political priority by most of the regional administrations since they have to implement Community policies and programmes (structural funds, research and development policies, etc.). Moreover, since 1986, the presence of Spanish business and social organizations in Brussels has been increasing. Big companies and organized general, and especially sectoral, interests use a double model of lobbying, combining internal and supranational action. On the one hand, they provide information, assessment and technical advice to national and regional civil servants, including the implementation of Community policies and programmes, as do the Chambers of Trade and Industry. On the other hand, they work in Brussels through national delegations and Euro-federations in order to keep information and establish contacts with EC officials during the preparation of Community bills. Nevertheless, Spanish interest groups are still more reactive than preventive, having recourse to professionals when they try to deal with specific problems. Private interests are still reluctant to establish contacts with MEPs, and the role of consultative bodies – particularly the ESC – is largely seen as a pure formality. Worried about the increasing difficulties faced by national and regional administrations in enforcing Community acts, environmental groups and consumer rights associations exert pressure which often results in complaints against the Commission.

Conclusion

Entry into the EC has meant for Spain the end of a secular isolation in which it had been marginalized from the great European events. Democracy has also strengthened in this process. Certainly, during the 1980s political stability and economic growth have so far favoured Spanish integration into the EC. In addition, until now European integration has produced more benefits than losses in terms of financial resources and political influence. Structural funds have managed to shape a regional development policy which did not exist previously. At the same time, EC membership has had a consistent impact on public administrations whose structures and procedures have undergone a process of adaptation in order to conform with Community standards. Furthermore, domestic administrations are also more and more sensible of how the knowledge and expertise of interest groups can improve their negotiation capacities in Brussels. Spain's entry into the EC in 1986 has been crucial for the development of its environmental policy. In spite of the difficulties in enforcing Community rules, Spain has developed a relatively successful bargaining strategy combining both a claim for special treatment, according to its specific and its relative industrial delay, and the demand for additional funds to enable it to comply more quickly and effectively with Community requirements.

Public opinion as well as most political parties and interest groups supported the central government's strategy towards Economic and Political Union. Political ability has proved to be an important resource. Spain is a proactive Community partner which enjoys some of the privileges of the big member states and is the leader of the cohesion policy group at the same time. In December 1991, it succeeded in getting the new cohesion fund for itself, Portugal, Greece and Ireland and in doubling the quartet's receipts of regional aid. It was also Spain's insistence that led to the entry price in terms of grants and loans for Norway, Finland, Sweden and Austria to join the European Economic Area and later on the European Union.

At the Maastricht summit the Spanish government succeeded in having its proposal on European citizenship included in the treaty. In addition it was one of the main supporters of subsidiarity conceived as an evaluation standard to reach the EU aims, but not as a way of limiting the Community powers. According to the Spanish Memorandum on Subsidiarity presented in Edinburgh:

> The EU Treaty does not create a federal structure and thus it is still too early to fix the list of Community exclusive competences … The real extent of subsidiarity, which only affects shared competences, has to be progressively established by the Court of Justice.

However, the regions fear that the national government will confine subsidiarity to the relations between the member states and the EU, avoiding the involvement of other levels of government. Due to the positive effects of EC membership, there has been very little political debate in Spain about the constitutional consequences of the increasing transfer of powers to the EU. It is commonly accepted as a matter of fact that the integration process inevitably implies a loss of internal competences. This is in contrast with Catalonia and the Basque Country, where political elites worry about the impact of European integration on regional competences and interests in terms of re-centralization. The regions' claims for participation in the EC led in 1992 to the institutionalization of a Conference on Community Affairs which does not satisfy Catalan and Basque traditional aspirations to enjoy an official or, at least, a more influential status in the European arena. Both regions strongly support the strengthening of European institutions since it erodes the nation-state powers and offers many opportunities for a growing cooperation with other European regions. Their calculation is that, in the long term, the process of political and economic union will lead to the reshaping of the European space on the basis of some coherent and competitive macro-regions. According to this logic, only those regions provided with economic and social capacities and historic identity should be able to lead the process.

The main weaknesses of the Spanish institutional system regarding EC/EU matters can be summarized in the following points. Firstly, the integration process has had a negative impact on both the horizontal and the vertical division of powers. As in other member states the national parliament is almost excluded from EC decision-making and this loss of powers is far from being compensated by the Mixed Committee for Community Affairs. As regards the regions, their constitutional position has been weakened by the transfer of internal competences to the EC/EU although they are directly involved in the implementation of Community policies. A second salient feature is that central administration officials feel dissatisfied about both the impact of European integration, which implies growing public management competitiveness, and the decentralization process which is dismantling the traditional settlement of the central state. In addition, Spanish ministries are not internally coordinated when they deal with European policies. The lack of internal coordination affects the various interministerial structures and even the permanent representation in Brussels. Concerning the internal transposition of EC directives that can be complemented and adapted by the regional governments, central authorities are not in a position to prescribe specific measures or to control the way in which these authorities carry out their tasks. The formulation of Community programmes very often depends on information provided by the regions. Thus, the policy process appears highly fragmented and insufficiently coordinated both horizontally and vertically. These shortcomings could explain the increasing number of infringement procedures initiated against Spain since 1990. Finally, the economic crisis and political constraints linked to economic convergence have given rise to tensions and reticences among political and social actors which have dramatically changed the previous idyllic image of the EC, while public opinion has become more sceptical about European integration.

Select bibliography

Barrachina, E., *Las instituciones de la CE* (Barcelona: PPU, 1988).

García de Enterria, E. et al., *Tratado de Derecho Comunitario Europeo* (Madrid: Civitas, 1987).

—— 'Spanish Report', in J. Schwarze et al. (eds.), *The 1992 Challenge at the National Level* (Baden Baden: Nomos, 1990).

Mangas, A., *Derecho Comunitario Europeo y Derecho Español* (Madrid: Tecnos, 1987).

Molina del Pozo, C. L., *Manual de Derecho de la CE* (Madrid: Trivium, 1990).

Morata, F., *Autonomia Regional i Integració Europea* (Barcelona: Institut d'Estudis Autonòmics, 1987).

Muñoz Machado, S., *El Estado, el Derecho Interno y la CE* (Madrid: Civitas, 1986).

The Netherlands

Fundamentals of the Netherlands in EU affairs

The historical and cultural background

Life in the Netherlands, including politics and administration, has always been strongly influenced by the outside world. Since commerce and trade are the lifeline of the country, open communication and intensive exchange of goods and ideas developed relatively early in the country's history. As a refuge for dissenters from abroad, the Netherlands entertained and tolerated a variety of religious and political ideas within its borders. Compared to other countries in Western Europe, notions of self-government struck roots deeper and earlier. After the successful rebellion against Spain in the seventeenth century, a sense of national identity developed within a rather loose structure of government, based on local and provincial autonomy. Although nationalism or chauvinism never made a strong appeal – or, one could say, never made sense – among the Dutch, the identity of the Netherlands (language, culture) was never questioned and a strong national self-confidence developed. Economic growth and colonial expansion only added to this self-confident notion of Dutch citizenship. Against this historical background, political thinking in the Netherlands developed some striking characteristics which are still evident today.

Firstly, there is the notion that 'the government belongs to us'. Whereas in other countries the government is in charge and takes care of its citizens, in the Netherlands the citizens consider themselves in charge of their government. They have felt like this for centuries, even though the number of citizen-participants was small in the seventeenth and eighteenth centuries, and increased only in the nineteenth and twentieth centuries. Through an elaborate system of inputs (consultation, representation etc.) the Dutch citizens tell their government what to do. Policies are always the result of an elaborate process of negotiation and compromise. Therefore, they usually have a strong base of support, but there is always the risk of opposition and defiance. Respect for government and obedience can never be taken for granted. A prevailing middle-class culture, and a dislike of extremes – 'just be normal, that is crazy enough' is a common saying – makes for modest government and for self-conscious citizens.

Secondly, there is a strong sense of privacy (the sovereignty of the home, the church, the voluntary association), putting limits to government intervention, a tolerance for diversity in behaviour, culture and lifestyle, and a strong preference for consensus and compromise over disagreement and conflict. The geographical, historical and economic necessity of maintaining trading contacts with strongly different groups, of overcoming the threats of nature and of maintaining unity among a number of minorities – a clear and permanent majority could never develop – have embedded these political notions solidly in the country's social and economic life.

Thirdly, the culture and structure of the Dutch governmental system show some striking paradoxes, all of them related to the characteristics mentioned above. The country is a monarchy with a strongly republican culture, and it is a unitary state with a federal, or even confederal, history. The country was a confederal republic for more than 150 years (1648–1815). The unitary kingdom of the Netherlands should not be taken at its face value. It can only survive as such, by allowing considerable leeway, both formally and informally, to popular indifference towards the monarchy as an institution and to the demands of local and other 'lower' entities. The monarchy is based on the personal popularity of the queen/king rather than on reverence for the institution of the monarchy, let alone an ideology of monarchism. The national government is constitutionally bound to respect the long-standing historical autonomy of provinces and municipalities, which was only strengthened by the twentieth-century political system of 'consociationalism' and 'pillarization' in order to ensure stable and democratic government. European federalism is, therefore, clearly in line with the history of the Netherlands, even though explicit (con-)federalism was abolished in 1815.[1]

The attitude of citizens towards government in the Netherlands was characterized not by 'majority' or 'sovereignty' but by a busi-

---

[1] Federalism is a way to prevent, rather than to establish, a super-state in Europe.

nesslike mentality and a preference for coalition and compromise among minorities. Completing this paradoxical picture, there is moralism, i.e. a strong preference in Dutch political culture for moral justifications. From the founding years in the seventeenth century onwards, public life in the Netherlands has had strong religious and moral overtones. The founding myth of the state was formulated in religious terms – a war against Catholic Spain for religious freedom, against papal suppression, for true Christianity. Calvinist church ministers and lawyers set the tone and the trend of public debate. This pervasive moralism characterizes public debate until this very day, regardless of political ideology. From left to right, there is preaching and telling others what is good or bad; hypocrisy and a lack of realism are its logical consequences. As a result, the Dutch are often pictured as 'merchant-ministers' trying to combine the profitable and the morally just, and to have the best not only from this world but also from heaven.

Dutch foreign policy

For the survival of the Netherlands as a state, the balance of power in Europe has always been crucial. England being its main rival in foreign trade and colonial empire-building, and France being a major threat on the continent, the Netherlands made an extensive use of balancing and counterbalancing mechanisms, trade-offs and buffers (e.g. in today's Belgium) in its foreign policy, in order to minimize foreign influence while maintaining and cultivating international contacts. After the nineteenth-century rise of Germany in European politics, there was a clear tendency to rapprochement towards Germany – based on language, religion, royal family, and the economy – without, however, antagonizing the French and the British too much. The game became more and more complicated and was put to some difficult tests, e.g. in the Luxembourg question in the 1860s and the Boer War at the beginning of this century. Still, the Netherlands managed to remain neutral during the First World War. In the early years of this century, the country considered itself a major middle power with strong worldwide colonial and economic resources.

This self-image, however, was completely shattered in the economic depression of the 1920s and 1930s, and the ensuing war years. The country suffered military defeat, economic decline and destruction, and the loss of its colonial empire. Post-war Dutch society, in several respects, made a clear break with the past. Cultural life, including education, turned away from its pre-war ties with Germany, and became completely Anglo-Saxon in its orientation. Also, foreign policy took a radically different course. The disillusions of world politics and the priority of economic recovery brought about an almost exclusive focus on the immediate economic and security interests of the country, i.e. Nato and European cooperation. The transatlantic ties, especially with the US, became a major pillar of Dutch foreign policy, in spite of American support for Indonesian independence. Atlanticism, however, was to be combined with a strong pro-European stand.

In the Dutch view, European cooperation would bring about a supranational, federal state in Europe. These 'United States of Europe' (USE) should be open to the outside world – maintaining the world trading network has always been a major national interest of the Netherlands – and within this USE a small country like the Netherlands would benefit from the 'levelling off' effect (i.e. in European policy-making the power of larger members would be equalized, neutralized and reduced) and from the equal rights of all member states. This view, as time went by, has not been able to stand the full test of hard political reality, but it served as a doctrine justifying Dutch missionary activism in the development of European cooperation.

Aside from this, there were other motives behind Dutch pro-Europeanism. During the war years, resistance groups had become disillusioned with pre-war national politics and demanded radical innovations after the war, including the construction of a new Europe. The administration of American aid required European collaboration, and after the initial success of the European Coal and Steel Community (ECSC) there was a bandwagon effect drawing more and more economic groups and sectors into the process. Agriculture, for example, was afraid to 'miss the boat' after industry had joined. There was also a clear interest for the Dutch economy as a whole in the unification and expansion of the European market. Thus, without serious opposition, the Dutch government could embark upon a strongly supranational European policy.

The EC decision-making cycle and the participation of national institutions

The data
By analysing the network of interlevel official contact one can dis-

cover how the agenda of European policy develops; if, on the whole, an EC-wide system of increasingly coordinated and integrated policies develops; or if policies are fragmented, re-nationalized or even disintegrating. To understand a developing system of cooperative states, interlevel interaction and interlevel learning among public office-holders centred around the EC institutions offers a vital line of research. The remainder of this chapter will try to shed some light on this interaction, as far as the Netherlands are concerned.

As can be expected in research about the 'black box of government', there are limits to the information that can be obtained, both in quantity and quality. The mass media focus on 'hot' political issues or personalities – interlevel official interaction does not make attractive reading or listening. Still, sometimes, as a by-product of EC media events, information transpires about interaction, coordination – or the lack of it – among public officials, i.e. politicians or bureaucrats. From the specialized media about the EC, or journals for public administration, one will get more information and a better view of EC-related interaction. Even then, however, the quality of the information is limited: impressions and opinions abound, formal procedure is sometimes presented as reality. In general, it is very difficult to check the reliability of data and to distinguish facts from values.

Solid political science research on Dutch behaviour in the EC is very scarce: only a handful of publications have come out.[2] The best research, moreover, recognizes its limits for generalizations – the most solid basis is also a small one, at present. Therefore, in the following paragraphs on the Dutch role in the EC system of cooperative states one will find not only hard facts but also impressions and (informed) opinions. We will, first, look at government institutions and their involvement in 'Europe'. Political parties, interest groups and the public at large will be presented after that.

National administration

Since the EEC treaties were signed by the national government of the Netherlands, the national ministries were the first to become involved in the EC policy process. During the early years of European cooperation, the major participants and rivals were the ministries of Foreign Affairs and Economic Affairs. In the handling of the post-war Marshall Aid, but also in the ECSC negotiations, the Ministry of Eco-

---

[2] See bibliography at the end of this chapter.

nomic Affairs took the lead through its directorate-general of Foreign
Economic Relations and a special Task Force. This Task Force, however, was transferred to the Ministry of Foreign Affairs after the
phasing-out of Marshall Aid. Political and administrative dominance
moved away from Economic Affairs. In order to deal with tensions
between the ministries, a Coordinating Committee for European
Cooperation (CoCo) was established in 1956. This committee of civil
servants, chaired by a minister (or under-minister), still plays a central role in the present EU policy coordination structure. Because of
its administrative character, and because of the inability of the Dutch
Council of Ministers to make clear-cut decisions, the tensions
between the two ministries simmered on.

In 1963, a ministerial council ('*Raad voor Europese Zaken – REZ*')
was established at the highest political level. The chairman and the
deputy chairman of CoCo were members of this REZ, as well as other
ministers involved in EC policies. The number of participants in this
political coordination body increased through the years: in 1987, nine
ministers and two under-ministers were members (Foreign Affairs,
Economic Affairs, Finance, Transport and Water, Agriculture and
Fisheries, Social Affairs, Housing and Environment, and Health and
Wellbeing). Coordinating powers in EC matters were allocated in
1972: the Minister of Foreign Affairs became coordinating minister at
the political level (REZ), the Under-Minister of Foreign Affairs
became chairman of CoCo. This structure is still operative and valid
at present, albeit with one proviso. Since the European summits
became more and more important, the Prime Minister and his (small)
Ministry of General Affairs entered the scene, especially under Prime
Minister Lubbers who developed a strong interest in European affairs.
The coordinating structure did not change, but some public confrontations between the Minister of Foreign Affairs and the Prime
Minister on EC matters occurred in the late 1980s.

Which procedures are followed between the Dutch CoCo and
REZ, on the one hand, and the EC policy-making institutions, on the
other hand? In order to prepare decision-making in the EC Council
of Ministers, the Council working groups – permanent or *ad hoc* –
and COREPER play a crucial role. Here, a member state may introduce amendments to Commission proposals.

The procedure for these policy-preparing discussions from The
Hague is different for four categories of proposals. In case a single
ministry is involved, a distinction is made between technical and non-

technical proposals. Technical proposals are presented in the Council working groups in Brussels by an expert from the ministry concerned; non-technical proposals will always be presented by a member of the Dutch Permanent Representation. If more ministries are involved in a proposal, the same distinction is made. Technical proposals are coordinated in The Hague, either by formal or by informal consultation, and the experts from the ministries will dominate the Dutch delegation/presentation. Non-technical proposals are coordinated in The Hague by the Ministry of Foreign Affairs (directorate-general European Integration). It gives its instructions to the Permanent Representation, whose members will conduct the negotiations in the Council working groups. The Permanent Representation in Brussels, meanwhile, has developed from a classical embassy into a sizeable administrative coordinating unit.[3] Hosted and supervised by the Ministry of Foreign Affairs, it consists of the official representatives of every ministry except Defence. Each ministry has at least two officers in the Permanent Representation, except Interior and Justice (only one officer), so that coordination can take place at all times.

The next step in the process, i.e. the preparation of the actual Council meetings, involves COREPER. One day before COREPER meets in Brussels, interministerial coordination takes place at, and is chaired by, the Ministry of Foreign Affairs, either in The Hague or at the Permanent Representation in Brussels. These weekly 'instruction meetings' are attended by standing representatives from the ministries of Agriculture, Economic Affairs and Finance, and by specific other ministries, depending on the issues. The most involved ministry will present a draft instruction; if no agreement is reached, issues are left to the discretion of the Permanent Representative. Proposals on which agreement has been reached in a working group will not be substantially discussed in COREPER. Proposals on which COREPER has reached agreement will not be discussed in the Council. For items to be discussed substantially in the Council, the Dutch Council of Ministers prepares and coordinates the Dutch position; CoCo serves to prepare these (weekly) meetings, again under the direction of the Ministry of Foreign Affairs. It is said that this close linkage of the political and the administrative preparation explains the success of Dutch EC policy coordination.

---

[3] Similar developments took place in the permanent representations of the other member states. The Dutch Permanent Representation is among the smaller ones in Brussels.

How do the representatives of the Dutch national government operate in the web of policy bodies and procedures? First of all, due to the increasing specialization both in The Hague and in Brussels and the multitude of contacts by telephone, fax, train etc., deviations from this procedure occur, especially at the lower levels within the ministries. There is hierarchy, but also fragmentation. The ministries traditionally most involved in EC affairs, i.e. Foreign Affairs, Agriculture, Economic Affairs and Finance, play a more direct and active role in the process than the other ministries. Secondly, in the various coordination bodies, there is a strong desire for consensus – taking a vote on an issue is extremely rare. Thirdly, a very important role in coordinating EC policy is played by administrative units of a hierarchically junior rank in the ministries. This makes for very attractive work for junior civil servants. In the actual negotiations in Brussels, however, the political level (ministers) clearly dominates. For the Dutch national contacts with Brussels in general, time pressure – the Council meeting every week, dealing with a large number of items – is strong. The small size of the Dutch national administration, its consensus orientation and lack of clear-cut authority, makes for a 'team spirit' among the group of civil servants travelling to Brussels every week.

Dutch EC policy participation is a process where time constraints placed on the actors have led to a complete integration of both policy coordination and negotiation into a single collective decision-making process. Those who are politically responsible focus on resolving conflicts which their civil servants were not able or allowed to solve at lower levels. The civil servants play a dominant role in policy coordination, and a substantial role in the negotiation of relatively less important issues. Only in the negotiation of important issues does the political level come in strongly.

It should be noted, though, that the Hague–Brussels interaction works two ways. Not only do national politicians/civil servants influence the EC, they are also influenced strongly by the results of EC negotiations, which are a major input for Dutch EC policies. Another characteristic of this interaction is its lack of attention to overall issues. It is, often quite literally, a fight against the clock by a small group trying to keep up with a large number of mainly technical and limited issues. The expansion of EU activities will require more attention to overall and long-term consequences for the Dutch governmental system. New structures or task forces will be needed.[4]

The implementation of EC policies

The Dutch government has always been actively pro-EC. From the 1950s onward, Dutch politicians took initiatives for European integration and in international discussions they were more strongly, and more consistently, in favour of supranationalism than many other countries. One might expect, therefore, that Dutch implementation of EC legislation leaves little or nothing to be desired. Nevertheless, it is interesting to check some facts, focusing on EC directives.[5]

Since the early years of the EC, some 1,500 directives have been made, and the Netherlands have been sued in the European Court of Justice about twenty times. In nine cases, the Court verdict ruled against the Dutch government. At the end of 1993, some five cases were still *sub judice*. One recent case in 1991 concerned the legislation of electro-medical equipment, where the EC directives should have been implemented in 1986. If one looks at the three major steps of non-implementation of directives, i.e. violation of deadline for implementation, starting an infringement procedure by the Commission, and Court verdict, the first form prevails in the Dutch case. From scattered information, it becomes clear that this problem already existed in the 1970s: in 1978 the deadline of 1 January 1978 for 138 directives created between 1973 and 1975 was violated in sixty cases, i.e. more than 40%. On 30 September 1991, the number of violations of deadlines was seventy-nine; for some directives the deadline for implementation had passed nine or ten years previously. On 30 September 1993, sixty-eight cases had passed the deadline (1992: sixty-nine). Infringement procedures were started in fifty cases in 1991, in fifty-two cases in 1992 and fifty-one in 1993. Figures for earlier years (e.g. seventeen in 1989) suggest that the European Commission has taken much more action in the last few years.

What are the reasons for this considerable backlog in implementation and in information about it? One problem is the lack of coordi-

[4] See J. M. M. van den Bos, *Dutch EC Policy-Making. A Model-Guided Approach to Coordination and Negotiation* (Utrecht-Amsterdam, 1991).

[5] See A. F. Kellermann and J. A. Winter, 'The Netherlands', in J. Schwarze (ed.), *The 1992 Challenge at the National Level – A Community-wide Joint Research Project on the Realization and Implementation by National Governments and Business of the Internal Market Programme* (Baden-Baden, 1990), pp. 523–55.

nated supervision. For EC policy formation there is CoCo and REZ, but there is no competent body in the Dutch system to supervise and monitor its implementation. The Ministry of Foreign Affairs is responsible for reporting to the Commission about the implementation of EC directives, and the necessary information is provided by the individual ministries. Foreign Affairs depends on their willingness and ability to provide it. In case of non-implementation, this willingness may very well be limited. Apart from these reports, therefore, MPs have asked specific ministries for information about EC directive implementation. Also, in 1990 the government established an inter-departmental working group to investigate this problem under the responsibility of the Ministry of Justice (Commission for the Monitoring of Legislative Projects). This working group presented its conclusions in that same year.

The major cause of the backlog is the nature of the Dutch legislative process. Legislation of an implementative nature, elaborating specifics for practical use rather than giving broad principles and guidelines, has a low priority in the first place. Much time, and little attention is given to it. However, once it is taken up, there is a strong tendency to perfectionism: the adaptation of Dutch legislation is not limited strictly to the requirements of the EC directive, but other related problems are also put under scrutiny. Many advisory bodies are included in the consultation process, questions of responsibility – which ministry is in charge? – are avoided or taken up too late, and one is insufficiently aware of the urgency and necessity of implementation. In short, an EC directive is put into an extensive, cumbersome and thorough consultative machinery, which takes much more time than the Commission allows. This machinery involves not only the ministries or local/provincial administrations, but also numerous private associations representing social, economic or professional interests, recognized as official discussion partners by the ministries through official advisory or consultative bodies (in the case of agriculture, their status is based on law). Not only are these organizations consulted about all changes of government regulations relevant for their members, they also have their own internal rules which are to be adapted to new EC directives.

Only after all this has been accomplished will a ministry, through the Ministry of Foreign Affairs, report to the Commission that implementation has taken place. Table 7.1 shows some recent figures. It is striking that not only Agriculture and Economic Affairs appear on this list, but also some 'less central' ministries in the field of EC policy-making like Housing and Environment, and Health and Well-being.

Table 7.1 Non-implementation of EC directives by various Dutch ministries (situation at 30 Sept. 1994).

Ministry	Deadline passed	Infringement procedure	Court case, verdict
Agriculture	9	6	0
Housing, Environment	1	1	0
Health, Welfare	13	11	0
Social Affairs	1	1	0
Transport, Water	7	3	0
Economic Affairs	1	0	0
Finance	0	0	0
Justice	1	0	0
Education	1	1	0
Interior	0	0	0
Various ministries	3	2	0
Total	37	25	0

Source: Handelingen der Tweede Kame, rergaderjaar 1994–1995, 21.109, nr. 78 (Proceedings of Parliament).

The Dutch government in 1991 declared its intention to catch up with the implementation backlog by simplifying and speeding up the legislative process in EC affairs. It wants to prepare implementing measures in an earlier phase, it will involve advisory bodies in the adaptation discussion much less often, it wants to speed up parliamentary procedure and it will look for opportunities to delegate the implementation of EC directives.

It is not very clear what this latter idea would imply. One could think of specific and specialized task forces, inside or outside government, specifically in charge of Dutch legislative adaptation for 'Brussels'. It remains to be seen how soon these intentions will show results. Looking more specifically at the 'race for 1993', i.e. the implementation of the 282 measures from the European White Paper, it is somewhat embarrassing to see the weak performance of the Netherlands, at least by the end of 1991. Out of the 126 measures which should have been implemented before 31 May 1991, thirty-four had not been implemented by the end of that year. Within the EC, this put the Netherlands in eighth place. Since then, some 380 EC directives have been implemented (1991:90, 1992:149, 1993:141) by the Netherlands government. Although this figure does not specify the White Paper measures, one can assume that the Dutch score in this respect has improved.

As far as possible sanctions for non-implementation of EC law are concerned, Dutch opinion seems quite positive about the need for them. At least, expert lawyers have expressed themselves quite strongly in favour. There is an embarrassing contrast between the overall pro-EC stand of the Netherlands and the specific interests represented by its ministries, e.g. Ministry of Agriculture, Ministry of Economic Affairs and Ministry of Finance. A problem related to sanctions, of course, is who is to administer them? Self-punishment by national governments seems masochistic rather than realistic. Therefore, a withholding of payments from community funds, or a reduction of votes in the Council might be most effective.[6]

The national parliament

In comparison with the national administration, the interaction between the Dutch parliament, especially the Second Chamber, and the EC institutions is much more limited. Not only does the European Parliament often feel left out of the policy-making process, the Dutch parliament is also often confronted with *faits accomplis* in legislation due to EC rules. Sometimes, informal contacts within a 'policy community' like agriculture, where members of parliament, interest group representatives and civil servants at various levels interact frequently, will compensate for the lack of formal contact.[7] In general, however, members of parliament feel very handicapped in EC affairs. Not only the plenary meetings of the Second Chamber, but also its Standing Committee on Foreign Affairs/European Affairs are informed only afterwards, rather than consulted before EC policy decisions are made.

Parliament's feelings about decision-making in Brussels were aptly formulated by a Member of Parliament (MP) saying that 'European democracy is suffocated by civil servants from The Hague colluding with their colleagues from the other member states in Brussels, e.g.

[6] See A. E. Kellermann, 'The Netherlands in face of its Community obligations', *Common Market Law Review*, 20 (August 1983), pp. 297–333.

[7] See Ben J. S. Hoetjes, 'Nederlandse landbouwbeleid in West-Europa – schakels en problemen tussen internationale politiek en Nederlandse agrari ërs', *Internationale Spectator*, 14 (February 1989), pp. 99–106.

in Council working groups, rather than by the Commission's bureaucracy.' A current, and related, discussion concerns the 'double mandate' allowing a national MP to be a European MP at the same time.
It is argued that, before the introduction of the direct elections to the
European Parliament in 1979, links between the national and the
European parliaments were stronger, since European MPs were
recruited from, and combined with, national parliament membership.
Membership in the European Parliament was not considered to be a
full-time job. At present, indeed, Dutch EP members spend considerable time in The Hague with their national colleagues and party constituencies. Now that the Dutch parliament wants to streamline its
meetings, it is felt that reintroducing the double mandate could contribute to a more efficient use of resources and could formally
strengthen the links between the national and European Parliaments.

On the other hand, if this would imply a complete return to the
pre-1979 situation, doing away with the direct EP elections, distance
between the EP and the Dutch citizens would increase, and democracy would suffer. Even if the direct EP elections remain – which is
likely, because of their support in other member states – the double
mandate would probably renationalize the European Parliament's
election campaign. Thus, the EP elections might draw a higher voter
turnout, but would become less European. On balance, democracy
might win, but Europe might lose.

In the mid-1980s, especially after the Single Europe Act, the Dutch
parliament showed a growing interest in EC affairs. In 1986, a Permanent Committee of the Second Chamber for EC affairs was
installed. It consists of twenty-seven members from all political parties (the Dutch Second Chamber has 150 members in total). Aside
from this, the government annual reports on the EC were changed
into specific reports on the implementation of EC law from 1981
onwards. Since 1989, government submits a quarterly report on the
implementation of EC directives to parliament, specified by ministry,
as well as a half-yearly report on the progress of European cooperation. Also, there have been more *ad-hoc* debates on European integration in the 1980s than before.[8]

The Dutch parliament has shown a clear interest in the EC substantially in favour of the 'all-EC perspective', i.e. the bulk of parliament argues in terms of European rather than Dutch national

[8] See Kellermann and Winter, *op. cit.*

interests. However, as long as it sees a 'democratic deficit' at the EC level, it is unwilling to diminish any of its powers *vis-à-vis* the government. The recent discussions about the streamlining of the legislative procedures, speeding up the legislative process and reducing consultation procedures for draft legislation, made it clear that the Second Chamber takes '*je maintiendrai*' ('I will maintain my rights', i.e. the motto of the House of Orange) as its guiding line. A government proposal for a Decree Law enabling speedy implementation by short-cutting parliament was fiercely resisted. In the view of most Dutch MPs, their lack of influence in EC policy-making should not be compensated by giving more powers to the national parliament, but by strengthening the position of the European Parliament in the EC policy process. Only among small right-wing groups is a full renationalization of EC policies desired.

Provincial and local administration

The consequences of the EC treaties for provincial and local government had silently been ignored for a long time. After the SEA, however, the EC entered the sub-national scene. The old discussion about the reorganization of local and provincial government, which had been dragging on for years, was suddenly put into the perspective of European integration. Would the existing division of the country into 12 provinces and 700 municipalities, cooperating through voluntary agreements, stand competition with the other EC member states? Would Dutch sub-national government be able to operate at the European level, competing successfully for resources, investments etc.? The interest in 'Brussels' had more to do with the old discussion, however, than with Europe as such. Also, the SEA coincided with a general policy of decentralization by the Dutch national government, which revived local and provincial demands for power in more and more fields of policy.

The EC treaties did not affect the internal legal order in the Netherlands in a direct and formal sense. In this decentralized unitary state, the central government was the exclusive partner in EC policy. The autonomous powers of the provinces and municipalities were entrenched in law, but in practice were severely limited by their financial dependence on the centre. Indirectly, however, as time went by, more and more EC legislation came to affect Dutch sub-national government: in 1989, it was estimated that 15% of all Dutch legislation and regulation originated from Brussels. Binding EC legislation (regulations, directives, decisions) especially in the fields of environment policy, social security, health, veterinary/plant diseases had direct consequences for local and provincial authorities in charge of these fields. Also, the principles of non-discrimination and free movement of goods and services have to be obeyed by local government, e.g. inviting tenders and awarding public contracts. Moreover, the principle of EC loyalty requires that any government, including local or provincial, will abstain from any activity which might endanger the implementation of the EC treaties. The widespread neglect of EC-wide public tendering for projects above 1 million ECU by the Dutch local authorities is, therefore, all the more embarrassing. Next, there are the EC facilities, or subsidies, which are highly relevant for sub-national administrations. The structural funds (ERDF, ESF, EAGGF), and the EC funds for cross-border cooperation (Interreg) could facilitate local policies. Especially the border municipalities and regions Netherlands–Belgium and Netherlands–Germany have benefited from this. The old industrial areas in the east (Twente) and the southeast (South Limburg) as well as the rural regions in the northeast (Oost-Groningen) received considerable financial support from the structural funds.

There is also a national dimension to this. Now that central financial support is diminishing, EC funds are very attractive for the subnational administrations. It enables them to avoid raising local taxes, which would be very unpopular, or a cut-throat competition between rich and poor municipalities and provinces. Especially the provinces, which have been indicated as 'Basic Administrative Units' on the EC administrative map, hope to increase their resources and to strengthen their relative power *vis-à-vis* the national government and the municipalities.

After the SEA, there was the Schengen Treaty abolishing border controls and creating common policy arrangements. Although the EC as such was not involved and treaty coverage was smaller than the whole EC territory, for Dutch police authorities it opened the eyes for the European dimension of public order and the fight against crime. Crime has become a transnational problem. Police power, in the Netherlands, is in the hands of the Ministries of Justice and Interior, and, via the latter ministry, of municipal authorities. The mayor, in every municipality, is in charge of public order, police and security. In the larger cities (above 50,000) the police apparatus is municipal; smaller municipalities are served by the national police. Presently, the police service is in the process of reorganization, creating some 25 'police regions' and merging municipal and national police organizations. The Maastricht Treaty further strengthened European awareness in police circles, adding the fields of justice, police and public order to the policy concerns of the EC institutions. The Dutch sub-national level reacted to these recent developments by means of information, discussion, research, legislation, lobbying and representation. After the SEA, a publicity campaign was started. The Association of Dutch Municipalities, the Interprovincial Consultation Agency and the Ministry of the Interior established a Common Information Point in 1990, putting all relevant information about EC policies (application procedures, requirements, conditions etc.) at the disposal of sub-national administrations. Within the ministry, a permanent unit for European affairs was established.

Then, the discussion about the viability of the Dutch municipalities and provinces was renewed. A report on Dutch metropolitan policy ('Montijn Report')[9] argued that the present system is a handicap in the European context, and the three Randstad provinces Noordholland, Zuidholland and Utrecht initiated a study about a merger into a Randstad Metropolitan Region. There were two striking elements in this discussion: firstly, its focus on administrative effectiveness and competitiveness, neglecting political legitimacy, democracy and citizens' views; secondly, its clear preference for an increase in scale. 'Big is beautiful' seems to be the slogan of the day. Therefore, the local level is likely to become the victim of future reorganizations.

In March 1993, new legislation was presented to parliament (the 'Kaderwet Bestuur in Verandering') which will create some 25 regions as a new politico-administrative level between the municipalities and the provinces. This law, in force since 1 January 1994, will first be implemented in the urban areas: seven urban regions (in Amsterdam, Rotterdam, The Hague, Utrecht, Eindhoven-Helmond, Arnhem-Nijmegen and Enschede-Hengelo) will be established, and the rest of the country may follow later. The powers of the regions, as well as their personnel, are to be taken away from the municipalities and, to a lesser extent, from the provinces. The consequences for EC-related activities are still not quite clear, and implementation of this law is lagging behind.

During the 1980s there has been increasing lobbying from Dutch

[9] Externe Commissie Grote Steden ('Commissie – Montijn'), *Grote Steden, grote hansen* (Den Haag: 1989).

sub-national administrations in Brussels. The provinces and munici-palities on the periphery of the country, especially the north and east, had the advantage of being there first and knowing their way around in Brussels, but the others caught up quickly. Generally speaking, how-ever, this lobbying developed in a very haphazard manner. Provinces, municipalities etc. found it very easy to send a representative to Brus-sels or to use the services of EC consultants. They worked individually or by means of *ad hoc* 'combines' without much central guidance or coordination from the national level, and there was great optimism about the possibilities and resources to be obtained from the EC. After some sobering experiences, the 'Association of Dutch Municipalities' decided to station a representative in Brussels in order to promote the interests of all Dutch municipalities, and the Ministry of the Interior appointed a representative in the Dutch Permanent Representation in Brussels in 1991. This representative operates on an equal footing with the other members of the Permanent Representation and has the task of keeping an eye on all EC policies concerning his ministry (police, public order, security, minorities, local and provincial administration). On the whole, however, it can be said that the interaction of the Dutch sub-national level with the EC institutions is not yet in order. As an eager latecomer, it went through a period of over-enthusiasm followed by serious attempts to get itself organized in order to establish a solid and realistic working relationship with 'Brussels'.

The courts of justice
Although the courts are not considered as direct actors in the politi-cal process in general, and in European integration in particular, the actions of Dutch courts have a clear indirect impact upon EC law and, in their turn, are guided by existing EC law, acting as implementing and enforcing agencies. Since implementation and enforcement of EC law were discussed above, here we can mention, first, a major court case from the Netherlands influencing EC law, i.e. the Van Gend & Loos *v.* Dutch Tax Administration case from 1963. On the basis of a dispute about the rate of customs excise due by a firm for the import of a specific chemical product, it was established by the European Court of Justice (ECJ), after previous rulings by Dutch courts, that the EC treaties do create a direct legal effect within a member state and create individual rights which national courts must protect.[10]

[10] Case 26/62, Van Gend en Loos *v.* Nederlandse Administratie der Belastingen [1963] ECR 1, pp. 1–30.

Secondly, the Dutch courts frequently make requests to the ECJ for preliminary rulings, in order to incorporate EC law into Dutch jurisprudence. Between 1950 and 1989, there were 152 references from the ECJ to requests from Dutch courts. Only Germany has made more requests. In general, there is very active litigation from the Netherlands towards the ECJ. Most of the requests came from administrative courts (105, forty-five from ordinary courts and two from special courts or tribunals). In 80% of the cases, the Dutch courts took the ruling of the ECJ into account, and in 72% of the cases there was strict conformity. Most Dutch courts found the ruling of the ECJ helpful, and there were no special difficulties created for the ECJ by requests/references related to Dutch courts. The majority of the Dutch requests were from courts of last instance, and only a minority from other courts of appeal. In terms of topics, the Dutch cases were distributed over a wide variety of fields, similar to other member states. In general, it seems that the Dutch requests for pre-liminary rulings do not deviate from the average EC pattern.[11]

Public opinion, political parties and interest groups

Public opinion
There is little debate about European integration in the Netherlands. EC membership is not among the priorities in the Dutch political debate. There is more discussion about immigration, developments in Germany and Eastern Europe, fraud, taxes and the social security system, or even South Africa, than about the developments in the EC/EU. Sometimes attention flares up, e.g. when the Dutch Commissioner is succeeded or when there are rumours about the Dutch Prime Minister becoming President of the European Commission. Personalized stories rather than policy problems attract attention in the present post-ideology era. Still, there were, and are, arguments in favour or against the EC/EU appealing to the Dutch public at large and to specific groups in particular. Most reasons why the Nether-lands joined the EC have maintained their validity, new reasons have been added, but some 'second thoughts' have also come up.

In favour of the EC/EU is the Dutch curiosity and openness towards foreign countries, culture, people and travel. There is a strong inter-

---

[11] See J. Korte et al. (eds)., *Primus inter pares. Report on courts in the Netherlands* (The Hague, 1989).

est in things from abroad, and a certain underestimation of domestic products, traditions or even the language. Lifestyle, advertisements, fashion trends all emphasize the desire to be cosmopolitan rather than local. Dutch proverbs like 'what comes from far away, is better' reinforce this tendency. The Dutch self-image implies a strong outward orientation, as well as a tolerance for 'strange' cultures and hospitality towards foreigners. Whether this self-image corresponds with actual behaviour, e.g. *vis-à-vis* immigrants and refugees, is a different question. Secondly, there is a strong awareness in the Netherlands, that openness to the outside world is vital for the country's economic health and survival. From the late Middle Ages, the country has been involved in a worldwide economic network, which has become the basis of its existence. Cutting off external contacts never appealed to Dutch elites or the citizenry at large. When the country remained neutral in world politics, e.g. during the First World War, this served to maintain and increase external trade contacts and not to restrict them. Recently, e.g. during the Gulf War, the Dutch dicta 'trade ignores boundaries' and 'money never stinks' were again illustrated, sometimes in a rather embarrassing way. International economic contacts have a high priority, political loyalties or divisions play second fiddle. The establishment of the EEC in the 1950s, therefore, could count on a strong Dutch support.

This very argument, however, also puts certain constraints on Dutch enthusiasm about the EC. Historically, the Dutch international trading network has been worldwide and maritime rather than continental. Like the British, the Dutch have always been more interested in free world trade and transport than in the formation of economic blocks on the continent. In the 1950s, therefore, there was strong ambivalence in commerce as well as agriculture about joining the EEC. Membership was only acceptable if it would not endanger trade relations outside Europe. In discussions within the EC, the Dutch – and the British – position has always been in favour of free trade, both internally and externally. Protection, e.g. for agriculture, was accepted rather than promoted. The GATT negotiations with the USA and Japan put the Dutch in a rather awkward position within the EC. Even the Dutch farmers' protest against the 1993 GATT outcome was tactical rather than strategic. This worldwide orientation might also explain the limited interest in European integration among social scientists; interest in Third World affairs, for example, developed much earlier and stronger.

In the discussion about the pros and cons of EC/EU membership, however, some concern has developed, especially after the EC/EU demonstrated itself not only in name, but also in policy actions. Not only was the government in some cases unpleasantly surprised to find its hands tied by European regulations, e.g. concerning wages and labour conditions, but especially after the Single European Act it dawned upon the Dutch, that the EC would move into some areas of policy where the Dutch system of consociational democracy had created strong vested interests which might not stand free European competition. The broadcasting system, giving privileges to religion- or ideology-based corporations, and strictly regulating commercial influences, is a major example. Related to this, language became an issue, especially in higher education, where 'Europeanization' has made great progress. As a backlash to internationalization, the Minister of Education, Ritzen, in 1990 declared Dutch to be the only language of regular instruction in universities. Exceptions to this rule abound, and legislation will remain largely symbolic, but the political gesture, by itself, was revealing. Especially among the Protestant groups, where national identity and nationalism is relatively strong, the following question came up: will it be possible to have public office-holders, e.g. mayors or aldermen, of non-Dutch background? Will the Dutch language become a second-choice language for elite communication in the Netherlands? What will become of the monarchy? What of the 'consociational' educational system? The elaborate system of social security? Will EC harmonization imply a reduction towards the lowest common denominator? For agriculture in the Netherlands, the balance of costs and benefits of EC membership is turning: from a net beneficiary, it has become a net contributor to the EC/EU. Therefore, in the Dutch farming community doubts about the EC/EU are rising, and since this group partially overlaps with the Protestant community, commitment to the EC/EU may be weakened in the years to come. More and more groups have become aware that European integration implies not only opening up foreign countries for Dutch enterprise, but also opening up the Netherlands for foreign influences which are more than just economic. By way of a belated response, feelings of ambivalence and reluctance are growing. The EC/EU is no longer a cause advocated by a 'small island of Europeanists' in a sea of tacit agreement or indifference. A real debate has finally started.

Looking at public opinion in the Netherlands in general, however, one should not overestimate this debate about Europe. Even though media culture is very much internationalized, the political discussions in the media and its topics are very much domestic, or even local. Local and regional radio stations are increasingly popular. The Dutch national elite is the top news item for the media, and international affairs, including the EC/EU, are put in that perspective. International news is important, in order to be 'in touch with the world', but in political terms the formula of 'Dutch solutions to Dutch problems' is carefully maintained. Not only among the political parties, but also among the media, Dutch society, as the base of existence, is not called into question.

As can be expected from the stand taken by the political parties, the EC/EU is not a first-rank item of interest for the citizens. Comparative public opinion surveys during the last three decades show a moderate interest among citizens in EC affairs. Now and then it is in the focus of public attention, but often it is forgotten altogether. Because of the rather low level of permanent interest, short-term changes in public attention for the EC/EU occur relatively easily.[12] Still, non-instrumental support for the EC/EU, i.e. goodwill for the EC/EU without reference to other goals, has been quite high in the Netherlands throughout the years. In the 1960s, only 5–10% of the population opposed EEC membership, and 70–80% was clearly in favour. In the 1970s and 1980s, this did not change: most Dutch people are quite positive about the EC, and there is little concern about the loss of sovereignty. In instrumental terms, a large majority (more than two-thirds and growing) of Dutch citizens thinks that EC membership has more advantages than disadvantages, and helps to solve problems. Development assistance to the Third World, environment, and even defence and unemployment, people think will be handled best at the European level. Compared to other member states, Dutch public opinion during the last two decades has been very positive about the EC/EU, even though its interest is not high and its support not unconditional. An analysis of Dutch opinion makes clear that support for the EC/EU is not clearly related to age, sex, socio-economic status or occupation. In terms of political allegiance voters for all the four larger parties (Labour (PvdA), Christian Democrats (CDA), Liberal-Left (D'66) and Liberal-Right (VVD)) are

---

[12] See J. F. H. Jansen, 'Een Nederlands "nee" tegen "Maastricht"?', *Bestuurskunde*, 7 (1992), pp. 352–66.

in favour of the EC/EU; only among the rightist voters (orthodox Protestants, centre-democrats) and in the Green Left there is clear opposition to the EC/EU. The behaviour of Dutch voters in the elections for the European Parliament bears out these characteristics. Party choice in the EP elections follows national trends and patterns, but turnout is very low. For national parliament's elections some 80% of the voters turn out, but for the EP elections in 1979 58.1% showed up, in 1984 50.6%, in 1989 47.2% and in 1994 only 35.6%. From a viewpoint of democratic support, there is reason for considerable concern.

Political parties

The larger political parties, i.e. Christian Democrats, socialists, rightist liberals and leftist liberals, in principle were (and still are) all positively committed to the EC/EU and during the last decades they have all actively contributed to its growth. However, there have been limits to this. First of all, the EC was a tacit 'second-order' commitment rather than an outspoken, clear and high priority in public political discussion. Because central issues were domestic, and because EC issues were complicated, technical, far away from the voters, but broadly considered 'a good cause', much room for manoeuvre was available for the Dutch representatives in the EC to make it develop and grow. The EC could prosper in the shadow of other political priorities. Secondly, if one looks more closely at recent political discussions, the 'approaching of Europe' has created considerable confusion among Dutch political parties. In the 'language in education' issue, for example, a socialist minister of education took a strangely nationalist stand.

Among the rightist liberals there was resistance against the Maastricht Treaty. This was all the more remarkable, because the European MPs from this party were among the strongest fighters for Maastricht and the strengthening of the European Parliament. In Christian Democrat circles, especially among the Protestants, the issue of culture, identity and religion does create some ambivalence towards 'Catholic' Europe, but the most outspoken resistance against the EC/EU is found among the smaller parties on the right, i.e. the orthodox Protestant SGP (Staatkundig Gereformeerde Partij), the GPV (Gereformeerd Politiek Verbond), and the extreme rightist 'Centre Democrats'. The national symbol of the country, i.e. the present Queen, ironically, is quite positively interested in European integration.

The major background of mixed feelings about the EC/EU in the Dutch political parties is the immigration/minorities issue. The influx of refugees and immigrants especially from the Mediterranean has continued for the last thirty years. It was handled by a number of well-meant but inadequate policy responses and its recent increase combined with the economic recession brought an accumulation of negative consequences, e.g. anti-immigrant feelings among large sections of the Dutch population, especially the lower and the lower middle class. For electoral reasons these feelings can no longer be ignored, especially by the socialist party, which has lost its ideological foothold after the downfall of communism in Eastern Europe and which is in need of new electoral appeal. Christian Democratic commitment to the EC/EU has not really been affected. Its investment in the EC has been so large and so long-established that a serious deviation from the EC/EU-road would run counter to established party interest. Rightist-liberal (VVD) criticism of the EC/EU looks more tactical – depending on its status of opposition or ruling party – than strategic. Within the rightist liberal party, however, there are several currents. The business group is strongly international in its outlook, but the populist group could appeal to nationalist, anti-foreign sentiments among the voters. The leftist liberals (D'66), in spite of their long-time role as an opposition party, have been remarkably consistent in their pro-EC/EU stand. Their strength in parliament and government increased considerably in the 1993 elections. They joined a new government and their leader became Minister of Foreign Affairs. This could give a strong positive impetus to Dutch support for European integration.

Interest groups

Although no systematic data are available, some observations can be made on the development of Dutch interest group orientation towards the EC/EU. From the early EEC days onwards, Dutch business, industry as well as agriculture, has always been in close touch with EC policy-making. Through their European umbrella associations their views were put into the policy process, via ECOSOC, the Commission or the Council. In the field of agriculture, especially, a policy community could develop, where representatives of the Ministry of Agriculture, the farmers' associations, and DG VI frequently and intensively interacted along formal as well as informal lines. Industries also operated through ECOSOC. Trade unions, consumer organizations and environmental groups came later, but basically followed the same pattern.

What is new in recent years is: (a) the considerable increase in interest group activity from the Netherlands in the EC/EU; (b) the activities of small businesses and local authorities; (c) the shifting of the focus towards the European Parliament. 'Lobbying', which traditionally had a rather negative connotation in the Netherlands, seems to have lost its taboo. In the competitive, individualist culture of the late 1980s, it is openly advocated as important and useful. More and more groups or organizations turn to 'Brussels', sometimes using their own officials but, more often, using the services of the numerous 'EC consultancy agencies' in Brussels. New groups which previously felt no need to promote their interest in the EC/EU institutional network are presenting themselves. The establishment of DG XXIII, which until 1989 was part of DG III as the 'Task Force Small and Medium-size Enterprises', in a way provoked this increasing interest by offering a special channel for small businesses and their representatives. The Single European Act which was co-initiated and strongly supported by large Dutch firms like Philips had a similar effect on local and regional authorities in the Netherlands, as we have seen above.

The shifting focus of interest group activity towards the European Parliament was caused, on the one hand, by an unfounded optimism about the increasing powers of the European Parliament, and on the other hand by the ability of the European Parliament to be decisive in new fields of EC policy. In the financial crisis of the EC in the early 1980s, it became clear that established policy fields like agriculture were a dead-end street, and that new policy areas and initiatives were needed. The European Parliament would be the strongest supporter of this. The European Parliament itself, initially, welcomed this attention from the world of lobbying as a recognition of its importance. Soon, however, some second thoughts came up, because lobbying took chaotic and sometimes undesirable forms. A register, official recognition and a code of conduct for lobbyists were demanded by Dutch MEPs.

Conclusion

Concepts
From the previous pages, it has become clear that several concepts

from the Netherlands could contribute to a framework for the analysis of the European Union. The cornerstone for this analysis is the notion of 'political integration': the process of reorientation of loyalties, expectations and actions by political actors from various (national) systems towards a new political centre.[13] This centre has institutions at its disposal which have, and try to acquire, jurisdiction over the 'old' political systems. The concept of integration implies several dimensions: it can be considered as a process or as a condition resulting from this process, it can be negative or positive (the removal of barriers *v.* the development of common policies), scope and intensity of integration are variable, and the shifting combination of loyalties from national to a higher level is of strategic importance. Integration can only take place on the basis of respect for the autonomy of the constituent units and as a voluntary acceptance of the supranational 'higher' order. It is useful, therefore, to relate the notion of 'European integration' to the notions of (consociational) 'democracy' and 'federalism' as forms of limited government, and as the 'limiting conditions' for the integration process.[14] Looking at current EU dynamics of integration, one can observe that there is nothing linear or automatic about European integration. There are ups and downs, often occurring simultaneously in different fields, there is movement and there is standstill, and any theory of European integration will have to take standstill, crisis or paralysis into account. Secondly, it is important to realize that there is more to European integration than the newspaper headlines suggest. The news is only a part of the process. Less visible, but at least as important, is the ongoing production of European policy. In more and more fields of government intervention, the EU produces rules to which, sooner or later, national governments will have to conform. One could say the speed of this rolling snowball varies, but the movement and the direction are clear. There is to be more and more common European policy, both in quantity and in quality. The very existence, size and substance of EC policy output has created a momentum of its own. If the media report crisis or standstill at the political level, the everyday EC policy process will react to this, but will not disappear. A

---

[13] See Ernst B. Haas, *The Uniting of Europe: Political, Social and Economic Forces* (Oxford, 1950), p. 16.

[14] See Carl J. Friedrich, *Man and his Government* (New York, 1963); Carl J. Friedrich, *Limited Government* (Englewood Cliffs, 1974); Arend Lijphart, *Democracy in Plural Societies. A Comparative Exploration* (New Haven, 1977).

merged system of interstate cooperation[15] – which seems to be less a layer cake than a marble cake – is developing.

This brings us to a third observation. European integration takes place differently along the various dimensions. Economic behaviour, especially in private enterprises, has 'Europeanized' much more rapidly than social behaviour. Firms are used to operating across national boundaries much more than trade unions or other voluntary associations. Policy production has 'Europeanized' further than party politics, public opinion and culture, which are still very much nationalized. Civil servants are much more used to coordinating, negotiating, and operating within the EU than party politicians or journalists. Sometimes it seems that, in spite of the awareness of European interdependence and integration, actors are forced back into their national straitjackets in an inconsistent, or even tragic, way. It is this very discongruence among the dimensions of the integration process which causes friction, standstill, crisis and backlash and which could ultimately weaken and undermine the EU.

A fourth remark concerns the legitimacy of the EU system. Acceptance rather than enthusiasm seems to characterize most people's attitude towards the EU. Even within the European Movement in the Netherlands, a pragmatic and down-to-earth attitude prevails without eliciting much idealism or emotional appeal.[16] In this respect, the EU can be compared to 'multicultural federations' like Belgium or Canada, where common feelings are very weak. The consequences of this for the development of the EU system could be analysed comparatively, using these countries as 'cases-in-point'.

Problems and results
As has become clear from previous pages, the overall relationship between the Netherlands and the EC/EU is quite positive. As a strong sign of the Dutch attitude towards the EC/EU, there is their clear commitment to the strengthening of Europe from the very beginning in the late 1940s. Also, internationalism – travel abroad, the command of foreign languages – has a strong tradition in Dutch society, which serves as an asset in Europe. Another tradition, i.e.

[15] See Wolfgang Wessels, 'Staat und (westeuropäische) Integration. Die Fusionsthese', in Michael Kreile (ed)., 'Die Integration Europas', *Politische Vierteljahreszeitschrift*, 23 (1993), pp. 36–61.
[16] See the contribution of Gerhard Göhler in this book for the 'symbolic dimension' of European integration.

the willingness to find pragmatic solutions based on compromise, also contributes to the effectiveness of the Dutch in the European context. Nevertheless, there are problems and weaknesses. First of all, there is a loss of direction in Dutch politics in general. After the 'pillarization system' lost its hold in the 1960s and 1970s, attempts to establish a 'polarization system' (left–right, especially promoted by the left, thinking of itself as moral monopolist) failed, and since the left broke down in the late 1980s, the Dutch parties have lost their ideological compass and their appeal to the voters. Election turnout dropped during the 1980s, and about 25% of the voters can be described as floating. As a consequence, parties are looking for appealing issues and populist themes are gaining ground both in liberal and socialist circles. One of these is the 'threat from outside' theme related to crime and immigration, and this has a clearly anti-supranational ring. The image of the EC/EU as a superbureaucracy makes it even more vulnerable to populist attacks. Populism in the larger parties, especially Labour (PvdA) and Conservative Liberal (VVD), strengthened by xenophobia and nationalism from the small rightist parties, may create a considerable anti-European force in Dutch politics, frustrating Dutch commitment to a supranational Europe. In its participation in EC decision-making, the Dutch national government suffers from a lack of overall direction and control, and from fragmentation. A remedy could be to change the Dutch EC policy procedure, giving a clearer mandate to either the Prime Minister or the Minister of Foreign Affairs to overcome inter-ministerial disputes. The European work of the Ministry of Foreign Affairs has become more and more domestic in substance as well as in procedure. In substance, it is more and more taken over by the specialized ministries, and in procedure, it has become administrative coordination rather than international diplomacy. There is reason for scrutiny and reallocation of resources and powers among the coordinating ministries (Foreign Affairs, Interior, General Affairs, Finance). Also, there is a need to improve the supervision of EC policy implementation. Aside from this, a rotation of civil servants from one ministry to another, as well as a rotation from a Dutch ministry to the European Commission ('*detachement*') might improve integration and coordination in Dutch EC participation.

This brings us to the question of results, gains and losses: in 1990, an attempt was made to survey and evaluate Dutch membership in a variety of fields.[17] In the economic field, it came out that especially Dutch agriculture, trade and monetary policy in particular have, on balance, benefited from EC policy. In other economic areas, like industry or regional disparities, the balance of costs and benefits was more or less even. The Dutch steel industry could be restructured thanks to EC industrial policy support, but benefits for the peripheral regions of the country were very modest. In the field of overall government, a major gain for the Netherlands was seen in its ability to influence other countries and participate in European affairs much more effectively than it could ever hope to do as a single small country. Thus, for the Netherlands, the EC/EU is a major political investment.

In the social and cultural field, the gains and losses of EC membership for the Netherlands are rather unclear, and, also, are rapidly changing. The peculiar Dutch broadcasting system will have to face international competition and financial independence. Arts and monuments will be protected from extinction by a Delta Plan for the Arts. Publishing and language, however, are rapidly internationalizing.

Criminal policies (drugs etc.) will have great difficulty in the face of other member states' views, as will the social security system. Dutch government as well as interest groups will have to be clear about their priorities, and will need all the means at their disposal to retain them within the EC/EU in the years to come.

The developments in the 1980s – the accession of new members, the SEA, the 'Europe 1992' campaign and the Maastricht Treaty – have some important consequences for the Netherlands. First of all, the increase in members has clearly reduced Dutch influence in the EC/EU. In order to articulate Dutch interest and viewpoints, it is necessary to find allies among the other member states, and it is no longer sufficient to voice the Dutch view as 'the right one'. The Dutch moralistic tendency to overestimate the importance of morally just, pro-European stands has led to several failures and blunders. There is a need for a sober and realistic assessment of Dutch limitations within Europe, and for coalition strategies. Another consequence of the 'SEA and after' is the need to explain and justify 'Europe' to the Dutch public. The 'Europe 1992' campaign has awakened many groups in Dutch society – professional groups, local and provincial authorities, public opinion – and made them aware of the direct

---

[17] See M. Wolters and P. Coffey (eds.), *The Netherlands and EC Membership Evaluated* (London, 1990).

impact of 'Europeanization' on their own interests. The demands on European institutions have increased in terms of material benefits (subsidies, regulations), but also in terms of legitimacy. Those whose material interests will not be strengthened by the EC/EU and who will be or feel losers, will they turn away from European integration? If the EC/EU is only a source of money, accompanied by complex regulations, as an 'arrangement for business convenience', then its legitimacy will remain very weak and it may even become a source of alienation for citizens *vis-à-vis* their elites, i.e. a threat to the democratic system. At a time when more people in the Netherlands have become aware of Europe but the influence and the benefits of the Netherlands in Europe are decreasing, its commitment to Europe is fundamentally at stake. Therefore, the main challenge arising from the post-Maastricht era in the Netherlands is to strengthen the popular legitimacy of the European Union, to transform the 'Europhorie' of 'Europe 1992' into a sustained attitude in favour of Europe. This challenge will not be easy to face but it is of critical importance. Also, one has to note that prospects are far from hopeless. Interest in the outside world has always been strong and positive in the Netherlands. It offers a good starting-point for European awareness and lasting support for Europe, not just as a convenient arrangement, but as an indispensable means to safeguard the values of democracy, tolerance, prosperity, peace and the rule of law in the Low Countries.

Select bibliography

Bos, Jan M. M. van den, *Dutch EC Policy-Making. A Model-Guided Approach to Coordination and Negotiation* (Utrecht-Amsterdam, 1991).

Dommers, J., 'Hoeveel Europees werk in uitvoering? De uitvoering van EG-beleid kwantitatief bezien', *Bestuurskunde*, 4 (1993), pp. 181–91.

Europese Beweging Nederland, *De gevolgen van een Europese 'vierde bestuurslaag'* (Den Haag, 1991).

Externe Commissie Grote Steden (Commissie-Montijn), *Grote Steden, grote hansen* (Den Haag 1989).

Haersolte, Johan C. van, *Uitvoering EC-richtlijnen in Nederland 1958–1992* (Den Haag, 1993).

Hoetjes, Bernard J. S., 'Nederlands landbouwbeleid in West-Europa – schakels en problemen tussen internationale politiek en Nederlandse agrariërs', *Internationale Spectator*, 14 (February 1989), pp. 99–106.

—— 'Political Science in the Netherlands', in J. Bellers (ed.), *Politikwissenschaft in Europa* (Münster, 1990), pp. 128–44.

Jansen, J. I. H., 'Een Nederlands "nee" tegen "Maastricht"?', Bestuurskunde, 7 (1992), pp. 352–66.

Kellerman, Alfred E., 'The Netherlands in Face of its Community Obligations', Common Market Law Review, 20 (August 1983), pp. 297–333.

Kellerman, Alfred E. and Winter, J. A., 'The Netherlands', in J. Schwarze (ed.), The 1992 Challenge at the National Level – A Community-wide Joint Research Project on the Realization and Implementation by National Governments and Business of the Internal Market Programme (Baden-Baden, 1990), pp. 523–55.

Korte, J., 'Prejudiciële verwijzingen (art. 177 EG) in het kader van kort geding procedures door Nederlandse rechters', in Sociaal-Economische Wetgeving (1990), p. 103.

Korte, J. et al. (eds.), Primus inter pares. Report on Courts in the Netherlands (The Hague, 1989).

Lijphart, Arend, Democracy in Plural Societies. A Comparative Exploration (New Haven, 1977).

Pijpers, Alfred, The Vicissitudes of European Political Cooperation (Leiden, 1991).

Schendelen, Marinus P. C. M., Het Europese parlement (Utrecht, 1984).

—— Lobbyen – hoe werkt dat? (Den Haag, 1990).

Sloot, Thomas J. M., 'Verzuiling en pacificatie', in M. Wolters (ed.), Democratie en beleid in de Europese Gemeenschap (Alphen aan den Rijn, 1992), pp. 171–86.

Vree, Joop K. de, Political Integration. The Formation of Theory and its Problems (The Hague, 1972).

Wolters, Menno and Coffey, P. (eds.), The Netherlands and EC Membership Evaluated (London, 1990).

Zahn, Ernst, Das unbekannte Holland (Berlin, 1984).

France[1]

Fundamentals of France in EU affairs

For more than forty years, the emergence of the Community political system has confronted the French state with a gradual process of
'Europeanization'.[2] The mutations that are taking place within the
domestic institutions and political processes show this with an intensity that has increased since the entry into force of the Single European Act (SEA) on 1 July 1987. Since then, there has been an
acceleration of the effects of the European unification process on the
functioning of the state in France. Paradoxically, the French society
only became aware of this phenomenon with the signing of the
Treaty on European Union (TEU) on 7 February 1992.

Considering the French tradition of the nation state, a detour
through history appears useful to understand how much an element
of political and intellectual destabilization the European unification
process represents. In this respect, it is appropriate to go back as far
as the French Revolution because this historical event, for the most
part, laid the present foundations of the Republican nation state.
Article 3 of the Declaration of the Rights of Man and the Citizen of
26 August 1789 thus asserts that 'the principle of all sovereignty
resides in the nation. No group, no individual may exert any authority that does not emanate from it explicitly.' The draft of the constitution drawn up by Marat in 1789 also illuminates the foundations
of the French tradition by stipulating that 'the nation is the true leg-
islator of the state. To preserve sovereignty, it has to preserve its
independence. Thus the convocation of the assemblies ... the way of

[1] English translation by Bettina Döser, research associate at the Institut für
Europäische Politik, Bonn.
[2] Robert Ladrech, 'Europeanization of Domestic Politics and Institutions: The Case
of France', *Journal of Common Market Studies*, 32 (1) (1994), pp. 69–88.

proposing a question there, of opining, of decreeing, and that of making and sanctioning laws absolutely have to depend on it ... The absolute independence of the nation, therefore, has to establish the first constitution of the state.'[3] These excerpts point out two fundamental principles which have since been reaffirmed, in one way or another, in all the constitutions of the republics, including that of the contemporary Fifth Republic. The first principle is that there is no political entity outside of the nation, defined as a community of citizens with equal rights living within a limited territory. Sovereign, this nation is the source of the law. The second principle is that the unity of the nation is guaranteed by the state, conceived as both a concrete support and the expression of a collective identity.

Based on a plurality of competing sources of law no longer depending on the gathered representatives of the nation but imposing itself from outside, the European Community, from the beginning, proceeds from a fundamental disagreement with the French tradition of the nation state. This allows us to understand the reasons why each significant advancement of the European unification process leads to a resurgence of fears, which are neither the monopoly of the right nor or the left, about the end of the French model of the nation state.

The EC decision-making cycle and the participation of national institutions

The government and the ministerial bureaucracy

Numerous studies have shown that in Western Europe, the nation state has become a complex and segmented entity and, further, that it is no longer the only organizer of the 'social piloting'. Then, the phenomenon of administrative coordination can no longer be analysed as a search for harmony between the single politico-administrative actors; it has to take into account a broader social context. Nevertheless, this does not mean that specific forms of coordination, of which the objective remains the maintenance of coherence within the state, can no longer be distinguished. In France, there is a governmental coordination based on a hierarchical mechanism – i.e. the legacy of the Jacobin nation state – which, for the most part, has

[3] Cited by Antoine Winckler in 'La France, Etat et société face à l'Europe', *Rapport dactylographié aux entretiens de l'après-Maastricht* (Paris: Mouvement européen, 6 February 1993), p. 1.

been re-enforced during the Fifth Republic: the inter-ministerial realm. From a formal point of view, this mechanism appears as a combination of organs (the General Secretariat of the Government, etc.), meetings (inter-ministerial committees, inter-ministerial meetings, etc.) and procedures (e.g. the technique of arbitration) that supervise the cabinet of the Prime Minister and to some extent that of the President of the Republic in order to hierarchize the different public policies.[4]

In a very 'idiosyncratic' way, the French government has projected this hierarchical approach of coordination into the treatment of Community policies. Since the creation of the European Coal and Steel Community (ECSC), the definition of every position concerning several ministries before a Community Council is subjected to the filter of an organ composed of officials of different state administrations directly linked to the Prime Minister: the *Secrétariat Général du Comité Interministériel pour les Questions de Coopération Economique Européenne* (SGCI).[5] As an obligatory intermediary between the ministries and the French Permanent Representation to the European Union, the SGCI originally only intervened in the phase of formulation of Community policies. From 1986 onwards, it has also found itself entrusted with the coordination of the normative implementation of Community policies on the national level and, from 1994 onwards, with that of positions related to the third pillar of the European Union, i.e. justice and home affairs. In return, due to a strong resistance from the Quai d'Orsay (i.e. the French Foreign Ministry), the coordination of the Common Foreign and Security Policy (CFSP) has not been entrusted to the SGCI as the circles around Prime Minister Balladur would have wished. The SGCI only intervenes if a joint action of the CFSP calls on Community instruments or policies.

In most of the cases, the meetings within the SGCI allow for the definition of common positions before negotiations in the EC Council through a bureaucratic bargaining process. If a point of contest persists between the ministries, the SGCI submits it to the cabinet of the Prime Minister which attempts to organize a renewed coordination with the advisers of the ministers in inter-ministerial meetings.

[4] See Jacques Fournier, *Le travail gouvernemental* (Paris: Presses de la FNSP, 1987); Jean-Louis Quermonne, *L'appareil administratif de l'Etat* (Paris: Points/Seuil, 1991).
[5] See Christian Lequesne, *Paris-Bruxelles. Comment se fait la politique européenne de la France* (Paris: Presses de la FNSP, 1993).

Moreover, the most sensitive questions (like, for example, the issue of the General Agreement on Tariffs and Trade in 1993) may lead to a meeting of the concerned ministers under the presidency of the Prime Minister. This is thus known as the convocation of the *inter-ministerial committee* or – in a more informal phrasing – of a meeting of ministers. Resuming a practice that had become obsolete during the 1980s, Prime Minister Edouard Balladur brings together an inter-ministerial committee every month devoted to European affairs in order to get to the point with the members of his government on current 'big' issues and also to settle certain important positions. During these high level meetings in Matignon (i.e. the seat of the Prime Minister), the cabinet of the Prime Minister – knowing that the Secretary General of the SGCI often acts as an adviser – or the Prime Minister himself may arbitrate, which means intervening when ministerial positions conflict and deciding without reaching a consensus. The dyarchic nature of the Fifth Republic includes only one possibility of challenging this power of arbitration of the Prime Minister which is through the intervention of the President of the Republic. The conflictual atmosphere of the first cohabitation (March 1986 to March 1988) has reinforced this phenomenon on several occasions.[6]

As long as the scope of Community policies was limited to the customs union, energy policy, competition policy, agricultural policy, commercial policy and social policy and as long as the EC Council of Ministers was the dominant decision-making organ deciding by consensus, this hierarchical way of inter-ministerial coordination produced policy coherence. The progressive widening of the Community agenda from the mid-1970s and the institutional reforms introduced by the SEA and the TEU have since confronted it with serious limits by making the decision-making process more atomized.

Even if a circular from the Prime Minister of 21 March 1994 re-emphasized that it is essential for contacts between representatives of the administration and the services of the Commission to be prepared in concertation with the SGCI, it is in fact impossible for the latter to coordinate all the exchanges that the officials of the ministries have daily with those of the Commission and the representatives of interest groups in order to explore sector by sector the orientations of the Community policies. Despite the creation of positions responsible for

[6] See Lequesne, *op. cit.*

the relations with the European Parliament within the main ministries whose activities have to be coordinated by the SGCI, the latter is, in the same way, no longer in a position to control all relations developing between the officials of the ministries and the members of the European Parliament since the SEA. Finally, it would be even more illusionary for the SGCI to pretend to exercise a systematic control over the informal flows existing between the local political and administrative actors, the representatives of local economic interests, the services of the prefectures and those of the Commission for the implementation of EC regional policies.

Obviously, the French government is coping with the fact that the European unification process imposes new ways of making decisions based on horizontal and informal networking whereas its internal decision-making system was built according to the principle of vertical hierarchy. It hereafter has to accept that the formulation of Community policies means that each directorate, each ministerial cabinet or simply each official expresses the interests of sectoral networks woven with the elected (local, national, European), the officials (of the Commission, other member states, local communities) and the representatives of interest groups. If the SGCI is thus more than ever invited, in the official statements of the governments, to maintain the constraint of formal hierarchical coordination, this is because Community policies are more and more the product of an addition of 'micro-negotiations' and of 'micro-decisions' carried out in different political and administrative settings and no longer totally controllable. In such a new configuration of decision-making, governmental coordination means monitoring various administrative autonomies more than exercising from the centre an absolute control on the whole policy process.

The national parliament

In all EU member states, the growing interference of Community policies with domestic legislative activities has led the national parliaments to claim a closer association with the definition of positions negotiated within the Council. In France, this demand of the national parliament has grown up during the ratification of the TEU.[7] Taking advantage of the reform proposed by the President of the Republic

[7] See Françoise de la Serre and Christian Lequesne, 'France and the European Union', in Alan W. Cafruny and Glenda G. Rosenthal (eds.), *The State of the European Community. The Maastricht Debates and Beyond* (Boulder/London: Lynne Rienner/Longman, 1993), pp. 145–57.

with a view to rendering the constitution more compatible with certain clauses of this treaty, the National Assembly and the Senate adopted in June 1992 a new Article 88-4 which stipulates that:

> The government submits propositions comprising clauses of legislative nature to the National Assembly and the Senate as early as their transmission to the Council of the Communities. During or outside parliamentary sessions, resolutions may be voted upon ... according to modalities established by the statute of each assembly.

Even if these resolutions are in no way legally binding for the government, the possibility left to the parliament to resort to them is a sign that its powers concerning Community policies progressively advance from simple information to control. A circular from the Prime Minister of 21 April 1993 has completely reorganized relations between the French government and the national parliament derived from the application of Article 88-4.

Instructed about all propositions from the Commission, the SGCI is, in fact, responsible for distinguishing between two categories of texts. On the one hand, those susceptible of comprising 'clauses of legislative nature' (in the sense of the French law defined in Article 34 of the constitution of 1958) and required to be specifically transmitted to parliament according to the terms of Article 88-4: on the other hand, those that, according to the terms of a law of 10 May 1990, are, for simple information, transmitted to the *Delegations for the European Union* that have existed within the two assemblies since 1979. The propositions susceptible of depending on the procedure of 88-4 are thus transmitted to the Conseil d'Etat which may take fifteen days to render an opinion about their legislative nature. A follow-up sheet is also transmitted to the *Secrétariat Général du Gouvernement (SGG)* as well as to the SGCI, which, theoretically together with the concerned ministries but in practice often by itself, has eight days to examine the legislative texts that have to be modified or repealed. After an examination by its different administrative sections (and, in some cases, by its general assembly), the Conseil d'Etat emits an opinion which is transmitted to the SGCI and to the SGG. It is up to the latter to formally seize the Presidents of the National Assembly and the Senate. While for the government, the national parliament represented only a marginal constraint in the formulation of Community policies until 1992, the procedure of 88-4 has turned it into a 'binding link' of the inter-ministerial work.

The transmission to the parliament of Commission propositions containing dispositions of a legislative nature is based on a long bureaucratic procedure. It is, therefore, not astonishing that after one year of functioning, it was confirmed that on average, one month passed between the moment when the SGCI obtained the propositions of the Commission and when the SGG forwarded them to parliament in order for the latter to examine them and, if necessary, to vote resolutions. Hence the criticisms formulated by the parliamentarians, particularly within the National Assembly, when some propositions were transmitted while the EC Council had already adopted them in Brussels. The debate on the deeper association of the French parliament with EC/EU affairs shows how difficult it is to reconcile domestic procedures depending on a certain agenda and decision-making speed with Community procedures corresponding to another agenda and decision-making speed. To avoid a situation in which parliament cannot comment on a text because it has not been consulted in time, a circular from the Prime Minister of 9 July 1994 introduced important changes. Inspired by the British example under the pressure of the French MPs, it invited the French Permanent Representative as far as possible to oppose the addition to the Council agenda of any proposition containing dispositions of a legislative nature on which the national parliament had not been able to comment, or else to subordinate the passing of votes in the Council to a later opinion by the national parliament. The principle of 'reserves' for parliamentary examination, for a very long time completely unacceptable to French governments because it was considered contrary to their constitutional monopoly in the sphere of international negotiations, has now been officially initiated. This evolution proves that Community policies are no longer assimilated with foreign policy within the French government. It also perfectly illustrates how a domestic political process can be gradually 'Europeanized'.

The local communities

In France, no procedure exists to associate the local communities systematically with the formulation of the positions that the government negotiates within the Council of the EC. Informal means nevertheless allow for the regions and other local communities ('*départements*' and '*communes*') to assert their opinion on Community policies to the government and the Community institutions, either by way of their representatives (in the national and in the European Parliament) or by that of interest groups.

In the domain of the Community's regional policy, the twenty-two French regions are not associated with the negotiations which allow for the interregional allocation of the credits allotted to the structural funds. It is, in fact, the state which negotiates the objectives of intervention and the zones of eligibility through the channel of the ministries, the Délégation à l'Aménagement du Territoire (DATAR), the SGCI and the Permanent Representation to the EC. The regions are, however, afterwards associated with the preparation of the Community Support Frame (CSF), this is to say, when it comes to presenting the regional plans, following the criteria and envelopes determined by the Commission. In the phase of the implementation of structural aids, the participation of the regions often depends on the more or less conflictual nature of the local political game. Case studies[8] thus claim that the administration of the state – in particular the services of the heads of regions – benefits from a position of neutrality in relation to the local political games, which allows for them to play a decisive role in the coordination, implementation and control of the Community programmes.

Since the SEA, however, the assertion of informal steps taken by the regions, the départements and the French cities toward Community institutions has been observed. In 1994, sixteen of twenty-two French regions retained a permanent outpost in Brussels. These offices are either individual ones (Nord-Pas-de-Calais, Rhône-Alpes) or constitute an association of several French regions (the office 'Grand Sud' thus represents the interests of meridional regions) or else an association together with a region of another member state (the Picardie region has thus opened a joint office together with the English region of Essex). All these offices undertake lobbying activities primarily directed to the Commission. The aim is to keep the public and private regional actors informed about the possibilities for financing and contracts offered by the different directorates general (DGs), to follow the elaboration of propositions that could have implications for the local economies and, finally, to favour activities

---

[8] See Richard Balme and Patrick Le Galès, *Stars and Black Holes: French Regions and Cities in the European Galaxy*, unpublished paper presented at the EUROLOG Conference (University of Twente, 23–26 September 1993); Richard Balme, *La politique régionale communautaire comme construction institutionnelle*, unpublished paper presented at the colloqium of the Association Française de Science Politique (Paris, 24–25 March 1994).

of cross-border cooperation which are the ones that offer the French regions the greatest independence from the state. The Commission encourages these kind of activities, especially by way of the programme INTERREG, of which 800 million ECUs concerned the French regions in 1990–1993. The realization of these programmes can be the object of strong tensions between the heads of regions and the local representatives where the latter find it more difficult to accept that the state tries to control the use of credits without itself complementing them.

The regional lobbying activity also takes place at the European Parliament because the cumulative mandates to which French representatives are accustomed allow for the consideration of territorial interests. The 'Atlantic group' of the European Parliament which assembles the European representatives of the Atlantic façade, and which is dominated by the French parliamentarians, thus seems to have played an important role in the widening of the eligibility criteria of the programme STRIDE (development of regional capacities in the field of research and technology) to rural and maritime zones. It also seems to contribute to the programming of the TGV-line Paris–Madrid, using the Atlantic axis.[9]

Interest groups

The neo-corporatist grid of analysis has never been applied to the case of France because institutionalized macro-negotiations between the state and the main social organizations could never establish themselves there.[10] In return, a mediation of sectoral corporatist type between the state administrations and the interest groups has, for a long time, allowed for the coherence of public action.[11] Considered 'inadapted as soon as the problems to be treated require an approach which no longer coincides with the existing cleavages,'[12] this kind of mediation has also been challenged by the European Community, in particular since the launching of the internal market programme.

[9] See Richard Balme, *op. cit.*
[10] See Andrew Cox and Jack Hayward, 'The Inapplicability of the Corporatist Model in Britain and France', *International Political Science Review*, 4 (2) (1983), pp. 217–40; Bruno Jorbert and Pierre Muller, *L'Etat en action* (Paris: PUF, 1987), p. 172.
[11] See Ezra Suleiman, *Les hauts fonctionnaires et la politique* (Paris: Le Seuil, 1976), pp. 202–13; Jorbert and Muller, *op. cit.*, pp. 171–206.
[12] Jorbert and Muller, *op. cit.*, p. 205.

Firstly, by allowing national interest groups to use in parallel several channels of pressure (Commission, European Parliament, European professional federations), the European Community has contributed to making the French model of sectoral corporatism evolve toward more pluralism.[13] Retroactively, this pluralism encourages competition and fragmentation of interests which less easily authorizes one French administration (or one body) to pretend to control the formulation or the implementation of one policy in symbiosis with what was traditionally called in France 'les professions'. In their study dealing with the 1992 reform of the Common Agricultural Policy, François-Gilles Le Theule and David Litvan show well that the system of fragmented representation of interests at the Community level is a factor (among others) that has contributed to the Ministry of Agriculture and the main French agricultural unions being incapable of producing a common position *vis-à-vis* the Commission and the other member states.[14] Conclusions heading in the same direction could be drawn, in the French case, from the import policy on Japanese cars (1991) or else the reform of the Common Fisheries Policy (1993).

Secondly, because the European unification process relies very often on frame-objectives ('*objective 1992*' being the most obvious example) to stimulate its development, it forces the actors to consider the agenda in a more anticipatory way. Hence the expertise function which, however, in the Community realm is rarely the monopoly of a single actor. On the contrary, there is a competition of expertises which are carried out in parallel and often without being coordinated with the Commission, the committees of the European Parliament, the socio-professional organizations and, of course, the national governments. For a long time concentrated within the SGCI, expertise on Community policies has, with the debate on the internal market, tended to diversify in France even if remaining within the state apparatus. One of the institutional translations of this evolution has been the development by the central administration of new mediating structures in order to hierarchize priorities with the interest groups. These

---

[13] See Wolfgang Streeck and Philippe C. Schmitter, 'From National Corporatism to Transnational Pluralism: Organized Interests in the Single European Market', *Politics and Society*, 19 (2) (1991), pp. 133–64.

[14] See François-Gilles Le Theule and David Litvan, 'La reforme de la PAC: analyse d'une négociation communautaire', *Revue Française de Science Politique*, 43 (5) (October 1993), pp. 755–87.

structures have mostly associated high ranking civil servants with local representatives, heads of business, bankers, unionists, academics or else representatives of non-profit associations. As examples one can cite the 'committee on economic reflexion for the preparation of the 1992 deadline' chaired in 1987–88 by Marcel Boiteux, honorary president of the EDF; or else the 'groups for study and mobilization' (GEM) initiated in September 1988 by Edith Cresson, Minister for European Affairs, and revived in 1991–92 during her short stay in Matignon. The analyst has nevertheless to be very cautious when considering the effects of these structures of mediation. The need for more 'outside' information and expertise relating to the 1992 deadline does not allow one to conclude that the decisions taken by the French governments have effectively taken into account the pressures of the interest groups. Besides, the effort to associate the social actors with the managing project of the internal market was not applied to the more political project of the European Union. During all the negotiations leading to the Maastricht Treaty, expertise was the monopoly of the central state administration (and among it of a specialized network of ministers and high-ranking bureaucrats) which pursued it in a situation of splendid isolation. The parliament and the society discovered the treaty *a posteriori* during the ratification debate.

Conclusion

Even if the French state continues to be based on the Jacobin principles of hierarchy and dependency by which it was inspired, it has not escaped, since the end of the Second World War, the tendencies towards more sectorization and segmentation that the European unification process has re-enforced. From this results a general evolution of the French policy style from hierarchy towards more bargaining. Political processes, like the relations between the government and the parliament or else the forms of mediation between the state and the interest groups, are all affected by this 'Europeanization' mostly characterized by incremental adaptation.

Select bibliography

Briseul, Jean Paul, 'Structures territoriales françaises et construction de l'Europe', *Défense nationale*, 1 (1993), pp. 17–27.

Buffotot, Patrice, 'Le référendum sur l'Union Européenne', Modern and Contemporary France, 3 (1993), pp. 277–86.

Collard, Sue, 'Political Union Revisited: From de Gaulle to Mitterand 1960–1990', in Wadia Khursheed (ed.), France and Europe (Paris, 1993), pp. 18–35.

Drain, Michel, 'La France et la construction européenne: de l'acceleration aux incertitudes', Relations internationales et strategiques, 9 (1993), pp. 135–46.

Dreyfus, François-Georges (ed.), France and EC Membership Evaluated (London: Pinter, 1993).

Guigou, Elisabeth, 'Les Français et l'Europe, regard d'une pro-Maastricht', in Societé Française d'Enquete par Sondages (ed.), L'Etat de l'opinion 1993 (Paris, 1993), pp. 87–90.

Haywood, Elisabeth, 'The European Policy of François Mitterand', Journal of Common Market Studies, 31 (2) (June 1993), pp. 269–82.

'L'administration française face aux nouvelles échéances européennes', Revue française d'administration publique, 63 (1992), pp. 459–89.

Lequesne, Christian, Paris-Bruxelles. Comment se fait la politique européenne de la France (Paris: Presses de la FNSP, 1993).

Lequesne, Christian and de La Serre, Françoise, 'Frankreich', in Werner Weidenfeld and Wolfgang Wessels (eds.), Jahrbuch der Europäischen Integration (Bonn: Europa Union Verlag, 1992, 1993 and 1994).

Moravcsik, Andrew, 'Idealism and Interest in the European Community: The case of the French Referendum', French Politics and Society, 1 (1993), pp. 45–56.

d'Orcival, François, 'La France devant l'Europe allemande?', in Philippe de Saint Robert (ed.), l'Europe déraisonable (Paris, 1992), pp. 53–60.

Pinton, Michel, 'La monnaie européenne unique est-elle utile à la France?', in Philippe de Saint Robert (ed.), l'Europe déraisonable (Paris, 1992), pp. 91–8.

Sabourin, Paul, 'Le Conseil d'Etat face au droit communautaire. Methodes et raisonnements', Revue du droit public et de la science politique en France et à l'étranger, 2 (1993), pp. 397–430.

Seguin, Philippe, 'Les Français et l'Europe, regard d'un anti-Maastricht', in Societé Française d'Enquête par Sondages (ed.), L'Etat de l'opinion (Paris, 1993), pp. 93–7.

Denmark

Fundamentals of Denmark in EU affairs

To the extent that it is possible to speak of countries as having a specific 'state culture', that of Denmark is characterized by duality and tension between a centralized culture rooted in the strong absolutist state and a decentralized culture dating back to the democratic revolution in the middle of the last century with its unique alliance between farmers and intellectuals.[1] The Danish democratic revolution was a peaceful one led by intellectuals in Copenhagen, but supported by the powerful farmers and smallholders. Unlike in other European countries, democracy was granted to the people by the king. The high degree of mobilization of the countryside convinced a far-sighted king of the need to make concessions. The Danish revolutionary inheritance is thus an odd mixture of popular involvement in politics and a state apparatus with long and unbroken traditions, but also perhaps aided by the institution of the monarchy blessed with a certain image of benevolence.

Like France Denmark is an old unitary state, but in domestic affairs decentralization is nowadays considerable. Nearly 70% of total public expenditure is administered by the regions and municipalities.[2] In Denmark there are three territorial levels of government: the national level, the fourteen regions (*'amter'*) and the 275 municipalities (*'kommuner'*). The growth of the EU system in recent years has meant that the lower levels in the vertical division of labour are increasingly affected by EC decisions. The Danish regions are mainly affected by harmonization and mutual recognition of norms and stan-

[1] See Tim Knudsen, *De danske Stat i Europa* (Copenhagen: DJØF Forlag, 1993).
[2] Henning Bregnsbo and Niels Christian Sidenius, 'Denmark: The National Lobby Orchestra', in M.P.C.M. van Schendelen (ed.), *National Public and Private EC Lobbying* (Aldershot: Dartmouth, 1993).

dards notably in the area of transport and equipment for hospitals, areas which fall under the competence of the regions. The new chapter on health policy in the Maastricht Treaty will also require adaptation in the Danish regions. The Danish municipalities are mainly affected by EC rules in the areas of social policy (notably projects fostering new employment), the environment (where Danish districts are responsible for implementation), culture and education. So far the municipalities have not undertaken any major adaptation to EU membership. Only the largest cities – Copenhagen, Aarhus, Odense, and Aalborg – plus the medium-size town of Vejle have their own representation in Brussels. However, some municipalities of above medium size are currently considering sending lobbyists to Brussels. In addition, the national association of districts ('*Kommunernes Landsforening*') has a lobbyist in Brussels. The joint municipalities' EU secretariat is planning to open an office in Brussels.

The horizontal division of power in Denmark is not very strong. Montesquieu's doctrine, though mentioned in the constitution, is of little importance in Denmark. There is no sharp demarcation line between the legislative and the executive powers in Denmark. Government and parliament normally work very closely together in what has rightly been called a 'cooperative democracy'.[3] In this century one party has only once enjoyed an absolute majority in parliament. This has created a tradition of broad majorities with most laws being passed by more than two-thirds of the Folketing. The close interconnectedness between parliament and executive is also reflected in the fact that most ministers are members of parliament. The Danish judiciary is very weak and is overshadowed by the strong parliament. The legal profession in Denmark has talked about 'absolutist parliamentarianism' in Denmark. In a comparative perspective, it is interesting to note that the Danish High Court has never declared a law unconstitutional, not even during the German occupation from 1940–1945.[4]

Denmark adopted the Single European Act (SEA) after a referendum, but enjoys a special status as regards the Maastricht Treaty negotiated at the Edinburgh summit in December 1992 and approved at a referendum in May 1993. Denmark will not take part in the third

[3] Henning Sørensen and Ole Wæver, 'State, Society and Democracy and the Effect of the EC', in Lise Lyck (ed.), *Denmark and EC Membership Evaluated* (London: Pinter Publishers, 1992), pp. 3–26.

[4] Tim Knudsen, *op. cit.*, p. 130.

phase of monetary union; nor does it take part in the West European defence cooperation outside NATO.

The EC decision-making cycle and the participation of national institutions

The government/ministerial administration

In a comparative perspective, Denmark belongs to the EU member states which have opted for centralized administrative procedures in EC decision-making. In this respect, Denmark can be placed in the same category as France and the UK – like Denmark old nation states with well-established national bureaucracies. Thus, one reason for the considerable centralization of the Danish EC decision-making process seems to be the strength of the national bureaucracy and its vested interests. Another reason is that EC membership was, right from the start of the EC debate in Denmark in the beginning of the 1960s, a controversial and divisive issue. As pointed out by Grønnegaard Christensen, the sensitivity of Community relations was from the early days of EC membership seen to require the establishment of strong coordination procedures both at the inter-departmental level and between government and parliament. Besides, the centralized coordination apparatus was seen as a guarantee against a gradual undermining of Danish sovereignty due to domestic ministers' expected acceptance of any Community measure giving short-run profits to their clientele but disregarding more long-range immaterial consequences for national sovereignty and Danish identity.[5]

Over the years there has been a certain weakening of the coordinating function of the Foreign Ministry. The Danish EC decision-making process reveals some of the same tendencies towards 'sectorization' and 'decentralization' as does the normal decision-making process. A recent investigation concluded that three factors in particular tend to activate the coordinating machinery, thus enhancing the degree of centralization:[6]

---

[5] See Jørgen Grønnegaard Christensen, 'Blurring the International-Domestic Politics Distinction: Danish Representation at EC Negotiations', *Scandinavian Political Studies*, 4 (3) (1981).

[6] Jørgen Grønnegaard Christensen, Peter Germer and Thomas Pedersen, *Åbenhed, offentlighed og deltagelse i den danske EU-beslutningsproces* (København Udenrigsministeriet, 1994).

1 whenever decisive, national interests are at stake (i.e. interests relating to Danish sovereignty, security and national economy);
2 whenever there are clashes of interests between sectors leading to open controversy regarding the handling of an issue;
3 whenever there are internal problems of coordination in the ministry concerned.

The main bodies involved in the Danish EC decision-making process are the government ministers, national civil servants, national interest groups, the opposition parties assembled in the *European Committee*, and in some cases the national parliament *in toto*.[7] National regional chambers do not exist in Denmark, but at the preparatory stage regional interest groups are involved in the work of some special committees set up by the national administration. A coordination machinery has existed since Denmark's entry into the EC. It consists of coordination committees on three levels (see Figure 9.1):[8]

1 the *special committees*;
2 the *EU committee*;
3 the *cabinet committee on EU affairs*.

The *special committees* largely reflect the division of labour in the Commission's directorates and in the Council's working groups. At present, there are twenty-four groups. Members are civil servants from the ministries most concerned and, more recently, also representatives from the major interest groups in the sector concerned. The special committee undertakes the technical analysis and coordination of the Danish negotiation position. The Ministry of Foreign Affairs is a member of all committees and chairs six of them. The *EU com-*

---

[7] The Market Relations Committee will be renamed the European Committee ('*Europaudvalget*') dating from the start of the new parliamentary session in October 1994.

[8] For overviews of the Danish administrative procedure regarding EC legislation, see Jørgen Grønnegaard Christensen, 'Da centraladministrationen blev international', in N. Amstrup and I. Faurby (eds.), *Studier i dansk udenrigspolitik* (Aarhus: Forlaget Politica, 1978); Jørgen Ørstrøm Møller, 'Danish EC Decision Making: An Insider's View', *Journal of Common Market Studies*, 21 (3) (March 1983); Karsten Hagel-Sørensen and Hjalte Rasmussen, 'The Danish Administration and its Interaction with the Community Administration', *Common Market Law Review*, 22 (1985) pp. 273–300. For an early analysis which retains some value, see Svend Auken, Jacob Buksti and Carsten Lehmann Sørensen, 'Denmark Joins Europe', *Journal of Common Market Studies*, 15 (1976), pp. 1–36.

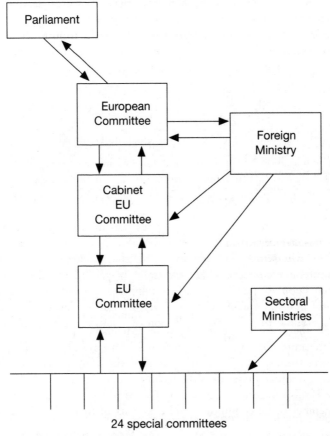

Fig. 9.1 Model of the Danish decision-making process in EC/EU affairs

mittee is the highest coordination body at the level of civil servants. In principle it is composed of the heads of department ('*departementschefer*') from the ministries most concerned. In practice, however, members are often lower-level civil servants. Nine ministries plus the Ministry of Foreign Affairs which chairs the sessions are represented on the committee. It has been pointed out that the EU committee's contribution to coordination is limited; often the draft from the special committee is simply rubber-stamped, and in case of disagreement the serious discussion will usually take place in the government's Common Market Committee. The EU committee is thus rather anonymous, an assessment confirmed by some recent case studies.[9] The *Cabinet Committee on EU affairs* is the ministerial coordination body in which the government ministers most concerned assess and, if necessary, revise the negotiating draft. The Prime Minister is a member of the Cabinet Committee. The committee is of fundamental importance for internal political coordination in the government. Significantly, the chairman of the EU committee, who comes from the Foreign Ministry, is also secretary of the Cabinet Committee and is present at the meetings of the parliamentary European committee (see below). Normally he also attends the meetings of the Council of Ministers and thus follows a case through all stages, which helps to establish some continuity and at the same time gives the Foreign Ministry a crucial role in the Danish EC decision-making process.

During the *preparatory phase* the sectoral ministry (i.e. the ministry most concerned) has the initiative alone. It is the sectoral ministry which sends representatives to the Commission's expert committees, where drafts for proposals not yet submitted are commented upon. Depending on the Commission's responsiveness, the sectoral ministry therefore has a certain influence on the Commission's original proposal. Consultation of relevant interest groups is also carried out by the sectoral ministry, which integrates the responses from those groups in a basic draft, which forms the basis of the Danish position on a given proposal of the Commission. This draft paper also forms the basis of the meeting in the special committee, which is chaired by the ministry most concerned. According to some specialists, coordination has become less frequent at the preparatory stage over the years. Now national experts taking part in the working groups of the Commission sometimes act under instruction from their own ministry only.[10] As coordination tends to strengthen the Ministry of Foreign Affairs at the expense of the sectoral ministry, this tendency, which is in part due to the growing quantity of EC legislation, suggests a certain loss of power for the Foreign Ministry.

[9] See Christensen, Germer and Pedersen, *op. cit.*
[10] See Hagel-Sørensen and Hjalte Rasmussen, *op. cit.*, p. 276.

In the *decision-making* phase, in which the Council is the pivot, the sectoral ministry still undertakes most of the administrative tasks and retains the initiative:

- the sectoral ministry appoints the Danish representatives in the Council's working groups;
- the sectoral ministry maintains close contact with the sectoral attaché at the Danish Permanent Representation in Brussels;
- the sectoral ministry prepares the draft negotiating instruction for the permanent representative, which is then approved by the Danish coordination bodies and is given its final shape by the Foreign Ministry;
- the sectoral ministry is represented by its minister at the Council meetings.

With the important exceptions referred to earlier, there is thus a basic tendency towards 'sectorized' decision-making, the decisive influence being located in an alliance between the individual ministry and important interest groups in the policy sector.

In the *implementation phase* civil servants play a predominant role. In a small but interesting research project, a Danish researcher examined seventeen randomly selected directives in order to establish how they were implemented in Denmark. It emerged that of the seventeen directives only one was implemented by law, i.e. in accordance with the constitutional requirements of three parliamentary hearings.[11] This shows that in Denmark parliamentary control in the implementation stage is very limited: a conclusion which is supported by the fact that since 1973 the Danish Folketing has to a considerable extent inserted clauses in newly adopted laws indicating that ministers are in the future empowered to implement new EC directives by means of (internal) regulations. The Danish compliance with EC legislation is widely considered to be exemplary. Along with the UK and France, Denmark has topped the list of national implementation records in recent years. This is reflected in the generally harmonious relationship between the Danish authorities and the controlling bodies at the EU level. During the period from 1982 to 1992 a total of 338 opening letters were sent to Denmark; this led to fifty-one reasoned opinions and finally to sixteen proceedings before the ECJ (see Table 9.1). One detects a steady

---

[11] The results of the project are summarized in Mark Dovey, 'Demokratiets trange kår i EF', *Berlingske Tidende*, 23 November 1990.

growth in the number of cases during the period 1982–92, but this is probably more due to the growth in the number of EC legislative acts and to intensification of the Commission's control than to a deterioration in the quality of Danish implementation of EC legislation. Most of the cases against Denmark were solved at the early stage of the opening letters and only a small percentage resulted in proceedings before the ECJ. It should be added that in recent years there have been several more serious conflicts between Denmark and the EU, e.g. the Great Belt case (infringement of public procurement rules), in which the Danish state lost the case at the ECJ, and another lost case concerning illegal employer contributions ('the AMBI case').

Table 9.1 Number of opening letters, reasoned opinions and cases against Denmark before the ECJ 1982–1992

Year	Opening letters	Reasoned opinions	Cases before the ECJ
1982	16	10	1
1983	13	3	3
1984	21	3	1
1985	27	4	2
1986	26	3	1
1987	36	6	0
1988	29	6	3
1989	36	4	1
1990	36	5	3
1991	52	3	1
1992	46	4	0
TOTAL	338	51	16

Source: Fifth and Tenth Annual Report to the European Parliament on Monitoring the Application of Community Law, COM (88) 425 final, 3.10.88; Com (93) 320 final, 28.4.93.

If one looks more specifically at the period 1988–92 in which most of the legislation work for the realization of the internal market has been done, one can discover quite a few differences according to different policy fields (see Table 9.2). In fact most of the opening letters have been sent in the field of the internal market and agriculture; the rather high number of opening letters in the field of environment and employment/social affairs is quite surprising for Denmark, which has a strong socio-ecological bias. However, if one looks at the number of reasoned opinions during the same period, one discovers that the high number in the field of the internal market is still there, whereas in the field of the environment and social affairs Denmark fully implemented the EC law. It is more the comparatively high number of reasoned opinions in the field of customs and excise duties which is unexpected. There have been no steps taken at all against Denmark in the field of economy and finance (see Table 9.3).

Table 9.2 Number of opening letters according to policy fields 1988–1992

Issue area	1988	1989	1990	1991	1992	Total
Internal market and industry	13	15	12	13	12	65
Environment	4	2	5	4	4	15
Agriculture	10	10	1	16	21	58
Employment and social affairs	0	1	3	6	1	11
Transport	0	0	4	1	1	5
Customs and excise duties	0	1	0	1	0	2
Fishery	1	0	3	0	0	4
Economy and finance	0	0	0	0	0	0
Information, communication, culture	0	0	0	0	1	1

Source: Tenth Annual Report to the European Parliament on Monitoring the Application of Community Law, Com (93), 320 final, 28.4.1993.

Table 9.3 Reasoned opinions against Denmark 1988–1992

Issue area	1988	1989	1990	1991	1992	Total
Internal market and industry	2	1	3	2	2	10
Environment	1	1	0	0	0	2
Agriculture	0	1	0	0	0	1
Employment and social affairs	0	0	0	0	0	0
Customs and excise duties	2	1	1	0	0	4
Economy and finance	0	0	0	0	0	0

Source: Tenth Annual Report to the European Parliament on Monitoring the Application of Community Law, COM (93), 320 final, 28.4.1993.

The number of cases in which the ECJ has intervened has been very small. Between 1973 and 1991 the author has registered twelve cases of court actions against Denmark. Of these Denmark won three and lost nine (see Table 9.4). In general the time lapse for Danish compliance in lost cases is short (see Table 9.5).

Table 9.4 Decisions by the ECJ in which Denmark was a party 1973-1991 (direct action)

Case no.	Issue	Outcome	Date of verdict
100/90	Duties conc. travel	Denmark loses (infringement of dir. 78/1033/EØF)	17/10–91
208/88	Duties on border trade (beer)	Denmark loses (infringement of dir. 87/198/EØF)	6/12–90
302/86	Packing for beer	Denmark loses (infringement of EØF art. 30)	20/9–88
349/85	Export restrictions conc. EUGFL and beef meat	Denmark wins (Commission used wrong interpretation of word 'beef meat')	27/1–88
348/85	Fishing quota	Denmark wins (annulment of Commission decision 85/451/EØF)	15/12–87
278/85	Infringement of treaty, dangerous substances	Denmark loses (infringement of dir. 79/831/EØF)	14/10–87
106/84	Duties on fruit wine	Denmark loses (infringement of treaty art. 95/1/EØF)	4/3–86
252/84	Free exchanges of services and right of establishment	Denmark loses (infringement of treaty art. 59 and 60 EØF)	4/12–86
143/83	Equal pay	Denmark loses (infringement of dir. 75/117/EØF)	30/1–85
158/82	Free movement for goods and health control	Denmark loses (infringement of treaty art. 9 and 13 EØF)	9/11–83
211/81	Legal harmonization	Denmark wins	15/12–82
171/78	Internal duties on alcohol	Denmark loses (infringement of treaty art. 95/1 EØF)	27/2–80

Source: Table compiled by the author.

There has not been a significant number of cases of non-compliance, and the average lapse of time was approximately twelve months. But it should be added that in most cases the reaction time is lower, the normal reaction time being between three and five months. The relatively high average is due to one or two 'abnormal' cases, e.g. the case of equal pay, in which the reaction time was fifty-one months.

Table 9.5 Time lapse for Danish compliance in lost cases

Case no. and subject	Sentence	Date of Danish juridical reaction
171/78 internal duties, on alcohol, 'the snaps case'	27/2–80	Law 153 6/5–80. Subm. 29/2–80
143/83 Equal pay	30/1–85	Law 243 19/4–89. Subm. 16/10–88
158/82 Free movement of goods. Health control	9/11–83	Regul. 142 2/4–84
252/84 Service insurance	4/12–86	Regul. 565 23/9–88
106/84 Duties on fruit wine	4/3–86	Law 341 4/6–86. Subm. 30/4–86
278/85 Treaty infringement. Duty on notification for dangerous substances	14/10–87	Law 285 13/5–87
302/86 Packing for beer	20/9–88	Regul. 124 27/2–89
208/88 Duties on border trade (beer)	6/12–90	Regul. 160 18/3–91

Source: Table compiled by the author.

The parliament

In formal terms and in large part also in practice, the Danish parliament plays a bigger role in the EC decision-making process than other national parliaments in the EU. The Folketing's *European Committee* is in many ways a unique construction in the EU. Similar bodies exist in Germany and France, but the Danish EC stands out because of its greater ability to exert control over the executive in EC policy. As such it has attracted the attention of a number of other national parliaments in the EU and has indeed been a source of inspiration for parliamentarians in Germany and France seeking greater control over their country's EC policy. The European Committee is one of the Folketing's twenty-three standing committees and consists of seventeen members, the political parties being represented according to size. The information provided by the government in the European Committee is confidential. According to the act of accession, the government is required to notify the committee on proposals for Council provisions which will become directly applicable in Denmark or the implementation of which requires action by the Folketing. The involvement of the Danish parliament in EC decision-making facilitates Danish implementation of EC legislation, as the consent of a majority in the European Committee normally guarantees that a directive adopted in the Council of Ministers can pass unhindered through Parliament at the implementation stage. The involvement of the committee also helps Danish minority governments to test the resistance in parliament to individual pieces of EC legislation.[12]

The original right of the European Committee to be notified was widely seen to be rather weak and had indeed been reinforced later. Following pressure from parties in parliament, a (politically binding) report from the European Committee (then the Market Relations Committee) of 29 March 1973 stated that 'the government shall consult the Committee on Market Relations on matters which involve market policy and which are of major importance'. The report adds that this should be done in a way that respects both parliament's influence and the government's freedom of action. The latter wording left the government (in fact the Ministry of Foreign Affairs) with some latitude. Furthermore, the report states that the government shall (where relevant) give the European Committee an oral explanation of its initial stance. The important point is that the government is not obliged to secure a positive approval of its policy from the European Committee. It merely has to ensure that there is not a majority against its negotiation position ('negative parliamentarianism'). A report adopted by the European Committee in 1974 reiterated most of the points of the 1973 report, but added that it was still for the government to decide which EC matters were of such importance that the European Committee should be consulted. It also said that the negotiation (in the EC) was still the full responsibility of the Foreign Minister.[13]

In 1983 a parliamentary crisis concerning Danish participation in economic sanctions against the USSR revealed the fragility of the committee's powers. It became clear that there was scope for serious

[12] See Jørgen Ørstrøm Møller, *op. cit.*, pp. 257ff.
[13] Beretning fra Markedsudvalget (afgivet 14 juni 1974), *Folketingets Forhandlinger* 1973–74, pp. 984ff.

misunderstandings between government and opposition as long as government submissions in the European committee were purely oral. This crisis led to a certain improvement of the consultation procedure in the European Committee. A report from the committee in June 1983 stated that in future the ministers must specify beforehand on which points of the agenda they are going to submit a negotiation position. The submission will be taken down in short-hand by the secretary of the European Committee. However, the Minister of Foreign Affairs declared that the contents of the protocol of the committee could not bind the government legally irrespective of the fact that the contents had been taken down in short-hand.

Despite its rosy image abroad, the European Committee suffers from a number of weaknesses.[14] First of all, notwithstanding the continuous strengthening of the role of the committee, it is worth emphasizing that the improvements in the parliamentary consultation procedure have taken place without any amendment of the Act of Accession.[15] The legal character of the obligations of the government has not been discussed, nor has the possibility of introducing sanctions. Secondly, the European Committee is involved in EC decision-making at a very late stage, once Danish civil servants have in most cases already taken a position *vis-à-vis* other EU member states. This makes it difficult for the committee majority to modify the Danish stance without appearing to damage the Danish negotiating position. Thirdly, the growth in the rate of activity of the EC/EU in recent years has led to a significant increase in the workload of the European Committee. This enhances the risk of overlooking problems in EC legislation. Fourthly, in most cases members also have other parliamentary responsibilities and they do not receive administrative assistance earmarked for EC/EU affairs. The European Committee draws upon the expertise of other parliamentary committees only to a limited extent. Only in the case of environmental issues has it become customary to seek advice from the expert committee. This means that committee members are in fact expected to be experts in a number of different issue areas. As this is rarely the case, European Committee debates tend to become highly political and technically rather superficial. The fact that the European Committee has now for

[14] See Christensen, et al., *op. cit.*
[15] See Hagel-Sørensen and Hjalte Rasmussen, *op. cit.*, p. 284.

a couple of years had an EC/EU consultant to assist it in preparing committee meetings appears to have improved the situation only marginally. Fifthly, members receive EC/EU documents only a few days before committee meetings. Finally and probably most importantly, the information provided by ministers has often been lacking in quality.

In the spring of 1994, Denmark lost two important political battles in the EU concerning additives in foodstuffs. This episode (along with other setbacks for Denmark which put the executive under pressure) drew attention to some of the flaws in the Danish system of parliamentary control. As a result the Folketing decided on a number of reforms to remedy one of the key problems referred to above, the problem of insufficient and imperfect information. The main reform was to formulate stricter requirements as to when and how the government shall inform the European Committee, parliament, and the general public about the political battles in the EU in which Denmark is involved. It was thus decided to introduce a new system of so-called 'factual notes'. The notes are to provide information as to how a given Commission proposal will affect Danish laws and what the budgetary consequences of the proposal will be. The notes will also contain information regarding the criticism a given proposal has received from interest groups, etc. during the preparatory phase. The notes which are to be prepared by the government will be submitted to the European Committee, the relevant sectoral committees in parliament, and to the Danish MEPs. To the extent possible, the factual notes are to be submitted immediately after the Danish government has received the proposal in question from the Council secretariat and in any case before the EP deadline for amendments. Due to practical difficulties the new procedure will at first only apply in areas where Danish standards are affected, i.e. environmental policy, health, working environment and consumer policy. It is foreseen that the new procedure will later be applied to all 'major' cases on the Council's agenda, including pillar II and III cases. Other changes were introduced as well. The European Committee is planning to arrange hearings. It was decided to set up a *Council for European Policy*, consisting of a wide range of representatives of interest groups and grassroots organizations as well as opinion leaders in the EU area. The Council will arrange hearings and conferences, its purpose being to foster a greater and broader consensus. Finally, parliament has set up an *EU information centre*. In general the new reforms must be described as major improvements, probably constituting the biggest step forward in the democratization of Danish EC/EU policy since 1973.

Public opinion, political parties and interest groups

Danish EU politics are characterized by a discrepancy between a political elite and a corporate sector which now largely subscribes to the goal of a European Union, and a general public which remains opposed to the political dimension of European unification. One must distinguish between Danish EU opponents who object to membership of both the present EU and the earlier EC, and EU sceptics who can be defined as those in favour of a watered-down Union epitomized by the Danish opt-outs in the Edinburgh agreement. It is interesting to note the broadening of the support for European unification as such among the Danish political parties. Thus, seven parties including the erstwhile EU opponents in the Socialist People's Party (SF) managed to agree in October 1992 on the so-called 'National Compromise' regarding Denmark's relationship with the EU. The Socialist People's Party accepts European Union but only in the watered-down version of the Edinburgh Agreement. Danish public opinion is, however, characterized by a strong current of opposition to EU membership reflected in the first Danish 'No' to the Maastricht Treaty in 1992 and in the high number of 'No' votes in the 1993 referendum.

The EP elections in June 1994 were seen as a victory for the EU opponents. The diehard EU opponents in the People's Movement against the EU scored 10.3%, the slightly more pragmatic opponents in the new 'June Movement' who favour some kind of binding regional integration in Europe registered an impressive 15.2%. The total anti-EU vote was thus 25.5%, a major improvement on the 18.9% obtained by the People's Movement in 1989. Some of the new anti-EU votes clearly came from traditional supporters of the Socialist People's Party (SF), which has changed sides on the fundamental issue of European unification since 1989. Thus, in 1989 the SF obtained 9.1%, and in 1994 8.6%. One's overall assessment of the outcome of the EP elections in 1994 depends on whether one counts the SF as pro-EU or anti-EU. Given the fact that the present SF leadership only accepts the EU in the watered-down Edinburgh version, it is probably most correct to categorize the party as EU sceptics. The general trend in Danish popular attitudes seems to be one of increasing polarization with the moderate left-wing SF caught in the eye of the storm.[16] This pattern was reflected in the national elections in Denmark (September 1994), in which a radical left-wing party, the Unity List, became represented in parliament for the first time by capitalizing on the anti-EU issue.

During the first decade after Danish accession to the EC, membership was not a salient political issue, mainly due to the lack of momentum in European integration which made the EC a *de facto* economic entity. Since the mid-1980s, Danish EC policy has on the other hand been intensely politicized. In 1986 the controversy surrounding the adoption of the Single European Act provoked a referendum, which was won comfortably by the adherents, with 56% voting in favour. It has been shown that the outcome was very much dependent on the 'yes' side's ability to shape popular perceptions of the options available: since a majority of Danes were known to support continued membership of the EC, the 'yes' side pursued the strategy of describing adoption of the Single European Act as a precondition for continued Danish EC membership. In this it succeeded. The opponents of the SEA failed in their attempts to separate the reforms from membership itself.[17] The campaign prior to the first referendum on the Maastricht Treaty was different. For the first time in the history of Danish EC membership, the adherents of further integration argued their case mainly in political terms. A (small) majority of the Danes did not subscribe to the goal of a political union. This ought not to have come as a big surprise. Danish resistance to political unification was well known and it was only because of the predominance of economics in the Single European Act and the tactical skill of the 'yes' side in the 1986 campaign that this resistance did not surface earlier. In fact seen from a historical perspective what was surprising about the outcome of the 1992 referendum was not so much the victory of the 'no' side as the high score of the 'yes' side.

What were the motives of the adherents and opponents of the Maastricht Treaty? Polls show that in a battle fought with political weapons the supporters of further integration were in for a tough

---

[16] See Karen Siune, Palle Svensson and Ole Tonsgaard, *Fra et nej til et ja* (Aarhus: Politica, 1994), p. 205.

[17] See Torben Worre, 'Denmark at the Crossroads: The Danish Referendum of 28 February 1986 on the EC Reform Package', *Journal of Common Market Studies*, 26 (4) (1988).

fight. Apparently, the adherents also failed to impress on their supporters the political nature of the choice facing them. Concern about economic marginalization and a loss of welfare were the main motivating factors for the 'yes' side. The main concern of the no-voters was the loss of national freedom of action in a Union with a strong measure of political integration. Fear of becoming a satellite of the big member states and especially Germany was not strongly articulated by respondents (only some 2% said this was an important consideration behind their 'No'), but it may have played a bigger role as an underlying concern. The democratic deficit in the EC was also an important motivating factor, but contrary to what was argued by some international observers, it was not decisive.[18] What appears to have caused a number of opponents of Maastricht to change their minds in the second referendum in 1993 was partly satisfaction with the Edinburgh agreement, partly an effective 'yes' campaign which successfully shifted the emphasis from politics back towards economics and the costs of isolation.[19]

The EC/EU activity of private interest groups in Denmark is aided by the traditionally very close relations between the public sector and the large associations within industry, agriculture and the service sector.[20] There is a clear pattern of sectorization in Danish EC decision-making, and smooth relations with relevant ministries and their channels to Brussels have tended to compensate for weak direct links with the EC/EU. Most private lobbying is performed through or by associations. Euro-associations seem to play a limited role for Danish interest groups except for the agricultural sector. But so far the associations have not invested very great resources in the direct representation of interests in Brussels, an exception being Danish agriculture which has an office with nine lobbyists in Brussels. Only 13.4% of manufacturing companies have direct contact with the EC/EU. A few major companies such as Lego, Danfoss, Scanvægt and the partly state-owned Dansk Stålvalseværk (the Danish Steel Rolling Mill) have, however, mounted major lobbying initiatives.

[18] See Siune, Svensson and Tonsgaard, *Det blev et nej* (Aarhus: Politica, 1992).

[19] See Siune et al., *Fra et nej til et Ja, op. cit.*, and Nikolaj Petersen, 'Game, Set and Match. Denmark and the European Union from Maastricht to Edinburgh', in T. Tiilikainen and Ib Damgaard Petersen (eds.), *The Nordic Countries and the EC* (Copenhagen: Copenhagen Political Studies Press, 1993).

[20] This section is mainly based on Henning Bregnsbo and Niels Christian Sidenius, 'Denmark: The National Lobby Orchestra', in M. P. C. M. van Schendelen, *National Public and Private EC Lobbying* (Aldershot: Dartmouth, 1993).

Conclusion

The Danish EC decision-making system is what could be called a system of 'parallel coordination': the Foreign Ministry acts as coordinator in the executive branch, the European Committee in the parliamentary branch of the system. Both coordinating bodies have come under some stress in recent years. The Danish administrative system with regard to EC/EU affairs is characterized by a balance between decentralized planning and negotiation, on the one hand, and centralized coordination on the other. Individual ministries have extensive responsibilities in the field of EC policy. At the same time, the inter-ministerial coordination system, in which the Foreign Ministry plays a central role, ensures that Denmark generally acts as a unitary actor in Brussels. On balance the centralist features outweigh the decentralist ones. But as the policy scope of supranational integration increases, it evidently becomes more difficult for the Foreign Ministry to coordinate EC/EU policy.

The procedures for parliamentary control are elaborate and have sometimes been the object of critical comments from other EU member states with speedier democratic procedures. However, a *modus vivendi* has gradually been reached, and in recent years there have been few cases of open confrontation between government and opposition in the European Committee. However, the recent decision to strengthen significantly the position of Parliament and the European Committee in relation to the executive has made it more difficult for the Foreign Ministry to coordinate Danish EC/EU policy effectively. The advantages of the Danish system for democratic control should not be overlooked either. The system is indispensable in a political system with a high frequency of minority governments. It also ensures that EC legislation generally enjoys a high degree of acceptance. While the institution of the European Committee has been functional from the point of view of the political system *senso strictu*, it may, however, have had certain negative effects for the wider political system. Through the European Committee, parliamentary debate on the EC/EU has largely been confined to a small group of politicians in parliament which has enjoyed privileged access to the government's policy process. The involvement of parliamentarians in general has been limited. There is thus an element of 'parliamentary sectorization' and co-optation in the institution of the European Committee. Characteristically, the recent changes in the role of the committee were in part prompted by criticism from parliamentarians outside the committee and from the media. The legitimacy of the current system is thus under some pressure, although there are no signs of imminent changes in the fundamental structures of Denmark's EC/EU decision-making system.

Select bibliography

Auken, Svend, Buksti, Jacob and Sørensen, Carsten Lehmann, 'Denmark Joins Europe', *Journal of Common Market Studies*, 15 (1976), pp. 1–36.

Bregnsbo, Henning and Sidenius, Niels Christian, 'The National Lobby Orchestra', in M. P. C. M. van Schendelen (ed.), *National Public and Private EC Lobbying* (Aldershot: Dartmouth, 1993).

Christensen, Jørgen Grønnegaard, 'Da Centraladministrationen blev International', in I. Faurby and N. Amstrup (eds.), *Studier i Dansk Udenrigspolitik* (Aarhus: Politica, 1978).

—— 'Blurring the International-Domestic Politics Distinction: Danish Representation at EC Negotiations', *Scandinavian Political Studies*, 4 (3) (1981).

Christensen, Jørgen Grønnegaard, Germer, Peter and Pedersen, Thomas, *Åbenhed, offentlighed og deltagelse i den danske EU-beslutningsproces* (København: Udenrigsministeriet, 1994).

Hagel-Sørensen, Karsten and Rasmussen, Hjalte, 'The Danish Administration and its Interaction with the Community Administration', *Common Market Law Review*, 22 (1985), pp. 273–300.

Pedersen, Thomas, 'Danish EU Policy from the Perspective of Federalist Theory', in *Proceedings from the Jean Monnet Colloquium in Tübingen*, 1-4 July 1993 (Brussels, 1994).

Petersen, Nikolaj, 'Game Set and Match. Denmark and the European Union from Maastricht to Edinburgh', in T. Tiilikainen and Ib Damgaard Petersen (eds.), *The Nordic Countries and the EC* (Copenhagen: Copenhagen Political Studies Press, 1993).

Siune, Karen, Svensson, Palle and Tonsgaard, Ole, *Det blev et nej* (Aarhus: Politica, 1992).

—— *Fra et nej til et Ja* (Aarhus: Politica, 1994).

Ørstrøm Møller, J., 'Danish EC Decision-Making: An Insider's View', *Journal of Common Market Studies*, 21 (3) (March 1983), pp. 245–60.

Greece[1]

Fundamentals of Greece in EU affairs

The Hellenic Republic signed the first Association Agreement with the EC[2] in 1961 (applied in 1958, and in force since 1962). The 'Athens Agreement' was aiming at the accession of the Hellenic Republic into the EC within twenty-two years. The Agreement was partly frozen for seven years (1967–74), at the initiative of the Commission of the EC, as a reaction to the military regime that assumed power in Athens in 1967 and re-entered into force on the restoration of a liberal parliamentary regime in 1974. Almost immediately after the collapse of the military regime (as a result of the Turkish invasion of Cyprus and of a deepening economic crisis) the government then in power under K. Karamanlis, crowning its novel political project of liberal bourgeois modernization,[3] applied for full membership to the EC, early in 1975. The Hellenic Republic joined the EC, as its tenth member, in 1981.

Generally speaking the debate in Greece on the 'European system of cooperation', either before or after the accession of the country into the EC, has been conducted within a small circle of bureaucratic and party political elites without wider participation. To a large extent this reflects the *modus operandi* of the Greek political system.

[1] I am greatly indebted to numerous colleagues at the Department of Political Science and Public Administration at the University of Athens for their comments on earlier drafts of this paper, in particular Professor A. Fatouros. Needless to say, all errors and any conceptual and other deficiencies are entirely my own responsibility.

[2] After the Treaty on European Union (TEU) the EC is a pillar of the EU. In this paper the terms 'Community', 'Communities', 'EC' etc. are used interchangeably and refer to the EC of the Treaty of Rome as it was modified by the Single European Act (SEA). By 'EU' is understood the new European Union after Maastricht.

[3] See G. Mavrogordatos, 'The Greek Party System: A Case of Limited but Polarized Pluralism?', *West European Politics*, 7 (4) (1984), pp. 156–69.

Centralization, hyperpoliticization,[4] absence of rules for the game, virtual non-existence (with some exceptions) of civic organizations and a weak but paternalistic state are some of its typical characteristics. Although parliamentary institutions were introduced comparatively early in the Greek political system, these were never fully embraced by the Greek soul; as is the case with Western liberal ideas in general.[5] Diamandouros pointed out that this is due to a number of factors such as the impact of the illiberal, patriarchical Ottoman rule, the dire experiences inflicted by the behaviour of Western powers towards Greece, the weakness of the Greek bourgeoisie, the powers of traditionalist elites, the dominance of nationalist and irridentist ideologies as well as the absence of long and stable links with the European Enlightenment.[6] These inadequacies, although possibly not to the same extent, are still with us today designating the quality of the Greco-EU relations. In a recent contribution Fatouros[7] pointed out that the issue of the entry of the country into the EC was entangled in the old cleavage between 'Westernizers' and 'traditionalists'. This cleavage draws its existence in the years before the independence of the modern Greek state in 1831. This cleavage refers to the age-old question as to whether Greece belongs to the 'East' or to the 'West'. The 'Westernizers' (modernizers) historically identified, *grosso modo*, with the rational inquiry and the political liberalism of the continent, a sometimes cosmopolitan view of the world, whereas the 'Easterners' (traditionalists) were represented chiefly by the Orthodox Church advocating the defence of the status quo, e.g. religion, tradition and social hierarchy.[8] The Greek case in the EC/EU, therefore, is not and could not be a success story. This, *inter alia*, may be due to the fact that the country joined the Community on political rather than economic grounds. Certainly, it seems, the charismatic

[4] Spourdalakis talks of a case of 'apolitical hyperpoliticization' referring to an expedient for public affairs arising out of the need to serve one's own interests. See M. Spourdalakis, *The Rise of the Greek Socialist Party* (London: Routledge, 1988).

[5] See on this D. Kioukias, 'Political Ideology in Post-Dictatorial Greece: The Experience of Socialist Dominance', *Journal of Modern Greek Studies*, 11 (1993), pp. 51–73.

[6] See N. Diamandouros, 'Greek Political Culture in Transition: Historical Origins, Evolution and Current Trends', in R. Clogg (ed.), *Greece in the 80s* (London: Macmillan, 1988).

[7] See A. A. Fatouros, 'Political and Institutional Facets of Greece's Integration in the European Community', in J. H. Psomiades and B. Thomadakis (eds.), *Greece, the New Europe and the Changing International Order* (Pella, 1993), pp. 23–42.

[8] *Ibid.*, p. 24ff.

authority and consummate statesmanship of the then Prime Minister K. Karamanlis was instrumental in the success of the Greek application, as much as it was a result of the influence of the French understanding (Giscard d'Estaing/Helmut Schmidt) in the EC.

In Greek eyes, the country's new (from 1974 onwards) situation in regard to its neighbours necessitated additional structures of support in its international relations. In internal political terms the EC was seen as

- the additional support required for the protection of the new and fragile liberal parliamentary regime;
- the political and economic context which would facilitate the economic development of the country.

Karamanlis's strategy was based on a theory of 'induced modernization', e.g. that the country as a whole would have had to adjust to its much more competitive environment or perish. The underlying Westernization philosophy symbolizes the gamble that the country nearly lost during the PASOK years. 'Right' *v.* 'Left', 'East' *v.* 'West' (and possibly 'Third World' *v.* 'East' and 'West'), these cleavages (and their by-products) marked and are still marking the development of Greco-EC/EU relations.

The EC decision-making cycle and the participation of the national institutions

The government/ministerial administration

During the association years Greco-EC relations were the responsibility of the then Ministry of Coordination (Ministry of National Economy since 1983), including the permanent representation in Brussels, since this was the ministry responsible for the international economic relations of the country, although most ministries created European affairs divisions after 1976.[9] The Ministry of Foreign Affairs only appeared in the picture after the accession of the country to the EC. By Law 1104/80, representation of the country in the Community became the responsibility of the Ministry of Foreign Affairs and indeed of the minister and his junior minister and/or under-secretary of state for European affairs to the extent that min-

---

[9] See on this A. Makridimitris and A. Passas, *The Greek Public Administration and the Decision-Making Process in the Greco-EC Relations* (Athens: EKEM, 1992), p. 17.

isters participating in the various sectoral Councils must, by Law 1104/80, act in concert with the Minister for Foreign Affairs.[10] In the Ministry of Foreign Affairs (YPEX), for example, the agency for EC affairs and the Department on European Political Cooperation (EPC) are predominant in policy-making.[11] The new PASOK government introduced a *Secretary General on EC Affairs* in November 1993 above the YPEX and the department on the EPC, thus somewhat shifting the centre of power upwards and facilitating the political control of both agencies.

As a result of EC membership the style of policy-making has become more open, involving experts from other departments and ministries as well as independent experts.[12] Responsibility for European issues was given to the *Ministry of the National Economy and the Council of Economic Advisers (SOE)* – a unit of strategic importance within the Ministry of the National Economy – both of which at the time under Minister Arsenis (as was previously the case under Minister Manos and under the now late Minister Genimatas) had almost absolute authority on issues of economic policy broadly conceived, a politics/economics dichotomy. Gradually though, under the influence of a certain 'economism' in the perceptions of the implications of the Single European Act (SEA) and of the Treaty on European Union, but also due to the poor comparative economic performance of the country, the Ministry of National Economy has aquired the best part of the responsibility for European Affairs. Of course this is a source of tension between the various ministries which is compounded by the fact that to all intents and purposes the EC Council of Ministers is a 'legal fiction'.[13] Tension has also been built up as a result of the more recent changes in the 'European System of Co-operation' with the SEA and the extension of the competences of the Community to new areas of cooperation. Conflicts between the various ministries are resolved at a higher level, which is the cabinet

[10] *Ibid.*, pp. 18–20.

[11] See P. C. Ioakimides, 'Greece in the EC. Policies, Experiences and Prospects', in Psomiades and Thomadakis (eds.), *op. cit.*, pp. 405–20, especially pp. 414ff.

[12] *Ibid.*, p. 415.

[13] See on this W. Wessels, 'The EC Council: The Community's decisionmaking Centre', in Robert O. Keohane and Stanley Hoffmann (eds.), *The New European Community. Decisionmaking and Institutional Change* (Boulder: Westview, 1991), pp. 133–54, esp. pp. 145ff. See also by the same author 'Administrative Interaction', in W. Wallace (ed.), *The Dynamics of European Integration* (London: Pinter, 1990), pp. 229–41.

level (KISIM)[14] or even personally by the Prime Minister.[15] It must be said, however, that in general the effectiveness of such bodies of collective responsibility as KISIM is at best dubious, at least in European policy issues. Information from the Ministry of Foreign Affairs suggests that the SEA was not even discussed within KISIM![16] The reason for this phenomenon may relate to the fact that foreign policy lies traditionally within the domain of the prime minister and the prime minister's office within the Ministry of Foreign Affairs.

Anastopoulos in line with Makridimitris and Passas discusses the problems that the Greek public administration faces within the EC.[17] Hellenocentrism, a defensive attitude, a narrow financial approach as well as inflexibility are some of its major shortcomings. As a result the credibility of the Greek administration in the EC is seriously impaired.[18] Passas points out that in organizational terms the main problem seems to lie in poor coordination between the vertically organized units, the understaffing of those units and the wide mobility of personnel mainly through party political activity.[19] With regard to the last point, the speech delivered by Mr Pangalos, the under-secretary for foreign affairs, responsible for European affairs, of the PASOK government, is illustrative of the situation:

> When the time comes for the implementation of agreed policies with regard to the personnel in the administration ... the Minister, any Minister, on personal or party political considerations chooses the people to be sent to Brussels or that will become heads of the EC relevant departments within these ministries. As a result there are people in charge with no knowledge of the subjects involved whatsoever or that cannot even speak a foreign language.[20]

[14] See Makridimitris and Passas, *op. cit.*, p. 33; KISIM stands for 'Kivernitiko Simvoulio' which is a cabinet-like institution in which the prime minister, the two vice-chairmen of the government and the ministers of National Economy, Finance, Defence, Internal Affairs and Education participate.

[15] *Ibid.*, pp. 31ff.

[16] I owe this point to P. C. Ioakimides at the Ministry of Foreign Affairs. See also P. C. Ioakimides, *The EC and the Greek Public Administration*, paper presented to a conference organized by EKEM on 'Greece in the European Community' (May 1991).

[17] See D. I. Anastopoulos, 'The Greek Public Administration and the European Community. Necessary Adjustments in the Greek Administrative System', in EKEME-EIPA, *National Administration and Community Law* (Athens, 1993), pp. 33–49; Makridimitris and Passas, *op. cit.*

[18] See Anastopoulos, *op. cit.*, p. 35.

[19] See A. Passas, 'The Organisational and Functional Adjustment of the Greek Civil Service in View of its Community Obligations', in EKEME-EIPA, *op. cit.*, pp. 243–54.

[20] See T. Pangalos speech delivered in the EKEME-EIPA conference in 1993, *op. cit.*, pp. 281–2.

Anastopoulos proposed a number of changes in the system[21] which should be 'rationalized' and which should include the *Government Committee of European Policy (KYSEP)* in order to coordinate EC policies at the level of government, a vice-president of the government responsible for EC affairs[22] under the prime minister, a General Secretariate of EC affairs under the vice-president for EC affairs and a *Permanent Committee of Interministerial Coordination (DISEP)*.[23] Finally, task force units within each ministry for the planning of the European policies of each ministry (and whose head should participate in DISEP) are suggested as well as the development of institutionalized linkages between the national and the supranational bureaucracies with the introduction of interlocutors in each agency at the level of directors. Some increase is also foreseen in the role of the regions concerning the programming coordination and implementation of the EC-financed projects (with some transfer of power towards the regions). This completes the galaxy of the main proposals. There are other proposed measures of lesser magnitude regarding the upgrading of the personnel in the administration, even through transfers from the private sector as in France. At the end of the day financial considerations seem to lie in the way of administrative reforms, especially on issues related to EC affairs. Unfortunately, none of the above proposals has been implemented as yet. The new PASOK government (as of October 1993) has remained idle in most policy areas of its time in office so far.

The courts and the Greek implementation record

According to one account during the period 1981–5 there were 108 cases in which the Commission of the EC had initiated proceedings for breach or failure to comply with Community law.[24] This is quite favourable compared with Belgium (109), France (197) and Italy (189), but rather unfavourable when compared with the United King-

---

[21] See Anastopoulos, *op. cit.*, pp. 285ff.

[22] A view shared also by T. Pangalos, *op. cit.*, possibly leading to the formation of a bi-partisan agreement on the lines of the civil service reform. See also on this the view of Makridimitris in *Oikonomikos Tahidromos,* 14 Aug. 1993.

[23] All these proposals are included in the *Memorandum for the Modernization of the Civil Service* of 1990 and the subsequent *Proposal for the modernisation of the Greek Civil Service* of March 1992.

[24] See P. Bernitsas, 'The Breaches of the Community Law by the Greek Republic', in P. Kazakos and K. Stefanou (eds.), *Greece in the EC. The first five years* (Athens: Sakkoulas, 1987).

dom (61) and the Netherlands (69). Moreover, in the period 1982–4, there were 297 cases in which third parties notified the Commission of a breach of Community law by the Hellenic Republic, whereas the Commission identified another eighty-nine on its own.[25] According to another account, however, up to October 1987 only thirty-three cases have been brought before the European Court of Justice (ECJ), of which eleven have been struck off the Court's register after *a posteriori* compliance by the Hellenic Republic.[26] In their view the Greek courts seem to have accepted wholeheartedly the supremacy of Community law over national law on the basis of Art. 28(3) of the 1975 constitution. Table 10.1 shows all cases in front of the European Court of Justice for the period 1981–93 for breach or failure to comply with Community law by the Hellenic Republic.

Table 10.1 Cases before the ECJ against the Hellenic Republic 1981–1993

Year	no. of cases before the ECJ
1981	–
1982	–
1983	–
1984	3
1985	10
1986	13
1987	10
1988	14
1989	10
1990	10
1991	9
1992	4
1993	4

Source: Tenth and Eleventh Report of the Commission to the European Parliament on Monitoring the Application of Community law, 1992 and 1993. COM (93) 320 final, 28.4.1993; COM (94) 500 final, 29.3.1994.

As Table 10.1 shows, there were eighty-seven cases of breach of the Community law by the Hellenic Republic which were referred to the

---

[25] *Ibid.*, p. 8.
[26] See D. Kerameus and D. Kremlis, 'The Application of Community Law in Greece, 1981–1987', *Common Market Law Review*, 25 (1988), pp. 165ff. Some of the cases identified by the authors are also included in Table 10.1 in this chapter.

ECJ.[27] The table is exhaustive for the period 1981–93. Table 10.2
shows the ministry responsible for the policy area in which there was
a breach of the Community legislation. The importance, though, of
these cases for the interests of the Hellenic Republic varies. For example there are six cases which are not considered as important if only
because of the low level of respect that these issues enjoy in Greece.[28]
Indeed, it seems that the Hellenic Republic will become one of the
better clients of the ECJ on environmental issues in the 1990s, in spite
of being awarded responsibility for environmental issues by the
Delors III Commission. Already in 1992 there were six cases for
which the Commission issued an opinion under Art. 169 TEU, and
all of them concerned environmental issues under the responsibility
of the Ministry of Energy and National Resources (YPEHODE).[29] In
other words the message is that only cases with important financial
consequences are deemed as important in this country, or those that
appeared in order to protect a particular political clientele of a sufficient political (financial) weight, usually in the name of the national
interest.

Two other cases exemplify this point since these were due to the
political will to protect an influential banana producer in Crete from
the competition of better and cheaper foreign products.[30] On the other
hand case 132/85 on the failure of the Hellenic Republic to comply
with the first and second Community directive on capital movements
was deemed as very important on account of the poor performance of
the macro-economic indices in the country (although similar actions
over the years have not prevented Greek subjects from depositing an
estimated sum of US$ 17bn – a sum roughly equal to the foreign debt
of the country – in Swiss banks). Similarly the case on tax treatment
of imports is a very important one which gives account of a long practice in Greco-EC relations, going back to 1968 when the customs
union between the two sides was formed following the 1962 Associa-

[27] Since 1991 the responsibility for the defence of the country before the ECJ has
been transferred to the Legal Council of the State ('*Nomiko Synvoulio tou Kratous*').
[28] Case 123/86 on the quality of water for shellfish; case 187/86 on surface water;
case 187/86 on waters for live fish conservation; case 190/86 on directive 75/442; case
187/86 on water for swimming and case 187/76 on surface drinking water.
[29] These concerned directive 79/409, directive 88/610, directive 87/101 and two more
cases concerning the Lake Vegoritis and the river Soulos. Data reported in the daily
Kathimerini, 26 Jan. 1993, p. 5.
[30] Case 241/85 on bananas from ACP countries and case 194/85 on banana imports
from the EC.

tion Agreement. Indeed, since 1968 all forms of tariff barriers to trade between the two sides have been abolished, a fact which did not prevent the continuation of the protection of the Greek industries through a complicated array of internal taxation measures designed to counteract imports. At the end of the day this issue was finally solved in 1987 through the application of the so-called 'adjustment tax', a *contra legem* measure in itself as Bernitsas[31] has pointed out. Finally there are two case which are much more serious from a *communautaire* point of view, since they relate to the failure to comply with rulings by the ECJ.[32] The same comment applies to case C 45/91 on the river Kouroupitos for which, although there has been a ruling by the Court, a recent report informs us that no measure of compliance has been introduced as yet.[33] In those cases where there is compliance with EC law, this does not happen before the lapse of sixteen months on average for those cases referred to in Table 10.1. On the other hand, in spite of the fact that the problem with the incorporation of EC legislation relates to that included in directives, the Hellenic Republic has a very good record in the implementation of the directives on the Single European Market, having incorporated 165 directives by December 1992 and nearly 200 by December 1993.

The EKEME/EIPA study identified four areas of interest to the Greek government with regard to the application of Community law.[34] These areas are:

- health and safety of employees during work;
- the Greek border regions;
- telecommunication services;
- nationalized industries.

On the issue of health and safety the policies of the Greek government have been described as a case of harmonization and non-application. The situation is much more complex with regard to the second issue which concerns the country's border regions and the Community legislation. Perrakis rightly points out that in the case of the country's border regions, a host of legal, political and economic

---

[31] See Bernitsas, *op. cit.*, p. 173. The introduction of this tax was a result of a political agreement between the Greek Republic and the EC institutions.

[32] Case 328/90 on the implementation of a decision of the ECJ; case 159/89 on the ECJ decision Gaston-Schul.

[33] See *Kathimerini*, 26 Jan. 1993, p. 5.

[34] See EKEME-EIPA, *op. cit.*

factors mix, giving rise to a very convoluted and politically conse-
quential situation in the relation between Greece and the EC.[35]

Table 10.2 State bodies and ministries 'responsible' or 'co-responsible' for
cases before the ECJ 1981–1991

Body/ministry	Responsible	Co-responsible
Ministry of Health (YYP)	0	2
National Drug Organization (EOF)	0	2
Ministry of National Economy (YPETHO)	3	18
Ministry of Energy and National Resources (YEFP, since 1987 YPEHODE)	0	1
Agricultural Bank of Greece (ATE)	0	1
Ministry of Agriculture (YG)	8	6
Ministry of Trade (YPEM)	15	3
Minstry for the Environment (YHOP)	1	7
Ministry of Finance (YPOIK)	5	2
Ministry of Justice (YDIK)	1	2
Bank of Greece (TE)	0	2
Ministry of Defence (YEA)	0	1
Ministry of Foreign Affairs (YPEX)	0	1
Ministry of Education (YPED)	2	0
Ministry of Transport (YPMET)	2	1
Ministry of Coordination *YPS, since 1983 YPETHO)	0	1
Ministry of Employment (YE)	1	0
Ministry of Industry, Research and Technology (YVET)	1	4
State Chemical Laboratories (GHK)	1	2
National Tourism Organization (EOT)	0	1
Ministry of Culture (YPP)	1	0
Ministry of Environment, Physical Planning and Public Works (YPEHODE, since 1987)	3	3

Very briefly, via a number of laws dating back to the inter-war
period, the Greek state has explicitly banned non-Greek subjects
from buying property in those areas designated as border regions
(practically 51% of the territory of the country). The ban was relaxed
de facto during the 1960s and early 1970s at the initiative of the then
government of the country. Two decisions by two courts (30/1981
and 75/1981) relaunched the debate on this issue which internally

[35] See E. S. Perrakis, 'National Administrative Rigidities in the Application of Community Law. The Black–White Logic in the Case of the Greek Border Regions', in
EKEME-EIPA, *op. cit.*, pp. 81–99.

ended with decision 425/83 of the Supreme Court. After action had been taken by the Commission of the EC on the basis of Art. 169 EC, the case finally ended with decision 305/87 of the European Court of Justice (case no. 305/87). The ECJ concluded that the said ban violated Arts. 48, 52 and 59 of the Treaty of Rome. The Greek Supreme Court had entered this debate with its decision 425/1983, referred to above, which states, *inter alia*, the following: 'this decision (i.e. the previous decision by a lower court) was dictated by reasons of supreme national interest, for the protection of the territorial integrity and the national security of the country given the obvious dangers that can be foreseen as a result of foreigners buying up property in border regions'.[36] This quotation from the decision of the Supreme Court highlights the extreme sensitivity that the Greek state in general applies when approaching issues that might have security implications. Nevertheless, a *posteriori* the Greek government complied with the ruling of the ECJ, kept the ban in force, but excluded from the prohibition subjects from the EC member states.[37] Finally the new Treaty on European Union (Art. 73b) on the liberalization of capital movements is expected to give rise to a plethora of legal problems regarding the border regions.[38]

The third issue above relates to the telecommunications market in the EC as well as in Greece. Nowadays it is quite a topical issue with reference to the privatization or quasi-privatization policies of the previous New Democracy government (and of the current PASOK government although with differences in emphasis) regarding these services. Spathopoulos pointed out the various legal problems that the 'Organismos Tilepikinonion Elados' (OTE), the country's Telecom company, faced after the accession of the country to the EC,[39] and especially after the ECJ's judgment on the British Telecom (BT) case, on very much similar grounds to those in the BT case.[40] Directive 90/388 should have been incorporated in the Greek legal order by 31 December 1990. By December 1991 the Commission of the EC

[36] Quoted in Perrakis, *op. cit.*, p. 82.

[37] This happened with Law 1829/90, Arts. 24–32. See on this G. Kremlis, 'Aspects of the Border Regions Problematique and New Developments in Community Law', in EKEME-EIPA, *op. cit.*, pp. 107–12.

[38] *Ibid.*, p. 111.

[39] See F. Spathopoulos, 'The Creation of a Common Telecommunications Policy', in EKEME-EIPA, *op. cit.*, pp. 143–81.

[40] See OJ L 360/36 of 21 Dec. 1982.

had already issued an opinion. The government complied with the requirements of the Community law by July 1992 (Law 2075/92). This, however, is a 'framework law' whose implementation requires the issuing of several presidential decrees none of which has been published as yet.[41] Karageorgiou goes a little further than that by suggesting that the 'Greek government ignored the international trends in the telecommunications market as well as the policy intentions of the Commission at all phases of this process'.[42] The author pointed out that at the end of the day Law 2075/92 by which the Greek government complied with directive 90/388 EC was based on a philosophy diametrically different from that of the Commission. Instead of whittling away the ideas about the existence of physical monopolies in the sector, the said law reaffirmed them. *Plus que ça change, plus c'est la même chose!*

The fourth issue above relates to the nationalized industries in Greece. This is one more politically impressionable story which has been at the top of the political agenda for quite some time. By Law 1386/83 forty-four industries with 30,000 employees and a total debt of 250 billion drs were nationalized (the process of nationalization ended in 1985). A new organization was set up, 'The Organization for the Reconstruction of the Industry' (OAE). The forty-four companies were divided into two categories[43] depending on whether they were thought likely to survive market pressures if reorganized. The 'experiment' lasted for eight years and failed at an estimated total cost of over 1 trillion drs[44] to the state budget. The Commission of the EC did not react to the setting-up of the OAE. It was only in 1987 that the Commission issued a decision by which it demanded changes to certain aspects of Law 1386/83 as contravening directive 77/91/EC on company law. The Hellenic Republic was asked to comply within three months but it took much longer than that, namely forty months.

Generally speaking, the compliance of the member states with the rulings of the Court has been remarkable considering that the latter

[41] That is by January 1995.

[42] See I. S. Karageorgiou, 'Telecommunication Services and Community Rules on Competition', in EKEME-EIPA, *op. cit.*, pp. 183–91; here: p. 190.

[43] Twenty-three companies were thought able to survive the market pressures, if reorganized, whereas twenty-one were thought to be unable. All in all 250 companies have applied to be included in Law 1386/83.

[44] At 1983 prices; see Ministry of National Economy, 'Bulletin of Information' (June 1992).

lacks the means to enforce its rulings.[45] Cases, however, of non-compliance should not be tolerated. Similarly, the idea of inflicting sanctions of various kinds on member states that violate EC law (the withholding of Community funds seems to be the most efficient measure in this respect) deserves some serious reflection. For Greece such a possibility would help to discipline and rationalize the political system, an argument similar to that used in the public debate of this country in favour of joining the EMS (before the imposition of the new 'temporary' 15% margin in August 1993) as soon as possible. The Treaty on European Union though followed a different formula in its Art. 171. According to this article, if a member state fails to comply with a ruling of the Court of Justice, a penalty or a lump sum will be imposed. If decisions of the Court on such a penalty will not be compromised at the political level, this article of the TEU may prove useful for the future functioning of the European Union.

Fifteen of the cases referred to in Table 10.1 above were related to the agricultural sector in general, i.e. 17.5% approximately. These range from illegal subsidies for the selling of agricultural machinery to farmers, to the criteria for organizing producers' organizations of olive oil. Thirty cases or 24% are related to the failure to incorporate EC directives into the national legal order, thus maintaining in force measures of equivalent effect to taxes or quotas, or in any other way discriminating against imports of industrial goods from the other EC countries. For some of these cases, however, the Hellenic Republic complied *a posteriori* with the Community legislation and as a result the initiated proceedings had been dropped.

As Table 10.2 above showed, the ministries of Trade, National Economy, Agriculture and Finance were responsible or co-responsible for sixty out of seventy-nine cases before the Court between 1981 and 1991 or 76% of them. Most of the cases before the ECJ are of concern to ministries with an economic orientation. The breaches of Community legislation are in those areas where the 'European System of Cooperation' is more developed, e.g. in those areas that are re-regulated at the supranational level. Finally, in a number of instances the Hellenic Republic and/or Greek natural or legal persons brought cases to the ECJ. Kerameus and Kremlis identified twelve such cases

---

[45] See on this *inter alia* G. F. Manchini, 'The Making of a Constitution for Europe', in Robert O. Keohane and Stanley Hoffmann (eds.), *op. cit.*, pp. 177–94.

up to October 1987, eleven of which were directed against the Commission and one against the Council.[46]

The parliament

It is probably fair to suggest that the overall influence of the parliament in foreign policy formulation is marginal. This is true in the case of the European policy of Greece which is regarded as part of the international relations of the country in spite of occasional declarations to the contrary by various influential individuals inside and outside the main political parties. A trend also towards the marginalization of the parliament seems to be in train regarding its position in the inter-institutional balance of power within the Greek political system in general. The reasons for this marginalization of the parliament are not dissimilar in their substance to the reasons outlined in the relevant international literature for other (West) European political systems.[47] A mixture of political and legal constraints combine with the structural obstacles associated with the development of the post-industrial societies. Papadimitriou identified two categories of constraints for the entanglement of the parliament in the foreign policy formulation process:[48] (a) *de jure*-constitutional, and (b) *de facto*. In particular, the most important function that the 1975 constitution recognizes in the field of foreign policy for the parliament is the ratification of international treaties, on the count provided for by the new Art. 36 para. 2. Papadimitriou suggests that the constitution affords to the parliament an increased presumption of competence in this field since the will of the 1975 Constitutional Assembly has been in favour of increased powers of the parliament (in conjunction with Art. 26, para. 2 of the constitution).[49] Papadimitriou concluded that

[46] See Kerameus and Kremlis, *op. cit.*, pp. 170ff.

[47] See on this *inter alia* P. Norton (ed.), 'Parliaments in Western Europe', special issue of *West European Politics*, 13 (3) (1990), pp. 1–156. See also M. Tsinisizelis, *Democratic Deficit. A View From the South*, paper presented to the annual PSA conference in Lancaster, United Kingdom. On the role of the Greek parliament in the foreign policy formulation process see T. Kouloumbis and D. Konstas (eds.), *The Greek Parliament in Foreign Policy 1974–1984* (Athens: Sakkoulas, 1986). From the voluminous international literature see the more recent contributions by F. Jacobs; and R. Corbett and M. Shackleton, *The European Parliament* (Harlow: Longman, 1992).

[48] See G. Papadimitriou, *The (Greek) Constitution and the Process of European Integration* (Athens: Sakkoulas, 1982).

[49] See S. Vassilouni, *The National Parliament and the European Community*, Greek Parliament, Scientific Committee (February 1990).

the parliament during the decade 1975–85[50] exercised its ratification powers without a substantial debate either on the whole or in parts of these agreements which is a remarkably consistent practice throughout the decade under examination. Additionally, a large number of international agreements are excluded from the ratification procedures of the parliament in spite of specific constitutional provisions. According to Papadimitriou there exists a transfer of powers to the executive. The same conclusion can be drawn with respect to the 'regular' means of parliamentary control since neither the constitution nor the rules of procedure differentiate between them for the purposes of foreign policy.[51] The 1975 constitution does not recognize any specific role for parliament in the formulation of the foreign policy of the country, including its European policy.

This position of the country in the 'European System of Cooperation' is usually discussed in parliament on the occasion of more general debates on 'the state of the country' between party political leaders, or on the eve of major European Councils; this is a practice mostly used during more recent years due to the rapid developments in the EC since the mid-1980s. At any rate debates of this sort are always conducted in the context of the foreign policy of the country and the information provided during these meetings is at best trivial. The only exceptions to this rule so far have been the debates on the occasion of the ratification of the Treaties of Accession of Spain and Portugal and of the Single European Act.[52]

Through the procedure of oral and written questions individual members of parliament can control the executive or demand information and documents of the various ministries which are involved in the European policy-making process. This possibility seems to be under-utilized by MPs in European affairs since they prefer issues of 'domestic' importance. This is true for both government and opposition MPs at the same time.

The relevant international literature, both in the field of law and political science, has concluded that the nature of Community legislation and especially its direct effect and direct applicability (in the case

---

[50] The dates (1974–77, 1977–81, 1981–85) show the years that general elections were held after the 'Metapolitefsis' of 1974. These were four in all up to 1985.

[51] See Papadimitriou, *op. cit.*, pp. 17ff.

[52] See parliamentary debates of 4 November 1985 (Accession of Spain and Portugal) and of 14 January 1987 (SEA).

of regulations and also of directives after the SEA)[53] had adverse effects on the influence of parliamentary institutions throughout the EC. Since the mid-1980s with the entry into force of the SEA (1987) and of the more recent Treaty on European Union (TEU), the question of the democratic deficit has absorbed much of the time of the discussions inside and outside the EC. It is no surprise, therefore, to find out that the role of the Greek parliament in the field of incorporation of EC legislation is minimal. Indeed Law 945/79, by which the accession treaty was ratified, stipulates that the final responsibility for the incorporation of EC legislation in the Greek legal order rests with the executive of the country on the basis of the general authorization of Art. 43, para. 4 of the 1975 constitution, i.e. through presidential decrees.[54] Table 10.3 shows the number and the contents of the legislation relevant to the EC that has passed through parliament.

Table 10.3 is exhaustive for the period 1981–9 (1 January 1981 to 1 October 1989), i.e. the years of PASOK in government and also of the two interim governments of 1989–90. In the period between 1975 and 1979, i.e. during the last phase of the association agreement, the parliament has been involved four times in legislation relevant to the EC.[55] Once in the Community, and in a period of nine years, only thirty laws were ratified by parliament.[56] Most of this legislation concerned the EC's external relations and institutional affairs.

Another indication specific to the Greek parliament may be given by the sad fact that although the government was required to submit to parliament an annual review of its European activities (Art. 3 of law 945/79 by which the accession agreement was ratified), it did so only once on April 1989 in the space of nine years (1981–9), only three months before losing the June 1989 general elections.

The procedure that originated in the accession treaty for the incorporation of EC legislation through presidential decrees was continued and extended in law 1338/83 on the 'implementation of the Commu-

[53] See on this J. Pelkmans, 'The New Approach to Technical Harmonization and Standardization', *Journal of Common Market Studies*, 25 (3) (1987), pp. 249–69.

[54] See S. Yassilouni, *op. cit.*, pp. 5ff.

[55] Law 278/76 which created an EC information and press service in Athens; Law 499/76 on an additional protocol in the Association Agreement; law 477/76 on a Greco-EC interim agreement and Law 746/78 on the second Greco-EC financial protocol. See N. Frangakis, 'The Greek Parliament and the Participation of Greece in the EC, 1974–1981', in T. Kouloumbis and D. Konstas (eds.), *op. cit.*, pp. 85–95.

[56] This number includes all the 'major' pieces of EC legislation such as the Accession Treaty, the SEA, the TEU etc.

nity law' which contained the special delegation of authority of Art. 43, para. 2 of the constitution for the publication of regulatory decrees or of regulatory acts by the executive.[57] As Vassilouni observes, Law 1338/83 provided for the administration of EC legislation by means of ministerial decrees or other regulatory acts from other sections of the executive. By way of Art. 1 of the same law the final responsibility for the incorporation of Community legislation rests with the government.

Table 10.3 Number and contents of relevant EC legislation decided upon by the Greek parliament

Number	Law	Issue
1	1180/1981	MEPs to the European Parliament
2	1255/1982	EC Press and Information Office
3	1338/1983	Implementation of Community law
4	1402/1983	Adaptation of customs and tax legislation to EC law
5	1420/1984	Ratification of additional protocol for the transportation of animals
6	1427/1984	Voting rights for non-resident Greeks on the 1984 EP elections
7	1440/1984	Greek participation in the EIB, ECSC capital and EURATOM
8	1447/1984	Adaptation of internal taxation to the EC regime
9	1531/1985	LOME/EC-ECSC ratification
10	1572/1985	Ratification of the accession of Spain and Portugal to the EC and EURATOM
11	1505/1986	LOME IV/EC
12	1603/1986	ECSC (Austria/Switzerland: transportation of coal)
13	1640/1986	Set-up of special Legal Service on EC issues
14	1681/1987	Ratification of the Single European Act and of annexes to that
15	1682/1987	Means and institutions of regional policies, Integrated Mediterranean Programmes and public investment
16	1690/1987	Greek participation in the 'European School'
17	1714/1987	ECSC/India
18	1716/1987	EC/Tunisia
19	1717/1987	EC/Lebanon
20	1718/1987	EC/Israel

[57] See S. Vassilouni, *op. cit.*, pp. 9ff.

21	1719/1987	EC/Morocco
22	1720/1987	Ratification of additional protocols to agreements with Lebanon, Morocco, Israel, Egypt, Jordan, Syria, Algeria, Tunisia and the ECSC
23	1721/1987	EC/Egypt
24	1722/1987	Ratification of EC/Kartalena Agreement
25	1723/1987	Ratification of additional protocols to the agreements between ECSC and Austria, Norway, Sweden, Finland, Liechtenstein, Iceland
26	1724/1987	EC/Jordan (ratification of additional protocol)
27	1725/1987	EC/Yugoslavia
28	1726/1987	EC/Algeria
29	1727/1987	Technical obstacles to trade
30	1814/1988	Ratification of Agreement
31	2008/1992	Treaty on European Union

Source: S. Vassilouni, *The National Parliament and the European Community*, Greek Parliament, Scientific Committee, Annex II (February 1990).

Law 1338/83 is also important for another reason: it signifies the change in PASOK's attitude with respect to the EC. More specifically, the said law was published fifteen months after the expiration of the general authorization to the executive contained in Law 945/79 by which the Accession Treaty was ratified. That is to say that for a period of fifteen months (from 1 January 1982 to 17 March 1983) no Community legislation was incorporated into the Greek legal order, which had no unimportant consequences for the relations between Greece and the EC. It was the memorandum to the EC of March 1982 which was the main factor behind the publication of Law 1338/83.

The Greek parliamentary *Standing Committee on European Integration (or on European Community Affairs* as is the name preferred by the parliament's rules of procedure) is a mixed committee consisting of twenty-nine parliamentarians (fourteen MPs and fourteen MEPs) and one vice-chairman of the House as the chairman of the committee. It is one of the more recent committees of the seven standing committees of the House and was set up by a decision of the chair of the House on 13 June 1990.[58] Both MPs and MEPs are voting members and are chosen on the basis of the electoral strength of their parties in both the National and the European parliaments, although the

[58] Decision of the Chair of the House (the Speaker) 3076/2008 of 13 June 1990.

electoral system is not the same in both instances.[59] The tasks of this committee were defined in the same decision. Thus, the committee deliberates on: (a) institutional issues of the EC; (b) the cooperation between the national parliaments and the European Parliament; (c) the EC legislation due for incorporation into the national legal order; (d) the decisions of the *ad hoc* or standing parliamentary committees of relevance to the EC.[60] Neither the tasks of this committee nor its synthesis are defined in the rules of procedure of the parliament. As with the other standing committees of the House the number of participants in this committee may be changed following a decision of the chair. With the creation of this committee the parliament simply confirmed the earlier decision of its chair referred to above and modified its rules accordingly. The rules, however, stipulate that the committee shall monitor the convergence process and the process of European integration in general and that it 'can submit reports twice a year on which there can be a debate at the plenary' but no vote will be taken on these reports.[61] Similarly the rules allow for the possibility that ministers may be summoned in front of the committee to supply information on EC matters especially on the eve of Council meetings as is the case with the other standing committees of the House. The very wording of the rules, however, may raise doubts as to the existence of the necessary political resolution in the setting-up of this committee. To make things worse the penultimate paragraph 4 of Art. 32 A states that 'for the purposes of this committee Art. 37.2 shall not be applicable'. This means that there is no remuneration to the members of the committee for their participation in the committee work. Suffice to point out that this is the only standing committee of the House in which Art. 37.2 is not applicable. Nevertheless, it was by the relative increase in power of the European Parliament after the SEA and the introduction of the cooperation procedure between the EP and the Council that the necessary impetus for the creation of this committee was established. However, the necessary evidence for its practical significance regarding parliamentary

---

[59] In the European elections the electoral system is one of pure proportional representation as opposed to the national elections where the system is under continous revision. Since 1974 every government has put forward a tailor who remade the electoral system before each general election. Most of these systems were of the proportional representation type, but a pure representative system similar to the one at the EP elections was never put forward.

[60] Article 5 of decision 3076/2008.

[61] Article 32 A, 2 of the rules of procedure of the House.

scrutiny on EC affairs has not been supplied yet. After the entry into force of the TEU, changes in direction were contemplated but nothing has happened yet.

Local government

At the level of local government, the situation is similar to that concerning interest group activities within the Greek political system (see below). The '*Topiki Autodioikisi*' ('local self administration' if directly translated), which originated from the 'communes' during Ottoman rule,[62] is not recognized as a source of power independent from the state under Art. 102 of the 1975 constitution. It is allowed, though, to exercise those powers that have been delegated to it by the state. Art. 102 of the 1975 constitution stipulates that the local authorities are responsible for the management of 'local affairs'.[63] The definition of what constitutes a 'local affair' has been a constant source of tension in the relations between the state and the local authorities (municipalities). These latter are divided into '*demoi*' and '*koinotites*' on the basis of their population. All municipalities with more than 10,000 inhabitants are classified as '*demoi*', while those with less are classified as '*koinotites*' (communes); 84% of which have less than 1,000 inhabitants. However, the communes altogether represent only 19% of the total population of the country. Overall there are 5,999 '*koinotites*' and only 304 '*demoi*'.

The vast majority of the bottom tier local authorities are communes in spite of having only a small percentage of the total population of the country. Through this irrationality of the territorial multidivision the powers of the 'centre' and its policy choices are facilitated considerably. The situation is aggravated by the extreme financial dependence of the local authorities upon the uninhibited flow of resources from the centre. The absence of elected intermediary bodies such as regions – in spite of the existence of room for a development in this direction in the 1975 constitution and despite the tripartisan agreement on the subject during the oecumenical government of 1989/90 – also facilitates the muddling through of the policies of the centre.

[62] See on this B. Andronopoulou and M. Mathioudaki, 'Administrative History of Modern Greece. Regional/Local Administration', *Dioikitiki Metarithmisi* (1988), pp. 18–34.

[63] See on this S. Flogaitis, *The Greek Administrative System* (Athens: Sakkoulas, 1987).

Administrative regions have been introduced as a direct result of the country's membership of the EU in order to accommodate the Integrated Mediterranean Programmes (IMPs) of 1985. Indeed Law 1622/86 and the presidential decree 51/87 divided the country into thirteen regions and in six of them IMPs were implemented.[64] This development, however, should not be interpreted as a parallel process of devolution which followed the introduction of the IMPs (or the reform of the structural funds for that matter). Instead, since the new structure which was formed for the management of the Community's structural policy was not empowered with the necessary legal means to carry out its tasks, it is safe to describe the situation as one of 'nominal devolution'.[65] In January 1993 the 'Decleris commission' appointed by the Minister of the Presidency presented its report on a programme of 'administrative modernization'[66] whose self-acknowl-edged *raison d'être* has been defined as a reaction to the prospective entry into force of the Treaty on European Union. The committee proposed, *inter alia*, the reduction of the number of regions to seven or eight, and even more importantly it suggested regional ministries headed by junior ministers and/or under-secretaries of state, along the lines of the already existing Ministry of the Aegean and the Ministry of Macedonia and Thrace. The purpose of these measures according to the words of the documents were 'the design, planning and the coordination of regional development and the execution of regional programmes'. The answer to the challenges of the Treaty on European Union is not devolution but further state control. This comes as a natural consequence to the very limited part played by the regions, or the local authorities for that matter, with respect to the new role (as from 1988 onwards) afforded to the structural funds and the introduction of the new 'partnership' procedure involving the national and supranational institutions in the choice of projects for financing. Such a conclusion is applicable for the implementation phase of the Community structural policy although local interest groups through their local chambers and party political connections

[64] For the purpose of the IMPs the country has been divided into six administrative regions: Aegean Islands, Attica, Central and Eastern Greece, Crete, Northern and Western Greece, Peloponnese. Law 1622/1986 was introduced shortly after the sub-mission of the first IMP; the seventh IMP was a sectoral one on informatics.

[65] On the issue of regional planning in Greece see F. Papageorgiou and S. Verney, 'Regional Planning and the Integrated Mediterranean Programmes in Greece', in *Regional Politics and Policy*, 1 (2) (1992), pp. 139–161.

[66] Reported in the newspaper *To Vima*, 24 Jan. 1993.

seem to enjoy added currency. More generally the centralization of the political system and the position of the local authorities as well as the absence of elected intermediary institutions are among the principal reasons that the Treaty on European Union ·is creating problems in Greece. More specifically, subsidiarity, a key concept in the new Maastricht Treaty (Art. 3b TEU), is not really understood in its practical consequences and adds unwelcome pressures towards the devolution of authority in the political system. At the end of the day the general characteristics of the Greek political system seem to be reproduced. The experience from the application of the first Community Support Framework (CSF) 1988–93 seems to be a case in point. Funds from the CSF were allocated to 10,000 different projects (where the choice of projects for financing seemed to have been random with no overall strategic objectives to be obtained) in the best traditions of clientelistic politics, reducing thus the overall development impact of the EC's financial help.[67]

Public opinion, political parties and interest groups

Public opinion

Public opinion in Greece is, on the basis of the data presented by Eurobarometer, inside the trend found for the rest of the EU member states. Table 10.4 provides some details.

A big majority has been recorded in favour of the unification attempts in Western Europe. In fact to the first question in Table 10.4 on the efforts to unify Western Europe 67% (average between 1980–90) replied that they were strongly in favour, or in favour to some extent and even 79% in 1993, whereas only 15% (12% in 1993) were found to be against to some extent or very much against the unification attempts. Thus there was a net gain of 15 points over more than a decade concerning the favourable opinion in Greece with regard to European unification. This finding is supported by the data provided by the second question in Table 10.4 referring to the evaluation of the respondents to Greece's EC membership. During the eleven years shown in this question those of the respondents that considered the EC as a 'good thing' were considerably more than those that considered it as a 'bad thing' by a factor of 4. In 1993 this factor

[67] See on this D. Mayes, I. Begg and M. Tsinisizelis et al., *A New Strategy for Economic and Social Cohesion*, European Parliament Research Report, no. 19 (1991).

Table 10.4 Greek public opinion and European integration[68]

QUESTIONS	1980s %	1993[69] %	DIFFERENCE[70]
For or against efforts to unify Western Europe	1980–90		
FOR: very much/some extent	67	79	+12
AGAINST: very much/some extent	15	12	−3
Membership of Greece in the EC a good or a bad thing?	1981–90		
GOOD	52	68	+16
BAD	13	8	−5
NEITHER	24	18	−6
Has Greece benefited from EC membership?	1983–90		
BENEFITED	60	72	+12
NOT BENEFITED	20	18	−2
NO REPLY	20	11	−9
Favourable or unfavourable impression of the EP on what has been read or heard?	1982–90		
RATHER GOOD	52	56	+4
RATHER BAD	12	11	−1
NEITHER	29	30	+1
Favourable or unfavourable impression of the Commission on what has been read or heard?	1987–90		
GENERALLY FAVOURABLE	59	51	−8
GENERALLY UNFAVOURABLE	6	13	+7
NEITHER	28	33	+5
For or against a European government responsible to the EP?	1987–90		
FOR	51	62	+11
AGAINST	16	12	−4
NO REPLY	34	26	−8

grew to 8.5. Does this data suggest that there exists a wide appreciation of the EC experiment *per se* or is this due to underlying changes

[68] The numbers in the table are averages for the respective time period unless otherwise indicated; most of them are taken from Eurobarometer trends 1974–90.

[69] Eurobarometer, no. 39 (1993). All figures for 1993 in the table are from the same source.

[70] Differences between the two columns in absolute terms.

in social and attitudinal structures of the modern Greek society? This is the theme for another more in-depth reflection but it should be pointed out that according to Inglehart's typology Greece has joined the post-materialistic cohort of countries.[71]

The above observations, regarding the bases of support for the EC, are strengthened if we take into consideration a certain 'mismatch' in the data between the first and third questions. This latter refers to the feeling of the respondents as to whether their country has benefited from membership of the EC. Indeed only since 1989 onwards do the percentages in favour of European unification match with those who feel that their country has benefited from the EC. In every other instance up to 1989 (1980–88) those of the respondents who thought that their country had benefited from the EC were more, by a factor of 3, than those who thought the opposite. At any rate they are considerably less than those in favour of European unification in the earlier question. Nevertheless if we observe the trend in both questions we may conclude that the anti-EC attitude is declining at the beginning of the 1990s.

The last three questions in Table 10.4 relate to the institutions of the EC. The first of these refers to the impression that the respondents had of the European Parliament. The data suggest that there is an adequate coverage of the EP in the media, although Greek TV, both public and private, and newspapers tend to overstate its importance in the EC's institutional system perhaps because the EP tends to be more 'sympathetic' to Greek positions.

From 1987 onwards there is a reversal of the previous trend of the period 1981–87.[72] The percentage of the respondents who had a 'rather good impression' of the EP were more than those who had a 'rather bad impression' by a factor of nearly 4.3 up to 1990 and by a factor of 5 from then onwards. It is interesting to notice that those who answered 'neither good nor bad' have remained at about 30%. Unfortunately the question is put in such a way that it is not possible to reach any other conclusion on the attitude of the population on the EP. Some indication though is offered by the replies to the last question on the creation of a European government accountable to the EP.

[71] See R. Inglehart, *Culture Shifts in Advanced Industrial Societies* (Princeton: Princeton University Press, 1990).

[72] See for more details Eurobarometer trends 1974–1990, table B9, p. 127.

Greek public opinion is overwhelmingly in favour of such a development by a factor of 3 over the period from 1987 to 1990 and by a factor
of 5 in 1993. In spite of these favourable opinion polls on the current
and the future role of the EP, the elections of the EP are considered of
lower importance in Greece than the national elections. In fact this
seems to comply with the 'second order model' developed by Reif.[73]

A similar positive attitude is recorded for the European Commission, becoming overwhelming between 1987 and 1990 with the 'generally unfavourable' reply virtually disappearing. These results,
however, should be treated with some caution (like all results from
similar exercises) considering that there exists a certain confusion
with regard to the exact role and powers of this institution. To the
very poor information on the functions of the European institutions
is added a linguistic/translation problem (*'Epitropi'* = Commission =
committee). In 1993 a rather sharp increase was recorded in the percentage of the respondents with an unfavourable opinion of the Commission. This was of the order of 500%. At the same time positive
responses to all the other parts in question 5 have worsened considerably. It is very difficult to account for this drop in the public's
appreciation of the Commission. One explanation of this development is more in terms of a reaction to the Macedonian issue than in
terms of a growing anti-Maastricht sentiment.

Regarding the ECJ it is very difficult, if not impossible, to appraise
its impact on Greek public opinion. I would guess that its role and
significance are not understood or worse that it is an unknown institution for the public at large. From the data presented in Table 10.4
it seems that there exists a generally favourable climate on the EC
and the advancement of the integration process. This point is seem-
ingly sustained by the inferred low level of legitimization of the internal political system but also as a result of the widespread feeling
among the Greeks that the country has benefited from EC membership (in spite of recent political difficulties).

These findings are on the whole supported by opinion polls conducted in the country on behalf of political parties and which
appeared in the daily press. One of those worth mentioning, however,
showed a strong anti-EC feeling, almost equally distributed throughout the country, of the order of 54% among the sample on account

---

[73] See K. Reif, 'The Second Order Elections', in K. Reif (ed.), *The European Elections* (Aldershot: Gower, 1985), p. 8.

of the Macedonian question.[74] There is a feeling among experts that most such polls are poorly and hastily prepared and should be treated with caution.

The political parties

The collapse of the military regime in 1974, the '*Metapolitefsis*', had important consequences for the political system of the country. Firstly, experiences from seven years of military rule led to the legalization, in the collective consciousness of the population, of parliamentary government, a fact that could not be easily assumed during the pre-coup years. The Greek Communist Party became legal after being banned for almost thirty years (since 1947) and was allowed to contest in the first democratically held elections after the collapse of the military regime in 1974. Indeed KKE and KKE-interior, the two Communist parties (as a result of the 1968 split of KKE), managed to capture almost 9% of the electorate. The anti-communist ideology, a pillar of the pre-coup state, was driven *ad absurdum*.[75] Combined with the relegalization of the parties of the Communist left, the monarchy was brought to an end through the December 1974 referendum, in completion of the 'liquidation of the past image'[76] policy pursued by the New Democracy government of the day. The composition and structure of the political personnel changed radically. This change was more obvious with regard to the middle and lower party political personnel than at the level of the leadership of the parties. An illustration of this statement is the Panhellenic Socialist Movement (PASOK) under Andreas Papandreou which challenged the Union of Center Forces–New Powers under G. Mavros for the vote and the support of the social layer that supported the Union of the Centre before the military coup. Papandreou captured 14% of the vote in 1974 (as opposed to 21% for G. Mavros) which proved good enough for the leader of PASOK to absorb Mavros's party in time

[74] Mori poll conducted for and published in the daily *Eleftherotipia*, 14 Feb. 1994. The question put to the sample was the following: 'Are you satisfied or not by the way that the EC in general reacted to the Skopje (FYROM) issue? Would you accept withdrawing from the EU if Greek demands are not met?' Answers: 54% yes, 26% no, 20% no reply or another reply.

[75] See E. Katsoulis, 'The Human Capital in the Process of Modernisation. The Greek Defence Society in Front of the year 2000', in E. Katsoulis, P. Kazakos and T. Giannitsis (eds.), *Greece Towards 2000. Politics, Economics and External Relations* (Athens: Papazisis, 1990), pp. 35–49.

[76] See G. Mavrogordatos, *op. cit.*, p. 158.

(see Table 10.5) to the extent that during the elections of 1981 which PASOK won, Mavros was elected MP on the PASOK list.

Table 10.5 Results of Greek parliamentary elections 1974–1981

Parties	1974 Votes in %	Seats	1977 Votes in %	Seats	1981 Votes in %	Seats
Extreme Right	1.1	–	6.8	–	51.7	–
New Democracy	54.4	220	42.9	173	35.9	115
Centre	20.6	60	12.0	16	1.5	–
PASOK	13.6	12	25.3	93	48.1	172
KKE Esoterikou	9.5	3	2.7	2	1.4	–
KKE		5	9.4	11	10.9	13
Extreme Left	0.0	–	0.5	–	0.2	–
Others	0.9	–	0.4	–	0.4	–
Total	100.0	300	100.0	300	100.0	300

Source: T. G. Mavrogordatos, 'The Greek Party System: A Case of Limited but Polarised Pluralism?', *West European Politics*, 7 (4) (1984), p. 157.

Both the socialist and the Communist left adopted policies consistent not only with their broad ideological stance but also with the treatment that had been afforded to them since the years of the civil war. Indeed what a number of commentators have described as sometimes 'too much of a police state'[77] was not particularly kind to opposition ideologies to say the least. This 'right' *v.* 'left' cleavage that frustrated the country for almost thirty years until 1974 had spilled over to the level of the international relations of the country right from the beginning on account of the British and American intervention (Truman Doctrine) in the 1946–9 civil war against the Communist-led ELAS (National Liberation Army) in the context of the (later called) American 'containment policy'. Anti-American feelings on the part of large segments of the population grew on the fertile background of the role of foreign powers during the recent history of the country. This anti-Western attitude of the populace was revitalized in 1974 due to British and NATO inaction to prevent or reverse the Turkish invasion of Cyprus, their alleged action to prevent the Greek army from landing on the island and the support

[77] See R. Clogg, *A Short History of Modern Greece* (Cambridge: Cambridge University Press, 1979); K. Tsoukalas, *The Greek Tragedy* (Athens: Papazisis, 1974).

of the USA with regard to the military regime. It was also against this background of 'xenophobia' that owes its existence to the history of the modern Greek state since 1831, that the political parties representing the broad 'left' flourished in the period from 1974 onwards. A population accustomed to real or perceived threats to its national integrity throughout the years of its existence in an independent state would be easily attracted by populist slogans. Andreas Papandreou's PASOK[78] played brilliantly on Greek nationalism and xenophobia and in the space of seven years after its appearance and in the 1981 elections it received 48% of the vote and a handsome majority in parliament. PASOK would almost double its share in three consecutive elections in 1974, 1977 and in 1981. The irony of history had brought to power a political party that was elected on a ticket to withdraw from the EC, at a time when the Hellenic Republic was becoming a full member of it. The antipathy of the major parties of the broad left to the EC (PASOK and KKE mainly, since the smaller KKE-interior was more concerned with the terms of the accession to the EC) was practically exemplified by the fact that both parties walked out of parliament during the discussion on the ratification of the Treaty of Accession to the EC in 1979. As a result the Treaty was only ratified by the majority party in parliament at that time, i.e. New Democracy.

PASOK's EC years (1981–9) went through a number of phases. Initially, during its opposition years, the leadership of the party was caught in a North–South paradigm which almost naturally resulted in the rejection of the EC as a solution for the problem of the economic development of the country. It was also opposed to the EC on national sovereignty grounds. Although this is not the place to discuss the ideological foundations of the party's analysis it is important to note that, electoral considerations aside, this impassioned anti-EC stance of the party during its opposition years was to a large extent responsible for a good part of the problems that the country faced inside the EC. This attitude educated accordingly the grassroots and more importantly the cadre of the party, that is to say the very people who were responsible for the implementation of government policies both in Greece as well as in the EC institutions. The second phase of the PASOK attitude was marked by the 'Memorandum to the EC' of March 1982; the

[78] For a good analysis of PASOK see C. Lyrintzis, *Between Socialism and Populism: The Rise of the Panhellenic Socialist Movement*, unpublished PhD thesis (London School of Economics and Political Science, 1983).

change was completed with the support of the SEA. In essence, nearly half of the time that PASOK spent in government was required for the party to decide whether the country should stay in the EC or not. The other political parties of the right (New Democracy) and the left (KKE-interior and its offspring in the 1980s 'The Alliance of the Left and Progressive Forces' or '*Sinaspismos*') remained in favour of the EC with the exception of the KKE which adopted a highly volatile position on the issue, being in favour from 1986 onwards of returning to its old rejectionist position after the TEU.

Interest groups

The Hellenic Republic has a reputation in the literature of comparative European politics for being one of the most centralized countries, if not the most centralized one in contemporary (Western) Europe. There are a number of reasons for this. The history of the modern Greek state since its independence in 1831 is almost exclusively a history of irredentism and national liberation struggles which ended in victories and in tragedies alike. The modern Greek state grew up in a hostile neighbourhood whose continuous turbulence triggered a series of political crises internally. Thus the centralization of the political system was the inevitable result, with the Greek state in the role of a modern 'Leviathan' or a 'Colossus' but with 'feet of clay' as Mouzelis[79] colourfully suggested. As a plethora of studies indicates, however, the magnitude of the modern Greek state has never meant that this was a strong state.[80] For a long period in modern Greek history a fragile political system whose endurance was always in doubt has been its central feature. Traditional political parties with extensive networks of clientelistic relations, offering, *inter alia*, public sector enrolment, became the chief stabilization mechanism in support of the system. Clientelism, and possibly bureaucratic clientelism as well, are considered as the dominant *modus operandi* of the Greek political system in spite of being under attack on several grounds by a number of researchers.

Generally speaking, the Greek political system has been defined as state corporatist, as a party state, as an anarchic corporatist state or

[79] See N. Mouzelis, 'Greece at the Margins. Whose fault?', *To Vima tis Kiriakis* (30 Dec. 1990).
[80] See for example A. Manesis, 'The Evolution of the Political Institutions in Greece: In Search of a Difficult Legitimisation', *Les Temps Modernes*, special edition in Greek (Athens, 1986).

a case of limited but polarized pluralism. Researchers have used different definitions over the years but the above seem to describe the Greek reality better although a combination of these would perhaps be more appropriate. Charalambis examined the peculiarities of the Greek political system with emphasis on the development of the Greek state before the Second World War and after the civil war in 1949.[81] He showed that the state apparatus has been the acknowledged mechanism of consensus formation, through the wide offer of employment and the distribution of all sorts of monetary and non-monetary benefits to 'dangerous' social groups. The Third Greek Republic, says Charalambis, is a party democracy because the political parties inhibit any other form of political representation. Mavrogordatos convincingly concluded that party parliamentary divisions were reproduced at the level of organized interests through a series of structural changes initiated by the PASOK governments between 1981 and 1989,[82] and stressed the introduction of a proportional representation system as the vehicle for party intervention in the internal affairs of these organizations. Katsabanis identified similarities between the Greek trade union movement and its European counterparts.[83] The Greek trade unions represent mostly the skilled and specialized workforce drawing their members from the big public, semi-public and nationalized companies (banks, electricity, telecommunications). Katsabanis stressed the lack of political autonomy from the main political parties as the main (political) problem of the Greek trade union movement. In effect, the relevant literature unanimously concluded that party political divisions are reproduced at the level of organized interests.

An examination of the European policies of the main organized interests, i.e. the GSEE (workers), the PASEGES (farmers) and the SEV (industry),[84] shows the close relationship between these organizations and the government of the country during the period 1985–9

---

[81] See D. Charalambis, *Clientelistic Relations and Populism. Extra-Institutional Consensus Formation in Post-Civil War Greece* (Athens: Papazisis, 1989).

[82] See G. Mavrogordatos, *Between Pitiokamptis and Prokroustis. Professional Organizations in Contemporary Greece* (Odisseas, 1990).

[83] See S. Katsabanis, 'Problems and Prospects of the Greek Trade Union Movement', in Katsoulis et al., *op. cit.*, pp. 150–9.

[84] GSEE stands for '*Geniki Sinomospondia Ergaton Ellados*' (General Confederation of Greek Workers' Unions); PASEGES is the '*Panellinia Sinomospondia Enoseon Georgikon Sineterismon*' (Panhellenic Confederation of the Unions of Agricultural Cooperatives); and SEV stands for '*Sindesmos Ellinikon Viomihanion*' (Union of Greek Industries).

regarding policy-making at the EC level.[85] PASEGES was founded in 1935 and along with GESASE and SYDASE represents the 'macrocosm' of the farmers' union movement in Greece.[86] In 1938 PASEGES was abolished but re-established in 1945. It is the umbrella organization of the farmers' cooperative movement and since 1981 has been a member of COPA/COGECA, the farmers' umbrella organization at EC level. The organization has an office in Brussels which is mainly used for the collection of information on developments in the Common Agricultural Policy (CAP) at the Commission and at the Council of Ministers. The rather poor financial situation of PASEGES in recent years has not permitted an adequate development of the office which has a volatile number of personnel employed, ranging between five and ten. The office is situated in the same building as COPA/COGECA which saves money and time in the collection of information. The people of the organization believe that the most efficient way of collecting information at the EC level is through personal contacts with the staff of the Commission especially in DG VI. The information collected is then transmitted to the specialized working groups (one for each product of relevance to Greek agricultural production) of the organization which serves as a preparation to the board of the organization in decision-making.[87]

The board of PASEGES consists of members with known party political affiliations, a practice used since the days of beginning the political control of the organization, given its extreme financial dependence upon state funding.[88] This picture of the organization as

[85] The issue of interest-group intermediation at the EU level has not been adequately or systematically assessed over the last few years. The rationale of the intermediation of the organized interests is basically threefold: (1) Eurogroups perform the function of an exchange of information; (2) they perform the function of putting pressure on the EU authorities on behalf of their affiliates; (3) they perform the function of the transmission of information from the EU towards the national centres of power. Nevertheless the research agenda on interest group politics between the two levels of state authority is large and the debate is still inconclusive.

[86] GESASE and SYDASE are also members of COPA/COGECA. GESASE stands for *'Geniki Sinimospondia Agrotikon Sillogon Ellados'* (General Confederation of Greek Agricultural Unions) and SYDASE stands for *'Sinomospondia Dimokratikon Agrotikon Sillogon Eladas'* (Confederation of Democratic Agricultural Unions of Greece).

[87] The board of the PASEGES is the decision-taking body of the organization. It consists of twenty-one members elected for three years (Arts. 15–23 of the charter of PASEGES).

[88] Mainly through the 'Agricultural Bank of Greece'; see on this K. Kostis, *Agricultural Economy and the Agricultural Bank of Greece* (National Bank of Greece editions, 1987).

the transmission belt of governmental choices is very slowly changing with the entry into the picture of GESASE (dominated by PASOK
mainly and the Communist left) and SYDASE (New Democracy),
whose poor finances, however, are a serious obstacle to their effort
to attract membership away from PASEGES, thus breaking the
latter's monopoly of representation of the farming population. In this
direction leads also the extremely bad financial situation of the agricultural cooperatives, the vast majority of which are also heavily in
the red.

On the EC issues PASEGES and the Greek government manage to
adopt a unanimous stance in the Community arenas in most cases
through a process of consultations.[89] This may also be explained with
reference to the importance of the agricultural economy for Greece.
Indeed, agriculture contributes 17.4% of the gross national product
in Greece and accounts for 31.3% of the value of total exports. Still
30% of the total labour force is employed in the agricultural sector.
The existence of the CAP has been the chief parameter of successive
governments in their decision to associate, join and finally stay in the
EC, in spite of comparatively poor support for Mediterranean production under the CAP regulations. The defence of the national interest, therefore, requires unanimity at EC level. On the whole,
PASEGES utilizes strategies described by Averyt, i.e. through the
Eurogroup (COPA) and the national government, depending on the
circumstances,[90] in order to adapt to a changing political environment, ranging from the relative calm of state corporatism to the turbulence of transnational pluralism.

GSEE was created in 1918 with the participation of 214 unions representing at the time approximately 65,000 workers.[91] GSEE is one of
the two peak unions (the other one is ADEDY, representing only
public sector employees)[92] and is a member of the ETUC, i.e. the
worker confederation's umbrella organization at the EC level. GSEE
appears at the top of an organizational pyramid in which the unions
of the private as well as the wider public sector (banks, common util-

[89] This view comes out of interview material with key actors in PASEGES.

[90] See W. Averyt, 'Eurogroups, clientella and the European Community', *International Organization*, 29 (4) (Autumn 1975), pp. 949–72.

[91] See G. Koukoules, *Greek Trade Unions. Economic Self Sufficiency and Dependence: 1948–1983* (Athens: Odisseas, 1984).

[92] See D. Kioukias, *Organizing Interests in Greece: Labour, Agriculture, Local Government and Political Development since the Metapolitefsis*, unpublished PhD thesis (University of Birmingham, 1991), pp. 72ff.

ities organizations etc.) are represented. At a lower level in the organizational pyramid are to be found sectoral federations and labour centres which are members of GSEE and are organized on occupational and geographical lines. Finally at the bottom of the pyramid there exist first rank unions along sectoral and occupational lines.[93] Today the picture is one of extreme apportionment as there are over 5,000 first rank unions and 84 federations. A measure of the lack of political autonomy of the organization may be given by the fact that in every instance until 1989 the leadership of GSEE was of the same party political affiliation as the government of the country. Nevertheless, at the national level the organization has developed a network of linkages with the Ministry of Employment, although the country lacks a forum for dialogue between the social partners. Until 1981 there existed the 'Council of Social and Economic Policy' (SKOP) which was renamed after 1982 the 'National Council of Development and Programming' (ESAP). Like the majority of macro-corporatist arrangements in Europe, these institutions exhibit great instability. The lack of political autonomy on the part of organized interests resulted in the very poor legitimacy of their policies and did not contribute to establish conditions of industrial peace.

The SEV ('Union of the Greek Industries') was created in 1907 and has currently over 500 members. It is an active participant in UNICE. The SEV consists mainly of big industries (two out of three are the most profitable industries of the country) including those representing multinational capital. In contrast with the other two organizations referred to above, the SEV exhibits a higher degree of political autonomy which is probably better explained with reference to the importance of its political resources, i.e. its significance in economic terms. The SEV is probably the best organized interest with a strong personnel (forty people) and a budget of 400 million drs. per year (1992). It contributed significantly to the public debate in this country over the years. The objectives of the Union are *inter alia*, the supply of information, of in-train services and of representation of its members within the Greek state and in the European forums. Internally the organization has developed four specialized sub-sections (research and analysis, membership and employers' organizations,

---

[93] Until the publication of law 1264/82 on the 'democratization of the labour union movement' many of the mass unions were excluded from GSEE on account of their political affiliations whereas a plethora of rubber stamp unions formed the majority of the organization.

state and institutional agencies, international cooperation). Central to the international cooperation sub-section is the Brussels bureau. The bureau is responsible for the representation of the SEV in UNICE and participates in the various committees of the umbrella organization at the EC level. During 1991 the organization was represented in fifty-two working groups which met 124 times. Through its bureau, the SEV participates in the Permanent Council of UNICE with one permanent representative. The bureau has developed independent links with the EC institutions and especially with the Commission. This is probably the most important function of the bureau, especially its informal contacts with individuals from all the EC institutions, including the COREPER and the Greek Permanent Representative, the Economic and Social Council and the European Parliament. At the national level the role of the SEV as well as of other interest groups may be assessed with reference to its attitude to the Greek public administration. An example of this may be given by recent legislation on the Community Support Frameworks (CSFs). The Greek government passed a bill through parliament by which it created in July 1991 ELANET (Hellenic Development Company).[94] The responsibility of this company has been defined as making proposals to the government on the allocation of the structural funds between the public and the private sectors of the economy, the participation in the preparation and negotiation of the national proposals submitted to the EC in the context of the CSFs, the contacts with the Commission with the purpose of identifying new programmes and/or ways to improve the existing ones and the evaluation of submitted proposals. The founding members of ELANET were the SEV, the EEF (Union of Greek Ship Owners), the EET (Confederation of Greek Banks) and POX (Panhellenic Union of Hotel Owners). All of them are employers' associations but more importantly all of them were political friends of the New Democracy government at that time. GSEE was asked to participate but it declined the offer for reasons that are not entirely clear, but seem to be dictated by party political considerations. Nevertheless, with the pretext of rationalization and avoidance of red tape this seems to be a fine example of what is probably societal corporatism in the making.

---

[94] See P. Kazakos, *Private Sector and the Community Structural Policy*, Working paper 10 (EKEM, 1992).

Conclusion

The relations between Greece and the European Community have evolved through a number of different phases over the years. The EC experiment was doubted by the majority of the political parties in parliament for the best part of the time that Greece has been a full member in the EC. The reason is that the issue was entangled in the right *v.* left cleavage that has tormented this country for more than forty years since the end of the Second World War. The 'pendulum theory'[95] that was used to describe Greco-EC relations has some explanatory value. Nowadays the pendulum seems to have been stabilized since the three major parties in parliament, i.e. New Democracy, PASOK and the smaller Alliance of the Left (Synaspismos) share the view that the country must positively adapt to the 'New European Community'. In July 1992 the parliament ratified the Treaty on European Union with a huge majority although, again, without much prior public debate. Whichever the position of the pendulum, the policy style is the same.

The Greek government has pursued in the period 1981–9, either in the EC or the EPC (until the entry into force of the SEA), a policy of 'uneasy interdependence' in an effort to maintain the maximum possible degree of freedom in the conduct of its internal and foreign policies. This attitude may have helped the creation of an 'anti-communautaire' image of the country within the EC. To this is added the political climate in which the three consecutive elections were held between 1989 and 1990 which were characterized by bitter exchanges about scandals and economic corruption to such an extent that political commentators in and outside the country were wondering whether such things could happen in an EC member state. The election result of April 1990 for the first time normalized the situation. However, the introduction of a tough austerity and rationalization programme by the government gave rise to social unrest especially during the summer of 1992, which was paralleled by internal (Supreme Special Court) and external (Skopje) problems and led to a chaotic political climate.

The European policy of the Hellenic Republic is primarily the responsibility of the central government. Internally the government enjoys a near monopoly position since there are no other powerful

[95] See P. Ksazakos, *Greece Between Marginalisation and Incorporation. Choices for the Next Decade in the Greco-EC Relations*, in Katsoulis et al., *op. cit.*, pp. 474–88.

institutions capable of challenging its authority. French-style dirigisme is the *modus operandi* of the system. Intermediary organizations at the state level are mere transmission belts of government choices. There are no elected regional councils and the approximately 6,000 *demoi* and *koinotites* of the country ensure that through this geographical multi-division the power of the centre remains intact. At the societal level the pattern seems to be the same; party political intervention ensures that no other form of political representation is capable of challenging the government's authority. The 'Greek *etatisme*' promoted the allotment of the civic society in order to avoid unwelcome challenges to its authority.

At the European level relations between the government and organized interests project 'a billiard ball image' as different actors promote the same positions in different forums. To a certain extent this is a structural problem in the sense that the differing level of economic development between Greece and the other EC member states facilitated an internal compromise on the need for more resources from the various Community funds. This has been the main concern of the Greek European policy since 1981. This attitude of the various Greek governments postulates an intergovernmental view of the 'European System of Cooperation', although the official rhetoric denies such a standpoint. Indeed throughout the two intergovernmental conferences of 1990/1991 the Greek government was among the staunchest supporters of the advancement of the integration process, i.e. a member of the 'federalist camp' in the Council.

Select bibliography

Ioakimides, P., *European Political Union* (Athens: Themelio, 1993).

Katsoulis, E., Kazakos, P. and Giannitsis, A. (eds)., *Greece Towards 2000. Politics, Economics, External Relations* (Athens: Papazisis, 1990).

Kazakos, P. (ed.), *The Integration of the Internal Market and Greece* (Athens: Ionian Bank of Greece, 1989).

Kazakos, P. and Stefanou, K. (eds.), *Greece in the EC. The First Five Years* (Athens: Sakkoulas, 1985).

Kouloubis, T. and Konstas, D. (eds.), *The Greek Parliament in Foreign Policy, 1974–1984* (Athens: Sakkoulas, 1986).

Maravegias, N. and Tsinisizelis, M. (eds), *European Integration. Theory and Politics*, 3rd edn (Athens: Themelio, 1993).

—— *The Integration of the European Union. Political, Legal and Economic Aspects* (Athens: Themelio, 1995).

Tsinisizelis, M., 'Greece and the European Community. A Bibliographical Essay', *Modern Greek Society*, 18 (1990), pp. 1–120.

Tsoukalis, L. (ed.), *Greece and the EC. The Challenge of Adaptation* (Athens: EKEME/Papazisis, 1993).

United Kingdom[1]

Fundamentals of the United Kingdom in EU affairs

The analytical context

Over the last decade or so there has been a growth of interest in institutional analysis within the academic community. In Germany this development has been reflected in the programme of research supported by the Deutsche Forschungsgemeinschaft. More well-known in the Anglo-Saxon world is the growth of new institutionalist analysis emanating from North America, although this 'new' approach has been treated with some scepticism in the United Kingdom (UK).[2] In this chapter an attempt will be made to demonstrate that institutionalist analysis can offer important insights into explaining the way in which the UK interacts with its partners in the European Union (EU). At the same time, the paper will attempt to offer an empirical exposition of the way in which the UK's institutions and political forces have enmeshed themselves in the supranational level of governance.

How will institutions be understood in this chapter? In line with Gerhard Göhler's contribution to this volume, we see institutions as making up one of the three components of political life. That is to say, if political activity is divided up into political forces, polity and policy, then institutions make up the second of these categories. However, the analysis which follows goes somewhat beyond Göhler's approach (and most German institutional theory) and regards insti-

[1] In what follows Kenneth Armstrong was responsible for consideration of the implementation of European policy and the legal analysis; Simon Bulmer for the making of European policy and the political analysis. We are grateful, for their comments, to Martin Burch, John Peterson and Willie Paterson. The usual disclaimer applies. We acknowledge the financial support of the UK Economic and Social Research Council (award no. W112351014 on rule-making in the Single European Market).
[2] For a sceptical view, see G. Jordan, 'Policy Community Realism versus "New" Institutionalist Ambiguity', *Political Studies*, 38 (3) (1990), pp. 470–84.

tutions as political structures which intermediate between political forces and policy.[3] Thus institutional characteristics will be utilized in an explanatory manner, reflecting the American new-institutionalist approach. The situation may thus be seen as one where institutions occupy an important mediating role between political forces and policy outputs:

Political forces → political structures (institutions) → policy

In practice, this means that the opportunities open to political forces are influenced by the institutional structures of the state. This argument has been articulated by Thelen and Steinmo, who argue that institutions shape not only '... actors' strategies ... but their goals as well, and by mediating their relations of cooperation and conflict, institutions structure political situations and leave their own imprint on political outcomes'.[4]

But what are 'the institutional structures of the state'? In addition to the well understood notion of the institutions of government, we follow the new institutionalists in including 'beliefs, paradigms, codes, cultures and knowledge'.[5] Political institutions do not just comprise the formal structures of government for making authoritative policy decisions. They also entail a symbolic dimension. Beliefs, paradigms, codes, cultures and knowledge thus approximate the symbolic dimension – or ritual – which knits together and highlights what is common and persistent for all members of the particular institutional community.[6] The distinction between the symbolic and instrumental roles of institutions is an important one. It is particularly evident when institutions are subject to reorganization with a view to achieving new goals. Success in such purposive reform will not be assured unless symbolic ritual also adapts. Over the postwar period the United Kingdom has faced many new challenges. However, adaptation of the symbolic and/or cultural-normative context of its political institutions has

[3] See also his discussion of the theories of institutions in G. Göhler, 'Institutionenlehre und Institutionentheorie in der deutschen Politikwissenschaft nach 1945', in G. Göhler (ed.), *Grundfragen der Theorie politischer Institutionen* (Opladen: Westdeutscher Verlag, 1987), pp. 15–47.

[4] K. Thelen and S. Steinmo, 'Historical Institutionalism in Comparative Politics', in S. Steinmo, K. Thelen and F. Longstreth (eds.), *Structuring Politics: Historical Institutionalism in Comparative Analysis* (Cambridge: Cambridge University Press, 1992), p. 9.

[5] J. March and J. Olsen, *Rediscovering Institutions: The Organizational Basis of Politics* (New York: The Free Press, 1989), p. 26.

[6] This passage draws on the discussion of Arnold Gehlen's work in Gerhard Göhler's contribution to this volume.

has often been 'sticky'. Thus, the attempt to introduce French-style economic planning failed because it was insufficiently embedded in the institutions and culture of the British state. We should not be surprised, then, if membership of the European Community since 1973 has presented challenges both in terms of institutional adaptation and for the symbolic and cultural-normative context of the British polity.

In examining the interaction between the UK and the EU, we are concerned with a multi-tiered set of institutions. Thus, it is important to be clear about the level at which analysis is conducted. The principal focus here is on the institutional characteristics of the UK's political system. Clearly, the logic of this volume is not that membership of the EU has a harmonizing effect on how each member state handles the various supranational policy issues. Rather, the assumption is that there are divergencies in the approaches of individual member states.

A further issue concerns the degree of aggregation in the analysis. Many observers of public policy have come to recognize that it is not possible to identify national patterns of policy without running the risk of generalization.[7] Thus we should be alert to the possibilities of different institutional forms and norms within the different component parts of national European policy-making. To put it more concretely, we should anticipate different organizational arrangements and normative circumstances as between, say, Britain's participation in EC budgetary policy-making and its involvement in the EU's Common Foreign and Security Policy (CFSP).

Institutional characteristics

If institutions are to have an important explanatory role in our analysis, the key opening questions are:

- What are the principal characteristics of the British polity?
- How have they shaped the formulation of European policy?
- And what has been the impact of the institutional structure upon policy itself?

The principal characteristics of the British political system are as follows:

- it is a unitary state;
- it is a constitutional monarchy, with the formal seat of power residing in the Queen in parliament (parliamentary sovereignty);

[7] See M. Wright, 'Policy Community, Policy Network and Comparative Industrial Policies', *Political Studies*, 36 (4) (1988), pp. 593–612.

- parliamentary sovereignty also embodies the principle that the government in parliament has the ultimate power to make or unmake any law (i.e. no law can bind a successor parliament);
- there is no formal, written constitution and no British constitutional court vetting parliamentary legislation or acting as a check on government;
- the English legal tradition (Common Law) differs from that of continental Europe;
- the rules of the electoral system tend to assure single-party majoritarian government;
- the institutional structure of the state encourages the conduct of adversarial politics between Her Majesty's Government and Her Majesty's Opposition;
- the prime minister has considerable potential power resources at his/her disposal, and can call upon the centralized machinery of Whitehall, coordinated through the Cabinet Office, to reinforce leadership;
- in horizontal terms, state power in policy-making has been centred on government, with very few agencies having effective autonomy (e.g. no independent central bank);
- the direct involvement of the state in economic governance is relatively limited by comparative European standards;
- the civil service is well qualified, under pressure to be efficient, and theoretically neutral (i.e subservient to the objectives of whatever party is in power);
- in vertical terms, state power is concentrated on central government, with local government having a weak position;
- the UK nevertheless comprises different national identities (Scots, Welsh etc.) within its unitary state;
- historically, British government extended beyond the domestic boundaries of the UK state as a result of the colonization process;
- finally, the constitutional order – of England in particular – has evolved peacefully over many centuries, with no breach of territorial or constitutional integrity.

Institutions and symbols

At a general level, then, these are the principal characteristics of the governance of the UK. These institutional characteristics are embedded in cultural-normative terms and, in many cases, have a symbolic dimension. It is worth mentioning a selection of these, particularly those with some potential impact upon the conduct of British European policy.

Parliamentary chambers are often an interesting starting-point for separating out the role of symbols and instrumentalism in political institutions. It is interesting, therefore, to note the contrasting adaptation of the two houses of parliament to the institutional challenges posed by European integration. The House of Commons has devoted much time to such challenges and, in particular, the question of parliamentary sovereignty. The concentration upon this theme has had rather more to do with the symbolic than the instrumental side of politics. Thus the assumption in much of the debate in the House of Commons has been that a sovereign parliament is the central locus for policy-making. In reality, however, executive control over the Commons severely curtails parliamentary sovereignty. The debate, in consequence, has been largely symbolic. Moreover, despite politicians' claims that the UK is virtually unique in undertaking vigorous parliamentary debate on major issues of integration, such discussion as occurs is frequently adversarial ritual rather than reasoned scrutiny. A more instrumental – rather than symbolic – approach to European policy-making might consist in the creation of a powerful scrutiny committee, such as occurred in the Danish parliament, the Folketing.[8]

Paradoxically, it has been the House of Lords – through its *Select Committee on the European Communities* – which has taken on a more effective scrutiny role. Although a chamber even more steeped in ritual it is much less able to play upon the symbolic significance of parliamentary sovereignty since this resides in the House of Commons. Judge sees the roots of the lower house's parliamentary sovereignty in the English constitutional settlement of 1689, which effectively transformed the upper house into part of the 'living dead of the constitution'.[9] The House of Lords also lacks the democratic credentials necessary to playing the sovereignty card. So, with the symbolic politics of parliamentary sovereignty set to one side, and in its attempt to preserve a role in political life, it has developed a highly respected system for scrutinizing draft legislation emanating from Brussels. In consequence it has a procedural approach attuned to membership of the EU. For the Lords an instrumental role has taken precedence over symbolism.

[8] See the chapter by Thomas Pedersen in this volume.
[9] D. Judge, *The Parliamentary State* (London: Sage Publications, 1994), p. 3; the 'living dead of the constitution' is the description coined by Kingdom.

The strict government–opposition cleavage – or adversarial values – engendered by the organization of parliament and by the electoral system creates a highly competitive context within which the party system operates. This adversarialism contributes to the pattern of policy-making. Thus the idea that 'the winner takes all' leads to a situation where cooperation between the parties is limited within the House of Commons even if, as at the time of ratifying the Maastricht Treaty on European Union (TEU), both parties claimed to favour most of the TEU's contents.

A similar situation exists outside the immediate parliamentary context. For example, there is no notion of proportionality, i.e. an institutional representation of the diversity of political opinion in the agencies clustered around the state. Nor do corporatist notions of the representation of the diversity of interest group opinion come into play in the manner characteristic of, say, Germany. This situation combines with the centralization of power on the government-in-office to enable belief-systems, ideology and norms to be highly specific to a particular government. Thus new political ideas – such as Friedman's monetarism or deregulation – can take a persuasive hold of British politics with comparative speed. Yet it is striking that some of the neo-liberal ideas of the Thatcher governments, such as on liberalizing telecommunications, took quite a long time to gain wider acceptance in continental Europe. Of course, not all new ideas are successful, so the UK is not necessarily the beneficiary from this situation. Perhaps of greater significance is the fact that the UK may be institutionally predisposed to holding beliefs and values out of synchronization with its EU partners. Is it entirely a coincidence that the collective stance of the EC/EU has, after a time-lag, moved towards British policy on CAP reform, the EC budget, economic liberalization, with signs also emerging of movement towards loosening labour market regulation?

Such changes in governmental values typically may occur in respect of attitudes towards state–market relations, for there is not the need to maintain the consent of both sides of industry on policy substance.[10] Similarly, the strong position of central government – and the absence of constitutional checks – means that the interests of the

---

[10] For analysis of the contrasting case of Germany, see S. Bulmer and P. Humphreys, 'Kohl, Corporatism and Congruence: The West German Model under Challenge', in S. Bulmer (ed.), *The Changing Agenda of West German Public Policy* (Aldershot: Dartmouth Publishing/ASGP, 1989), pp. 177–97.

English regions, or of Wales and Scotland, may be subordinated to other political values to which the governing party gives priority. It is purely a speculative point, of course, but would the British government have pursued so vigorously a policy of trying to limit EC regional spending if there had been a stronger regional counter-balance to the Treasury's influence in Whitehall?

Finally, the continuity of territorial integrity and constitutional evolution have created considerable pride in British political institutions. These values are, of course, subject to generational change. However, this pride in national sovereignty is a further source of resistance to the constitutional challenges posed by membership of the EU. It is often difficult to distinguish between national sovereignty and parliamentary sovereignty, but their roots differ. National sovereignty may be seen as directed at influences from outside the UK, whereas the roots of parliamentary sovereignty lie in internal constitutional development. Concerns about national and parliamentary sovereignty are mutually reinforcing components in the institutional and cultural-normative interaction between British politics and the European Union.

Institutions, symbols and UK European policy

How, then, do these institutional and symbolic characteristics of the UK's political system assume explanatory importance in the specific context of British European policy? The centralization of power within the executive branch of government contributes to a relatively coherent presentation of policy within the institutions of the EU. When combined with the competitive, even confrontational, characteristics of senior ministers – for these are valuable behavioural attributes for success within British parliamentary politics – the result can be British toughness in supranational policy-making. It was not merely Mrs Thatcher who demonstrated these characteristics but also individual ministers, for instance James Callaghan as Labour Foreign Secretary during the renegotiation of the terms of EC membership in 1974/75. When constitutional change is under consideration within the EU and, for ratification purposes, within the British polity, the parliamentary arena potentially becomes much more involved in policy-making. This dimension adds a new institutional context, replete with its own political symbols. Thus national sovereignty and parliamentary sovereignty become valuable weapons with which opponents of government policy can seek to score political points.

Moreover, these are the kinds of issues which find an echo in public opinion.[11]

The British parliament is not just an arena within which this debate takes place but, rather, its characteristics – institutional and symbolic – can influence government policy. Two points are critical in this respect. Firstly, the government needs to secure a majority in the House of Commons if it is to enact legislation or ratify treaty changes. Thus the size of the governmental majority is of critical importance. Secondly, a small majority, such as that enjoyed by John Major's government following the 1992 general election, creates greater risks than the larger majorities enjoyed by Mrs Thatcher. However, a further important factor is how far the House gives opportunities to dissenters within the parties, and particularly the governing party.

It was the combination of these two factors which in large part explained the different fates of the Single European Act (SEA) and the Maastricht Treaty on European Union in the House of Commons. The SEA was ratified at a time when Mrs Thatcher held a parliamentary majority of well over 100 seats so that the limited dissent from within the Conservative Party was not salient. In fact, Mrs Thatcher was able to use parliamentary procedure to expedite ratification of the SEA through the House using the guillotine procedure. This episode is interesting for three reasons. Firstly, it indicates that EC/EU-constitutional issues do not automatically develop into major parliamentary debates. Secondly, it indicates how parliamentary sovereignty does not automatically come into play. In other words, it has a deep symbolic character but it is not automatically given an instrumental role. Thirdly, we can see that the reason for this paradox is that the government can more easily control proceedings in the House of Commons when it has a clear majority.

The contrast with ratifying the Maastricht Treaty is striking, not least because the SEA had been much more unequivocally a rein-

---

[11] For purposes of comparison, it was arguably only with popular concerns over the fate of the Deutschmark in a future Economic and Monetary Union that this kind of debate about European policy took place within the German context. In the UK, by contrast, it has been beneath the surface since the early 1970s. Accession to the EC; renegotiations; the 1975 referendum; the budgetary crises (1979–84), which coincided in part with Labour Party's policy of withdrawal from the EC; the TEU debate (1992–93); and the parliamentary exchanges in early 1994 concerning the voting arrangements in the Council of Ministers after the EFTA enlargement: these are amongst the EU developments which have reopened the debate periodically.

forcement of the supranational character of the EC. Despite the TEU having strong elements reinforcing intergovernmental cooperation, ratification was much more problematic. John Major's government had a ruling majority of twenty-one. Thus a vocal group of Eurosceptics within the governing party was in a position to put that majority in jeopardy. Moreover, the Labour Party – Her Majesty's Opposition – acted out its institutional role of seeking the government's defeat, despite its support for the TEU. Thus in July 1993 the rules and procedures of the House of Commons were of decisive importance to the fate of the TEU.[12]

Seductive as it may be to concentrate analysis on such major constitutional decisions concerning integration, the full involvement of parliament in European policy is relatively infrequent. A much more representative pattern is one of 'technical' policy developing in a relatively harmonious manner within a specialist group of negotiators. To be sure, the SEA and TEU may interrupt the routines of policy-making. However, the majority of British EU policy-making takes place away from the spotlight, in negotiations undertaken between officials and interest groups. Moreover, the routines are essentially similar to those established from the British accession in 1973, for there has been no systematic reorganization such as through the creation of a 'minister for European affairs'. A final comment in this contextual introduction must be reserved for the adjustment of the UK's constitutional-legal structure to European integration. The fundamental challenge in this respect arose when the UK joined the EC. The conflicting doctrines of parliamentary sovereignty and the supranational character of EC law were recognized at that time. However, there were some ambiguities, as Josephine Steiner has pointed out:

> namely, the *extent* to which the United Kingdom as a state had transferred sovereign powers to the Community; and secondly the impact of membership on the principle of *parliamentary* sovereignty; was that transfer of sovereignty absolute, or subject to revocation or qualification according to the will of Parliament?[13]

In fact, both these ambiguities have been resolved largely in the EC/EU's favour rather than that of parliament. As Steiner points out,

[12] For an account of the problems of ratifying the Maastricht Treaty, see D. Baker, A. Gamble and S. Ludlam, 'The Parliamentary Siege of Maastricht 1993: Conservative Divisions and British Ratification', *Parliamentary Affairs*, 47 (1) (1994), pp. 37–60.

[13] J. Steiner, 'Legal System', in S. Bulmer, S. George and A. Scott (eds.), *The United Kingdom and EC Membership Evaluated* (London: Pinter Publishers, 1992), p. 125.

the increasing amount and scope of EC law, the extension of scope in the direct applicability of EC law, and the increased use of majority voting following the SEA (and subsequently the TEU) account for the growth in the extent of transfer.

As regards the constitutional principle of parliamentary sovereignty, this holds that parliament is free to derogate from prior legislation, including EC legislation. How has this principle been affected by the supremacy of EC law, as established in the 1964 *Costa v. ENEL* case? Hitherto, this dimension of parliamentary sovereignty has also been resolved in favour of the EC/EU, as was demonstrated with the 1990 *Factortame* v. *Secretary of State for Transport* case where a British statute was disapplied on the grounds of incompatibility with EC law. Nevertheless, there remains in theory the possibility of parliament repudiating EC law.[14] Thus, in respect of parliamentary sovereignty, the SEA and the TEU have entailed not the crossing of some new constitutional-legal threshold but a creeping development of constraints upon parliament. In turn, these have resulted in procedural refinements within the House of Commons.

In what follows we outline the institutional characteristics of European policy-making in Britain. This outline presents the context for the argument that institutions shape the pattern of policy. Two broad patterns of policy-making may be identified. The 'route one' approach is characteristically British. Just as in the style of (English) soccer often given this label, where the ball is played directly into the goal area, so European policy matters quickly enter the parliamentary arena for political debate. The route one approach is 'triggered' by concerns about sovereignty, is more politicized and is subject to the adversarial context of the House of Commons. As has been argued, the sensitivity to sovereignty – whether external (national sovereignty) or internal (parliamentary sovereignty) – derives from institutional characteristics of the UK. The 'route two' approach is the default position. Thus, where the concerns about sovereignty do not arise, policy is largely conducted at a specialist level with interest groups, often in discrete institutional settings. Where policy coordination is required, this will be presided over by the Cabinet Office. Policy-making at the specialist level is likely to be well coordinated. Thus the character of the domestic 'veto points' in the formulation of British European policy differs between the two routes: in the

---

[14] For full discussion, see Steiner, *op. cit.*, pp. 127–30.

former case it is a matter of parliamentary politics; in the latter case it is a matter of interest group lobbying but with institutional checks designed to ensure policy coherence. Finally, routes one and two merge at the implementation stage. Here, the situation is more straightforward. The centralized character of the state, the government's majority in parliament and the UK's administrative culture assure a smooth transposition of supranational legislation.

The EC decision-making cycle and the participation of national institutions in EU decision-making

A point to be made at the outset is that the UK has tended to be rather reactive and 'awkward' in its general approach to European integration.[15] The roots of the awkwardness lie principally in Britain's status as a late member of an established 'club'. It consequently did not like some of the rules already in force, such as those concerning the Common Agricultural Policy, the 'own resources' budget and so on. Much effort, in consequence, was devoted to trying to attain a better match between EC policies and British interests. Moreover, British ministers have not been inclined to indulge in pro-European rhetoric. Their proposals for the further development of integration have generally been highly pragmatic in nature rather than conjuring up grand visions of a European future.[16]

The pragmatic approach also has been evident in other respects. In the context both of the creation of the Intergovernmental Conference (IGC) which drafted the SEA and, five years later, of the creation of the IGCs in which the TEU was negotiated, the British government was reluctant to agree to procedures leading to formal constitutional change. To some extent this reflected an unfamiliarity with this kind of constitutional politics, due to the lack of a codified British constitution. However, it also derives from a failure to take seriously, and share, the normative political support for integration that is present in other member states. Once again, domestic institutions and their norms have an explanatory value.

The principal institutional link between national politics and the European Union is through the national governments, which are often

[15] S. George, *An Awkward Partner: Britain in the European Community* (Oxford: Oxford University Press, 1990).

[16] See for instance the statement of HM Government's policy in 'Europe – the Future', *Journal of Common Market Studies*, 23 (1) (1984), pp. 74–81.

seen as occupying the role of gatekeepers. This designation derives from their central institutional role at the intersection of national and European decision-making. The national government comprises different levels, of course, and it is important to be alert to these in what follows. Thus, the growth of the European Council since 1975 has brought with it a major involvement on the part of heads of government. The ministerial level is extremely active in the various formations of the Council of Ministers. The civil service is active in the preparation of policy. It is also involved at the European decision-making stage by supporting the appropriate national minister or through participation in the Committee of Permanent Representatives (COREPER) and its associated specialized working groups. The involvement of civil servants in EU negotiations may occur in the form of the Whitehall-based officials. Equally, the role of the UK Permanent Representation in Brussels (UKREP) must be considered. Finally, civil servants and ministers have an involvement in transposing Community law into national law where this is necessary. Enforcing EC law is a separate task which also falls in part to central government due to the lack of a regional level of government.[17] A significant number of policy areas entail the local authorities' involvement.

It is also possible to identify two apparently contradictory patterns in the management of British European policy. On the one hand, there has been a growing involvement in European integration on the part of the prime minister. Moreover, a European Secretariat was created within the Cabinet Office with the brief of ensuring policy coordination. These features suggest a centripetal effect: a coordination at the top political level and within the administration of the work of government. On the other hand, upon entry in 1973, EC business was integrated into the existing departmental structure of government, with virtually no major inter-departmental reform since. This integration of a European dimension into existing ministries brings with it quite serious possibilities for undermining policy coordination. The principal reason for this situation is that ministers and their civil servants are able to invoke 'Brussels' as a reason for pursuing their own departmental norms and beliefs at the expense of the collective governmental view. Moreover, the institutional structure of

---

[17] The so-called 'Next Steps' reforms under elaboration in the civil service aim for a much clearer distinction between its policy-making functions and those concerned with policy implementation. The latter will increasingly become the responsibility of separate executive agencies.

the EC/EU becomes an additional political resource for departmental ministers and civil servants. It may be all too comforting to find that one's counterparts in the other member states have exactly the same problems. It may even prove to be a valuable resource to utilize against one's colleagues from other departments in Whitehall.[18] How, then, are these two dynamics reconciled? The principal explanation lies in the fact that the prime minister's concern has been limited to the guidelines of policy and those issues of party political salience within the UK, and the House of Commons in particular. Most other matters, however, have been left to the departmental specialists within Whitehall.

The prime minister

The role of the prime minister in British European policy may be regarded as having greater importance than in other member states. The prime minister's participation in the European Council is important, of course, given that institution's responsibilities for, *inter alia*, the strategic development of the EC/EU, policy development and crisis management. However, this situation does not set the British prime minister apart from his counterparts. There are two other, UK-specific, factors which give the prime minister increased salience.

The first derives from the power resources available to the office-holder. It would be dangerous to equate the power potential of the prime minister with the personality of one incumbent. Nevertheless, Mrs Thatcher's control over the direction of policy – including European policy – demonstrated the potential for exploiting power resources. Under John Major, particularly with his much smaller parliamentary majority since the 1992 election, it has not been politically feasible to keep such a firm hand on policy direction. Nevertheless, there are still procedural decisions open to the prime minister that can have an impact on the nature of policy discussion that follows.

[18] One clear comparative example of this situation can be drawn from German experience. There, the federal ministry of agriculture found it had considerably greater capacity to pursue policies supporting its agricultural community than when it was subject to the immediate control of the finance ministry within Bonn. Within the UK, by contrast, it has been relatively uncommon for one ministry to pursue a policy completely at odds with the wishes of another. For more on German European policy-making, see Dietrich Rometsch's contribution to this volume; also S. Bulmer, *The Domestic Structure of European Community Decision-Making in West Germany* (New York: Garland Inc., 1986).

One example would be in choosing which ministers are to exchange views on specific European issues before they go to full Cabinet. Moreover, a system of majoritarian government still offers greater potential power than the precarious coalitions which sometimes characterize the UK's partners. The extent of prime ministerial power has been at the heart of an ongoing debate in British public administration circles.[19]

The second factor derives from the continued party political salience of European policy within the UK. Sensitive issues of European policy, such as the Exchange Rate Mechanism (ERM), Economic and Monetary Union (EMU), the TEU's social protocol and constitutional reform are examples of areas which the prime minister neglects at his or her peril. Even an arcane issue such as the weighting of votes in the Council of Ministers may have a politically sensitive sovereignty dimension, as was the case in early 1994 in the context of the fourth enlargement of the EU. The critical point, therefore, is that the prime minister must have good antennae for picking up signals from the political environment concerning both the government's collective policy actions and his/her own actions. It is instructive to remember that Mrs Thatcher's negativism at the October 1990 Rome European Council meeting, in trying to block EMU, was exploited by her political opponents and contributed to her fall from power. Nevertheless, Britain's exit from the ERM in October 1992 and the tortuous process of ratifying the TEU, even with an EMU opt-out clause, resulted in John Major having to embrace precisely that negativism in order to cling on to power![20]

The prime minister is able to rely on advice from ministers and the Civil Service. However, it is worth mentioning other sources of advice which developed an important role under Mrs Thatcher independently of the more long-standing office of the prime minister.[21] The *Prime Minister's Policy Unit* became an important source of

---

[19] See, for instance, P. Dunleavy and R. A. W. Rhodes, 'Core Executive Studies in Britain', *Public Administration*, 68 (1) (1990), pp. 3–28.

[20] It is precisely such changes in circumstances and opinion that remind us that the explanatory power of institutions is not deterministic, for they only play an intermediating role between politics and policy.

[21] For a discussion of prime ministerial advisers, the prime minister's political office, private office, policy unit and press section, see Martin Burch, 'Prime Minister and Cabinet: An Executive in Transition', in L. Robins (ed.), *Governing Britain in the 1990s* (London: Macmillan, 1994).

policy ideas, although its impact upon EC business is unclear.[22] However, as well as this prime ministerial 'think-tank', Mrs Thatcher also brought in advisers who were neither in the Policy Unit nor in her political office. Thus Sir Anthony Parsons was adviser on foreign affairs: a source of advice alternative to the Foreign and Commonwealth Office (FCO). More significant for EC policy was the appointment of Sir Alan Walters as economic adviser. He was no enthusiast of the European Monetary System, which he regarded as 'half-baked' and this oppposition became a source of tension with the then Chancellor of the Exchequer, Nigel Lawson, who had been shadowing the Deutschmark and advocating full membership of the EMS. This disagreement led ultimately to the resignation of both Lawson and Walters in 1989. These advisers, although in some cases seconded from the civil service, are not in practice subject to the same rules of political neutrality. Sir Charles Powell, seconded from the civil service, gave political advice on European matters. Mrs Thatcher felt that diplomats from the FCO were too closely involved in negotiations with foreign partners for them always to be able to identify British national interests. Overall, the strengthening of advisory arrangements introduces further centralization of policy but increases the risk of conflict with individual ministers.

The departmental ministers

If this consideration gives the impression that the prime minister is at the centre of European policy-making, this impression must be dispelled. In comparison, the involvement of other ministers is more continuous, since it is dependent neither on the relatively infrequent meetings of the European Council nor on the fluctuating political salience of European policy issues. The Foreign Secretary and the Minister of Agriculture are particularly affected in this way. The European dimension of ministerial work has not been an 'easy ride' for several of the incumbents. Amongst the casualties of senior office on European policy-related grounds have been the following: Michael Heseltine/Leon Brittan (1986), Nigel Lawson (1989), Nicholas Ridley (1990) and Sir Geoffrey Howe (1990). The circumstances of these resignations or dismissals – all during Mrs Thatcher's premiership – have varied. The dismissal of Norman Lamont, who had presided

[22] D. Willetts, 'The Role of the Prime Minister's Policy Unit', *Public Administration*, 65 (1987).

over both the pound's exit from the ERM in October 1992 and over the Council of Economics and Finance Ministers during the British presidency (July–December 1992), was not entirely unconnected with European matters. There were also some resignations from the junior ministerial ranks, occasioned by the debates concerning the ratification of the TEU. Disagreements between ministers over European policy – e.g. in the late 1980s over the question of ERM membership – have had a minor impact on the conduct of British policy within the EC. However, it is important to note that these divisions have normally arisen from strongly held views of individual politicians; they do not indicate a deep-seated sectorization in the British policy-making process.

Foreign Secretary
(Chair)

Chancellor of the Exchequer
Home Secretary
President of the Board of Trade
Secretary of State for Transport
Leader of the House
Minister of Agriculture, Fisheries and Food
Secretary of State for Scotland
Secretary of State for Wales
Secretary of State for Northern Ireland
Secretary of State for Employment
Attorney General
Parliamentary Secretary – Treasury
Minister of State – Treasury
Minister of State – Foreign Office
UK Permanent Representative to the EC
Other ministries as business necessitates

Fig 11.1 Membership of the Ministerial Sub-committee on European Questions (OPD[E])

Source: 'Ministerial Committees of the Cabinet, Membership and Terms of Reference', Cabinet Office, 19 May 1992.

According to Stack's study,[23] conducted a decade ago, there is a regular slot in Cabinet meetings for ministers to report on EC developments. Due to the Official Secrets Act and the consequent problems of access no detailed information is available on how politically salient European matters are handled within the Cabinet.[24] The exceptions to this are where former (prime) ministers have published their memoirs but these are difficult to assess scientifically. However, the Major government's (limited) attempts to provide more open government resulted in the publication, on 19 May 1992, of the Cabinet committees then in operation. The list included the *Ministerial Subcommittee on European Questions*, whose composition is set out in Figure 11.1. In formal terms, this committee is subordinate to the Ministerial Committee on Defence and Overseas Policy.

The Civil Service departments
The overwhelming majority of European policy is conducted at the specialist level within the individual ministries. However, there are established procedures for the coordination of policy. Our attention is focused initially on the policy- and decision-making stages, that is to say on the period up to formal decision-making in the institutions of the EU. The decision to integrate EC affairs into the existing organizational structure of the ministries was taken upon British entry into the EC in 1973. Following general practice, coordination was entrusted to the *Cabinet Office*. The closest Britain came to having a 'Minister for Europe' was during the first year of membership, when the Chancellor of the Duchy of Lancaster was given responsibility for coordination.[25] Supervisory responsibility was passed to the Foreign Secretary, James Callaghan, upon the election of the Labour government in February 1974. In addition to its general coordinating role in government, the Cabinet Office was entrusted with European policy. It was considered to be a more neutral agency than the FCO for bringing together the wide spectrum of ministerial views, since the latter's expertise lay in diplomatic matters. Within the Cabinet Office

[23] See the chapter by Freida Stack in F. E. C. Gregory, *Dilemmas of Government: Britain and the European Community* (Oxford: Martin Robertson, 1983).
[24] For some discussion, see G. Edwards, 'The Presidency of the EC: The Case of the United Kingdom', in C. O. Nuallain (ed.), *The Presidency of the European Council of Ministers* (Beckenham: Croom Helm, 1985), pp. 239–43. Also see A. Seldon, 'The Cabinet Office and Coordination 1979–87', *Public Administration*, 68 (1) (1990), p. 112.
[25] See Stack, in Gregory, *op. cit.*

the *European Secretariat* is the principal focus for policy coordination. It is staffed by some six senior staff who are seconded from those ministries which are most affected by EC matters.[26] It acts 'as a clearing house for the dossiers that go to ministers as well as providing guidance for departments on others'.[27] The European Secretariat is one of four in the Cabinet Office but, of them, is particularly pro-active. The secretariat's tasks may include preparation of negotiating tactics.[28] The head of the European Secretariat is particularly influential in coordinating governmental policy and, in addition, briefs the prime minister prior to sessions of the European Council. A *coordinating committee* of senior officials – known as *EQ(S)* – is chaired by the head of the European Secretariat. For the purposes of cross-national comparison, it should be pointed out that the Cabinet Office is the part of the government responsible for putting into practice the principle of collective cabinet responsibility. It functions in an anticipatory mode; it does not have to contend with intra-coalition negotiations; nor does it expect to devote large parts of its time to solving crises which have already reached the Cabinet. These characteristics set it apart from some of its counterparts elsewhere in the EU.

The FCO plays a more technical kind of coordinating role. It is the final channel for communications between UKREP and Whitehall. It also assumes a greater role in policy coordination when the UK holds the presidency. The FCO has two divisions dealing with matters relating to the European Union: one dealing with external policy (including foreign policy); the other dealing with internal policy. Foreign policy cooperation amongst the member states has been a matter where the FCO has been wholly responsible for policy, although as security policy develops there is a logic pushing eventually towards the need to coordinate with the Ministry of Defence. Some indication of the workload associated with foreign policy cooperation is reflected in the figures for the diplomatic telex system (COREU) used for coordination between the member states. As European Political Cooperation has become the EU's Common Foreign and Security

---

[26] See S. James, *British Cabinet Government* (London: Routledge, 1992), p. 202.

[27] G. Edwards, 'Central Government', in S. George (ed.), *Britain and the European Community: The Politics of Semi-Detachment* (Oxford: Clarendon Press, 1992), p. 84. Also see J. Peterson, 'The European Community', in D. Marsh and R. Rhodes (eds.), *Implementing Thatcherite Policies* (Milton Keynes: Open University Press, 1992), pp. 152–69.

[28] See Seldon, *op. cit.*, pp. 107–9.

Policy (CFSP), so the number of COREU messages has increased: from 7,548 in 1990 to 11,714 in 1993.[29] Other ministries have had to accommodate the European dimension in a significant manner. The Ministry of Agriculture, Fisheries and Food (MAFF) is a prime example because of the extent to which national policy is integrated into the Common Agricultural Policy. Already in 1982 it was estimated that some 200 MAFF officials travelled to Brussels each month.[30] The principal departments affected by the EU are those set out in Figure 11.1. One or two of those ministries deserve explanation. For example, the President of the Board of Trade presides over the Department of Trade and Industry (DTI), this title having been taken up by Michael Heseltine after the 1992 election. The DTI's responsibilities within the EU are quite extensive and included the majority of the single market programme.

The Scottish, Welsh and Northern Ireland Offices also warrant comment, for they are often neglected in studies of European policy-making in the government.[31] As ministries in their own right, but not reflecting a separate, elected level of government, they have a twofold responsibility. On the one hand, they may represent their particular territorial interests at the policy-making stage, whether at ministerial or administrative level. On the other hand, they supervise policy implementation in their own territories. For instance, the existence of the separate Scottish legal system may necessitate different implementing legislation from the rest of the country. Unfortunately for simplicity of explanation, the three ministries do not have exactly the same responsibilities but they all have an interest in local government matters, regional policy and agriculture. The Scottish Office has a particularly strong interest in fisheries – on account of the size of the Scottish fishing grounds – and this may result in the Secretary of State for Scotland attending the Council of Fisheries Ministers. It is not impossible for these ministries to pursue policies – whether as advocates in intragovernmental preparation for the Council of Ministers or at the implementation stage – which differ from those pursued by their English counterparts. For instance, Peter Walker as Secretary of State for Wales pursued a pro-active industrial policy which appeared to bear little resemblance to that advocated by his prime minister,

[29] Figures quoted in *CFSP Forum*, no. 1 (Bonn: Institut für Europäische Politik, 1994), p. 1.
[30] Quoted in Edwards, 'Central Government', *op. cit.*, p. 73.
[31] These ministries are not even mentioned in Edwards, 'Central Government', *op. cit.*

Mrs Thatcher. Whitehall-centred analysis may ignore the potential for civil servants in Cardiff and Edinburgh to pursue subtly different political agendas. This is particularly the case in Scotland where a more distinct set of legal and financial institutions, together with the Scottish press, may lead to a different gloss being placed on European policy.[32]

The Attorney General's presence is attributable to being the senior law officer of government. It is worth emphasizing at this point that the UK civil service is staffed mostly by generalists, a situation which differs from the often pervasive presence of jurists in the administrations of other states. Of the departments in Figure 11.1, it is the Home Office which has the greatest potential for further 'Europeanization', should the third, Justice and Home Affairs, 'pillar' of the EU continue to develop.

Other agencies
All these departments and ministers are engaged in the preparation of policy. There will be consultation of other agencies outside the departmental structure of government as the need arises. The *Bank of England* is an obvious case in point in respect of monetary integration. However, hitherto it has not attained independent status, although both Nigel Lawson and Norman Lamont have advocated such a development, albeit after their respective tenures as Chancellor of the Exchequer. Under Kenneth Clarke the Bank of England has been given greater freedom as to when it may announce changes in interest rates. However, the actual decision to adjust rates essentially remains with government.

Other agencies are consulted on policy as necessary: for instance, the *Monopolies and Mergers Commission* and the *Office of Fair Trading* over the EC's Merger Control Regulation;[33] the *Health and Safety Executive* on EC legislation in that domain; the *Civil Aviation Authority* on air transport liberalization policy; and so on.

---

[32] An innovation for the early 1990s was the creation of 'Scotland Europa' as a Scottish business representation in Brussels. Attached to Scottish Enterprise (the Scottish economic development agency) but with local authority and private sector participation, it is not a policy-making body but provides a focal point for elites that is absent in England.

[33] S. Bulmer, 'Institutions and Policy Change in the European Communities: The Case of Merger Control', *Public Administration*, 72 (3) (1994), pp. 423–44.

The role of the UK Permanent Representation

UKREP is the principal governmental institution whose role remains to be outlined. Its involvement becomes more critical in the decision-making stage, although it is also responsible for keeping ministries briefed on developments in the supranational institutions. It has generally had a staffing level of some forty senior officials: one of the larger Permanent Representations in Brussels and with a spread of representatives from the ministries in Whitehall. The Permanent Representative returns to Whitehall on Fridays to discuss the broad strategy of British policy with the Cabinet Office and other interested ministries.[34] This regular participation in Whitehall's European policy-making is indicative of the latter's centralized nature; most other Permanent Representatives do not have this level of engagement in policy-making in their national capital.

The general pattern of British participation in European negotiations is one of following rather tight guidelines which, in the case of important meetings or those with cross-departmental significance, will have been worked out in the Cabinet, cabinet committee or one of the inter-ministerial committees. The involvement of the UK government in negotiations has been summarized well by Peter Pooley, formerly the senior official in UKREP from the Ministry of Agriculture, Fisheries and Food, in the following terms:

> the British are more predictable. They are very well briefed, they are very articulate, it's very easy to get hold of and understand their point of view. It's relatively more difficult to change it.[35]

This last comment highlights the fact that a highly coordinated European policy may bring inflexibility in negotiations within the EC. This situation – a product of the institutional characteristics of EC policy-making within the UK – may be compounded by the adversarial norms which British politicians bring with them to the Council and the European Council. Coming from an adversarial background, where 'political grandstanding' in the House of Commons is common practice, it may not be so easy to adapt to the cooperative norms which are needed in the more consensus-building intergovernmental institutions of the EU. More routine negotiations, where official-level bargaining is decisive, are not subject to these adversarial norms. Another pertinent observation is made by Geoffrey Edwards:

[34] Edwards, 'Central Government', *op. cit.*, p. 73.
[35] Quoted in Edwards, 'Central Government', *op. cit.*, p. 76.

If the pursuit of detailed policy objectives has generally been successful ... Britain's capacity to pursue a coherent overall strategy in the Community has been more questionable.[36]

The parliament

The role of parliament in shaping British European policy has three aspects to it. Firstly, the House of Commons is recognised as a 'talk' parliament rather than as a 'work' parliament. The consequence is that it is not especially attuned to the influential scrutiny of proposals emanating from the Commission. Secondly, the government's institutional origins lie in its majority in the House. Thus ministers need to be conscious of those European Union developments which might encounter serious criticism within the House. As already indicated, this anticipatory function becomes even more critical when the government-in-office holds only a small majority. The third aspect is the work of the House of Lords. By contrast with the lower house, its work is much more scrutiny-oriented.

The focal point of the work of the House of Commons lies in oral reports, debates and questions relating to the EU.[37] In the first category fall, for example, the reports made by the prime minister following a meeting of the European Council. Debates take place on EC proposals deemed to be of importance by the *Select Committee on European Legislation* (known as the Scrutiny Committee). Items sifted out by this committee were originally debated in plenary sessions. This was changed during the 1989–90 session because lack of parliamentary time often consigned such debates to unsocial hours, resulting in poor attendance. Instead, two special *standing committees* were established for the debate of different domains of EC legislation. However, such standing committees rarely capture public attention and party discipline generally ensures a fairly smooth passage. Parliamentary questions may be asked of ministers or the prime minister on European matters, although it would be difficult to attribute any significance to these upon the ultimate pattern of negotiations in the Council of Ministers. Finally, *departmental select committees* require a mention. They were an important development at the start of the Thatcher era. They are not, however, legislative com-

---

[36] *Ibid.*, p. 67.
[37] For more details of parliament's work, see S. George, 'The Legislative Dimension', in George (ed.), *Britain and the European Community, op. cit.*, pp. 91–103, on which this section draws.

mittees. As a result, their work tends to be ex post policy scrutiny of aspects of governmental policy, including on European affairs.

The work of the House of Lords is conducted in the *Select Committee on the European Communities*. This in fact comprises (1993–4 session) five *sub-committees* according to policy area. The reports are highly regarded in the UK and elsewhere in the EU. Alan Butt Philip has summarized the committee's work thus:

> The pressure of the peers, on a fairly apolitical, technocratic but *communautaire* basis, can be both politically persistent and yet unthreatening – hence its effectiveness, an indication that alternatives to adversary politics ... exist in the British political system.[38]

Parliamentary control over EC legislation is thus rather patchy and certainly raises questions as to why – other than for symbolic reasons – the sovereignty debate occasionally reaches fever pitch. Indeed, it was not until 1989 that the House of Commons Scrutiny Committee *was permitted* (i.e. by government) to look at anything other than formal EC proposals. Thus the Single European Act could not be considered prior to ratification, nor could the work of the IGC in which it had been negotiated. This executive control over the House even permitted the government to push through the SEA on the grounds that it was a technical matter designed to secure the main objective of the single market![39]

Policy implementation

It has become the convention to describe the UK as a combative negotiator in the Council of Ministers but a good performer in terms of the subsequent implementation of EC law. One explanation for the latter has been civil service efficiency. Moreover, there are in the UK no institutional features discriminating against EC legislation; indeed, as Butt Philip and Baron point out, administrators may not even be aware of the origins of the legislation.[40] Indeed, the importance of the administrative context may be developed further. The centralized nature of the UK administration may contribute to the positive performance. A federal state, by contrast, may create longer chains of

---

[38] A. Butt Philip, 'Pressure Groups', in George (ed.), *Britain and the European Community, op. cit.*, p. 157.

[39] See George, 'The Legislative Dimension', *op. cit.*, pp. 93–5.

[40] See A. Butt Philip and C. Baron, 'The United Kingdom', in H. Siedentopf and J. Ziller (eds.), *Making European Policies Work*, vol. ii, *National Reports* (London: Sage Publications, 1988), p. 639.

command. But, arguably as important is the culture embedded in the British public administration. Although the British administrative machinery is not populated by staff with a legal training, there is nevertheless a legalistic assumption that laws are made to be put into practice.

Control of the legislative branch of government by the executive is also a major contributory factor. Stephen George summarizes this aspect thus:

> It should be ... noted that it is much easier for the British Government to embody EC directives in national statutes than it is for the Governments of some other member states, because of the control that the British Government exercises over the parliamentary timetable, and the control it exercises over the vote in the Commons through the existence of a clear majority of members supporting the single party of Government.[41]

Finally, much EC legislation is enacted by way of delegated legislation under the terms of the European Communities Act of 1972, which set down the constitutional foundations of UK membership. This situation arises from the terms of the European Communities Act of 1972 (Section 2[2]); only EC measures imposing taxation, which are retrospective, or creating new criminal penalties must be implemented by primary legislation. Enactment of EC legislation through executive action results in relatively weak parliamentary supervision: technical scrutiny rather than policy oversight.

Taken together, these factors amount to a clear case of institutional characteristics explaining the UK's relatively good record on enacting European legislation. As an example of the UK's record on policy implementation, we can take the data on enactment of single market legislation into national law. As of 31 December 1993 the UK had enacted 92.3% of all binding EC directives (EC average = 90.40%), most of which are in the field of the single market legislation.[42] It stood third in the league table, behind the clear leader – Denmark (95.4%) – and almost joint second with the Netherlands (92.4%).[43]

---

[41] George, 'The Legislative Dimension', *op. cit.*, p. 97.

[42] See Eleventh Report of the Commission to the European Parliament on the Control of the Application of Community Law, 1993, OJ C 154, 6.6.1994, p. 7.

[43] Italy had made a concerted effort to improve its performance, having been in twelfth position only some two years previously. See for more details Marco Giuliani's contribution on Italy in this volume.

Compliance with European law

An alternative way of looking at the UK's record is by examining the extent to which the EC Commission has taken legal steps against the UK under Article 169 EC (see Table 11.1). In ascending order of gravity these steps take the form, firstly, of a 'Letter of Formal Notice' from the Commission addressed to the respective member state. The second stage is where the Commission, dissatisfied with the reply, gives a 'Reasoned Opinion'. The most serious situation is where the member state is still considered to be in dereliction of its duty, and formal proceedings are brought by means of a court case before the European Court of Justice (ECJ). As Snyder has pointed out, the effectiveness of Article 169 proceedings lies less in the judgments themselves.[44] Rather, it is the way that letters or reasoned opinions bring states into line. Thus the UK's ratio of 640 letters of formal notice to some thirty-two cases before the ECJ (1978-93) is also a relevant statistic. The UK seems to perform well above average as regards addressing Commission concerns so that full Court proceedings do not take place.

So how does the UK perform in the three categories in a comparative perspective? The overall picture is positive.[45] Letters of formal notice against the UK are rising significantly but following the trend in overall figures. In 1993 the UK was equal fourth in being the least subject to such letters. Reasoned opinions are issued by the Commission where it is unhappy with the national governments' response to a letter of formal notice. In 1993 the UK was second in being least the subject of such action. Those cases which the Commission pursues all the way to the ECJ are fewer in number, so taking one year's data is not representative. Taking the entire period 1988–93, the UK was in joint third place for 'good behaviour'.

None of this should hide the fact that the UK has been known to flout EC legislation. One example of this arose from the EC legislation on the mandatory fitting of tachographs in the cabs of lorries to monitor the time and distance travelled.[46] This caused considerable opposition in the road haulage sector and the UK failed to give effect

---

[44] F. Snyder, 'The Effectiveness of European Community Law: Institutions, Processes, Tools and Techniques', *Modern Law Review*, 56 (1993), pp. 19–54.

[45] See Table 14.1 in the conclusion of this book.

[46] See Butt Philip and Baron, 'The United Kingdom', *op. cit.*, pp. 675–710, for a case study of this legislation.

Table 11.1 Proceedings brought against the UK under Article 169 EC, by category, 1988–93.

Year	Letters of Formal Notice	Reasoned Opinions	Cases in the ECJ
1978	8	9	3
1979	24	7	2
1980	19	7	–
1981	20	8	2
1982	32	4	2
1983	20	7	1
1984	34	10	4
1985	29	11	5
1986	37	5	1
1987	44	9	2
1988	34	15	–
1989	37	13	5
1990	44	6	2
1991	63	11	–
1992	97	13	3
1993	98	15	–

Sources: Third Annual Report to the European Parliament on Commission Monitoring of the Application of Community Law 1985, COM(86) 204 final, Brussels, 3 June 1986; Fifth Report 1987, COM(88) 425 final, 3 Oct. 1988; Eighth Report 1991, COM(91) 321 final, 16 Oct. 1991; Tenth Report 1992 COM(93) 320 final, 28 April 1993 and Eleventh Report 1993, COM (94) 500 final, 29 March 1994.

to the legislation. This led to full proceedings being instituted by the Commission against the UK. In *Commission* v. *United Kingdom* (case 121/78) the ECJ found against the UK but the government then took two years to phase in legislation. Another illustrative case, *Commission* v. *United Kingdom (Re. Import of Poultry Meat)* Case 40/82, arose from a British ruling that imported poultry required a licence. The UK sought to justify its actions on the grounds that this measure would prevent the spread of 'Newcastle Disease'. The Court, however, found that this justification was spurious and that the licensing was designed to serve as an import barrier. Suffice it to indicate that sufficient time had elapsed before the case came to the ECJ for UK poultry farmers to benefit from the lack of foreign competition. British turkeys did not survive that Christmas! An analogous case arose concerning the import of UHT milk. Generally, the reaction of the UK to those cases it has lost in the Court has not been to flout the law in a brazen manner but perhaps to drag out compliance. It is worth adding two further connected points. Firstly, it was the British government which was a particular advocate of the imposition of fines on states not complying with EC law: a feature incorporated by the TEU into Article 171. Secondly, frustration at other member states' poorer implementation has even led to occasional suggestions that the UK should itself not be so assiduous in implementing EC law, and play the others at 'their game'.

The local government

The power of local government is quite restricted in the UK. Its powers can be changed by parliament: which in practice means at the will of the governing party. During the period of Conservative rule since 1979, there has been a quite sustained restriction of local authority power. Motivated by goals such as increasing local government efficiency, cutting public spending and increasing local accountability, the result has been to limit local authorities' power in an almost indiscriminate manner. At the same time as this development has been under way, there has been a growing impact of the EC upon local government. So how have the two processes interacted?

Many of the changes brought about by central government have not had a direct effect on local government's European role. The shift in local government financing falls into this category, as do changes in local authorities' involvement in school education. Other changes have had a greater impact. The abolition of the English metropolitan counties and the Greater London Council is a clear example. Many of these former counties contain areas eligible for structural fund aid. So, just as EC policy was beginning to demand a more integrated regional approach to applications for structural funds, so the metropolitan counties – complete with their economic development functions – had just been abolished. To take an example, the abolition of Greater Manchester Council (GMC) led to economic planning being taken on by the ten metropolitan boroughs which previously constituted GMC. As a result, there has been an inevitable duplication of resources in the boroughs. And this is not just the pattern in Greater Manchester but in all the metropolitan areas. Suffice it to say that the metropolitan boroughs are not brought together easily, even though this may be necessary to be successful in obtaining EC funds. The party in power may differ from one authority to another; there may be different political agendas; neighbouring cities may have an ongoing rivalry; economic and social problems vary from one authority to another; and so on.

At the beginning of 1994 the Conservative government considered the further reorganization of local government. In England it proposed single-tier authorities. The effect of this development will be the abolition of some county councils. Of potentially greater significance in the context of European policy is the government's abolition of the upper tier of Scottish local government, known as the regional councils. For an area such as Strathclyde, which claims to be Europe's largest local authority, there would be serious consequences for the economic development function which is important for seeking EC funding.

It is clear, then, that central government's control over the structure of local government has a major impact. If there is any compensation, it is that some EC funding is on a pluriannual basis, unlike central government assistance to local authorities.[47] Hence, EC support may bring with it greater financial certainty. Weighed against this consideration, however, is the fact that the UK government has sought to undermine the additionality principle, so EC funding may not represent extra money. Faced with challenges of this kind, the UK local authorities have sought to forge close relations with the European Commission. For its part, the Commission has encouraged such links. For instance, in the case of DG XVI (regional policy), the Commission has actually encouraged the emergence of an alliance of local authorities in the north-west of England – the *North-West Regional Association* – to assist with policy development.[48] Another example of the creativity at UK local authority level is Strathclyde Regional Council's promotion of an EC-wide lobby for Objective 2 areas, i.e. those regions of industrial decline eligible for assistance from the structural funds.[49] The UK is a major beneficiary from Objective 2 funding. UK local authorities have been prominent in forming other alliances aimed either at better positioning for EC aid or at increased appeal for investors, for instance Kent County Council's links with Nord Pas-de-Calais, facilitated by the Channel Tunnel project.[50] Some of the larger authorities – or consortia – have opened offices in Brussels.

[47] See J. Preston, 'Local Government', in George, *Britain and the European Community*, *op. cit.*, pp. 106–7.

[48] M. Burch and I. Holliday, 'Institutional Emergence: The Case of the North West Region of England', *Regional Politics and Policy*, 3 (2) (1993), pp. 29–50.

[49] See P. McAleavey and J. Mitchell, 'Industrial Regions and Lobbying in the Structural Funds Reform Process', *Journal of Common Market Studies*, 32 (2) (1994), pp. 237–48.

[50] I. Holliday et al., *The Channel Tunnel: Public Policy, Regional Development and European Integration* (London: Belhaven Press, 1991).

As far as their policy-making functions are concerned, local authorities have attempted to utilize the opportunities offered by the EC: in part as a way of regaining some power, given the impact of central government reforms. However, it is very difficult to judge what influence the authorities have over policy. Many of the funding decisions they seek to influence fit into an overall policy context, over which they do not have much power. This impotence derives from the fact that it is central government which is involved in the negotiation of the overall policy framework in the Council. Whitehall's consultation of local government has not been extensive because that has not always suited the Conservative government's political wishes. In some respects this centralized rule from Whitehall is being reinforced by the 1993 decision of the government to appoint 'regional prefects' to coordinate the work of different ministries in different regions, e.g. England's north west.

The role of the local authorities is not confined to seeking better EC funding. They are also entrusted with implementing significant parts of EC law.[51] As Preston indicates, the policy areas where local government is particularly involved are vocational training (where central government has subsequently taken greater control over policy); economic development (as discussed); environmental health; trading standards; and consumer protection. These responsibilities impose a significant workload. In essence it is a matter for the individual authority how it organizes itself with a view to implementing EC legislation, that is enacted within the UK. However, the Local Government International Bureau is an important resource, independent of central government, for assisting with this aspect of local authorities' activities. The principal challenge for local authorities lies with the establishment of the Committee of the Regions. Will this body enable UK local authorities to have a stronger input into the EU's decision-preparation and decision-making? This question cannot be answered until the committee establishes a track-record, and the performance of British representatives becomes clear.

The national courts
In order to gauge the level of acceptance of EC law in the national

---

[51] On this, see Preston, 'Local Government', *op.cit.*, *passim*; also Preston, 'Local Government', in S. Bulmer, S. George and A. Scott (eds.), *The United Kingdom and EC Membership Evaluated* (London: Pinter Publishers, 1992).

courts, we also need to consider the attitudes and actions of the UK judiciary. Over time, the UK courts have shown a strong willingness to accept their role in enforcing EC obligations. This development is in spite of the strong constitutional principle of parliamentary sovereignty and some early ambivalence shown towards the supremacy of EC law.[52] However, despite showing a willingness to give a purposive interpretation to national law to remove conflict with an EC directive, Lord Diplock in the House of Lords left open the question of what the national court should do if there was an express derogation from EC law in a national statute.[53] The courts have shown an increased willingness to give national legislation an interpretation that is in line with EC law, reflecting the ECJ's ruling in *Von Colson*.[54] However, the House of Lords was reluctant to interpret national legislation enacted *prior* to an EC directive to comply with later EC law.[55]

So, Article 169 EC proceedings alone are not enough for assessing compliance in the UK. Above all, the Commission does not have the resources to be especially thorough in acting as 'guardian of the treaties'. Indeed, in the context of the single market, there is considerable evidence that it is hoping that affected parties will take grievances to the law. Accordingly, important cases, such as Factortame (see below), have arisen as a result of Article 177 EC references by the national courts.

A further aspect of the adaptation of British institutions to the EC concerns the legal system. Have the British courts accepted the ECJ as having superior jurisdiction in the interpretation of European law? To address this question, attention must be given briefly to Article 177 EC proceedings, where national courts seek preliminary rulings from the ECJ (see Table 11.2). Between 1973 and the end of 1990 there had been a total of 118 such references (eight from the House of Lords, thirteen from the Court of Appeal and ninety-seven from other courts). These figures suggest that the national court structure has recognized the supremacy of the ECJ; this being especially the case for the English

---

[52] Compare Lord Denning's willingness to accept EC law with the greater reticence of the Court of Appeal judges in *McCarthy's Ltd.* v. *Smith* [1979] ICR 785.

[53] *Garland* v. *British Rail Engineering Ltd.* [1983] 2 AC 751.

[54] *Pickstone* v. *Freemans* [1989] AC 66; *Litster* v. *Forth Dry Dock and Engineering Co. Ltd.* [1990] 1 AC 546. *Von Colson* v. *Land Nordrhein-Westfalen* [1984] ECR 1891.

[55] *Duke* v. *GEC Reliance Ltd.* [1988] AC 618. The ECJ later ruled that there was an obligation to interpret national law to give effect to Community law regardless of whether the former was enacted before or after the latter: *Marleasing SA* v. *La Commercial Internacional de Alimentacion SA* [1990] ECR I–4135.

Divisional Court. One exception to this pattern came when the House of Lords refused to make a reference to the ECJ because it felt able to apply EC law without an interpretation from Luxembourg.[56]

Table 11.2 Article 177 proceedings by UK courts to the European Court of Justice

Category of court	Number of references
House of Lords	8
Court of Appeal	13
Others	97
TOTAL	118

Source: Court of Justice of the European Community, *Synopsis of the Work of the Court of Justice* (Luxembourg: OOPEC, 1992).

Although only rarely recognized within the UK in such terms, the courts' utilization of Article 177 references – including against UK public authorities – has served to undermine national sovereignty, for the government has no control over the judiciary's actions.[57] Another development of considerable significance for UK constitutional law was the decision of the ECJ that, pending the Court's decision on an Article 177 reference, the national court had to give interim relief to Spanish fishermen by way of a suspension of national law.[58] This decision gave the UK courts – in the context of European law – the power to disapply national law in a way that had previously been unconstitutional and which the House of Lords itself had refused to undertake.

In terms of the impact of Community law in empowering British courts in relation to parliament, it is worth highlighting the 1994 decision of the House of Lords declaring national legislation on part-time work as incompatible with EC law on sex discrimination.[59] Not only did the national court recognize the competence of the UK Equal Opportunities Commission to seek such a declaration and the com-

[56] *Freight Transport Association Ltd.* v. *London Boroughs Transport Committee* [1991] 3 All ER 915. Controversially, the decision of the House of Lords did not square with the substance of an earlier ECJ ruling against the UK.

[57] See J. Weiler, 'Journey to an Unknown Destination: A Retrospective and Prospective of the European Court of Justice in the Arena of Political Integration', *Journal of Common Market Studies*, 31 (4) (1993), pp. 421–3.

[58] *R.* v. *Secretary of State for Transport ex p. Factortame* [1990] ECR I–2433.

[59] *R.* v. *Secretary of State for Employment ex parte Equal Opportunities Commission and another* [1994] IRLR 176.

petence of the court to hear the action (as opposed to relying on Article 169 proceedings by the Commission before the Court of Justice), but it also found the UK government's justification for the discrimination between men and women to be insufficient. Indeed, the decision of the House of Lords went against the general direction of the Conservative government's labour market policy, including policy as pursued in the European arena. Clearly, EC law has empowered the British courts to scrutinize national legislation in a way hitherto impossible, given the court's traditional adherence to the legislative supremacy of parliament.

Public opinion, political parties and interest groups

Hitherto attention has focused on the institutions of government. This is not surprising, given the institutional analysis that has been employed. However, it is important not to neglect the political forces which shape the climate within which institutions function. These forces are public opinion, the political parties and interest groups. The EC/EU's impact upon them, and their response, cannot be treated in great detail here. Nonetheless, it is possible to give a brief portrait of how each of these political forces influences the policy-making process.

Public opinion

The role of public opinion plays a background role in shaping the political debate concerning European integration. There are, of course, numerous methodological pitfalls in conducting polls and in analysing data. Moreover, public opinion may not always be very well informed. For instance, a 1989 Gallup poll asked respondents how far they shared specific fears about the future of integration. The loss of parliamentary sovereignty was identified to a lesser extent than fears of increased drug smuggling, cross-border terrorism and – top of the concerns – the spread of rabies and plant diseases from the continent. Suffice it to indicate that the actual threat from rabies, not to mention perceptions of it on the continent, is negligible. Despite this caveat, some general observations can be made. Firstly, polls have revealed a clear majority of Britons supporting the process of integration, although the extent of the majority is lower than in the founding member states. Secondly, from the mid-1980s there has been a majority of respondents regarding the UK's membership of the EC as a good thing, but again a smaller majority than in the founding members. Thirdly, it was not until 1989 that a majority of respondents took the view that the UK had benefited from EC membership.[60] The lukewarm support for the EC has certainly been a factor which governments – both Labour and Conservative – have played upon when defending British interests. Nugent suggests that the Labour Party's policy towards the EC may have been influenced by trends in public opinion, namely its 1980 policy decision of favouring withdrawal; and then its gradual shift, from 1983 onwards, to a more supportive position.[61] The Conservative government's single market publicity campaign, 'Europe – Open for Business' (run by the Department of Trade and Industry) coincided with a more supportive British public opinion. Paradoxically, Mrs Thatcher's Bruges speech (in 1988), her opposition to EMU (1989–90) and the Conservatives' poor campaign for the 1989 elections to the EP all went somewhat against the tide of British opinion. This situation may have contributed to the feeling, within the Conservative Party, that she was increasingly out of touch with opinion: a feeling that culminated in her replacement.

Political parties

The role of the political parties in European policy-making is linked to some extent with that of public opinion. The party debate has a background influence but, in the absence of coalition considerations, no more than that. The one exception to this situation is where, within the House of Commons, there is a small governing majority. Then, the influence of backbench party opinion can have an impact on policy, especially when the government is reliant on the support of a handful of 'Euro-sceptics'. Because of the majoritarian electoral system and the centralization of power, there is little scope for opposition parties to influence policy. Over the period since 1973 the parties' views on the EC/EU have been quite complex. The Labour Party was deeply divided on European policy until the mid-1980s. Labour Prime Minister Harold Wilson (1974–6) had to use the device of renegotiations and a referendum to hold the party together. Then,

---

[60] For a survey, using various datasets, see Neill Nugent, 'British Public Opinion and the European Community', in George (ed.), *Britain and the European Community*, *op. cit.*, pp. 172–201.

[61] *Ibid.*, p. 195.

in 1980 the party conference adopted a policy supporting withdrawal. This also created divisions and was a primary factor behind
the creation of the Social Democratic Party, led initially by the
former Commission president, Roy Jenkins. The SDP's European
policy was supportive of integration and was very close to the policy
of the Liberals. Indeed, the two parties eventually merged to form
the Liberal Democrats.

For its part, the Conservative Party has held a consistently supportive policy towards the EC/EU but always based upon slow, pragmatic evolution. Moreover, the principal area of support has been on
creating the single market. Once the integration debate enters the
realm of ERM membership, EMU, strengthening supranational institutions and such matters, small groups of party MPs opposed to the
loss of sovereignty are identifiable. And the positions of several forceful political personalities – Mrs Thatcher herself but also the contrasting views of Edward Heath, Nigel Lawson and Michael
Heseltine – have led to substantive disagreements on the objectives of
policy. The salience of these disagreements, it is argued here, has been
a function of institutional factors. In other words, if the disagreements have threatened the Conservatives' majority in the House or
created inter-ministerial tensions, then they have assumed real significance. Otherwise, they remain an irritant for party managers and a
welcome opportunity for political torment from the opposition.

Interest groups
Interest groups are important political forces in the shaping of British
European policy. Their influence, however, is quite different from
that of parties and public opinion. Perhaps the only parallel with
those potentially adversarial arenas was provided by the trade unions'
initial anti-Europeanism, which was linked to Labour Party policy.
However, the development of the social dimension of European integration facilitated a rehabilitation of European integration in the
trade union movement from the mid-1980s onwards.

Most interest group lobbying takes place away from the public eye
and in specialist policy arenas. Provided that the issue under consideration is not sensitive in parliamentary terms, the adversarial character of politics is suspended. This means that interest group–civil
servant contacts take place on a specialist level. An array of discrete
policy communities thus exists, bringing together civil servants and

interest groups.[62] Generally speaking, interest groups are well-organized in the UK. There are not the ideological divisions which serve to fragment certain interests in France or Italy. On the other hand, group membership of policy communities is not formalized in the corporatist mode that characterizes Germany. One effect of this has been that the trade unions have had little influence over the Conservative government's policy; their views are deemed to be too close to those of the Labour Party. Hence trade union organizations have had to look to the European level to seek to influence policy. Lobbying of the European level is a well-established practice in British pressure groups, provided that financial resources permit. Usually, such lobbying is undertaken through the well-established route of European umbrella groups. However, the presence in the UK economy of a number of giant firms has also led to their establishment of offices in Brussels.[63] Such offices can offer multiple strategies of influence and avoid complete reliance on the UK government as a channel of influence. It is also worth noting that there are some asymmetries between UK private interests and those in partner states. For instance, British Airways (BA) has stood alone within the Association of European Airlines (AEA) as a privately owned 'flag-carrier'; the others are all partly or wholly state-owned. This situation may necessitate the use of multiple channels of lobbying, for the AEA was not especially receptive to air transport liberalization, whereas BA was more positively disposed. The extent to which UK utilities (telecommunications, power generators, water companies etc.) are in private ownership may give them interests which are different from those of their continental counterparts. Situations such as this suggest that the national channel of influence would remain an important part of their lobbying strategy.

To summarize, interest groups play a major part in UK European policy-making. Outside those areas where parliamentary sensitivities come into play, the government needs advice from interest groups in

[62] For more on this, see Butt Philip, 'Pressure Groups', in S. George (ed.), *Britain and the European Community*, op. cit., pp. 149–71; also S. Mazey and J. Richardson (eds.), *Lobbying in the European Community* (Oxford: Clarendon Press, 1993).

[63] See, for instance, the cases of the chemicals and automobile industries in, respectively: W. Grant, W. Paterson and C. Whitston, *Government and the Chemical Industry: A Comparative Study of Britain and West Germany* (Oxford: Clarendon Press, 1988); and A. McLaughlin, G. Jordan and W. Maloney, 'Corporate Lobbying in the European Community', *Journal of Common Market Studies*, 31 (2) (1993), pp. 191–212.

order to judge where British interests lie. The views may not always be taken up but the government is dependent on them for information. Interest groups' strategies are highly geared to exerting influence at the key access points in the EU/national institutional structures.

Conclusion

How, then, can the British pattern of European policy-making be characterized? It is certainly centralized. The governing party has the potential to place its stamp on policy, with public opinion and party politics acting only as background factors. However, parliamentary politics cannot be ignored. The result is a bifurcated approach. Thus many non-sensitive policy issues are decided in discrete (and discreet) policy communities, with relatively low key but effective coordination within the civil service ('route two'). More sovereignty-sensitive or ideology-sensitive matters are likely to enter the adversarial political arena ('route one'). This arena dictates closer policy coordination: up to Cabinet level, if necessary. Moreover, it is those policy issues which have entered the adversarial arena that tend to be the source of the principal conflicts between the UK government – of whatever political persuasion – and its partners in the EC/EU. It is precisely because of governmental coordination and the need for caution *vis-à-vis* the House of Commons that negotiations may become fraught within the Council of Ministers or the European Council.

The conclusion here is that this bifurcated approach has considerable explanatory value concerning the dynamics of British policy in the European Union. This conclusion must be unpacked somewhat, for it rests on several assumptions. Firstly, it rests on the assumption that domestic politics matter: to understand the UK's role in the EC/EU necessitates an understanding of the political and institutional dynamics within the UK.[64] However, the UK's negotiations in the EU involve it in a two-level game: the interaction between the two levels – domestic and European level – which takes place within the Council of Ministers determines whether British interests are influential.[65] Secondly, the UK government is seen as an intermediating force in the

[64] On this approach, see S. Bulmer, 'Domestic Politics and European Community Policy-Making', *Journal of Common Market Studies*, 21 (4) (1983), pp. 349–63.

[65] On two-level games, see R. D. Putnam, 'Diplomacy and Domestic Politics', *International Organization*, 42 (1988), pp. 427–61.

process of European policy-making. The 'domestic politics approach' does not equate to intergovernmentalism; it is recognized that other institutions along with political forces shape government policy. This occurs in the UK just as it occurs in, say, Germany; it is just that the circumstances differ, so policy differs.[66] Thirdly, and what is emphasized here in particular, a focus on institutions and their symbols can offer an explanation of the conduct of British policy in the EC/EU. Institutions and their symbolic dimension, it is argued, can offer an explanation of how the UK's bifurcated European policy is organized. But cannot a straightforward 'political forces' explanation do this? The answer advocated here is 'no'. And the reasoning is this. In quantitative terms, the majority of European decision-making is conducted away from major controversy and the public eye. This activity is as important in the representation of British interests as the eye-catching debates, such as on the Maastricht Treaty (which are open to a political forces explanation). By locating institutional factors at the centre of attention – indeed as mediating political forces – we suggest that a balanced view can be obtained of the UK's participation in the EU's operations.

What are the advantages and disadvantages of the UK's bifurcated approach? The advantages are that policy tends to be relatively clear to our EU partners; it tends to be presented coherently; and the key policy issues have usually been subject to domestic political debate (facilitating transparency). Moreover, the UK has a strong record on implementation EC legislation. In these respects the UK is far from being an 'awkward partner'. Indeed, it is much more predictable than some of its partners. The disadvantages are that the bifurcated approach excludes opposition parties from influence (thus hampering consensus); it excludes interest groups from influence if they oppose government ideology; it gives an inadequate voice to regional interests; the House of Commons (but not the peers) undertake negligible scrutiny of day-to-day matters; and the UK government may be an intransigent negotiator in Brussels.

What challenges lie ahead for the UK's institutions in the post-Maastricht era? Two are of major concern. First, how will the Committee of the Regions work? Will it afford an opportunity for UK

---

[66] For a domestic politics analysis of German European policy (prior to reunification), see S. Bulmer and W. Paterson, *The Federal Republic of Germany and the European Community* (London: Allen & Unwin, 1987).

regions, local authorities, Scotland and Wales to articulate their interests, as opposed to those perceived in Whitehall? Second, how will
democratic control be assured over the CFSP and the third pillar of
Justice and Home Affairs (JHA)? Democratic control over these
activities is not assured in the EP, for its powers are much weaker on
these matters than on EC activities. As government-centred activities,
democratic control has to be assured through national parliaments.
The clearer constitutional status given to CFSP and JHA affairs in
the TEU presents a clear challenge for Westminster.

Select bibliography

Bulmer, S., George, S. and Scott, A. (eds.), *The United Kingdom and European Community Membership Evaluated* (London: Pinter Publishers,
1992).

Edwards, G., 'The Presidency, the Case of the United Kingdom', in C. O
Nuallain (ed.), *The Presidency of the European Council of Ministers*
(London: Croom Helm, 1985).

Garel-Jones, T., 'The UK Presidency: An Inside View', *Journal of Common
Market Studies*, 31 (2) (1993), pp. 261–7.

George, S., *An Awkward Partner: Britain in the European Community*
(Oxford: Oxford University Press, 1990).

George, S. (ed.), *Britain and the European Community: The Politics of Semi-
Detachment* (Oxford: Clarendon Press, 1992).

Gregory, F. E. C., *Dilemmas of Government: Britain and the European Community* (Oxford: Martin Robertson, 1983).

Ludlow, P., 'The UK Presidency: A View from Brussels', *Journal of Common
Market Studies*, 31 (2) (1993), pp. 246–60.

Peterson, J., 'The United Kingdom', in D. Marsh and R. Rhodes (eds.),
Implementing Thatcherite Policies: Audit of an Era (Milton Keynes:
Open University Press, 1992), pp. 152–69.

Siedentopf, H. and Ziller, J. (eds.), *Making European Policies Work: The
Implementation of Community Legislation in the Member States*, vol. i:
Comparative Syntheses; vol. ii: *National Reports*, see contributions by
A. Butt Philip and C. Baron on the UK (London: Sage Publications,
1988).

Ireland

Fundamentals of Ireland in EU affairs

A small state

Ireland is one of Europe's many small states with a population of three and a half million and is located on the north-western periphery of the continent. Accession to the Community came in 1973 when agreement was reached on the first enlargement. Ireland is a relatively young state in European terms; part of the island (twenty-six counties) gained independence from Great Britain in 1922. Ireland declared itself a Republic in 1949 which ended all constitutional links with Britain. The republican features of the state are a written constitution with a Supreme Court and an elected President who holds office for seven years. The President exercises a reserve role in the political system. Executive power resides in the government of the day which must command the confidence of the parliament. The Taoiseach or Prime Minister (PM) is formally appointed by the President although nominated by Dail Eireann, the lower house of a bicameral legislature. The size of the government is limited to fifteen ministers by the constitution. Each minister is responsible to the parliament for the work of his or her department and the Cabinet as a whole is governed by collective responsibility. Ireland is a unitary state with a weak form of local government and limited decentralization within state agencies. A characteristic of the Irish public service is the important role played by state-sponsored bodies which were established for all of the major utilities but also as promotional agencies for the development and modernization of the Irish economy.

EC membership must be seen in an Irish context as part of a drive towards industrialization and modernization which began at the end of the 1950s. A desire to lessen Ireland's economic dependency on Great Britain formed part of the motivation. The Irish economy is very open with some 56% of GDP accounted for by exports. Moreover, the Irish economy is more dependent on agriculture, both as a source of employment and value added, than the average for the EC as a whole. The performance of Irish industry in the EC market is mixed; foreign multinationals located in Ireland have succeeded in penetrating the market whereas the performance of the indigenous firms has been weak. Population growth in Ireland has contributed to high unemployment and migration out of Ireland in the 1980s. Ireland is considered one of the lesser developed parts of the Community of Twelve and is a major beneficiary of EC financial transfers. All of these considerations have led Irish policy-makers and the Irish public to regard the Community as an economic entity. Ireland's neutrality during the Second World War and the subsequent non-membership of NATO serve to reduce the saliency of the political dimension of integration.

Membership of the Community imposed a severe burden on the Irish administration at the outset. It was ill-prepared for all that was demanded by involvement in the Community's intense negotiating process. The civil service had misjudged what personnel requirements would be necessary. There was also a continuing dispute between the Department of Foreign Affairs and the Department of Finance as to which should take the lead in the management of EC business. Ireland's Foreign Minister attended the opening of the accession negotiations flanked by the Secretaries (official head of a department) of the four main government departments. Foreign Affairs was not involved in the 1961 decision to apply for membership, a decision which was taken by a core group of Finance officials and the Prime Minister. During the 1960s, the department of Foreign Affairs was a peripheral ministry responsible for the UN. However, after accession, a government decision gave this department the main responsibility for managing the day-to-day issues of EC policy as this was the pattern in other member states. Ireland's first Presidency of the Council in 1975 served as the final apprenticeship for the civil service in adapting to EC membership. Management of the Council agenda and meetings for six months made Irish politicians and officials *au fait* with the nuts and bolts of the Community process. Thereafter, EC business became part of the normal flow of business in the administrative cycle.

Complex interaction
Since Ireland joined the European Community its political, adminis-

trative and judicial systems have had to adapt to the demands of EC policy-making and the development of the Community/Union. The Irish political system is no longer contained in a 'container', to borrow the phrase used by the French economist Perroux. Interaction with Brussels and bilateral contact with partners in other member states have served to internationalize public policy-making in Ireland. Decision-making in many policy sectors dealing with such diverse issues as the environment, agricultural policy, technical standards and regional policy take place within intergovernmental networks that reach from Brussels into sub-national government in the member states. The nature and intensity of the interaction and the balance between public and private actors differ from one policy sector to another.

Politicians, civil servants and representatives of interest groups straddle the EU domestic boundary in their day-to-day work. Public officials are no longer just agents of the Irish state; they are participants in an evolving polity which provides opportunities for political action but also imposes constraints on their freedom of action. A keen understanding of the dynamics of negotiations and the attitudes of one's partners and EC/EU institutions is as important as technical competence in the policy area. Judging the ebb and flow of complex negotiations in a multilateral and multicultural environment requires considerable skills. Judging just what might or might not be in the so-called 'national interest' is an uncertain process in the multi-levelled structures of the Union. The need for compromise, log rolling and package deals permeates the EU's policy process. The purpose of this chapter is to analyse the interface between the policy process in Brussels and Ireland.

The EC decision-making cycle and the participation of national institutions

When analysing the participation of national institutions in the Community's decision-making process, it is necessary to distinguish between different kinds of policy areas and issues. Each member state has its own set of issues that are accorded priority status either because of their economic importance or political sensitivity. There is a remarkable continuity concerning those areas of EC business that fall within the ambit of 'high politics' in an Irish context. The development of the Community itself, reform of the Common Agricultural

Policy (CAP), budget and regional policy, fisheries, monetary matters and certain aspects of foreign policy with a bearing on neutrality emerge as 'high politics'. Sectoral politics might cover such areas as company law, transport, standards, health and safety and environmental policy. Sectoral policy is largely managed by the policy community which surrounds that particular sector but may become items of 'high politics'. There are also those hundreds of low-key directives and regulations that are passed on a continuous basis in the Community system. Low policy issues are routine and absorbed into the standard operating procedures. Different styles of policy formation will characterize the different types of policy issues. 'High policy' issues are more likely to be dealt with by the Cabinet, inter-departmental groups and the parliament. Routine directives, on the other hand, tend to be dealt with within ministries and at relatively low levels of the administrative hierarchy. Sectoral policies, if important, will receive Cabinet time but tend not to have a significant interdepartmental dimension.

The government

The overall coherence of public policy is the responsibility of the Cabinet which stands at the pinnacle of the Irish system of government. The constitution limits the Cabinet to fifteen members which reduces the need for an elaborate system of Cabinet sub-committees. That said, there is a tendency to establish *ad hoc* cabinet committees to deal with major issues on the Community agenda. For example, committees have been formed to manage the Irish Council Presidencies, the Commission's May Mandate, the reform of the CAP and the National Development Plan for cohesion moneys. Usually the Cabinet deals with EC business as it deals with public policy originating within the state. The government is sent a memorandum by the relevant minister on all major issues that will reach the Council. Issues that fall within the realm of 'high politics', that are likely to involve a cost to the exchequer, that will require primary national legislation all reach the Cabinet table. The Cabinet is involved in deciding on negotiating strategies on major issues and would only deal with implementation in the event of a serious blockage or political problem.

The Taoiseach (PM) keeps a watching brief over major developments in the Community. The nature and intensity of ministerial involvement depends on their responsibilities. The Ministers of Foreign Affairs, Agriculture, Finance and Industry (enterprises) are intensively involved in EC matters. There are a number of ministers of state attached to their departments who deputize for them at Councils on occasion. The remaining technical or domestic ministries are largely concerned with their own policy domain. Ministerial briefs for Council meetings are prepared by the relevant government department. A minister would tend to have considerable leeway on sectoral and low-key issues and would check back with the Prime Minister on sensitive issues. The extension of the Union's policy scope and the extent of the transfers coming to Ireland from Brussels mean that almost all ministers have some EC involvement. That said, adaptation to the Community/Union has not altered how the Cabinet does its business. EC/EU matters are dealt with in the same manner as purely domestic issues.

The ministerial administration
There are sixteen government departments following the 1992 election which led to considerable administrative reorganization as part of the agreement on government between the coalition partners, Fianna Fail and the Labour Party. The arrangements for managing the interface with Brussels after accession endowed the Department of Foreign Affairs with primary responsibility for the day-to-day management of the policy process. This department is the main interlocutor with the Community system. Each domestic department manages those areas of policy falling within its competence. They service the relevant Commission expert groups, Council working groups and prepare briefings for their ministers for specialist Councils. Foreign Affairs services the General Affairs Council, the Development Co-operation Council, meetings within the second pillar and the European Councils in conjunction with the Department of the Taoiseach. In addition, Foreign Affairs prepares briefings on the 'A' points in all Councils. Table 12.1 gives an overview of the intensity of the involvement of government departments in EC/EU matters. This table shows that two-thirds of government departments have an important European dimension to their work. Put simply, since 1973 a 'Europeanization' of the policy process is evident. EC membership led to a transformation of the Department of Foreign Affairs. There have been a number of administrative reorganizations and a significant expansion in the staffing levels within the department since 1973. Keatinge argues that the institutional framework is 'characterised by increasing specialisation and the simultaneous fragmentation and growth of bureaucratic structures'.[1]

[1] Patrick Keatinge, *A Place Among the Nations* (Dublin, 1978), p. 215.

Table 12.1 Intensity of involvement in EU matters

Department	High	Medium	Low
Taoiseach (Prime Minister)	X		
Tanaiste's Office (Deputy Prime Minister)	X		
Finance	X		
Transport, Energy		X	
Communication		X	
Justice		X	
Environment		X	
Education		X	
Marine		X	
Agriculture and Food	X		
Equality and Law Reform		X	
Tourism and Trade		X	
Defence			X
Foreign Affairs	X		
Social Welfare			X
Health			X
Culture and Gaeltacht			X

Three divisions within the Department of Foreign Affairs are intimately involved in EC/EU matters: the European Communities Division, the Development Cooperation Division and the Political
Division. The *European Communities Division* with a staff of seventeen is responsible for monitoring the broad spectrum of EC matters.
Reports of working party meetings are lodged in the European Communities Division. It tries to ensure that the domestic ministries' service meetings in Brussels are adequately informed and that policy
developments in one policy sector do not impinge on general policy
priorities. By and large the European Communities Division does not
get involved in the details of domestic issues unless the General Council is dealing with them. This section takes the lead on new policy
areas, reform of major instruments or common policies, institutional
change and enlargement. The European Communities Division mon-
itors the implementation of EC law in the system, a facet of EC membership that has received far more attention since the Single European
Act (SEA). The Commission's monitoring of implementation and its
publication of league tables acts as an external pressure on the
domestic bureaucracy. The Foreign Affairs view is that Ireland must
fulfil its obligations under EC law. There is a regular discussion of
the pattern of implementation at the *inter-departmental European*

Communities Committee. A letter of notice from the Commission which comes via the Representation is usually enough to elicit compliance. Departments try to avoid going to the European Court of Justice (ECJ) because this requires the authority of the government. Blockages in implementation can arise when the Attorney General's Office is over-burdened with legislation. An extensive legislative programme at national level makes it more difficult to get the parliamentary draftsmen to draw up the legal instruments.

The *Political Division* is responsible for the second pillar of the Treaty on European Union (TEU), the Common Foreign and Security Policy. It has a staff of twenty-two and was created in response to the demands of European political cooperation. It is organized on the basis of regional desks and issues areas. The head of this division is the Political Director. This division services all meetings under the aegis of the second pillar and analyses the information received in the COREU network. Membership of the Community has blurred the distinction between foreign and domestic affairs and has meant that the Department of Foreign Affairs is more intensively involved in domestic issues than at any stage in the department's history.

The *Irish Permanent Representation* in Brussels is accorded a central role in the policy process because of the small size of the Irish bureaucracy. The Permanent Representative is a career diplomat and tends to be one of the most senior ambassadors. His or her deputy, Ireland's representative on COREPER 1, is also a career diplomat. Foreign Affairs supplies slightly less than half of the remaining officials in the Representation. The need to provide detailed coverage of substantive policy sectors ensures that the remaining civil servants are drawn from the domestic departments. There are usually twenty-five staff in the Representation although this is strengthened during an Irish Presidency. The balance of influence between the Representation and Dublin is difficult to establish. The preparation of dossiers and administrative coordination remains the prerogative of the national bureaucracy. The status and EC knowledge of the Permanent Representative ensures that his or her views carry considerable weight. The Representation acts as an early warning system and provides an insight on the thinking in the other member states.

The Department of Finance could be said to have discovered the European Community.[2] It was responsible for Ireland's first negotia-

[2] Dermot Scott, 'EEC Membership and the Irish Administrative System', *Administration* (1983), p. 151.

tions with the EEC in 1961. It provided the initial expertise on the Community and remains the most important government department. It is influential in determining Ireland's policy approach on monetary matters, structural funds, Community budget and the Community's general economic policy such as the Delors Report on Growth, Competitiveness and Employment. Although the department is primarily responsible for the national budget and public expenditure, Ireland's membership of the Exchange Rate Mechanism (ERM) and the doubling of the structural funds has enhanced the EC work of this department. The Finance Division is largely responsible for the drafting and implementation of the National Development Plan which forms the basis of the Community Support Framework. The department services the regional review committees and evaluates the operational programmes.

The significance of the Common Agricultural Policy (CAP) both in Ireland and in terms of Community policies ensured that the *Department of Agriculture* would undergo major structural change as a result of Community membership. The operation and implementation of EC schemes and regulations forms the major work of this department. Staffing levels in the department had to be strengthened considerably to deal with the implementation of the CAP. The rhythm of work on the CAP is regulated by the weekly meetings of the Special Agricultural Committee and the many Agriculture Councils. Meeting agendas are circulated to the relevant sections and briefing material is drawn up. All observations, substantive material and position papers must be ready by Thursdays for meetings taking place on the following Monday. Friday is allocated to defining instructions and ensuring the brief is coherent. All senior officials are involved in the process. The reform of the CAP and the GATT round have posed a considerable challenge to this department in the last four years.

The *Department of Enterprise and Employment* combines the old Department of Industry and Commerce and the Department of Labour. This department is responsible for a range of Community policies relating to the internal market, competition policy, industrial policy, social policy and the structural funds. It is heavily involved in the Community's regulatory policies. Hence it is responsible for some of the most complex and technical areas of Community policy. The specialist sections are responsible for negotiating and implementing the directives falling within their areas of responsibility. The department has a structural funds coordination unit and two units devoted to the evaluation of structural funds in training and industrial policy. This is a new feature of the management of the structural funds and reflects the interest the Commission is taking in the evaluation of the Community Support Framework. There is considerable internal specialization on EC matters in the department; the Commerce division deals with directives on insurance and company law.

The *Department of Trade and Tourism* has responsibility for the important Article 113 Committee on the Community's common commercial policy. There has always been an uneasy relationship between the Department of Foreign Affairs and this administrative unit dealing with trade matters. The tourism section of the department implements the operational programme on tourism which forms part of the community support framework.

The remaining departments are involved to a greater or lesser extent in formulating policy responses to proposals falling within their realm, in negotiating within the Council system and in implementing agreed decisions. All have an EC or an international division which coordinates EC business but the substantive work is the responsibility of the functional divisions. The small EC divisions do not have the expertise to undertake the detailed work of policy formulation. Functionalist specialists are now *au fait* with the Community system and tend to operate with ease at the European level. The roll of para-governmental agencies in policy formulation should not be neglected because of the technical nature of Community matters. Policies involving ionizing radiation, safety in the workplace, plant and animal diseases require scientific expertise. A myriad agencies such as the Agricultural Institute, the Nuclear Energy Board and the Health and Safety Agency are involved in policy formulation, thus extending the network of actors. Their role is particularly important because of the predominance of 'generalists' in the Irish civil service. Representatives drawn from these agencies attend Council working parties and provide technical backup for civil servants at the later stages of the negotiations.

The reach of the Community's policy process and the intensity of the negotiating process lead the member states to establish standard operating procedures for managing the myriad of proposals that must be negotiated and implemented within the national system. The preparation of briefs necessitates intra-departmental and inter-departmental coordination. Coordination is not limited to what might be termed 'administrative coordination'. Governments must pay attention to the overall development of the Union, the institutional balance and the promotion of their priorities. From time to time, the fragmented nature of the policy process breaks down and issues are dealt with on the basis of a package deal. The Delors package on financing the Union represents one such deal.

There are a number of different levels of coordination within the Irish system. The Cabinet is the juncture where major policy issues are resolved and the Taoiseach plays a leading role in determining governmental policy. At administrative level, the main institutional device for formulating national strategy and deciding on priorities is the *European Communities Committee* which actually pre-dates Ireland's membership. The central departments or 'overhead' ministries dealing with Brussels on a continuous basis are represented on the committee. These are Foreign Affairs, Finance, Agriculture and Food, Enterprise and Employment, Trade and Tourism and the Prime Minister's Department. The committee has undergone a number of changes since 1973. It was chaired by the Department of Foreign Affairs until 1987 when its composition was altered. The incoming Taoiseach, Mr Charles Haughey, who tended to regard the Department of Foreign Affairs as too pro-European and who had opposed the SEA while in opposition, appointed a Minister of State in his own department with responsibility for EC matters. The new minister, Mrs Maire Geoghegan-Quinn, took over the chair of the European Communities Committee. This added a political dimension to the committee and gave it the authority of the Taoiseach's department. Its work was overshadowed somewhat by the formation in 1988 of a *Joint Committee of Ministers and Secretaries* which met on a weekly basis to plan the Internal Market publicity campaign and the preparation of Ireland's National Plan for the Delors I round of structural fund moneys. The committee clearly signalled the political priorities of the Taoiseach and the importance he accorded to structural fund moneys. When the national plan was submitted to Brussels, this committee was transformed into a ministerial committee to manage the preparations of the Irish Presidency. Once the Presidency was over the European Communities Committee and the Ministerial Committee fell into abeyance and were not active during the intergovernmental conferences. When Albert Reynolds became Taoiseach in February 1992, he reactivated the European Communities Committee and gave a Minister of State, Mr Tom Kitt, responsibility for EC coordination.

The 'Kitt Committee', as it is known, meets on a monthly basis at Assistant Secretary level and provides a focus for coordination of the Irish approach and policy on all major strategic aspects of Community business. It is serviced by the Department of the Taoiseach and is attended by the Irish Permanent Representative. This committee deals with the big issues, particularly those involving a range of government departments. It will regularly review the programme of the member state holding the Presidency and periodically discusses implementation blockages within the Irish system. The committee establishes working groups on major issues. Although serviced by the Taoiseach's department, many of the detailed papers are compiled by the Department of Foreign Affairs or the relevant domestic ministry. While the removal of the secretariat of this committee from Foreign Affairs to the Taoiseach's department may have reflected a downgrading of the role of Foreign Affairs in relation to EC/EU matters, in reality, the addition of a political/ministerial presence and the authority of the Taoiseach's department has addeded to the status of the committee and the seriousness with which it is treated by the domestic departments. Day-to-day coordination resides with Foreign Affairs. Unlike other member states, standing inter-departmental committees on sectoral matters are not common in Ireland. In 1976 there were eleven policy groups dealing with areas such as fiscal harmonization, science and technology that might cross departmental boundaries. The Committees met infrequently and gradually fell into abeyance. It is now more common to establish *ad hoc* committees when the need arises.

Administrative management of the Community's policy process in Ireland is far less institutionalized than is the norm in other member states. There are fewer inter-departmental committees and those that exist meet far less frequently than those in other member states. Contact and consultation in other member states is more rigid and bureaucratic. The lead department in any particular area has considerable autonomy in working out the Irish response. Sectoral policy issues and low key issues are the preserve of the responsible departments. The emphasis is on telephone contact and written observations rather than formal inter-departmental committees. Irish civil servants appear hostile to elaborate procedures and bureaucratic 'lourdeur'. An understanding of this may be found in Ireland's administrative culture, the small size of the bureaucracy and the range of issues that are given high priority in Ireland. Personalism is a dominant cultural value in Ireland arising from late urbanization and the small size of the population. Personal contacts are extensive and easy to establish in a small administration. Irish civil servants know their counterparts in other departments, state agencies and representatives of the main interest organizations. The small nucleus of senior civil servants dealing with Brussels on a continuous basis meet frequently either formally or informally. This reduces the need for formalized committees.

Pragmatism, a legacy of British rule, is apparent in Ireland's administrative culture. Administrative adaptation to Community membership has been characterized by pragmatism. An emphasis on the immediate to the neglect of the medium to long term is a feature of this administrative culture. Policy-making in Dublin tends to be reactive rather than active in nature. Position papers and negotiating tactics are worked out at each stage of the policy process. This policy style is reinforced by the Community's decision-making process which is dominated by negotiations and is highly segmented. Irish policy-makers try to avoid isolation during negotiations by aligning with like-minded states on an issue by issue basis or hiding behind a larger state, if appropriate. Considerable attention is paid to the likely negotiating tactics of other member states. Irish representatives will only go it alone if they feel that the issue is of such importance that they have no choice. In fact on all occasions when Irish representatives accorded overwhelming political priority to an issue (ERM, Fisheries, 'milk-levy') they succeeded in getting special treatment and side payments. In each instance considerable political and diplomatic resources were invested in the negotiations. In a number of instances, the upper echelons of the civil service formed into a task force for the duration of critical negotiations. Size has implications not just for the policy process but for the range of issues that must be accommodated for Community negotiations. Interests are aggregated with greater ease in a small country as the potential for competing claims and conflict is reduced. Irish policy-makers have found it relatively easy to establish major priorities for the purposes of EC negotiations.

The parliament

The parliament (Oireachtas) is a bicameral legislature consisting of an upper and lower house. The lower house, the Dail, produces the government which is the product of a general election. The executive dominates the parliament and can go about its business in an unfettered manner provided it has the support of a majority of the MPs. While the decline of parliament is a common theme in the literature on liberal democracies, the Irish parliament is viewed as a particularly weak legislature.[3] Deputies and senators use traditional devices such as debates and parliamentary questions to elicit information about Irish policy towards the Community. The Taoiseach makes a statement to Dail Eireann after each European Council and the government produces a twice yearly report on developments in the European Communities which is laid before the Oireachtas. In reality these reports appear infrequently and are too tardy to be effective as a source of information for deputies and senators. The standard of debate on Europe tends to be low as few opposition deputies are willing to devote the kind of time it requires to become *au fait* with EC matters. Debate is usually limited to set piece discussion between the relevant minister and the opposition spokespeople. Parliamentary questions deal most frequently with the CAP and the structural funds. Parliamentary scrutiny of Ireland's EC business is uneven and limited.

In 1973 the Oireachtas established a *Joint Committee on Secondary Legislation of the European Communities* to oversee the implementation of EC law in Ireland. Subsequently its terms of reference were widened to include all Community legislation from the initial Commission document to the final stage when secondary legislation was being enacted in Ireland. The purpose of the committee was to ensure that ministers did not go beyond the powers delegated to them under the 1972 European Communities Act. The Committee had the power to propose the annulment of a piece of secondary legislation to the Oireachtas within one year of its coming into force. The committee was coterminous with the life of the Dail so that it had to be reconstituted after each election. The committee operated on the basis of four sub-committees which produced draft reports for the full committee. These reports could be debated in the full house although only three received debating time in the Dail. Because of the absence of a tradition of committees in the Irish parliamentary system, the committee had novel features when it was set up. Its development contributed to an expansion of the committee system in the Oireachtas and a strengthening of the links between the civil service and the parliament. It contributed to a breaking down of the excessive

[3] John Coakely and Michael Gallagher, *Politics in the Republic of Ireland* (Galway, 1992), pp. 112–34.

anonymity of the Irish civil service. Its capacity to act as a watchdog over the extensive range of EC policy was constrained because of its limited secretariat (two staff people) and the inexperience of Irish parliamentarians in working committees.

One of the main problems of the committee was that it did not have a specialized Foreign Affairs Committee to provide the policy context for its deliberations. The Fianna Fail–Labour Party coalition which took office in December 1992 made an explicit commitment to establish a Foreign Affairs Committee. Composed of twenty-five Dail deputies and five senators, the Committee held its first meeting in May 1993. A former Foreign Minister, Mr Brian Lenihan, was elected as chairman. The new committee subsumed the work of the Joint Committee on Secondary Legislation which became a sub-committee in addition to three other sub-committees on Northern Ireland, development cooperation and the UN. While it is too early to judge the effectiveness of the new committee, it does bring an added parliamentary focus to foreign policy matters and hence to the EC/EU. The Department of Foreign Affairs is working closely with the committee and has seconded an official to its secretariat. Foreign Affairs is also committed to supplying the committee with briefing papers and officials attend its hearings. The Foreign Minister, Mr Dick Spring, attended on one occasion. The presence of a former foreign minister in the chair gives added weight to its deliberations. The committee has the potential to provide a channel of informed debate on the many challenges facing Ireland and Europe in the post-cold war era. It may well act as a sounding board for changes in Irish security policy in the lead up to the 1996 intergovernmental conference. It can contribute to further changes in Ireland's parliamentary and administrative culture.

The regional and local level
Ireland is a highly centralized state with one of the weakest forms of local government in Western Europe. The abolition of rates in 1977 deprived local authorities of a form of local taxation and increased their dependence on central government. When the European Regional and Development Fund (ERDF) was set up in 1975 Irish local authorities anticipated that they would have direct access to the regional funds. In practice, local authorities had little impact on the planning of regional fund applications and the Department of Finance acted effectively in the role of gatekeeper. The reform of the

funds in 1988 and the Commission emphasis on partnership found Ireland ill-prepared to respond to the new policy environment. With its traditional pragmatism, the government established seven regional review committees in August 1988. Working groups and advisory groups were set up in each region to prepare submissions for the national plan. The groups consisted of the regional representatives of state agencies, local authorities and the social partners. The groups were transformed into monitoring committees for the Community Support Framework (1989–93).

The experience of the working groups and the contact this necessitated between Dublin-based agencies and the regions led to institutional learning. Each region received technical assistance from the Commission to help them prepare for the current round of structural funds moneys. These submissions formed part of the deliberations on the National Plan which was submitted to Brussels in autumn 1993. It is difficult to say whether or not this form of regional consultation is merely symbolic, designed to fulfil Commission policy preferences. There is no doubt that Ireland continues to be a highly centralized state, partly because of its size. Moreover, the analytical and administrative resources of the regions are weak. Central governments and state agencies have a predominance of resources. However, one of the important results of the regional groups is that it brings local officials, state agencies and the representatives of civil society together. Gradually they are developing strategies for development that go beyond their narrow sectoral concerns. The local input into central government planning is enhanced. The potential of local initiatives to fight unemployment and poverty and as a complement to national initiatives is receiving more considered attention. It could well be that there is a link between Ireland's relatively weak economic performance and an excessive centralization. The 1993 Development Plan contains a new chapter on local initiatives. The emphasis in the Union on subsidiarity finds a resonance within Ireland on the question of the distribution of power within the state.

The courts

Irish courts and the Irish judicial system have been open to seeking preliminary rulings from the European Court of Justice. It is estimated that about 50% of cases which involve points of EC law are referred to the European Court of Justice (ECJ). If a matter can adequately be dealt with by national law, an Article 177 TEU ruling is not resorted to. In 1989 only one case was refereed whereas in 1990 there were four cases, two by the Supreme Court. Courts at all levels, the Supreme Court, High Court, circuit courts and the district courts have all used the preliminary ruling process. The supremacy of EC law has not been questioned. In an early case (*Pigs and Bacon Commission* v. *McCarrenn*, 1978), Judge Costello stated explicitly that 'if according to Community law a provision of the Treaty is directly applicable so that rights are conferred on individuals which national courts must enforce, an Irish court must give effect to such a rule'.[4] An interesting feature of the interaction between Irish and EC law is the growing use of continental legal techniques and methodology in the Irish system. It is argued that Irish courts display a 'willingness to be influenced by European juridical methods and they do not share their English counterparts' rigid adherence to traditional common law principles and techniques'.[5] Community precedents such as 'proportionality' have been cited in domestic cases. Thus it could be argued that EC law has received a warm welcome.

In Ireland's first ten years of membership (1973–82) five actions were taken against Ireland. This rose to thirty-one between 1983 and 1990 which reflected the end of the transitional period. Infringement proceedings and particularly court cases are taken very seriously, and are avoided if possible. Judgments of the court are enforced by a procedure laid down by the European Communities (Enforcement of Community Judgments) Regulations 1972. Irish public authorities tend to comply with court judgments within one to two years of the judgment. Cases against Ireland have involved agriculture, fisheries, internal market issues, taxation and the environment.

Issues of constitutional law and the compatibility of EC treaties with the Irish constitution have been raised. In 1986 the government decided that it could ratify the SEA without resort to a referendum. It opted for a resolution and an Act of the Irish parliament. On 24 December just before the SEA was to come into force, a private citizen applied to the High Court for an injunction restraining the Irish government from lodging the instrument of ratification. The injunction was granted because of the seriousness of the matter. The High Court found that the Treaty was compatible with the constitution. Mr Crotty – a private Irish citizen – appealed to the Supreme Court

---

[4] See Paul McCutcheon, 'The Legal System', in P. Keatinge (ed.), *Ireland and EC Membership* (London: Pinter 1991), p. 220.
[5] *Ibid.*, p. 226.

which found in a majority decision (3:2) that Titles 1 and 2 of the SEA did not conflict with the constitution but that Title III codifying European political cooperation did. This meant that a referendum had to be held to enable Ireland to ratify the SEA.

A case sent by the High Court (*Society for the Protection of the Unborn Child Ltd* v. *Grogan*) was one of the most controversial issues sent by an Irish court. The case rested on the eighth amendment to the constitution (1983) which protected the life of the unborn (anti-abortion clause). The case was taken by SPUC (anti-abortion group) against members of the Irish Students Union who supplied information in Ireland about abortion clinics in the UK. SPUC sought an injunction against such information and publicity. The High Court referred the issue of Article 59 TEU on freedom to supply services to the ECJ. In case 159/90 the Court found in favour of SPUC on a technicality. The court ruled that the termination of pregnancy as legally practised in a member state was a service within the meaning of Articles 59/60 TEU but that because the students had no economic link with the UK clinics they could not rely on Art. 59 TEU. The eighth amendment to the constitution became entangled with the Maastricht debate because during the negotiations on Maastricht the Irish negotiators asked for a protocol to be appended to the Treaty (now protocol no. 17) saying that nothing in the Treaty shall interfere with the application in Ireland of the eighth amendment to the constitution. The protocol was a matter of considerable controversy during the campaign.

Public opinion, political parties and interest groups

Irish political parties do not fit readily into the pattern of Europe's political families. The critical cleavage is one between Fianna Fail and Fine Gael because of a split about the Treaty that granted twenty-six counties of Ireland independence from the United Kingdom in 1921. Since 1933, Fianna Fail is the only party capable of governing as a single party and has done so on many occasions. That said, the party system has become less rigid and government formation more complex. In 1989 Fianna Fail entered a coalition government, a major break with its traditional principles. There are a number of smaller parties, the Labour Party, the Progressive Democrats and the Democratic Left.

Unlike in other member states, the question of EC membership did not lead to splits in any of the political parties. The Labour Party opposed membership in 1972 but thereafter accepted the wishes of the electorate. It failed to adopt a party line during the SEA referendum because its rank and file remain sceptical about the Community. In the European Parliament, the party is part of the Socialist Group and is a long-standing member of the Socialist International. Fine Gael is a member of the European People's Party and could be regarded as the most pro-European of the parties. Fianna Fail is the least Europeanized because it forms part of a group in the EP with the Gaullists. There are no party to party links which isolates this party from what has been important to the other parties. The influence of EC membership is seen most readily among party activists who go to conferences and interact with their counterparts in other countries.

Interest organizations and pressure groups have had to adapt to an additional layer of government and an arena of influence. It is appropriate to distinguish between the involvement of interest groups at a macro and micro level in the political system. Political instability, a crisis in the public finances and weak economic performance led the government in 1987 to seek a consensus-based approach with the social partners in tackling the economic crisis. This materialized as a three-year formal programme entitled the Programme for National Recovery (PNR) that encompassed wage bargaining and wider issues of local policy. This was followed by the Programme for Economic and Social Progress (PESP) which included a chapter on the Community and Irish goals in integration. The PESP Review Committee was heavily involved in monitoring the implementation of the structural funds in Ireland. Hence the peak organizations, the Irish Congress of Trade Unions (ICTU), the Irish Business and Employers Confederation (IBEC) and the agricultural groups are intimately involved in macro policy-making in Ireland and have extensive involvement in the Brussels-based peak organizations, UNICE, ETUC and COPA. IBEC and the agricultural groups maintain offices in Brussels as part of their lobbying function. The Business Bureau of IBEC provides an extensive information service on EC funding and legal developments for its members. The ICTU cannot afford to maintain a permanent office in Brussels and thus relies heavily on its participation in the ETUC. The Congress has regularized its contacts with the Minister of Labour, now Enterprise and Employment, by standard meetings before each Social Affairs Council.

At a micro level, all kinds of interest organizations seek to influence the Irish response to EC law and Commission proposals. The social partners pay particular attention to social policy and company law. Producer groups of organizations affected by a particular directive will follow the issue through to implementation because the detail of implementation may be most important to them. Given the reach of the Community into most areas of public policy, interest groups, be they teachers, consumers, farmers, producers or women's groups, have developed a European dimension.

Irish public opinion has given its verdict on EC membership on three occasions: accession (1972 referendum), SEA (1987 referendum) and Maastricht (1992 referendum). In 1972 membership was endorsed by 83% of those who voted which reflected the political consensus on the issue. The SEA referendum was carried by 70% although the turnout was a mere 43.9% of the electorate. Maastricht was again carried by 69.1% with a higher poll of 55%. The size of the 'yes' vote was striking given the Danish 'no'. The pro-EC establishment (all political parties with the exception of the small Democratic Left), the employers, unions and farming groups faced a formidable challenge in the Maastricht referendum because the issue became embroiled in abortion politics. Anti-abortion groups, on the one hand, and feminists, on the other, campaigned against the Treaty. In addition there were the traditional Irish nationalists, supporters of neutrality and those arguing against the economics of Maastricht. This third endorsement of EC membership and the development of integration suggests that for a sizeable proportion of the Irish electorate the European Community, now European Union, is the main framework for the management of the Irish economy and the external projection of the state. European integration is a pillar of the Irish state. This confirms the trend in the Eurobarometer where 80% of Irish respondents in December 1991 felt that EC membership is a good thing for the country. These sentiments may have a strongly utilitarian basis and there is a danger that successive Irish governments have placed too much emphasis on financial transfers to Ireland as a means of legitimizing the Community.

Conclusion

Strengths and weaknesses

The Irish political and administrative system has adapted relatively easily to the demands of membership of the European Union. Standard operating procedures are in place and work most of the time. The lack of dense bureaucratic foliage allows senior civil servants and politicians to be selective in the areas that are accorded priority. Hence political and administrative resources are utilized most heavily in those areas that are considered important. Irish civil servants have internalized EC/EU business as part of the routine of their work and see it as a legitimate arena of public policy-making. Irish civil servants are by now well socialized into the norms and values of the Community policy. There is no in-built resistance to EC/EU involvement in a wide range of policy sectors provided that EC/EU decisions take account of the Irish situation. The small size of the bureaucracy facilitates a flexible response to Commission initiatives. The existence of a generally favourable public opinion makes Irish policy-makers less constrained in their dealings with Brussels apart from issues touching on security and public morality.

Five main weaknesses can be identified. First, the Irish political system has not always produced the kinds of public policies that were consistent with membership of a large and competitive market. Pragmatism and an emphasis on the short term produced a severe fiscal crisis in the 1980s. A major challenge for Ireland is to produce public policies that allow the Irish economy to deal with the competitive pressures of the EC/EU. There is some evidence that the government and the social partners are prepared to adopt cooperative strategies to manage the economic dimension of EC membership since the mid-1980s. Domestic economic management is critical to Ireland's ability to involve itself in EC policies, notably EMU. Second, the Irish parliamentary model and the brokerage role of deputies limits the scrutiny of EC business. The establishment of a Foreign Affairs Committee may well improve the parliament's involvement in the Community process. Third, a highly centralized system of government militates against the involvement of sub-national actors in the EC decision-making process. Hence Ireland is relatively immune to the growing regionalism in Europe. Fourth, there has been an excessive focus on receipts from the Community budget and a tendency to produce programmes that met the criteria without sufficient consideration given to the worth of the said programmes. The introduction of the community support framework has enhanced the weight given to evaluation and there is now a stronger planning focus. Fifth, there is little capacity within the Irish system for sustained thinking about the overall development of European integration and the role of small states. Size and limited staffing resources reduce the scope for reflective position papers and the development of a strategic view of the Community. The fact that the European Communities Committee did not meet at all between 1983/84 at a time of major development in the Community points to a certain institutional looseness. The decision in 1987 by the National Economic and Social Council to produce a major study on Ireland's membership of the Community marked an important move away from the *ad hoc* approach of the past.[6] A further attempt to develop a considered approach was the establishment in 1991 of an Institute of European Affairs in Dublin.

Challenges for the Irish institutional system

Irish policy-makers face a number of interrelated challenges in the post-Maastricht environment. First, there is the challenge of coming to terms with post-cold war Europe. This has a number of dimensions, notably, the enlargement of the Union, the variegated needs of a larger range of states, the consequences of German unification for the Franco-German relationship and leadership in the Union, and the need to adapt cold war institutions. Second is the need to assess the impact of the Maastricht ratification crisis, the recession and the breakdown of the Exchange Rate Mechanism (ERM) on the future prospects for integration. Third is the implications of enlargement for the Union's institutional balance and the role of small states in the EU. Fourth is the outcome of the continuing debate in the member states and the Union on growth, employment and competitiveness. It is far from clear what sort of Union is in Ireland's long-term interests. The NESC report[7] on Ireland's membership argued that an Economic and Monetary Union was in Ireland's interests provided that it had adequate macro-economic management and balancing redistributive mechanisms. Put simply, this was an argument for EMU with fiscal federalism. The prospects for this form of EMU, or even the more limited version in the TEU, appear bleak following the collapse of the ERM. It may well be that Irish policy-makers will have to respond to a Union in which 'variable geometry' is more prevalent. Underlying all of the above challenges is the question of small states in European integration. This issue was raised in relation to

---

[6] See *Ireland in the European Community: Performance, Prospects and Strategy*, report no. 88 (Dublin: National Economic and Social Council, 1989).

[7] See note 6.

representation within the Union's institutions. The larger states are addressing the question of the balance of representation in the system from their point of view given the prospect of many more states in the Union. Although changes in the institutional balance are not likely before 1996, there is a need in all small states to tease out the balance they must strike between representation in the system and the capacity of this system to take decisions. All of the above challenges highlight the need to monitor closely developments in European integration.

Select bibliography

Burns, B. and Salmon, T. C., 'Policy-making Coordination in Ireland on European Community Issues', *Journal of Common Market Studies*, 15 (1977), pp. 272–87.

Keatinge, P., *A Place Among the Nations: Issues of Irish Foreign Policy* (Dublin, 1978).

Keatinge, P. and Laffan, B., 'Ireland in International Affairs', in J. Coakley and M. Gallagher (eds.), *Politics in the Republic of Ireland* (Galway, 1992), pp. 200–21.

Laffan, B., 'While You are Over There in Brussels, Get Us a Grant: The Management of the Structural Funds in Ireland', *Irish Political Studies*, 4 (1989), pp. 43–58.

—— 'Political and Legal Systems', in P. Keatinge, *Ireland and EC Membership Evaluated* (London: Pinter, 1991), pp. 185–206.

Laffan, B., Manning, M. and Kelly, P. T., 'Ireland', in H. Siedentopf and J. Ziller, *Making European Policies Work* (Brussels: Bruylant, 1988), pp. 375–447.

McCutcheon, P., 'The Legal System', in P. Keatinge, *Ireland and EC Membership Evaluated* (London: Pinter, 1991), pp. 209–32.

Scott, D., 'EEC Membership and the Irish Administrative System', *Administration*, 31 (1983), pp. 147–99.

Portugal

Fundamentals of Portugal in EU affairs

The debate in Portugal on the semantics of integration goes back to the end of the 1950s, and to this day there is no single definition that would be universally accepted. Originally, the ideas behind the debate on integration contrasted with those on the Common Market in view of eventually joining it when taking part in the formation of EFTA. For Salazar and the nationalists (notably Franco Nogueira), there were two mutually excluding concepts, which were supposedly the underpinnings of EFTA and the EEC, respectively: cooperation, taken to signify that Portugal would in any circumstance have an equal vote and a veto, and integration, meaning that decisions could be forced on Portugal through majority vote.

Today, cooperation is no longer used 'against' integration and all political forces declare themselves in favour of European integration, although different meanings are implied by the word integration. What could be termed as the 'minimalist' notion of integration means solely participation in a given organization, in this case the European Community. For the Communist Party and the Conservative Nationalists, it means participation in the European Community provided the veto remains in practice, which in fact means close cooperation in a predominantly economic space, a free trade area, but not political integration. For most economists, it means a closer relationship between member countries mainly in what concerns trade and foreign investment, structural funds, monetary union, resulting in the acceptance of the 'common-marketization' of the Portuguese economy. Other sectors of the political elite see integration as a combination of economic federalism and political cooperation, although agreeing that in a number of political issues majority voting is acceptable. To Europeanists it means in essence gradually transferring a certain number of decisions, both in the economic and the political sphere, to supranational institutions, a long process of going beyond the nation state (this being the 'maximalist' definition).

In brief, integration, preceded by the word 'European', covers in Portugal a wide variety of notions, ranging from economic integration with the smallest possible political ingredient, to economic and political integration at least to the degree contemplated in Maastricht. The latter is seen essentially as intergovernmental, to a near-federalist approach; i.e. the current degree of political integration being considered as a step in a process to be taken further towards a supranational organization that would still fall short of a federal state. The definition which is perhaps more widely accepted is the second, if not in theory at least in practice (contradictory as this may seem). In Portugal, there are very few politicians who would define themselves as federalists, even among the most convinced pro-Europeans. Exceptions to this general rule are notably former President Mário Soares, and Diogo Freitas do Amaral and Francisco Lucas Pires, both former leaders of Centro Democrático Social (CDS).

A number of reasons are recurrently offered against transfer of powers from national to EU level, most of them playing on a nationalistic chord rather than trying to keep in touch with reality. Most of these reasons are actually put forward as if Portugal would have no part in taking decisions at EC level. Perhaps the predominant one is that in relinquishing even the tiniest bit of sovereignty, Portugal will inevitably lose identity. A variant of this same argument is that the Portuguese, like all other European citizens from smaller member states, will lose capacity to influence decisions that directly concern and affect them. On different grounds, a supranational power will be 'bureaucratic', as opposed to 'democratic' or 'transparent'. In the monetary field, where the arguments tend to be much less dramatic and far more sustainable, especially as a consequence of the turmoil in the European Monetary System (EMS), the major argument goes that with the single currency Portugal will be deprived of important policy instruments such as the possibility of devaluing its currency in order to enhance the competitiveness of Portuguese exports. Another argument that is often used, both in political and economic terms, is that to accept any further degree of integration, after German unification, means in reality to accept German hegemony through a European *directoire*.

On the side of the major arguments in favour of a furtherance of the process of integration · and consequently of the 'transfer of powers' it implies, the political ingredient is perhaps more present: the need to counter the re-emergence of nationalism, which has been the cause of intra-European civil wars, and to bolster democracy through integration (this last aspect is quite understandable in the light of the Portuguese experience). Germany is also a concern, of course, for those who want further progress of European integration, and think that this is necessary to balance the weight of Germany and to reinforce its links to other European partners. Integration is necessary for Europe to be able to face competition from the United States and Japan which no single European nation is able to do on its own. European integration will also translate into social and economic cohesion (this last aspect is particularly stressed in Portugal, which of course expects to be one of the beneficiaries). Another aspect seen as having particular relevance for Portugal, not only in view of its geographical closeness to North Africa, but owing also to its special relations with Southern Africa and Latin America, is that without integration and a common foreign policy dimension, and eventually a defence identity, Europe will not be able to act as a global power and to face the post-cold war security challenges on the continent, the Mediterranean and in areas of particular interest and concern to the member states.

From the government's point of view,[1] 'intensification of the European integration process ... must be directed towards two basic objectives:

(i) bringing the Community closer to the citizens by responding to their deepest concerns and by providing an area with genuine equality of opportunity in the framework of the harmonious development of all Community States and regions and in the light of the essential strengthening of economic and social cohesion;

(ii) strengthening the cohesion of Europe, giving it an increasingly active role in the modern world for the defence of the common interest of the Twelve.'

As to the institutional framework, the Portuguese memorandum pleads for the introduction of qualified majority voting as the general

---

[1] See 'Memorandum from the Portuguese Delegation – Political Union with a View to the Intergovernmental Conference', Ministry of Foreign Affairs, Lisbon, 30 Nov. 1993, in Finn Laursen and Sophie Vanhoonacker (eds.), *The Intergovernmental Conference on Political Union – Institutional Reforms, New Policies and International Identity of the European Community* (Maastricht, European Institute of Public Administration, 1992), p. 304 *et seq.*

rule in the Council decision-making process, with temporary exceptions for certain particularly sensitive matters where unanimity or an increased majority system should apply. For Portugal, the Commission's exclusive right of initiative should be maintained – although it should be accountable to the European Parliament if it fails to exercise that right – and its implementing powers developed, while the number of members per member state should be reduced to one. As to the European Parliament, the Portuguese memorandum considers that involvement of the European Parliament in the legislative process should be established as the general rule by extending the cooperation procedure to all areas in which the Council decides by a qualified majority, and looks favourably at closer contact between national parliaments and the European Parliament.

The Maastricht Treaty was debated and ratified by parliament, as required by the constitution, on 11 and 12 December 1992. As in other member countries, some previous amendments to the constitution were required, especially in what concerned the currency and the Bank of Portugal, and also 'sovereignty-sharing' in the political dimension as well. The relevant constitutional amendment in this last respect stipulates that 'Portugal may, under conditions of reciprocity, in accordance with the principle of subsidiarity and in view of implementing economic and social cohesion, agree upon the joint exercise of such powers as are deemed necessary to building the European Union.'[2] It is apparent from this formulation that whilst the 'joint exercise of powers' is explicitly made conditional to 'subsidiarity' and 'reciprocity', it is in fact made conditional to the principle and the practice of economic and social cohesion.

The debate on Maastricht took place not so much prior to the ratification itself, but during the discussions that led to these amendments (approved roughly a month before). Any amendment to the constitution requires a two-thirds majority, which means the Social Democrats need the support of the Socialists to pass an amendment. Both parties were decidedly in favour of the Maastricht Treaty, and consequently of the constitutional amendments required. The house is unevenly split into two camps: the larger pro-Europe camp (Social Democrats and Socialists), and the smaller anti-Maastricht-Europe camp (CDS and Communists). In a sense, discussions in parliament reflected the public debate in the media. At the time of the Danish

[2] Translation by the authors.

referendum, there was a public campaign and much debate in the media in favour of a national referendum in Portugal. However, this would have required a modification of the constitution, since it specifically excludes a referendum on either treaties or constitutional matters. Social Democrats and Socialists firmly opposed the idea of holding a referendum in Portugal, on the grounds that, being strictly 'forbidden' in constitutional terms, it would constitute a potentially dangerous precedent. Additionally, it was argued that the over-whelming majority of the Portuguese were in favour of membership of the EC/EU and supported the Maastricht Treaty, as substantiated by a variety of opinion polls.

Aside from a small number of members of the 'Partido Socialista' (PS) and the 'Partido Social Democrata' (PSD), who in spite of their pro-Europeanism wanted to see the constitutional obstacles removed and Maastricht 'ratified by the people' (an even smaller number were in fact against Maastricht), the national referendum campaign was launched by the CDS leader and backed by the Communists. The CDS was not openly campaigning against Maastricht, the rhetoric being rather 'let the Portuguese people decide' – although that they actually meant 'decide against' was pretty much obvious.[3] The Communist party, on the other hand, campaigned overtly for the referendum and against the Treaty. The President of the Republic was one of the few influential voices who, making no secret of his pro-European Union positions, spoke in favour of a referendum in Portugal, in spite of the constitutional obstacles. This has also to be understood, however, in the particular context of Portuguese domestic politics and the ups and downs of the existing 'cohabitation'.

The EC decision-making cycle and the participation of national institutions

The government

Portugal is clearly a country where decision-making lies primarily with the government, which has a near-monopoly in this respect.

---

[3] It should be noted that the pro-referendum campaign was launched shortly after a change in the leadership of the CDS. Most of the historical leaders actually left the party on the grounds of its about-turn in its European stances. Shortly after being re-baptized as 'CDS–Partido Popular' (CDS–People's Party), they were asked to leave the European People's Party on the grounds of their opposition to federalism and to Maastricht.

Power-sharing can meaningfully be used to describe only the relationship between central government and the two regional governments (Autonomous Regions of Madeira and the Azores). Regional governments are entitled to take part in any decision relevant to their region and this principle applies fully to EC matters. Both regional governments are represented at the *Interministerial Commission for the European Community* (CICE). Each region has one member of staff at the office of the Permanent Representative in Brussels with the task of following up dossiers which concern the region. It is customary that at important EC meetings (including Council meetings) in which issues relevant to the regions are discussed, a representative from the region will be part of the Portuguese delegation. The possibility has to be envisaged, however, that the principle of subsidiarity may be invoked, at a national level, by the regions to make a certain number of additional claims to the central government.

At the top of decision-making in European affairs is the *Council of Ministers for Community Affairs* (CMAC). The CMAC's monthly meetings are chaired by the Prime Minister, and attended by all cabinet members plus the Secretary of State for European Affairs. The Council produces the guidelines for Portugal's European integration policies and coordinates the follow-up of such policies. It has the final say in fundamental issues of European policy and essentially takes the initiative in this regard. Preparation of decisions and the development of guidelines of the CMAC is incumbent upon a *Government Commission for European Affairs* (CGAC), responsible for intergovernmental coordination of European affairs at a political level. The CGAC (meeting once every two weeks) is formed by a Secretary of State from each of the ministries involved in Community affairs and chaired by the Foreign Minister aided by the Secretary of State for European Affairs (in practical terms chaired by the latter). Horizontal cooperation between ministries, the definition of technical guidelines for the Portuguese positions in the various EC instances are coordinated by the CICE presided over by the Secretary of State for European Affairs (which meets every week) and formed by those directly responsible for European affairs in each ministry; the secretariat is incumbent upon the Director-General for the European Community at the Foreign Office.

The ministerial administration
As far as vertical cooperation within the different ministries is con-

cerned, this is, as a rule, coordinated by an *Office for European Affairs* ('*Gabinete de Assuntos Europeus*') in each ministry, normally headed by a Director-General, as is the case in the Ministry of Finance, the Ministry for Internal Affairs and the Ministry of Industrial Affairs. The European office in each ministry is not responsible for coordinating or implementing orientations or policies, but should forward matters to other departments within the ministry and follow them up. In the Ministry for Territorial Administration and Planning this task is performed by the '*Direcção de Avaliação e Acompanhamento*' (Direction for Assessment and Follow-up). Until recently, there had been no major restructuring of the administration as a consequence of the single market (because membership of Portugal coincided with the adoption of the Single European Act), apart from the creation of an Office for the Single Market at the Secretariat of State for European Affairs. Since Maastricht some restructuring is taking place, such as the creation of new forms of liaison, designed to meet the objectives of convergency. The general idea is to have the offices for European Affairs in each ministry working under already existing directorates-general which have executive responsibilities in areas deemed essential to guarantee that the objectives within the framework of convergency are met. At the Ministry for Territorial Administration and Planning, for instance, the Direction for Assessment and Follow-up was recently integrated into the Directorate-General for Regional Development and, at the Ministry of Finance, the Office of European Affairs will probably move to the '*Gabinete de Estudos Económicos*' (economic policy-planning staff). The concern for meeting the goals of convergency has also led to regular meetings of the Secretary of State for European Affairs, and the Finance, Interior and Social Affairs ministers. The Foreign Office has also been restructured to some extent. The former 'Secretariat of State for the European Communities' has been baptized 'Secretariat of State for European Affairs', and the portfolio for political and economic relations with the Twelve (and with the Council of Europe and the OECD) has been given to the Secretary of State for European Affairs, in an attempt to respond to the growing integration of political and economic affairs in EC policies.

In general the structure of the central administration (i.e. the civil service) as such has no significant role in what concerns the preparation of decisions and has a very limited capacity to influence the process, which lies essentially in the hands of the ministers' offices. It does, however, have a prominent and almost exclusive role (more clearly so in some ministries than in others) in the implementation of decisions and EC legislative acts, a field in which it is quite responsive. Many directives became due for transposal in 1992, most of them relating to the White Paper on the internal market. On 31 December 1993, Portugal had implemented 89.2% of all binding directives of the Community (1,052 from a total of 1,189 directives applicable, see Table 13.1).

Table 13.1[4] Portugal's record of implementation of EC directives 1993

	Directives applicable	Measures notified	%
Customs Union	9	9	100
Foodstuffs	66	60	91
Pharmaceutical	28	18	64
Chemicals	42	30	71
Motor vehicles	156	154	99
Equipment	86	84	98
Intellectual property	3	1	33
Telecommunications	6	5	83
Financial, tax law	53	44	83
Public procurement	7	6	67
Technical barriers	9	6	67
Indirect taxation	36	35	97
Establishment	44	42	95
Immigration	5	5	100
Diploma equivalence	61	59	97
Consumers	43	41	95
Competition	4	3	75
Employment	36	33	92
Agriculture	313	265	85
Transport	50	42	84
Environment	117	106	90
Energy	15	13	87
Total	1189	1061	89.2

In 1991, from a total of 853 established infringements, eighty-six concerned Portugal (thirty-nine of which were terminated after the Article 169 letter) and forty-four gave rise to reasoned opinions (forty of which were terminated after the reasoned opinion). In 1992, from

[4] See *Eleventh Annual Report to the European Parliament on the Monitoring of the Application of Community Law – 1993*, OJ C 154 (6 June 1994).

a total of 1,216 established infringements, 116 concerned Portugal. At 31 December 1992, thirteen were terminated after the Article 169 letter and no reasoned opinion was sent and in 1993 out of 1,209 infringement procedures 125 concerned Portual and none was followed by a reasoned opinion.[5]

Until 1 December 1993 only six infringement proceedings were brought before the Court of Justice by the EC Commission against Portugal. However, one can expect that the number of these proceedings will increase in the near future, owing to the substantial rise in the number of 'letters of formal notice' addressed to the Portuguese authorities during the last three years (from eighteen in 1988 and twenty-six in 1989, to 178 in 1990, eighty-six in 1991, 116 in 1992 and 125 in 1993). In 1990, Portugal was the member state which was addressed the largest number of reasoned opinions (sixty-nine from a total of 327) by the EC Commission.

At the end of 1993 no infringement proceedings were pending against Portugal, as all cases brought before the Court were terminated. In two of them, the Court ruled that Portugal had failed to fulfil its obligations under EC law. Those cases concerned (a) national legislation preventing persons other than official agents from making customs declarations,[6] and (b) barriers to swine imports.[7] Two other cases were removed from the register following compliance by the Portuguese authorities (directive on consolidated accounts[8] and directive on supply contracts).[9] In the two remaining cases the Court dismissed the applications (supply contracts to Lisbon airport[10] and alcohol monopoly).[11]

Inasmuch as there are only two cases in which the Portuguese Republic was considered not to have fulfilled its obligations under Community law, the lapse of time in which Portuguese authorities complied with the judgments of the Court of Justice is not relevant. In any case, as far as we know, measures to comply with the judg-

[5] *Ibid.*

[6] Judgement of 11 March 1992, *Commission v. Portugal*, Case C–323/90, [1992] ECR I–1887.

[7] Judgment of 26 May 1993, *Commission v. Portugal*, Case C–52/92, [1993] ECR I–2691.

[8] Case C–58/91, *Commission v. Portugal*, OJ 1992 C 10, p. 11.

[9] Case C–274/91, OJ 1992 C 182, p. 9.

[10] Judgment of 11 July 1993, *Commission v. Portugal*, Case C–247/89, [1991] ECR I–3659.

[11] Judgement of 19 January 1993, *Commission v. Portugal*, Case C–361/90, [1993] ECR I–95.

ment of the Court of 11 July 1992 in the 'customs case' (supply contracts to Lisbon airport) were adopted within a short period of time.

Special reference must also be made to the important number of
cases (approximately forty) where the Portuguese Republic intervened
before the Court of Justice in supporting the submissions of one of the
parties. Most of those cases concerned preliminary rulings of national
courts on the interpretation of the VAT directive, the EC rules applicable on social security matters, and cases where Portuguese natural or
legal persons[12] or specific Portuguese interests were involved.[13]

The changes contained in the Maastricht Treaty, especially in Article 171, should contribute to greater effectiveness as regards infringement procedures. However, before the Treaty is fully implemented on
this issue, it is too soon to be sure of practical consequences. Withholding payments from certain funds would seem, in the particular
case of Portugal, to have a greater impact, as far as effectiveness is concerned, than imposing any kind of fine. Of course the same will not be
true for other member states: a case-by-case approach would seem
more appropriate. Although this concerns less the case of Portugal,
there seems to be no reason why the Court of Justice should not be
able to annul national provisions in breach of Community law.

The parliament

Parliament (Assembly of the Republic) is in practice absolutely marginal to the EC decision-making process. The existing *Committee for
European Affairs* is kept informed of European affairs in general, and
its activity does not go beyond that. In November 1992, an amendment proposed by the Socialists, when the text of the Portuguese constitution was modified in order to ratify the Maastricht Treaty, was
adopted to accommodate a greater role for parliament in European
affairs: the Assembly of the Republic will be entitled to follow and
evaluate, in accordance with the law, the participation of Portugal in
the process of building the European Union, while the government is
required to forward in good time to the Assembly of the Republic the
information pertaining to that process. Although parliament saw its
European dimension slightly enhanced, the situation has not changed
significantly since then.

[12] See Case C–9/88, *Lopes da Veiga* v. *Staatsecretaris van Justitie*, 27 Sept. 1989,
[1989] ECR I–2989, and Case C–113/89, *Rush Portuguesa* v. *Office national d'immigration*, 27 March 1990, [1990] ECR I–1417.
[13] See Case C–225/92, *Matra* v. *Commission* (the Ford/Volkswagen aid case), 15 June
1993.

The courts

The process of adapting to the new reality represented by the EC judicial framework on the part of the Portuguese courts has been slow but sure over these last years. A sustained effort in the training of magistrates has been noticeable on the part of the '*Centro de Estudos Judiciários*' of the Ministry of Justice, and the results of that effort are beginning to show. A good number of missions of Portuguese magistrates to the Court of Justice and the Court of First Instance over the last couple of years should also be noted.

Nine preliminary rulings were submitted to the Court of Justice by Portuguese courts, three by the '*Supremo Tribunal Administrativo*' (Administrative Supreme Court), three by the '*Tribunal Fiscal Aduaneiro do Porto*' (Porto Custom Court), two by the '*Tribunal da Relação de Lisboa*' (Lisbon Court of Appeal) and one by the '*Tribunal da Comarca de Lisboa*' (Lisbon Court of First Instance). Most of these preliminary rulings concern the interpretation of EC tax and customs law as well as EC competition rules. All the nine preliminary rulings have been submitted to the Court of Justice between 1990 and 1993. It would seem this is too short a time period to reach conclusions as regards a change in attitudes.

There are three cases of explicit defiance, in declining to refer to the Court of Justice, which have occurred on the part of the high courts. In one case, the '*Tribunal Constitucional*' (Constitutional Court), although admitting it was subject to that obligation, considered that the matter was sufficiently clear as to make referring to the Court of Justice unnecessary. The other two cases both concern the '*Supremo Tribunal de Justiça*' (Supreme Court of Justice). In one of them, it judged that the Community law issue raised by the parties was not existent, and in the other it applied the Portuguese law, in spite of the apparent incompatibility with the provisions of one directive issued by the EC Council which had already been incorporated into national law. It is, however, possible that in a greater number of cases the Portuguese courts may have explicitly refused to refer matters to the Court of Justice.

Public opinion and political parties

The Portuguese public has hardly an opinion about the EC institutional system as such, i.e. can hardly differentiate between the institutional system and the European Community as a whole. What opinion polls do show, however, is a widespread support for the Community or the European integration process. Polls taken at the time of the Maastricht debate and the Danish and French referendums leave no doubt as to what the outcome of a referendum in Portugal would have been (in favour 54%, against 22%, don't know 24%). In our view, this should be understood as a yes to European Union in the sense of a yes to Europe, rather than a yes to the specifics of Maastricht. Having said this, the comments on the following institutions (see Table 13.2) are made distinguishing between public opinion, i.e. the population in general, and informed opinion, i.e. the elites.

Table 13.2 Attitude of the Portuguese on EC institutions

EC Commission	
'Visibility'(people who know of)	EC average: 45% Portugal: 58%
'Good or rather good opinion' of (as a percentage of the above)	EC average: 53% Portugal: 77%
European Parliament	
'Visibility' through the media	EC average: 44% Portugal: 61%
'Very/Important' role of the EP	EC average: 55% Portugal: 74%
A government for Europe?	
For/against European government	EC average: 55%/20%: Portugal 69%/9%

Source: Eurobarometer no. 37, June 1992 (during the Portuguese presidency of the EC).

The public sees the European Parliament as rather distant, as the marked increase in the proportion of abstention in the three elections for MEPs so far seems to show: 27.4% in 1987 (European and general elections held simultaneously), 48.7% in 1989 and 64.3% in 1994 (both European elections alone). On the other hand, the campaign of MEP candidates concentrated almost exclusively on domestic and not on European issues, and there are no indications that this will change in the near future. Elites, on the other hand, are inclined to think that the European Parliament is not representative enough, does not have enough powers (though they are against enlarging its powers any further), and think that a small country like Portugal will always have little influence in the European Parliament. The fact that the Social Democratic Party (PSD), in government since 1985, is a member of the Liberal-Reformist group and therefore does not belong to one of the larger European 'families' certainly contributes to this view. The federalist approach of many parliamentarians, including Portuguese MEPs, does not correspond, furthermore, to the dominant political culture in Portugal. What is said and done at the European Parliament has little echo in Portugal.

The political elite sees the Council of Ministers as the major guarantor of the intergovernmental character of the process of European integration. The public tend to see it as the main decision-maker in the political sphere (the extensive coverage of the Portuguese presidency in the media greatly contributes to this view; until then, there seems to be no clear distinction between the Commission and the Council).

As far as the Commission is concerned, the informed opinion is divided into two major trends: those who really deal with European matters tend to see it as an ally of smaller countries, and its president has a strong and positive image in Portugal. Those (largely in the ranks of the opponents to further European integration) who tend to see it as a huge bureaucracy taking up too much power, which is not subject to direct democratic scrutiny are especially concerned with its role in leading the European integration process which is perceived as far greater than it actually is. The public perceives the Commission, or more vaguely 'Brussels', as the principal body responsible for EC funds for Portugal.

The Court of Justice is the least publicized of European institutions and the least mentioned in the press. With the exception of legal publications, references to Community courts are not very common. In spite of this, the notion is beginning to take shape that there are Community courts to which matters may be referred. In particular, the appointment of a Portuguese national as President of the Court of First Instance of the European Communities, and some recent cases to which the press gave particular emphasis, contributed to a greater knowledge of this institution.

The figures given in Table 13.2 reflecting the opinion of the Portuguese people on EC institutions are taken from Eurobarometer, and they have to be considered as misleading in one respect: they portray an awareness of European affairs, a 'knowledge' of the Commission, Parliament, etc., greater than it is in fact among the Portuguese public. The majority of the Portuguese (especially the less informed, educated, affluent) look upon a vague entity with the name 'European Community' or 'Commission' provided it begins with the word

'Europe' or 'European', and they see it primarily as a good thing, since judging by their past and their present they think that their future and the future of the European Community/Union are closely linked together.

As far as the reactions from political parties to Maastricht are concerned, these could perhaps be summarized as follows: the PSD, in government, and the PS, the major opposition party, are decidedly and militantly in favour of the European Union. The Socialists would welcome greater powers for the European Parliament (and also for the national parliament: in return for their full support to the constitutional amendments required in order to approve Maastricht, the PS obtained from the PSD the concession that parliament be given some say in European affairs). The PSD is less enthusiastic about the European Parliament, and is in favour of the idea of a 'European Congress'. It should also be noted that the PSD, the government party since 1985, has consistently evolved to stronger pro-European stances, in part as a consequence of its own experience in government and of the government's participation in the whole EC process. This evolution was particularly noticeable during the Portuguese presidency of the EC in the first half of 1992.

Conclusion

Portugal is not immune to the current wave of 'Euro-pessimism'. The government, however, is fully committed to the European Union and Portugal is determined to be counted among the early members of EMU. The full blow of recession has not hit Portugal yet, and maybe it never will. Provided a general improvement of the economic situation in Europe occurs, which would probably pave the way for renewed Euro-optimism and renewed faith in a political Europe which so far has failed to materialize, the pro-European sentiment among the public is not likely to waver in Portugal, in spite of the noticeable nationalistic 'swing' in politicians' rhetoric which ironically could be observed during the campaign in the last European elections. It remains to be seen whether the currently prevailing pro-European sentiment will result in increased participation of the Portuguese citizens in the European process. This is a challenge for the Portuguese government to meet. And whilst much has been said about the need for 'democratization' and greater 'transparency' in European affairs in the wake of the Maastricht debate, the same is to a certain extent true at the national level. Whether this challenge will be met in Portugal, whether the government will be able to involve more closely first of all the parliament and other representative institutions in Portugal's European policy remains to be seen. In what concerns the relationship between the national and Community levels, it also remains to be seen whether the government will resist the temptation to avoid transferring further powers, invoking subsidiarity. So far there are no indications to that effect. 'Democratization' of the European process remains a fundamental issue, not only in the European but also in the Portuguese context.

Select bibliography

Álvares, Pedro and Fernandes, Carlos Roma, *Portugal e o Mercado Comum – dos acordos de 1972 às negociações de adesão* (Lisbon: Ed. Pórtico, 1980).

Ferreira, João Meneses, 'Partidos políticos, parceiros sociais e o desafio da CEE', in Mário Baptista Coelho (ed.), *Portugal – o sistema político e constitucional 1974/1987* (Lisbon: Instituto de Ciências Sociais da Universidade de Lisboa, 1989).

Lopes, Ernâni Rodrigues et al., *Portugal, o desafio dos anos 90* (Lisbon: Instituto Humanismo e Desenvolvimento, 1989).

Matos, L. Salgado de, 'O sistema político português e a Comunidade Europeia', in *Portugal e a integração europeia: balanço e perspectivas* (Lisbon: Análise Social, Vol. 27, 1992.)

Meirelles, F. de, 'Portugal and European Political Union', in Finn Laursen and Sophie Vanhoonacker (eds.), *The Intergovernmental Conference on Political Union – Institutional Reforms, New Policies and International Identity of the European Community* (Maastricht: European Institute of Public Administration, 1992).

Sousa, M. Rebelo de, 'A integração europeia pós-Maastricht e o sistema de governo dos Estados-membros', in *Portugal e a integração europeia: balanço e perspectivas* (Lisbon: Análise Social, Vol. 27, 1992).

Vasconcelos, Álvaro de, 'Portugal and European Political Cooperation', *The International Spectator*, 26 (2) (April–June 1991).

Vilaça, J. L. Cruz, Moniz, C. Botelho, Mota, A. Sassetti da and Miranda, A. Souto, 'Rapport portugais', in J. Schwarze, I. Govaere, F. Hélin and P. Van den Bossche (eds.), *The 1992 Challenge at National Level* (Baden-Baden: Nomos Verlagsgesellschaft, 1990).

Vilaça, J. L. Cruz and Pais Antunes, L. M., 'A integração portuguesa no sistema jurisdicional comunitário', in *Portugal e a integração europeia: balanço e perspectivas* (Lisbon: Análise Social, Vol. 27, 1992).

Conclusion: European Union and national institutions

Europeanization, fusion and convergence revisited: towards a common picture?

The picture which we get from the national chapters is quite ambiguous, containing divergent but also convergent patterns of institutional activity. We started from three hypotheses with regard to the institutional development in the EU: (1) the 'Europeanization' of national institutions, i.e. the shift of attention of all national institutions and their increasing participation – in terms of the number of actors and the intensity – in the EC/EU decision-making cycle; (2) the 'fusion' of national and European institutions in the policy cycle, i.e. the common sharing of responsibilities for the use of state instruments and the increasing influence of the EC arena on the vertical and horizontal interaction of national and European institutions; (3) the 'convergence' of the constitutional and institutional set-up in the member states, i.e. as a result of 'Europeanization' and 'fusion' institutions undertake similar innovations and adaptations which lead towards one common model and, as a result, to the disappearance of pre-existing differences among member states.

The fundamental observation we can make when examining, on the basis of the country reports in this book, the participation of national institutions – i.e. when looking into the national arena from the point of view of the *member states* in the preparation, making, implementation and control of binding EC decisions – is an increasingly intensive interaction between both national and European institutions.[1] The picture we sketch is strongly reinforced from the Brussels perspective. (1) National institutions in all member states have begun to make a constant effort toward European activity and participation in EC decision-making – what is understood as 'Europeanization' – in order to

[1] See the contribution of Wolfgang Wessels in this book.

cope with the requirements of the EC/EU political system. (2) Institutions on the national level – such as the governments, the ministerial bureaucracy, the parliaments, the regions and the courts – and institutions on the European level do not act independently from each other. Both are to an increasing extent cooperating, interacting and applying a parallel pattern of behaviour which is mutually interdependent. There is no clear-cut border line between 'national' and 'European' institutions and no clear division of competences as according to the understanding of the classical federal state where separate levels have their own competences and are using their own instruments of action relatively autonomously.[2] Quite the contrary: national and European institutions are cooperating to an increasing extent in EC decision-making. To this end they exchange views and information and exert their competences over the application of state instruments (such as law and budgetary means) in common. Thus, we can hardly locate the actions and responsibilities of national and European institutions since both are equally affected by, and involved in, the EC decision-making process. They are characterized by a trend towards 'institutional fusion' in terms of mutual influence and interdependence. (3) There are, however, quite divergent patterns of action and behaviour of national institutions in this respect which do not seem to converge into one common (state) model. An explanation for this is that the 'Europeanization' of national constellations and configurations must be understood as a larger development in which national institutions are embedded and which, to a varying degree, affects each type of institution, on all levels and in every member state. Within this 'macro-development' the trend towards institutional fusion is moulded and taking shape, without however leading to the convergence of the national constitutional settings towards one (state) model. However, in spite of the historical, political and constitutional differences, the EU member states have to a growing extent come under the pressure of a *certain* convergence in the sense of reaction and optimal adaptation when dealing with the EU institutional system. Some persistent patterns in this respect are: decentralization and flexibility, strong sectorization, high administrative coordination and low parliamentarization; there seems to be a trend in all member

---

[2] See Wolfgang Wessels, 'Die europäischen Staaten und ihre Union – Staatsbilder in der Diskussion', in Heinrich Schneider and Wolfgang Wessels, *Föderale Union – Europas Zukunft? Analysen, Kontroversen, Perspektiven* (München: Beck, 1994), pp. 51–69; here: pp. 53ff.

states to move in this direction. The longer-term development seems to be that member states in the EU become increasingly similar with regard to these basic features without, however, losing their specific politico-institutional structure and behaviour.

Thus, in short, we can say that the first and second hypotheses on 'Europeanization' and 'fusion' are valid, whereas the third on the 'convergence' of the political systems is only partly true. On the basis of the findings in the country chapters in this book, we will give in the following a more detailed overview of the effect of this hypothesized development on the different institutions in the member states.

The role of national institutions in the EC/EU: a comparison

The governments and the ministerial bureaucracy

In all member states the governments are and remain the core actors in EC/EU affairs. Through their representation in the Council of Ministers and the participation of the heads of state and government in the meetings of the European Council they clearly dominate the decision-making process of the European Union. The European level is matched by the national level particularly in the centralized countries of the EU (DK, EL, IRL, P, UK) where politicians have a powerful grip on EC/EU affairs and/or where the bureaucracy which is dealing with EC/EU matters is directly linked to the government and has developed effective means of participation in the EC/EU decision-making process (DK, F, UK). In some of these countries the national parliament does not play a major role in EC/EU affairs (EL, P). The decentralized (E, F, I, NL) and federal countries (B, D) are characterized by a stronger involvement of the regional/local level – with the effect that in Belgium and Germany regional ministers can participate in the Council's decision-making – without breaking, however, the preponderant role played by the central governmental actors.

Depending on the policy fields and the issue at stake in the Council, several different ministries are more or less intensively involved in the EC/EU decision-making process. Very roughly, we can differentiate between the 'pioneer ministries' – such as foreign affairs, economics, agriculture and finance – and the 'newcomers' – such as the ministries for the environment, education and research, industry, labour, women etc. – which have a different record of participation in EC decision-making but which are catching up if one looks at the list of the Council's meetings and its composition.[3] It is interesting to notice that the foreign ministry did not in all member states become the 'lead ministry' in EC matters (but in most of them such as B, DK, E, EL, F, I, IRL, P, UK). In some countries over the years of EC membership a rivalry between foreign ministry and economic ministry developed concerning the main responsibility with regard to the EC/EU (especially in D and NL). In other member states special units/advisory structures have been established which are directly connected to the head of government (B, F, NL, UK) or which are at least under a strong influence from the head of government (IRL). In all foreign ministries special departments or divisions have been created dealing with EC/EU matters, characterized to some extent by an intra-ministerial competition over the responsibility for the different pillars of the EU. The establishment of an own 'European ministry' has not occurred (so far) in any member state, with exception to a certain extent of France and Belgium. In the former there is a 'Ministre aux affaires européennes' and in the latter there has been a 'European Affairs Minister', but both without disposing of an own administrative sub-structure.

Except for defence matters all national ministries regularly send representatives to Council meetings or to meetings of the Council's working groups and the Commission's expert committees in Brussels. Estimating that there are about 250–300 working groups of the Council preparing the decisions of its 100 meetings a year and that there are about 600–700 committees of the Commission and that each member state sends an average of two civil servants and/or experts to meetings (which largly differ, depending on the issue at stake and the type of committee), there are, according to this very rough estimation, about 25,000 national officials involved a year (1994). Moreover, European matters are nearly always on the agenda of the national cabinet meetings. For instance in Germany the 'Cabinet Committee for European policy' which was established in the 1970s has not been used very frequently, since European questions were put on the agenda of nearly every cabinet meeting so that a specific committee was not necessary. In contrast to this, in Ireland a more pragmatic system of 'ad hoc cabinet committees' was installed whenever important issues were on the Communities agenda or during the Irish presidency. Thus the development of European policy-making has

---

[3] See Annual Reports of the Council of the European Community/European Union.

had a different impact on the national institutional structure. In all member states the EU Council and the national governments are closely related to each other and mutually influence their structure and policy agenda.

The increasing number of policy fields dealt with at the EC/EU level also had the effect of a more sophisticated coordination in the member states. The more ministries were affected by European policies, the more it became necessary to establish an effective system of inter- and intraministerial coordination and cooperation in order to reach common viewpoints and to develop a coherent negotiation strategy. Some member states – such as Denmark, France and the United Kingdom – are known for their streamlined and effective coordination mechanisms, which correspond to central bodies such as the 'Cabinet Committee on EU Affairs' in Denmark, the 'Secrétariat Général du Comité Interministériel' (SGCI) in France or the 'Cabinet Office' in the United Kingdom, and which allow them to formulate a coherent European policy and to develop successful negotiation strategies in Brussels. The latest development since the SEA and especially the Treaty on European Union suggests, however, that these more hierarchical ways of coordination are increasingly less able to cope with all issues, actors and flows of information (F) or have not prevented a tendency towards 'sectorization' and 'decentralization' (DK). In Spain the existence of a central coordination body – the Secretary of State for the EC (SSEC) which is linked to the Ministry of Foreign Affairs – did not prevent interministerial conflicts and difficulties in defining the Spanish position in the COREPER and the EC Council of Ministers. With the 'atomization' of the decision-making process in the EC/EU it is no longer possible (or perhaps appropriate) to control the internal coordination process through one central body. Other countries – such as Belgium and Germany – are 'by nature' more characterized by a fragmented policy-making and have developed more complicated internal coordination mechanisms with the result that their positions in Brussels are not always free from contradictions – such as in the case of Germany – or are handicapped by a cumbersome rotation system with the regions and communes, as in the case of Belgium. Sometimes this feature might be an advantage – in terms of the negotiation strategy or in order to get different viewpoints – though one should not draw any general conclusion from it. However, whether the coordination system is more or less streamlined and/or more or less sophisticated, in all member states the internal coordination efforts have substantially increased and are in some way 'dictated' by the European agenda.

In Portugal, the objective of reaching the convergence criteria for entering the third stage of EMU has increased inter-ministerial coordination efforts between the Secretariat of State for European Affairs, the Ministry of Finance, the Ministry of the Interior and the Ministry for Social Affairs. In Belgium a 'European coordinator' was introduced in each ministry in 1990 in order to supervise the implementation of EC legislation in the competent departments. Thus there is no leading ministry with a 'pilot function' which dominates the others – though in most cases the foreign ministry, the economic ministry, the finance ministry and the agricultural ministry play a central role and the other ministries participate to a varying intensity – but there is a permanent exchange and interaction of the individual ministers and their respective ministerial bureaucracies with the respective civil services in Brussels. This interaction – which very often is informal and *ad hoc* – takes place on all levels and is embedded in the national intra- and inter-ministerial coordination structure. In many member states there are clear signs of bureaucratic infights and inter-ministerial struggles for competence and responsibility in EC matters; to be present in Brussels, and to be involved in 'affairs' there, is generally considered to be a positive and necessary part of efficient sectoral policy-making. With Maastricht the internal distribution of competences and the question of the 'pilot function' has been put to debate, having (so far) only the effect of an increasing national incoherence. Most important is that there are apparently no longer clear-cut borderlines *within* and *between* the national and the European level; both are closely connected to each other and have started to move; responsibilities for policy decisions are shared and cannot, either vertically or horizontally, be attributed to one of them.

The heads of state and government play an important role during the meetings of the European Council. This institution has – in the terms of Göhler – an important symbolic function and gives, according to Art. D TEU, the broad political orientation to the integration process. Though the European Council very often takes concrete decisions which are highly important – such as in the case of the Delors I and II packages on the finances of the Community, in the case of the Ioannina compromise on the voting modalities in the Council or in the case of the appointment of Jacques Santer as the new President of the Commission – the preparation of the 'package deals' and the day-to-day technical questions are managed by the (political) state secretaries and the senior civil servants of the various ministries. It depends to a large extent on their capacity to internally coordinate the different views and to interact with their colleagues in Brussels to what extent the national governments are able to pursue a successful EU policy. Since Maastricht in all member states the preponderant role of the governments – and here especially the ministerial bureaucracy – has been diluted by a certain 'mood of concession', in the sense of a 'decentralization' of the internal decision-preparation and decision-making. In fact, during the process leading to Maastricht, national parliaments and regions have exerted political pressure on the national governments in order to improve their effective participation in the EC/EU decision-making process. The following paragraphs will show to what extent the parliaments and the regions were successful in this respect.

The parliaments
In nearly all of the country reports the national parliaments are perceived and/or described – with varying terms and because of different reasons – as the 'losers' of the European integration process until Maastricht (B, D, E, EL, IRL, NL, P). Taken together two main arguments can be found: firstly, due to the growing supremacy of the national governments in the EC decision-making process – due to the latter's quantity, i.e. in terms of the number of civil servants involved, but also due to their quality, i.e. in terms of the civil servant's information and knowledge of dealing with the sometimes rather technical issues and complex procedures in Brussels – the parliaments were left outside or were only marginally involved in the preparation and making of EC legislation (B, D, E, EL, F, IRL, P). Secondly, the national parliaments themselves did not show a high interest, did not want to and/or were unable to follow EC affairs closely because of their own cumbersome internal structures and complex procedures. This last argument is particularly mentioned in connection with the French 'Assemblée Nationale' and the German 'Bundestag' where the complicated internal handling of EC documents takes several weeks and reduces the capacity in these parliaments to react quickly to drafts coming from Brussels. In the German case one must add that the second chamber, the 'Bundesrat', in contrast to the 'Bundestag' – mainly due to the latter's own unwillingness – is much more efficient

in selecting and distributing the relevant EC documents to the competent committees. A further explanation for this certainly is that the 'Bundesrat' is much less a 'politicized' than a 'professionalized' body, which is primarily run by civil servants from the Länder governments. Also the House of Lords seems to be an effective (second) chamber due to its 'fairly apolitical' and 'technocratic' basis and is known for its highly regarded reports. In contrast to this the Spanish Senat does not seem to be involved in EC decision-making, except for matters concerning the autonomous regions.

There are different instruments available for national parliaments to influence the governments' EC policy-making. Many reports mention written and oral questions, reports and debates in plenary on the governments' European policy, especially after a summit of the European Council (D, E, EL, IRL, UK). The latter have primarily a control function with regard to the government and have only a limited direct influence on EC policy-making, due to the very often close links between the acting government and the majority in parliament and an effective party discipline (such as especially in IRL, UK).[4] The use of the above mentioned instruments is quite different, according to the national parliaments, and depends, among other factors, on the parliament's role in the political system and its characterization as a so-called 'talk' parliament (e.g. IRL, UK) or a 'work' parliament (e.g. D, DK).[5] Other parliamentary means are the involvement in the ratification of amendments to the Treaty of Rome – such as the decision on the Community's own resources or the act on the introduction of direct elections to the European Parliament – and the ratification of international agreements.

Parliaments were also to an increasing extent concerned with the incorporation of EC directives into national law – the number of EC directives per year grew from twenty-five in 1970 to fifty-nine in 1980 and reached seventy-one in 1990 – which became especially important in connection with the realization of the 1992 internal market. However, these activities were primarily limited to the *phase of the legal transposition* of decisions whereas national parliaments only

---

[4] This is still true for the United Kingdom in spite of the anti-disciplinary role of the 'Euro-sceptics' who are particularly strong because of the small majority in parliament of the Major government.

[5] 'Talk' parliament in the sense that a parliament's emphasis is on plenary debates, as opposed to a 'work' parliament which focuses more on committee work.

rarely intervened directly in the preparation and making of binding
EC law. To this must be added that in many member states the incorporation of directives into national law has mostly been done by delegated legislation, i.e. by the executive (D, EL, I, NL, UK). This
certainly also had to do with the attitude of national parliamentarians – including the party in opposition – to be more concerned with
'purely national issues' since these are more profitable in terms of
elections. Or – as in the case of Germany – there is a broad political
consensus on 'Europe' which explains why European issues rarely
lead to controversial debates between the parties of government and
the opposition. Moreover, parliamentary committees seldom bother
to look more closely at EC drafts given their correct impression that
they cannot change the major thrust of EC legislation.

A certain '*laisser faire*' attitude on the part of parliaments with
regard to EC decision-making changed substantially in connection
with the Maastricht Treaty. This was essentially due to two developments. On the one hand national parliaments realized that with Maastricht new policy fields and competences would be dealt with by the
European institutions without, conversely, improving the national
parliaments' role in the EC decision-making process. This would
strengthen the national governments and some EU institutions and
would lead to a further 'deparliamentarization' of the integration
process as far as national parliaments are concerned. On the other
hand the European Parliament was trying to improve the democratic
character of the Community and was looking for 'new allies' with the
same concern. During the presidency of Egon Klepsch national parliaments were not considered as competitors, but as useful partners in
this respect.[6] An improved cooperation with the national parliaments
could compensate the disappointment over the Maastricht Treaty and
would help to put more pressure on the Council and the European
Council. Some parliaments – but with Maastricht in force and applied
their number seems to shrink – responded positively to this and were
unwilling to diminish further their powers in EC affairs *vis-à-vis* the
governments as long as the democratic deficit at the EC level would
be upheld. The most extreme position in this respect was developed
by the Dutch Second Chamber (which is comparable to the first
chamber in other member states) where a debate on the reintroduc-

---

[6] Under President Klaus Hänsch this attitude has changed; Hänsch is more sceptical
with regard to a close interparliamentary cooperation and the 'Assises'.

tion of the 'double mandate' started in order to strengthen the links between the national parliaments and the European Parliament. Moreover Dutch parliamentarians – as well as parliamentarians in other member states – argued that their lack of influence in EC policy-making should be compensated not by giving more powers to the national parliament but by strengthening the European Parliament.

Thus Maastricht was accompanied by an 'awakening' of national parliaments with regard to the EC/EU decision-making process. In all member states the parliaments addressed demands to the national governments which concentrated essentially on two aspects. Firstly, parliaments were asking for *earlier and more comprehensive information* about legislative proposals of the Commission debated in the Council (B, D, DK, F). In Belgium the parliament insisted on the rule that it will be informed about an EC legislative act immediately after its transmission to the Council. In the German case the demand for better and earlier information was 'constitutionalized' through the introduction of the new Art. 23 in the Basic Law which strengthened the parliament's position with regard to the government. In France the parliament's demands led in 1992 to the introduction of a new Art. 88–4 in the constitution according to which the government has to inform the National Assembly (and the Senate) on all proposals of the Commission with legislative effect, immediately after they have been transferred to the Council. Moreover, according to a circular of the Prime Minister in July 1994, French ministers should give a 'vote on reserve' in the Council in case the parliament is not able to articulate before its opinion on a proposal of legislative nature. In Denmark a system of so-called 'factual notes' was introduced in spring 1994 in order to inform the parliament about the effect of a Commission proposal on Danish law, its budgetary consequences and the criticism raised by interest groups against it in the preparatory phase.

Secondly, parliaments were asking for a *more effective role during the decision-taking phase* of the Council and the *parliamentary control of decisions* taken by the governments. This latter aspect included a strengthening of the rights of the parliaments' specialized committees in EC/EU affairs. This was particularly true for France where the 'Delegation for the European Union' in the National Assembly has been more closely involved in the issuing of resolutions on an EC matter which are addressed to the government. In Denmark the already strong 'European Committee' (former 'Market Relations

Committee') became the addressee of the above mentioned 'factual notes' which strengthened its position, also with regard to other parliamentary committees. Moreover the Danish parliament decided to set up a 'Council for European Policy' consisting of a wide range of representatives from interest groups and organizations in order to arrange hearings and conferences. In Germany Art. 45 of the Basic Law was amended, establishing the new 'Committee on Affairs of the European Union' (*Unionsausschuß*). This new committee can be authorized to take decisions for the German Bundestag as a whole and must be seen in connection with the strengthened position of the Bundestag through the new Art. 23 of the Basic Law. The German government – by constitutional law – is bound 'to take into account' the Bundestag's opinion in its negotiations in Brussels. In the Netherlands the government was asked to submit more detailed reports on the implementation of EC directives and on the progress of European cooperation. And in Belgium the reports on the implementation of EC directives will be done by the Chamber of Deputies' advisory committee itself in order to appeal to public opinion and to put pressure on the government. In some countries these improvements of the parliament's situation resulted from the change of the national constitution (B, D, F, P) or led to important laws, declarations or reports of the national parliaments (DK, E, GB, I, NL) which bound the governments and improved the participation rights in EC/EU affairs of the national parliaments. Thus national parliaments in nearly all member states have strengthened their role in the EC/EU decision-making process. Though decision-making continues to remain primarily in the hands of the governments, the latter's mandate to negotiate in Brussels will to an increasing extent be monitored by the national parliaments, and here especially by their specialized committees (especially in D, DK, F). Hence it seems that parliaments no longer just 'accompany' the government's integration policy but try to 'prescribe' the government's actions in EC policy-making. It is expected that the further development of European integration will not take place without a more active role played by the parliaments, especially in the phases of the preparation and control of EC decisions.

Another approach consists in a more intensive interparliamentary cooperation. Since the end of the 1980s there are regular meetings of the presidents of the national parliaments and since 1988 their specialized committees in EC affairs meet once every half a year (with the same presidency as the Council Presidency) in the framework of the Conference of the Specialized Organs in Community Affairs (so-called COSAC meetings). In order to have an influence on the inter-governmental conferences preparing the Maastricht Treaty, representatives of the national parliaments and the European Parliament met for the first time in the framework of the so-called 'Assises' in November 1990 in Rome. These examples show that national parliaments and the European Parliament have intensified their relations; moreover there exists a multitude of bilateral parliamentary meetings and party political exchanges. The Maastricht Treaty explicitly welcomes the intensified cooperation between national parliaments and supports the convening of the 'Assises'.[7] However, in terms of the concrete participation in the preparation, making, implementation and control of binding EC law, the interparliamentary links have had little effect and, so far, have had primarily the function of attracting the attention of governments and public opinion. It cannot be overlooked, however, that efforts are undertaken towards closer cooperation between parliaments, which is particularly claimed by France, and that this constitutes a further, though a still weak, indicator of 'institutional fusion' in the EU.

The trend towards a closer parliamentary cooperation does not entail the convergence of their working structures and policy concerns. Quite the contrary: the reports from the different member states suggest that national parliaments have not substantially changed their peculiar outlook and characters and are – as in the case especially of the United Kingdom and France – an important element in the debate on national sovereignty. A further indicator for the continuing differences between national parliaments is the record of incorporation of EC legislation into national law. It not only reflects the divergencies in parliamentary efficiency and effectiveness when dealing with EC legislation but it also shows that, depending on the policy issue at stake, there are quite different attitudes in the national parliaments. The parliaments in Denmark, the United Kingdom and the Netherlands have the best record of incorporation of EC directives which is quite in contrast to the rather sceptical view towards European integration, especially in the former two countries.[8] It

[7] See declarations no. 13 and 14 in the Annex to the Treaty on European Union.

[8] See for more details the Eleventh Annual Report of the Commission to the European Parliament on Monitoring the Application of Community Law 1993, C 154 (6 June 1994), p. 7.

seems that in Belgium and Germany the less convincing incorporation record is, among other things, due to the federal structure of the countries. In Germany the involvement of the Länder in the legislative process – via the Bundesrat, where the opposition has mostly had the majority[9] – as well as the decentralized implementation of EC decisions in the German system of 'administrative federalism' might be an explanation. In Belgium the complex socio-political structure of the country and the recent federalization play a role which extended the competences of the regions and communes in EC affairs. But even before the state reform of 1993 the number of infringement proceedings of the Court against Belgium was among the highest (phase of cases before the ECJ), though the situation has improved at the beginning of the 1990s (see Table 14.1). In spite of their centralized structure, Greece and Ireland show a comparatively high number of infringement cases before the Court. The reasons for this seem to be in part political obstacles and a lack of efficiency in the parliamentary procedures which avoided a quick incorporation of EC law. A special case in this respect is Italy which was ranking among the last in the Community but which was able drastically to improve its incoporation record from 1992 onwards and consequently could reduce the number of infringement procedure referred to the ECJ. This improvement was primarily due to a special law, the so-called 'Legge La Pergola', which allowed an easy incorporation of EC legislation into Italian law – a kind of 'synoptical problem solving' – irrespective of the actual administrative follow-up. This approach certainly improved the statistical situation of Italy but did not contribute to solving the more general problem of the lack of effectiveness in the process of the incorporation and implementation of EC law in the country. In contrast to this the Dutch Second Chamber – under the motto 'I will maintain my rights' – resisted the government's intention to speed up implementation by short-cutting parliament's legislative role.

Thus in spite of the willingness of all parliaments to participate more actively in EC/EU affairs and notwithstanding the trend towards more intensive interparliamentary relations, substantial differences with regard to the actual role and function of national parliaments in EC/EU decision-making continue to exist.

---

[9] The Bundesrat's role is particularly strong concerning those laws which require its consent; on other laws the Bundesrat can at least raise an objection.

Table 14.1 Proceedings against member states by category in comparative perspective 1980–93

Type of proceedings State/Year	Letters of Formal Notice							Reasoned Opinions							Cases referred to the Court						
	1980–87	1988	1989	1990	1991	1992	1993	1988	1989	1990	1991	1992	1993	1980–87	1980–87	1988	1989	1990	1991	1992	1993
Belgium	358	52	66	68	71	110	98	32	21	32	46	22	26	169	78	10	14	13	8	6	7
Denmark	249	30	36	36	52	45	66	6	4	5	3	4	3	104	50	3	1	3	1	0	–
Germany	174	55	56	61	60	97	119	27	12	21	13	18	35	37	11	8	4	5	1	5	4
Greece	346	64	86	120	88	112	125	46	21	56	48	30	41	115	38	14	10	10	9	4	4
Spain	54	31	51	114	79	127	107	11	8	15	30	39	28	8	1	1	5	3	2	5	5
France	516	57	66	76	54	111	106	32	20	18	15	10	39	210	73	10	8	6	4	1	2
Ireland	255	40	51	52	59	88	91	23	13	17	27	13	25	86	25	8	2	3	3	9	–
Italy	509	107	115	111	115	137	108	70	58	62	76	40	49	260	139	14	36	25	24	11	6
Luxembourg	239	36	43	43	64	97	91	19	13	15	35	21	29	78	22	2	6	4	4	14	11
Netherlands	232	43	58	61	62	73	75	12	11	20	23	16	22	69	20	3	5	2	7	5	5
Portugal	13	18	26	178	86	116	125	7	5	12	84	22	40	0	0	0	1	2	2	1	–
United Kingdom	235	34	37	44	63	97	98	15	13	6	11	13	15	61	17	0	5	2	0	3	–
Total	3180	567	691	964	853	1210	1209	300	199	279	411	248	352	1197	474	73	97	78	65	64	44

Note: In reading the columns covering the period 1980–7 it must be recalled that Greece joined the EC in 1981 and Spain/Portugal joined in 1986.
Sources: Table compiled by the authors on the basis of the Annual Reports of the Commission to the European Parliament on Monitoring the Applications of Community Law.

The regions

With the extension of the policy fields dealt with at the European
level, the rights and competences of the regional and local level have
been affected to an increasing extent.[10] Especially in the fields of education, culture, research, social security, health, environment, infrastructure, agriculture and fisheries, many regions have specific tasks
or competences (D, DK, B, E, F, I, NL, UK). The growing legislative
activities of the Community in these fields led to the demand of the
regions to participate actively in the EC decision-making process.
This claim for effective participation in EC legislation did not take
place in all regions in the same way and the same intensity. In some
member states it was accompanied by a certain rivalry among
national regions (B, E, F and to some extent also in D) or it became
entangled in the conflicts of local politics (F). In the United Kingdom
the regional claim for competences was in opposition to the Conservative government's policy since 1979 to restrict local government
power. In all member states the claim for more participation rights
was most actively pursued by the executive level and to a minor
degree only by the regional parliaments. Not only the regions as such
were active but in some member states also big cities (DK, NL) and
associations of regions, counties or municipalities (D, DK, F, IRL,
NL, UK), which acted very often with the encouragement and financial support of the Commission. Due to their federal structure the
demands were particularly strong in Belgium and Germany. Only the
German Länder and the Belgian regions and communes could substantially increase their rights in the context of Maastricht, whereas
in Greece, Ireland and Portugal the regional level – because of its virtual non-existence in terms of their own institutions – could hardly
articulate an opinion. In some countries where a regional level exists
and disposes of its own rights and competences – such as in Spain,
Italy, France and the Netherlands – the regions had difficulties in
articulating their views *vis-à-vis* the governments and could only
slightly improve their position with regard to EC affairs. A certain
exception is in Catalonia, Spain, where demands were facilitated by
the party political dependence of the Socialist government on the
Catalan nationalist coalition's support. However, in spite of these
particularities, representatives of all regional and/or communal levels

[10] See Christian Engel and Joseph Van Ginderachter, *Trends in Regional and Local
Government in the European Community* (Louvain: Acco, 1993).

are today present in the new Committee of the Regions (in which there are also representatives of cities and local municipalities). Thus despite the differences in the structure of the member states – ranging from the federal states (B, D), to the more decentralized states (E, F, I, LUX, NL) and the centralized states (DK, EL, IRL, P, UK) – there seems to be a trend towards the growing involvement of the regional and communal level in EC affairs.

In some member states the regions and communes have gained a more institutionalized outlook due to the structural and regional policy of the Community. In fact, the development of specific aid programmes (such as Interreg) and the distribution of structural money necessitated the establishment of a regional level with its own authorities and administration. For instance in Ireland seven 'regional review committees' have been created which did not exist before in this way; advisory groups were set up in each Irish region which brought together local officials, state agencies and representatives of social and economic life in order to prepare the submissions to the national development plan. They were later transformed into monitoring committees for the 'Community Support Framework' 1989–93. In Greece thirteen administrative regions were established, six of them in order to implement the Integrated Mediterranean Programmes (IMPs). However, in contrast to the Irish case where the EC's regional policy led to some kind of 'institutional learning' between Dublin and the regions, in Greece the IMPs led only to a 'nominal devolution' of power to the regions. The suggestion to establish regional ministries at the centre indicates that, at the end of the day, the EC's regional policy had the effect of further state control by Athens and did not enhance the role of the Greek regions.

Many regions or big cities have their own representations in Brussels (B, D, F, DK, E, NL) and/or are members of transregional or transcommunal associations (such as the Assembly of the Regions in Europe or the International Union of Local Authorities) which have offices in Brussels. The municipalities and districts have very often set up a national association which has an office in Brussels (D, DK, NL). In the case of Portugal the regions (Azores, Madeira) even have their own staff at the national Permanent Representation in Brussels and in the French case they are in an indirect way represented at the European level through regional interest groups or politicians from the regions who have a seat in the European Parliament. In the United Kingdom, Scotland, Wales and Northern Ireland have their own ministries and may thus put forward their territorial concerns at the ministerial and administrative level. The Scottish Office which is interested in fisheries may attend the Council of Fisheries Ministers. Thus there are various direct and indirect ways of interest representation of the regional and communal level in Brussels which differ in scope and impact.

The creation of 'Euro-Regions' and the inter-regional cooperation in the framework of the 'Arge-Alp', the Union of Capital Regions of the EC or among the four most advanced regions in Europe – to mention only a few – are further elements of a growing involvement of the regions in European affairs. Although these latter activities have less to do with EC/EU decision-making as such, they nevertheless contribute to the self-consciousness of the regions and to their willingness to become an 'institutionalized third level' in the EC/EU decision-making process.

Besides the effort of regions and communes to seek direct or indirect contact with the EC/EU institutions (and here especially with the Commission) and to establish an 'institutionalized' relationship with the European level, some regions can also make use of the 'legislative way' through the 'second chamber' of the national parliament – in case such a chamber exists and represents somehow regional concerns – in order to participate in EC decision-making (especially in B and D). In Germany the Länder have been quite successful in extending their participation in EC policy-making through a more powerful role of the Bundesrat. In connection with the ratification of the Maastricht Treaty the German constitution has been amended (especially Art. 23 GG) which improved the Bundesrat's right of information in EC/EU affairs; Art. 52 GG enables it to convene a 'Euro-chamber' in order to react quickly to legislative acts of the Union. In contrast to this the Spanish Senado cannot be considered as a territorial chamber which has strengthened the role of the autonomous regions in EC affairs. The Spanish regions followed a different strategy and were trying to strengthen their direct links with Brussels and were negotiating with the central government in order to get more competences and participation rights in EC/EU matters (especially the Basque Country and Catalonia). The result was the establishment of an informal body of cooperation between the regions and the central government, the so-called 'Conference on Community Affairs'. However, in spite of this institutionalized multilateral participation, the Spanish regions continued to develop bilateral contacts with Madrid and – as in the case

of the Basque Country and Catalonia – continued to seek an arrangement on a special EU status with the central authorities. Thus, the
demand for a more active involvement of the regional level in EC/EU
affairs did not necessarily lead to a decentralization in policy-making
but, in some cases, even led to a recentralization (E, EL, I).

The regional level very often plays an important role in the implementation and application of EC law (B, D, DK, E, F, NL, UK and
to a certain extent also in EL and IRL). Especially in Germany the
Länder administration is responsible for implementing laws, either as
'own affairs' or 'on instruction' of the federal level. This is to a certain extent also true in Belgium and Italy; in Spain the central administration disposes of field executive services at the regional and
provincial levels. In other member states such as Ireland and Greece
local authorities play a limited role in the implementation of EC legislation. There is not only extreme financial dependence by the local
authorities on the centre but they also lack the legal and infrastructural means to carry out their tasks. In this respect the money from
the EC funds is an instrument for the local authorities to gain in
(political) power and to ask for changes in the internal distribution
of competences. Some regions see the principle of subsidiarity as a
further instrument in this respect (D, IRL, P).

The implementation function of the regions and communes
becomes especially important in case a member state is accused of the
infringement of Community law by the European Court of Justice
because of a too late or an unsatisfactory implementation of an EC
directive. As a consequence the central and the regional levels of the
member states have to cooperate and to coordinate in European
affairs more closely in order to avoid law suits before the ECJ. In
some member states special agreements have been made between the
central government and the regions which are binding for both and
which should improve the cooperation and coordination between the
two levels (D, B, E). In Germany this form of legally binding cooperation has happened already for quite some time – and which is
known as the German 'cooperative federalism'[11] – and is also used for
the internal non-EC decision-making procedure. In the case of Belgium the cooperation between centre and periphery led to a complex

---

[11] See Fritz Scharpf, Bernd Reissert and Fritz Schnabel, *Politikverflechtung: Theorie
und Empirie des kooperativen Föderalismus in der Bundesrepublik* (Kroneberg/Ts.:
Scriptor, 1976).

rotation system of central, regional and community ministers concerning the representation and cooperation in the Council of Ministers. Furthermore, the latest constitutional change in Belgium introduced the so-called 'substitution power' to the central state in case the regions or communes are not able to implement an EC law which falls under their competences. Although in Spain most of the autonomous regions have adapted their organizational structures to EC policy-making and to the management of finances from EC funds, EC directives are not effectively implemented. The decentralization in Spain which has been undertaken in the context of the Internal Market has increased the internal complexity and there is a lack of central monitoring – either by the government or the Commission – of the implementation of EC law.

To summarize, the EC/EU has become – not least by financial transfers – an important 'point of reference' for regions and municipalities. The various Community programmes have to some extent strengthened regional and local authorities but have also induced a certain 'artificial' regionalization in member states which in some cases was also to the benefit of the centre (E, EL, IRL). Regional and local authorities have adapted their structures to the EC policy-making process and have put forward claims – with different success – to the central governments for more competences and a better participation in EC/EU affairs. However, this did not lead to comprehensive constitutional changes in the member states but only to a partial institutional adaptation and learning process which differs widely according to the national context.

The courts

The national courts can also be qualified as political institutions since they participate in the institutional interaction within the EU system. They come in at the end of the policy cycle, i.e. during the phase of application and control of Community law. The national courts are the institutions which are also, but in a different way, affected by the increasing 'institutional fusion' which we observe. According to their specific functions within the political systems they participate much less in the general trend of cooperation and mutual interaction with their European counterparts, either in horizontal or in vertical terms. The reason is that the courts are less dependent on a permanent and direct exchange of views. However, they are nevertheless part of the interaction process between the national and the Community level.

They become active when a case is brought before them and they pronounce their judgment on the basis of the national law, the EC/EU treaties, previous judgements and well established legal rules and principles. And most importantly of the latter: all courts in the European Union act in respect of the principle of the primacy and direct applicability of EC law. Thus they have an important indirect influence on the shaping of Community law and the EC/EU institutional system as such.

In different cases and over different periods of time high national courts showed reservations concerning the respect of Community law. Especially the German 'Bundesverfassungsgericht', the German Finance Court, the Spanish High Court, the French 'Conseil d'Etat', the British House of Lords (in its function as the highest court of the United Kingdom) and to some extent also the Portuguese Constitutional Court explicitly expressed doubts. However, this did not lead to a non-uniform application of Community law and did not undermine the primacy of EC law over national law. In the case of the German Bundesverfassungsgericht the reservation is particularly strong. In fact, from its decision on the Maastricht Treaty in October 1993 one can conclude – and this argumentation is in a sense in continuity with its previous 'Solange I and II' decisions – that the Bundesverfassungsgericht still has some doubts as regards the protection of fundamental rights in the Union by the ECJ. In the future, as the German Bundesverfassungsgericht stated in its Maastricht decision, it has the intention of exerting jurisdiction on fundamental rights 'in cooperation' with the ECJ. This has been interpreted as a kind of control over the ECJ as regards the fundamental rights. It is interesting to notice that the Spanish Constitutional Court expressed a similar view as regards the protection of fundamental rights in the EU. Another extreme, but different, case is the British House of Lords which in the past has been reluctant to make reference to the ECJ since this would directly imply a weakening of the principle of parliamentary sovereignty. However, these examples are unique and constitute exceptions which do not reverse the general trend among national courts of an unequivocal acceptance of the principle of the primacy of EC legislation. Although national courts play a more discreet role, they have considerably contributed to the establishment of the 'Community of law' (*Rechtsgemeinschaft*) without which the integration process would not have been possible. The national courts together with the European Court of Justice were continuously following the path of an 'integration through law'.[12]

The national courts' interaction with the ECJ essentially takes place in the framework of the preliminary ruling procedure which allows national courts to refer to the ECJ in the case of a question concerning the interpretation of Community law, concerning the validity of acts of Community institutions or concerning the inter-pretation of the statutes of bodies established by the Council (Art. 177 TEU). Thus, when making use of this procedure the national courts implicitly accept the authority of the ECJ in questions con-cerning EC law. In total the preliminary ruling procedure has been used 2,590 times since 1958, which led to 2,111 decisions by the Court. German courts are the most active in referring to the ECJ. In fact one-third of all Art. 177 proceedings come from German courts, followed by Dutch courts. Due to their later entry into the European Community, but also because of a certain unawareness of the Art. 177 procedure, Portuguese and Spanish courts are those which have made the least reference to the ECJ (though the figures have increased in the last few years). In the German case 20% of all preliminary rul-ings are initiated by courts of last instance; in contrast to this the majority of the Dutch and the Portuguese preliminary ruling pro-ceedings are made by courts of last instance and in the Irish case all levels have equally made requests to the ECJ. Thus there is not a common pattern of behaviour of national courts as regards Art. 177 TEU. This is somehow surprising since only courts of last instance are obliged to make reference to the ECJ in the cases mentioned in Art. 177 TEU. A common trend only seems to be that most of the Art. 177 requests are made by Higher Administrative Courts and Higher Finance Courts, since many cases concern the interpretation of the EC tax and customs law and the EC competition rules.

With the exception of a few cases – especially by courts in Spain, France, Germany and the United Kingdom – national courts have always addressed the ECJ in an affair which falls under the latter's jurisdiction. Today the principle is accepted that pending the ECJ's decision on an Art. 177 TEU reference, courts have to disapply national law. This principle has especially strengthened the right of British courts to scrutinize national legislation which – because of parliamentary sovereignty – was in this respect impossible in the past.

[12] See Mauro Cappelletti, Monica Seccombe and Joseph Weiler (eds.), *Integration Through Law. Europe and the American Federal Experience*, 2 vols. (Berlin/New York: de Gruyter, 1986).

Moreover, although the high national courts have raised critical tones during the European integration process – such as the French Conseil d'Etat on the citizenship of the Union or the German Bundesverfassungsgericht in its decision on the Maastricht Treaty – they never declared a legislative act of the Community unconstitutional or definitively stopped the transfer of competences to the EC/EU because of the incompatibility with the national constitution. In connection with the ratification of the Maastricht Treaty there have been interventions of the national constitutional courts (B, D, E, F, P) which concerned above all the new rights of EU citizens to participate in communal elections and the participation of the regional level in EC decision-making and led to constitutional amendments. Thus national courts and the ECJ share today the view that (primary and secondary) Community law and the constitutional law of the member states are in principle compatible and are not in competition, but are complementary to each other. Only Ireland constitutes a certain exception in this respect due to the constitutionally based protection of the unborn child. This led to some juridical controversies in connection with the ratification of the Treaty on European Union and explains the insertion of a specific protocol in the Treaty on European Union referring to the Irish constitution. However, today it seems that this question is less a problem of the compatibility of the Irish constitution with the EU's legal system than of Irish internal politics.

The adaptation of national courts to the EU system is difficult to assess. The growing amount of EC legislation and the number of cases involving Community law has in all member states increased the requirement for national judges and lawyers to be familiar with European law. In Portugal specific efforts have been undertaken to train magistrates in European legal matters. In Ireland it is interesting to notice that the interaction between Irish and EC law has led to a growing use of continental legal techniques and methodology. Apparently this is not shared in the same way by British courts where the adherence to traditional common law principles and techniques prevails. Thus also national courts seem to be affected – at least partly – by a learning and adaptation process.

Concerning the infringement procedure according to Art. 169 TEU national courts are not directly involved. However, they are indirectly affected since Art. 169 decisions of the ECJ have an impact on the national legal and institutional system as a whole. National courts have to apply and implement Community law in the member states which has been 'repaired' by an Art. 169 decision. There have been many decisions of the ECJ on infringements of the treaties by member states. The number of decisions of the ECJ against member states and the types of issues at stake were quite different. Between 1980 and 1993 there has been a total of more than 100 court decisions against each of Belgium, France and Italy (see above), whereas against Germany, the Netherlands, Portugal, Spain and the United Kingdom there have been only 20–30 cases per country in the same time period. There is a broad variety of issues dealt with by the ECJ which does not show a common pattern; each member state has its own specific problems with Community law. In spite of this diversity in substance, member states have in common that a decision by the ECJ is taken seriously and puts pressure on the national institutions, especially the government, the parliament and the ministerial administration (see above). This is particularly the case when an affair ranks high in public opinion, such as the non-implementation of an EC directive on travel insurances in Germany. After a travel operator had gone bankrupt and many German tourists could not return back home from their holidays, the German government almost immediately transposed the directive into national law. Conversely, a national government might complain against a Council decision before the ECJ – as did the German government in the case of the regulation of the banana market – in order to demonstrate 'at home' that it did its best to fight against the (in its opinion) misleading decision. Thus the interaction with the European Court of Justice has in two ways an important function for national institutions, i.e. decisions of the ECJ exert pressure to implement and effectively apply Community law and thus settle legal conflicts; and they offer an opportunity for member states to complain against other member states or the EU institutions and in this way are sometimes used as an 'alibi function' for internal politics.

Taken together the overview on the comparison of national institutions in the EC/EU shows a picture of broad variety and heterogeneity. There is no single pattern of institutional behaviour and activity which can be identified in all of the member states. Many of the described actions and performances in the member states result from the specific constitutional and politico-institutional structures. This should not prevent us attracting the reader's attention to some trends which can be extrapolated on the basis of the observations made so far and to attempt to give an outlook on future institutional development in the European Union.

Institutional trends

Interaction and 'Europeanization'

The increasing involvement of national institutions in the work of the EC/EU institutions is described in the literature as a 'multi-tiered system of government',[13] which is characterized by intensive interaction and a process of mutual influence between – in strictly legal terms – the 'national' and the 'European' institutions. Thus the EC/EU's institutional system is not a 'closed club' but it is open towards national institutions and their participation in decision-making. Conversely, national institutions are not restricted to their national sphere of action but they are to an increasing extent oriented towards 'Brussels' and have an interest in participating in the decision-making process there. This phenomenon of interaction and mutual influence between European and national institutions and administrations has intensified and broadened since the beginning of the European integration process and is not limited to the top of the institutions but affects today nearly all levels within the institutions.[14] Seen from the perspective of the member states we can call this observation the basic trend towards 'Europeanization' of national institutions. The argument is that the longer and the more intensive the – strictly speaking – EC institutions back in 'far away Brussels' work and produce legislative 'output' which affects the member states, the more national institutions and political and social actors are pushed and pulled to participate in the EC/EU's decision-making process in order to have an influence on the outcome of the negotiation process. Besides this rational (re)orientation of institutions there is also a more unconscious – and thus less rationally but very often symbolically determined – (re)orientation of national institutions. From this point of view the EC/EU would be a new type of political organization which has established a new political and economic environment with its own norms, principles and values to which national actors respond by adapting their interests and beliefs to this 'regime' to which they belong. Ger-

---

[13] See Simon Bulmer, 'The Governance of the European Union: A New Institutionalist Approach', *Journal of Public Policy*, 13 (4)(1994), pp. 351–380; here: p. 355.
[14] See Wolfgang Wessels, 'Administrative Interaction', in William Wallace (ed.), *The Dynamics of European Integration* (London: Pinter, 1990), pp. 229–41.

hard Göhler would argue that the EC/EU makes use of symbolic features – such as the 'Internal Market 1992', 'Maastricht' or more recently the '1996 revision conference' – which serve as decisive factors of orientation to the member states, their institutions and consequently the people. However, Göhler complains that these 'symbols' of the European Union are too weak to integrate the people and do not lead to the establishment of a common identity.[15]

The central question is to what extent the trend towards 'Europeanization' had a similar or divergent effect in the member states. What does 'Europeanization' mean in concrete terms for the individual countries and their national institutions? Can we observe a converging pattern of institutional reaction and adaptation, in the sense that national institutions adapt in a similar way to the process of European integration, or do we observe a more diverging pattern of institutional reaction and adaptation, in the sense that national institutions show a rather different behaviour?

As a first result the country reports in this volume suggest that there is a common trend towards 'Europeanization' of national institutions. The Europeanization does not take place in a 'wild' and unregulated manner but seems to be more a step by step development in which each institution is looking for its 'European counterpart' and tries to find its specific mode of European and national participation and action.[16] Thus, bureaucracies – depending on the type and the policy sector – send civil servants to the working groups and committees of the Council and the Commission. Bureaucrats are involved in the Union's decision-making process quite differently from, for instance, representatives from national parliaments who participate in other forums and with different intensity (such as in COSAC or in the meetings of the presidents of parliament, see Table 14.2).

To these horizontal divergences between institutions of different kinds must be added the divergences between the member states where we can observe a broad variety of institutional behaviour. Thus there is a double cleavage concerning the type of institution and the member state to which they belong. The general observation here is that the basic trend towards Europeanization of national institu-

[15] See the contribution of Gerhard Göhler in this book.
[16] See Wolfgang Wessels, 'Institutionen der Europäischen Union: Langzeittrends und Leitideen', in Gerhard Göhler (ed.), *Die Eigenart der Institutionen. Zum Profil politischer Institutionentheorie* (Baden-Baden: Nomos, 1994), pp. 301–30.

tions differs in scope and intensity according to the member states. There are differences among the institutions in each member state which suggest that there is not one single pattern of institutional behaviour and participation but that there exists a great variety of possible combinations and options within the general trend of Europeanization. The assumption is that there is a 'basic institutional trend' in the institutional system of the EC/EU which is located between two cleavages: on the one hand 'Europeanization' and 'convergence' and on the other hand 'nationalization' and 'divergence'.

Table 14.2 Patterns of interaction between national and European institutions

	National governments	*National administrations*	*National parliaments*	*National courts*	*Regions/ local authorities*
EU Council	95 Council meetings (1993)	COREPER meets approx. once per week representatives in 250–300 working groups			[German Länder have representatives in 122 Council working groups]
EU Commission	Participation in Council meetings	Members in 300 committees and 600–700 study and expert groups			[German Länder have representatives in 217 commmittees/ study groups]
European Parliament	Informal meetings		Bi-annual COSAC meetings of the Presidents of parliament		Informal meetings
EC Court of Justice				preliminary ruling procedure (Art. 177)	
Committee of the Regions					4 plenary meetings in 1994; 8 committees and 4 sub-committees

From a 'Brussels' perspective 'convergence' is defined here as the gradual process of constitutional, institutional, procedural, organizational and behavioural innovations and adaptations to EC/EU decision-making by national political institutions and which, in the long-term perspective, could lead to one common politico-constitutional system in the member states, characterized, above all, by the disappearance of pre-existing differences. 'Divergence' in this context would mean the lack of innovations and adaptations of national institutions to the European institutional system and the maintenance of the politico-constitutional differences in the member states. Many member states seem to move towards 'Europeanization' and 'convergence' which can be concluded from the findings of the country reports of the book. The basic thesis is that the more member states 'Europeanize', the more national institutions are pushed towards 'convergence'; the 'fusion' of national and EU institutions in the policy cycle is a logical intermediary step to this. Conversely, the less member states 'Europeanize' and thus move towards 'nationalization' the more their institutions show a diverging pattern of behaviour; as a logical consequence no 'fusion' of national and EU institutions takes place. As a result the fusion of national institutions and the convergence (or divergence) of the national constitutional systems are dependent on the degree of Europeanization in the individual member states.

Degrees of 'Europeanization'
When summarizing the findings of the national reports in this volume, we can differentiate between various degrees of 'Europeanization' of national institutions. Applying the perspective of the national political institutions, we can distinguish between three categories and thus differentiate between 'low', 'medium' and 'high' Europeanization.

Depending on the type of institution (national government, national parliament, national courts, regions/communes, national administration) and its activities, each category must be evaluated differently. Certainly, in addition to this each category can differ according to the member state (e.g. the Europeanization of the regions/communes in Denmark is different from that in Spain) and must be seen in relation to the specific national context. However, this latter problem of comparison has been evaded by the formulation of some general patterns which can be applied to the institutions in several member states.

Low Europeanization By this we understand that an institution is not very active in European integration matters and plays a resistant role in the integration process; it is not very keen to participate in the EC/EU decision-making process; it has not exerted pressure on the other national institutions since Maastricht in order to get more rights and competences in European affairs or to improve its efficiency and effectiveness in EC/EU matters. Examples are the government in Greece and the United Kingdom; the parliaments in Belgium and Italy; the regions and local authorities in Denmark, Greece, Ireland, Portugal and the United Kingdom; and the administration in Greece and Italy.

Medium Europeanization By this we understand that an institution is relatively active in European integration matters and has increasingly gained a European outlook, especially since Maastricht. According to the different institutions the following peculiarities can be distinguished:[17]

1 *Government* (DK, E, I, IRL, NL, P): It plays a constructive role in the European integration process and generally does not block decisions in the Council; in spite of its central decision-making position in EC/EU affairs it is relatively open towards the other national institutions concerning their role in EC/EU decision-making.

2 *Parliament* (D, E, EL, F, IRL, NL, P): Europe has increasingly become part of its political debates; it has quite a good record in incorporating EC law and has had a specialized committee for European affairs for quite some time already; since Maastricht it has tried to extend its powers in EC/EU decision-making with some success and has adapted its internal working procedures in order to be more effective in the EC decision-making process.

3 *Courts* (B, D, DK, EL, F, IRL, NL, P): With some exceptions they have almost totally accepted the primacy of EC law and are actively making use of the preliminary ruling procedure (Art. 177 TEU).

4 *Regions/local authorities* (E, F, I, NL): They have been increasingly active in EC/EU affairs and have partly established their own representations in Brussels; since Maastricht they have put pressure on the governments with some success in order to extend their com-

---

[17] Belgium = B, Germany = D, Denmark = DK, Spain = E, Greece = EL, France = F, Italy = I, Ireland = IRL, Netherlands = NL, Portugal = P, United Kingdom = UK.

petences in EC decision-making, especially concerning the structural funds from Brussels.

5 *National administration* (B, D, E, IRL, NL, P): It is seen to have a relatively good record concerning the administrative handling of EC law and does not make a distinction between EC legislation and national legislation; it has to some extend adapted its structures and procedures to the growth of regulations coming from Brussels.

High Europeanization By this is meant that an institution has been very active in European integration matters and has developed its own active initiatives towards the EC/EU which classify it among the 'pioneers' of European integration. According to the institutions the following peculiarities can be distinguished.

1 *Government* (B, D, F): It is seen to play the role of an 'engine' in European integration; though it is still the central decision-making body, it has transferred some of its powers to other national institutions in order to enhance their role in EC decision-making; however, in political terms it is still preponderant and gives important impulses to European integration.

2 *Parliament* (DK, UK): It has intensively discussed EC/EU matters and thus contributed to a widespread public debate on Europe, but it also has a very good record in incorporating EC law into national law; its specialized committee for European affairs has got new powers in EC/EU affairs and its internal procedures work comparatively efficiently; it has extended its powers and competences particularly with regard to the government's central position in EC/EU matters and has put through an amendment of the constitution in this respect.

3 *Courts* (E, I, UK): They have accepted without reservation the primacy of EC law and have always addressed the ECJ in case of the interpretation of Community law according to Art. 177 TEU.

4 *Regions/local authorities* (B, D): They have become serious actors in EC decision-making, especially after Maastricht, in policy fields where they have own competences and/or which are of particular concern to them; they have established their own representations in Brussels which are effectively working; since Maastricht there are new constitutional provisions which allow them to send representatives to the Council of Ministers and to take decisions which bind as a whole the member state to which they belong.

5 *National administration* (DK, F, UK): It has a very good record concerning the administrative handling of EC law and has effectively applied Community norms; it has adapted and improved its structures and procedures to the growth of EC regulations.

Europeanization and convergence

The differences in degrees of Europeanization in the member states suggest that there are at least two basic directions of the institutional development in the EU and the member states. They imply that there is a causal link between Europeanization and convergence, but also between nationalization and divergence.

Divergence through nationalization? By this we mean that institutions primarily follow national objectives, irrespective of what similar institutions in other member states are doing; the results are behavioural divergences and, in a long-term perspective, the maintenance of the politico-constitutional differences in the member states. Since the institutions' aim is not to participate on a European level and to cooperate, but to solve their problems autonomously, primarily on a national level, they do not meet their European counterparts (or only very seldom) and are thus isolated and follow their own ways and ideas. The more recent member states – such as Greece, Spain and Portugal – come from this tradition and the assumption is that this is also true for the new members which joined the EU in 1995. We presume that with EU membership they will start moving in the direction of Europeanization and convergence whereas countries outside the EU – such as the Central and Eastern European states – will not follow this direction until they have gained full membership.

Convergence through Europeanization? By this we mean that institutions which are more and more participating in the EC decision-making process – and thus Europeanizing – must adapt their organization, procedures and behaviour in the direction of convergence, i.e. they must follow the development of their counterpart institutions in the other member states and the Union. The consequences are changes in the politico-constitutional systems of the member states, accompanied very often by a new discourse on European integration. Institutions adapt mainly for two reasons: firstly, they meet their counterpart institutions on the European level in

Brussels (e.g. the governments in the Council or the European Council, the parliaments in the framework of COSAC and the administrations in the various committees of the Commission etc.; see Table
14.2 above) and react to their behaviour. Secondly, because they
would like to improve their participation in the EC decision-making
process and aim to maximize their benefits when participating in the
preparation, making, implementation and control of binding EC decisions.[18] There are of course various national constraints (such as
national elections or the history of a country) and international influences (such as specific foreign policy relations) which have an impact
on the institutional adaptation and behaviour and which explain why
the EU member states are not all moving on a somewhat hidden
'ideal line' of Europeanization and convergence but have different
developments. However, the main observation at this point is that in
all member states there is, with certain limits, a common trend
towards deparliamentarization, sectorization and regionalization
which goes in the direction of Europeanization and convergence;
no member state seems to move towards divergence and nationalization.

However, in reality such 'pure' developments are difficult to identify, since patterns of institutional life and development are more
complicated than that. The contents of the country reports suggest
that in many cases we find an intermediary stage of the two directions of development or even a 'crossing' combination of both. In
more general terms it seems that the basic politico-constitutional
structure and the institutional behaviour and activities are directly
linked to each other.

Not a single model
The overview suggests that there are differences according to the
national institutions and the member states concerning their 'degree
of Europeanization' and their 'direction of development'. What seems
to be important is less the 'ranking' of each member state or institution but the (still) existing differences among them. Although there
seems to be a common trend towards Europeanization of national
actors in terms of the growing and intensified participation of

[18] See Gerhard Göhler quoted in Wolfgang Wessels, 'Staat und Westeuropäische Integration. Die Fusionsthese', in Michael Kreile (ed.), 'Die Integration Europas', *Politische Vierteljahresschrift*, special edition, no. 23 (1992), pp. 36–61, here: p. 36.

national institutions in EC decision-making, looked at in more detail
the institutional behaviour in the member states can be quite divergent. There does not seem to be 'one model' of an 'institutional mix'
in the member states, measured in terms of Europeanization, nor is
there one type of institution which shows the same profile in all of
the member states. The national *governments* of Greece and the
United Kingdom, for instance, are characterized by a low degree of
Europeanization (see above) which is quite contrary to the 'high
Europeanization' in Belgium, Germany and France. What is important in institutional terms is that nearly the opposite is true when we
look at the national *parliaments* (see above) in the same countries: a
high degree of Europeanization in the United Kingdom (in terms of
the intensity of discussion on the EC/EU, of the incorporation of EC
directives and of the control of the government's EC/EU policy), but
a rather low degree of Europeanization in Belgium and Germany. A
similar divergence can be found when we add to this the results of
the national administrations or the regions/local authorities. There is
no 'leading' or 'losing' country and there is no 'perfect' or 'imperfect'
institution in terms of Europeanization but there is a divergent mix
which does not reflect the development towards one model, either in
institutional or in political terms. What can be observed is that the
national political systems and constitutional elements do matter –
which explains why the country chapters in this volume follow the
order ranging from the federal, over the decentralized to the centralized member states – but they do not result in a similar pattern of
institutional behaviour in EC/EU affairs. The only trend which all
member states seem to follow is that the more they are located at one
or the other extreme (purely federal or purely centralized country),
the more they are inclined to show a divergent picture of institutional
behaviour (e.g. Germany, Belgium v. Denmark, Greece and United
Kingdom).

Thus, we have a picture of heterogeneity which reflects the institutional differences between the member states with regard to the
process of European integration. With the exception of broad trends
– such as deparliamentarization, sectorization and regionalization –
there are no indicators, at least when examining the institutional
behaviour in the EU, that the national politico-constitutional systems
converge beyond that into one pattern with similar institutions, distribution of competences and decision-making procedures etc. in all
member states. Though the European integration process has lasted

for over forty years, the national politico-constitutional set-ups are still 'obstinate'. The national constitutional and political constellations have been influenced and adapted, but they have not been 'revolutionized' and overturned as regards their basic features. The EC/EU continues to constitute a major challenge to the national institutional set-up and to national policy-making styles. However, it leads neither in the direction of a purely federal model which is subdivided into similar models of member states, nor in the direction of a purely intergovernmental model in which the member states are not affected by the EU's institutional development and maintain their national politico-constitutional structure. The observation we make is something in between, that could be best circumscribed by the term 'fusion model', and which is characterized by an intensive institutional interaction between national and European actors, a medium to high degree of Europeanization of national institutions and a low trend of convergence towards a single politico-institutional system. There is certainly not one optimal model of institutional participation which can be characterized as such, neither in the centralized, nor in the decentralized or federal member states; and there are no easy lessons to draw from this, but the 'fusion model'[19] can help us to understand some general patterns of institutional development in the EC/EU.

Patterns of institutional development

One phenomenon seems to be of specific importance when reading the country reports: we observe that the national administrations – especially the ministerial administrations – are directly involved in the preparation, the making and the implementation of EC decisions and have clearly gained in influence. The national administration, together with the administration on the European level, with the help of its expertise and qualified staff, has become one of the key actors in the European integration process. This has enhanced the tendency towards the 'bureaucratization' of the European integration process and contributed to its growing intransparency. The national courts have more or less accepted this process and have, on the basis of the principle of the primacy of EC law, contributed to the establishment of the 'Legal Community' (*Rechtsgemeinschaft*) and to the concentration of the decision-making power in the hands of the executive.

---

[19] See the contribution of Wolfgang Wessels in this book.

In connection with the ratification of Maastricht some national high courts have raised critical tones, but after all they did not directly intervene since the principles of democracy and of the sovereignty of the people according to their opinion were respected. Thus, the courts can be considered as 'benevolent observers' in the European integration process, supporting the 'triumphal march' of national ministerial bureaucracies in EC/EU affairs.

The observation made above that there is a common trend of Europeanization but not the development towards *one* institutional mix or *one* politico-constitutional model does not mean that there is not a similar institutional behaviour recognizable in the member states. During the 1970s and 1980s it has been discovered that the process of European integration has been paralleled – especially in connection with the new dynamics of the internal market programme – by a process of 'deparliamentarization'.[20] In fact the growing number of legislative acts decided by 'Brussels' were not – or only to a limited extent – debated in the national parliaments. The incorporation of EC directives and regulations into national law was mostly done by means of secondary law decided by the governments, thus by-passing national parliaments.[21] It could happen that parliaments were able to debate a European issue and to vote on a resolution, but this happened at a moment when the respective norm was already decided by the Council in Brussels.[22] The reason for this delay was, among other things, that national parliaments were informed too late or only in an incomplete way by their governments which did not allow them to take the appropriate action. To this must be added that the instruments and the capacity to control the governments – often because of internal procedural obstacles – were not very much developed in the national parliaments and did not contribute to an effective influence on the negotiations and decision-making process in

[20] See Klaus Hänsch, 'Europäische Integration und parlamentarische Demokratie', *Europa-Archiv*, 41 (7) (1986), pp. 191–200; Klaus Pöhle, 'Europäische Union à la Maastricht. Eine ernste Herausforderung für die Parlamente in der EG', *Zeitschrift für Parlamentsfragen*, 1 (1993), pp. 49–63; see also Andrew Moravcsik, *Why the Community strengthens the state: Domestic Politics and International Cooperation*, unpublished paper presented at the conference of Europeanists (Chicago, April 1994).

[21] See Heinrich Siedentopf and Jacques Ziller, *Making European Policies Work. The Implementation of Community Legislation in the Member States*, vol. i (London: Sage 1988), pp. 42ff; see on this also the respective parts in this book on 'implementation' or 'The parliament', especially in the contributions of Brigid Laffan, Francesc Morata, Thomas Pedersen, Dietrich Rometsch and Michael Tsinisizelis.

[22] See Hänsch, *op. cit.*, p. 197.

Brussels. Thus national parliaments – to a varying degree – lost in decision-making competences in all member states, whereas the national governments, with the help of the bureaucracy, could strengthen their position and extend their scope of competences. This distinction between the 'winners', i.e. the executive branch, on the one hand and the 'losers', i.e. the legislative branch, on the other hand can to some extent also be observed on the regional level.[23] In those countries where a regional tier of government exists, there is a trend towards a more active involvement of the regional/local governments and bureaucracies, whereas the elected regional parliaments/councils are kept outside this process and are losing in competences. The creation of the Committee of the Regions since Maastricht is an indicator that the role of the regions/communes has become more important in EC decision-making (though it is mostly limited to representatives from the executive level). Since Maastricht politicians and civil servants from the regions and municipalities are directly involved in the EC decision-making process and are present in Brussels. Although they cannot really be counted the 'winners' of the integration process, they can be considered as forceful 'latecomers' who are slowly approaching an institutionalized status in EC decision-making. It will to a large extent depend on their own creativity and effectiveness in the upcoming years to extend this position. Taken together it seems that within the EC/EU there is a trend towards 'policy sectorization', accompanied by inner-bureaucratic battles over competences and a trend towards 'deparliamentarization' accompanied by decentralization and regional *engrenage*.

Future outlook

The 'vicious circle'

The distinction between 'winners' and 'losers' and the 'benevolent observers' of the European integration process is not a static situation.

[23] In *party political terms* there are very often close relationships between both, since the majority in parliament is of the same political party (or par*ties* in cases of coalition governments) as the government in power; thus there is not a clear-cut borderline any more between the executive and the legislative, but both are – depending on the country and the issue at stake – working together and are depending on each other (the latter is particularly true in Denmark and the United Kingdom where parliament and government have developed a very close and direct relationship; see the contributions of Thomas Pedersen, and Kenneth Armstrong and Simon Bulmer). However, in *institutional* terms one has to distinguish between government and parliament since they have a different role and function in the decision-making process.

Quite the contrary: the European integration process is characterized by a dynamic development which is unknown on the national level. With regard to the institutional development the dynamics of the European integration process has established a threefold trend characterized by a growing complexity of the institutional system; by a more and more intensive controversy about this system; and by an increasing necessity for institutional adaptation.[24] Institutions from the national as well as from the European level are interacting in this context of complexity, controversy and adaptation, thus reinforcing these trends and being at the same time their 'victims'. National and EU institutions seem to be trapped in a 'vicious circle' (see Figure 14.1): (a) in order to participate in the EC/EU decision-making process, institutions adapt to this process and improve their effectiveness;

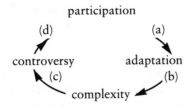

Figure 14.1 The 'vicious circle' of the institutional dynamics in the EU

(b) the growing involvement of more and more actors increases the complexity of the institutional system and disturbs its functioning; (c) this leads to a more intensive debate, in which conflicts can arise, about the role and function of the EC/EU; the necessary steps to be taken are discussed in order to improve its effectiveness in decision-making; (d) the latter increases the EU's importance and attracts new actors who want to participate in the preparation, making and implementation of binding decisions; this leads to institutional adaptations, an increase in complexity and new reflections about the reform of the institutional system etc. This rather abstract process of participation, adaptation, complexity and controversy does not have the same effect on every institution and does not take place in any particular phase of the European integration process. What is important is that there

[24] See the introductory chapter of Wolfgang Wessels to this book.

is not a fixed situation but there are changing patterns of influence and adaptation in which no single (set of) institution(s) is (are) dominating or being dominated.

Fusion without limits?

We started our reflections on the institutional development in the EC/EU with the discussion of three constitutional models, i.e. the intergovernmental model, the federal model and the fusion model. Although all three are in a sense 'ideal type' models – and thus can only describe 'reality' in a schematic way – we come to the conclusion that the latter seems to be best adapted to explain the processes of Europeanization, of increasing institutional interaction and of limited systemic convergence in the Union. The 'fusion model' puts an accent on the 'checks and balances' among national and EU institutions in the preparing, making, implementing and controlling of binding decisions. It focuses on the mixing of national and EU competences and the shared responsibility of institutions for the combined use of state instruments such as law and budgetary means. According to this model a clear-cut division of competences and responsibilities is not possible and can even be considered as unnecessary. More important in this model is the multitude of institutional interactions and cooperations both in vertical and horizontal terms. In terms of performance the balance is mixed, above all because of the complexity and the increasing number of actors. It is characterized by a development towards deparliamentarization and bureaucratization. Although institutional adaptations are undertaken and reform proposals are discussed, the 'fusion model' does not drastically change its appearance and functioning; quite the contrary: institutions seem to be trapped in a 'vicious circle' of participation, adaptation, complexity and controversy from which there is no easy way out. National and EU institutions are the 'victims' of their own dynamics.

Within the member states national institutions have 'Europeanized', in the sense that they are to an increasing extent pushed towards cooperation and coordination with European institutions and institutions in the member states, without converging, however, into a single politico-institutional model. Thus national institutions are in a permanent process of action and orientation in vertical and horizontal terms; a separation of their organizational structures and a clear attribution of the policy output seems to be neither adequate for the policy cycle nor really possible any more. Hence 'fusion' becomes also 'confusion' since we are increasingly less able to make individual institutions and persons accountable for their action. Thus the process of 'institutional fusion' is characterized by an increasing complexity, heterogeneity and intransparency; without strong involvement of national parliaments the decision-making process is hardly understandable and its output lacks a deeper-going acceptance. The participation of a multitude of actors in the system, which has the advantage of pluralistic decision-making, becomes at the same time its main deficiency: a high complexity and a low trend of convergence towards a single politico-constitutional model; symbolic features which could serve as elements of orientation are largely missing. The measures to be taken in this model with regard to the problem of democratic legitimacy would need further debate. However, we think that the extended participation of national institutions – especially of national parliaments – in such an institutional system will not be a sufficient answer. Further convergence of national systems will not take place since national parliaments – and national institutions in general – do not participate in a system with the future perspective of 'dilution' in an increasingly fusioned institutional 'hotch-potch'. They will try to keep their independence and will participate in the system as long as it seems useful for the fulfilment of their tasks and their own survival. Thus the development towards a 'federal system' seems to be unlikely; nor can we observe a turning back to an 'intergovernmental model';[25] more likely seems to be a further degree of institutional fusion and a higher procedural complexity in the upcoming future from which there is no easy way out. However an institutional 'de-Europeanization' will not take place; there are no signs of a withdrawal from the system but more of an institutional learning and re-equilibrium.

---

[25] See the contribution of Wolfgang Wessels in this book.

Index

Numbers in *italic* refer to tables or figures.